# Becoming ASIA

# Becoming ASIA

Change and Continuity in Asian International Relations Since World War II

**Alice Lyman Miller**
**Richard Wich**

STANFORD UNIVERSITY PRESS
*Stanford, California*

FOUNDATION® BOOKS

Delhi • Bengaluru • Mumbai • Kolkata • Chennai • Hyderabad
Pune • Thiruvananthapuram

Published by
**Cambridge University Press India Pvt. Ltd.**
under the imprint of Foundation Books
Cambridge House, 4381/4 Ansari Road, Daryaganj, New Delhi 110 002

**Cambridge University Press India Pvt. Ltd.**
C-22, C-Block, Brigade M.M., K.R. Road, Jayanagar, **Bengaluru** 560 070
Plot No. 80, Service Industries, Shirvane, Sector-1, Nerul, **Navi Mumbai** 400 706
10 Raja Subodh Mullick Square, 2nd Floor, **Kolkata** 700 013
21/1 (New No. 49), 1st Floor, Model School Road, Thousand Lights, **Chennai** 600 006
House No. 3-5-874/6/4, (Near Apollo Hospital), **Hyderguda**, Hyderabad 500 029
Agarwal Pride, 'A' Wing, 1308 Kasba Peth, Near Surya Hospital, **Pune** 411 011
T.C. 25/ 2731 Lukes Lane, Ambujavilasam Road, **Thiruvananthapuram** 695 001



This edition has been published by Cambridge University Press India Pvt. Ltd. by arrangement with Stanford University Press.

First South Asia Edition 2012

ISBN 978-93-82264-10-1

**Published by Manas Saikia for Cambridge University Press India Pvt. Ltd. And printed at Akash Press, New Delhi – 110 020**

*To Avis and Joyce*

# CONTENTS

# ILLUSTRATIONS

**MAPS**



**TABLE**

to conform more closely to Washington's other bilateral alliances and to appear less unequal to Japanese eyes. The revised treaty dropped the provision for use of American forces to quell internal disturbances, and it added a provision for termination by either side after ten years (the original treaty had permitted termination after a year's notice). Nonetheless, the revised treaty was adopted by the Diet amid widespread protests, reflecting considerable neutralist sentiment in Japan, and the turmoil it provoked prompted the cancellation of President Eisenhower's planned visit. In its revised form, again reflecting Japan's constitutional and political constraints, the treaty still departed from pattern by obligating the two sides to respond to attacks on areas under Japan's jurisdiction, not—as in the other mutual defense agreements—on U.S. territories in the Pacific region as well. In the case of the treaties with the Philippines and with Australia and New Zealand, the mutual defense obligation extended to the treaty partners' metropolitan areas, that is, to the American mainland as well as to territories in the Pacific. (It was this provision that Australia invoked after the terrorist attacks on the United States in September 2001, as did America's NATO partners.)

Why did Washington not simply follow the NATO model and create a multilateral collective security organization in Asia? Such an arrangement had in fact been contemplated, and a draft of a "Pacific Pact" was produced by Washington in the period after the jolt of the Korean War's outbreak mobilized American policymakers to press forward on a peace settlement with Japan. This organization would have comprised only island nations along with the United States, namely Japan, the Philippines, Australia, New Zealand, and possibly Indonesia, the latter's willingness to participate being in question. The draft prefigured the formulation used in the bilateral and ANZUS treaties in calling on the parties to act to meet the common "danger" if any side was attacked. (An annex to the draft takes care to make the point that the proposed Pacific Pact differed as follows from the NATO treaty: In the NATO accord, each side "agrees" that it would take appropriate action in case of an attack on any participant, whereas in the Pacific Pact the parties "declare" that they would do so.) Britain was conspicuously absent from the proposed membership, omitted because of U.S. Defense Department objections to a commitment to defend Hong Kong (and inclusion of the British would have raised the question of adding France with a commitment to defending Indochina). Not surprisingly, the British objected to the plan, and it was not seriously explored during the negotiations with the Japanese leading up to the peace treaty and bilateral pact concluded later that year. Thus the hub-and-spokes system emerged as the answer to U.S. security concerns in East Asia and the Pacific.

One inhibition against a collective security system for the region may have been the strong animosity Japan's former victims felt toward that country, making it difficult to induce them to enter a security body alongside their recent oppressor. Moreover, the constitutional limitations on Japan's military role militated against its participation in a collective defense alliance. But why not have an Asian organization without Japan, just as West Germany was not originally a member of NATO? This may have reflected the Europe-first strategy that prevailed in American thinking: an Asian NATO might have been too ambitious and costly an undertaking given the resources being allocated to Europe. (This consideration was reflected in an early 1952 article by future secretary of state Dulles, who

# PREFACE

The authors were prompted to undertake this work by their experience in teaching courses on Asian international relations since World War II. We found that the literature lacked a single, comprehensive, systemic account of this complex subject. For teaching purposes we improvised by splicing together selections from books and other sources, but this still left a need for an integrated approach to the subject. We hope that the result of our approach will serve the interests of various readerships, scholars and students, diplomats, journalists, military and intelligence personnel, members of international organizations and businesses, and others interested in how Asia became what it is today, playing an increasingly consequential role in global political, economic, and security affairs.

Our discussion of Asia is to be understood in a geopolitical sense, not including the Middle East. One of our objectives has been to integrate developments in South and Central Asia along with East Asia into the story of how the region developed from extensive colonial dependence into the vibrant, assertive Asia that it had become by the turn of the new millennium. Another objective was to provide perspective on one of the topics of compelling interest today: the rise of China. Because of China's central place in the international relations of Asia, from the time when it represented a power vacuum in the early postwar years, to its turbulent role during the Cold War, and now to its position as a major geopolitical and economic force, we devote a full chapter to the remarkable trajectory of the People's Republic.

As reflected in our subtitle, we address elements of both change and continuity in the period since the watershed events of World War II. There have been transformative events such as decolonization, the end of the Cold War (in which Asia played a crucial role), and the increasing salience of transnational issues such as terrorism. At the same time, many deeply rooted issues have persisted in the most militarized region of the world. Issues such as the division of Korea and its implications for nuclear proliferation, the Taiwan issue and its potential for catastrophic regional conflict, and the Indian-Pakistani dispute and other sources of instability in South Asia figure in our story from the early postwar years to the present.

We believe that contemporaneous documents—leaders' talks and speeches, international agreements, secret policy assessments—enrich accounts of events by what they show of policymakers' assumptions and perceptions at the time. We encourage readers to look into the original sources we have cited, and to whet their appetites we have scattered boxed excerpts of key documents throughout the text.

We are grateful to the undergraduate and graduate students and faculty members who have participated in our classes and stimulated our ideas on this subject at the Johns Hopkins University's School of Advanced International Studies, at Stanford University, and at the U.S. Naval Postgraduate School over the past two decades. We also express our gratitude to academic and government colleagues with whom we debated the issues and trends we recount in this book over many years. Finally, we owe thanks to the two anonymous reviews for the publisher, whose suggestions have improved the book, and to the staff at Stanford University Press for their congenial and professional assistance. Each of the coauthors is convinced that all remaining flaws in the book are the fault of the other.

# BECOMING ASIA

offensive against Taiwan. Consistent with this proviso, the ROC was induced to abandon the distant offshore islands, the Dachens, which were not stepping-stones for an invasion of Taiwan.

An easing of tensions in the Taiwan Strait coincided with Beijing's turn to a moderate approach to foreign relations. As noted in Chapter 6, this approach was especially on display at the first Asian-African conference, in April 1955, which provided the stage for Zhou Enlai's offer to enter negotiations with the United States on reducing tensions in the Taiwan area. Talks began in Geneva that August (and lasted until early 1958, when they were discontinued by Beijing after Washington had downgraded them to below ambassadorial level). Beijing brightened the atmosphere further with gestures toward the Nationalists, including suggestions of a "peaceful liberation" of Taiwan and conciliatory offers to the Nationalists. This phase of Chinese policy was paralleled by similar moderation in Soviet behavior (reflected, for instance, by establishment of diplomatic relations with Japan). After the Chinese turned back onto a militant path in 1957, they again probed the firmness of the U.S. commitment to Taiwan and the offshore islands in renewed artillery attacks in August and September 1958. On that occasion, however, the real test was the one posed to Beijing's alliance with Moscow. A watershed now loomed in that relationship.

## CONTAINMENT, COMMITMENT, AND CREDIBILITY

The structure of security relationships had given formal expression to the extension of the U.S. containment policy to Asia. Though there were elements of ambiguity, and the obligations undertaken by Washington to its Asian allies were somewhat weaker than those contained in the Rio and NATO treaties, the array of Asian alliances lent credibility to the American commitment to containment of Communism. As SEATO demonstrated, however, with its sparse representation from the area itself, the structure of U.S. alliances had large gaps due to the neutralist countries' aversion to bloc politics.

The greater clarity of commitment, with its intended deterrent effect, came at some cost to the treaty partners. The weaker side sacrificed some freedom of maneuver in exchange for enhanced security—a price the neutralists were not prepared to pay. Having renounced war as an instrument of policy, Japan in effect surrendered some of its sovereignty in the price of U.S. military protection. The Japanese parlayed this bargain into a concentration on economic development that produced the second-largest economy in the world. One result was to extract an added cost from the United States in the form of intense and at times bitter economic competition between these allies, and this was exacerbated by a perception among Americans that the Japanese were enjoying a free ride under the U.S. strategic shield. In other cases, the weaker partner was able to manipulate Washington's concern over the impact on its broader strategic interests of a defection by its ally, thereby complicating U.S. policymaking. These complications, for example, figured in the often-tortuous U.S. relations with Saigon during the Vietnam War. (Moscow had its own problems along this line, for example, restraining East Germany on sensitive German issues, or dealing with the independent policy proclivities of Warsaw Pact ally Romania.)

# 1 INTRODUCTION

To borrow Prince Metternich's characterization of Italy before its unification, Asia was not much more than a Western geographical expression at the end of World War II. Before the war, most of the region had been colonized or, in the case of China, dominated by foreign powers, and then during the war much of East Asia was forcibly embraced by the Japanese Empire. In the wake of the war, an upsurge of nationalist movements dispossessed the colonial powers. The postwar emergence of nation-states in most of the region for the first time had a transformative effect, with the new states ardently committed to the Westphalian concept of sovereignty. However, the evolution of nation-states in Asia was complicated by the importation of the U.S.-Soviet Cold War from its European cockpit. Even after the end of the Cold War, the effects of broader influences continued to shape the geopolitical landscape of Asia as a new century unfolded.

This history is an effort to provide a systemic perspective on these complex developments, focusing not on the outlook and actions of any single state but on the interactions of states and other forces within both a regional and a global context. The goal is to provide an interpretive account of how Asia became a region of increasingly consequential nation-states, leading to a shift in the global center of gravity toward the region—and prompting some observers to descry the advent of "the Asian century." Another aspect of this effort is to identify deep-seated continuities, in particular to track the origin and evolution of key issues still at the top of the international agenda, such as the division of Korea and nuclear proliferation, the Taiwan issue, the rise of China, Japan's role, the Kashmir issue and the now nuclearized Indian-Pakistani conflict, and the increasing salience of transnational issues such as terrorism.

Key documents, some public at the time and others later declassified, are used to examine the mind-sets and policy choices of the various protagonists in order to assess their goals and evaluate the effects of their decisions, anticipated and not. Excerpts from some of these documents appear throughout the text.

## TWO MAJOR NARRATIVE THEMES

The narrative of this history interweaves the two threads that have dominated Asia's international relations since World War II. One is the competition between the great powers of the postwar era—the United States and the Soviet Union—to enlist the region's states as assets in their global competition, the Cold War. The other is the struggle of Asian nationalistic leaders to establish independent nation-states and to develop the domestic support and the elements of national power to sustain sovereignty in a dangerous international context.

The interplay between these two trends was a direct consequence of World War II, which, from a global perspective, was a genuine watershed. The structure of international relations after the war was fundamentally different from that preceding it, the war having decisively altered the cast of great powers that had played major roles both globally and in Asia. Also, in the aftermath of the war, statesmen's ideas and approaches regarding international affairs, though they were based in part on lessons they drew from the war and its origins, were different from those that led them into it. Finally, the war set in motion trends that continued to define the features of the international landscape into the next century. For these reasons, the war makes a natural starting point.

The Cold War emerged almost immediately from the geopolitical environment created by World War II. During this period, the United States and the Soviet Union—the first superpowers in world history—built powerful alliance systems and contended in an ideological, political, military, and economic struggle for global power and predominance in every part of the globe. Asia was one of the principal arenas of this struggle, and the Cold War had a powerful impact on the region, shaping relations among the Asian states and their interactions with the rest of the world.

From a regional perspective, World War II reshaped the place of every Asian society in the international order. At the beginning of this period, the imperial powers that had colonized nearly every part of Asia over the course of the preceding four centuries—Britain, France, the Netherlands, Japan, and the United States—lost those colonial empires. Japan lost its East Asian empire, acquired over the preceding fifty years, as a direct consequence of its defeat in the war. The end of Britain's and America's colonial control in the early postwar years came about largely through political means. In contrast, the French and the Dutch were forced to quit their colonies after failing to reimpose colonial administrations through military means in the early postwar years.

World War II itself played no small part in this outcome. On the one hand, the war weakened the European colonial powers and their capacity to maintain their prewar empires in Asia and elsewhere; on the other, it helped enflame and mobilize simmering nationalistic sentiments within the colonies and created opportunities for indigenous elites to build independence movements immediately after the war was over. Although the British, French, and Dutch sought in different measure to restore colonial holdings, each abandoned or was forced to give up these ambitions in Asia in the early postwar years. Having accepted by the end of the war that recouping its position in India, the "jewel in the crown" of the British Empire, was no longer possible, London sought through negotiations in the early postwar years to preserve as strong as possible an association with an independent and sovereign India. The independence of Burma, until the mid-1930s a part of British India, was now a foregone conclusion, and independence for British Malaya followed in train, delayed for several years only by the decision to suppress a Communist insurgency.

Paris and The Hague less easily accepted the fate of their colonies. They saw recovering their empires as essential to restoring their status as major powers in the postwar international order. Each therefore fought brutal struggles to reassert its hold over Indochina and the East Indies, respectively. By 1949, however, the Dutch—under international pressure—were forced to accept the dissolution of their East Indies colony, and by 1954 the French withdrew from Indochina following their humiliating defeat at the hands of Vietnamese Communist forces in the siege of Dienbienphu and the political settlement at the Geneva Conference the same year.

Though far from weakened by the war—quite the opposite—Washington followed through on its prewar promise to grant its Philippine colony independence in 1946 (evocatively, on the Fourth of July). The United States maintained a strong and enduring presence in the Philippines, however, and retained its post–World War I mandates over western and South Pacific islands, as well as control over islands seized by force from Japan in the course of the war.

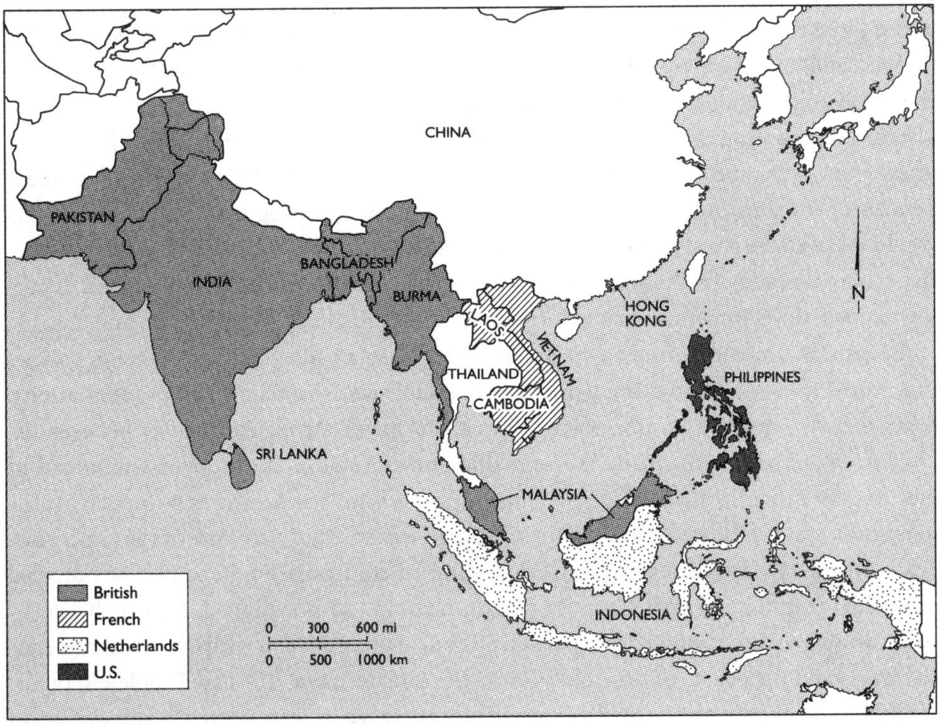


**Map 1.1** Postwar Colonial Possessions in Asia

The second major narrative theme emerged as a direct consequence. The dissolution of the European, American, and Japanese empires in Asia created new nation-states in a region that had until the war been almost completely subordinated under or colonized within the great-power empires over the preceding four centuries. In place of the prewar British colonies in Asia there emerged in the early postwar years the new nation-states of India, Pakistan, Burma (now Myanmar), Ceylon (now Sri Lanka), and Malaysia. Singapore emerged later, and the sultanate of Brunei much later. The French Empire gave way to the nation-states of Vietnam, Cambodia, and Laos. Out of the Dutch East Indies came the Republic of Indonesia. Only Thailand managed to escape outright colonization, preserving its autonomy by bandwagoning with the region's prevailing hegemon—the British in the mid-nineteenth century, the Japanese during World War II, and the United States after the war.

Although never colonized outright, the Republic of China (ROC), founded in Beijing in 1912 and reconstituted in Nanjing in 1928, used its participation in the war to win acquiescence in 1943 by the leading great powers—Britain and America—to end the treaty-port system that had encumbered full Chinese sovereignty for a century. At the same wartime conference in Cairo at which Chiang Kai-shek (Jiang Jieshi) won the end of the treaty-port system in China, the prospect "in due course" of an independent and sovereign nation-state of Korea, which had fallen under Japanese suzerainty in 1905 and under direct colonial rule in 1910, was registered.

World War II and the subsequent dissolution of the prewar empires marked the establishment of the Westphalian nation-state system of international relations (created in Europe in the seventeenth and eighteenth centuries) both in Asia and in what came to be called the third world. By the early postwar years, the dynamics of international relations in Asia could no longer be discussed in terms of competing empires; rather, they dealt with the competing agendas of newly created sovereign nation-states. Each of these new Asian states faced daunting challenges of consolidating statehood and sovereignty. At home their leaders had to channel the emotions of the aroused nationalism that had fueled their independence struggles and brought them to power into an enduring national consensus that would make stable governance possible. They had to find ways appropriate to their respective economic endowments and acceptable to their particular social constituencies to pursue national development, which was critical to their prospects, both at home and abroad.

Externally, the leaders of the new nation-states of Asia had to configure foreign policies that would allow them to defend their newly established sovereignty in an international order that very quickly became polarized in a new global struggle for power between the United States and its principally Western allies, on one side, and the Soviet Union and its bloc, on the other. In their efforts to come to terms with the pressures of bipolarity, the new Asian states followed varied paths. One way was to align with one of the superpowers, creating a polarized region in which the line of confrontation in some cases divided individual countries. Another was to remain neutral and nonaligned, a path chosen by India, among others, though it was pushed off course by a collision with China over territorial issues and the effects of the Cold War on the subcontinent. The new People's Republic of China, wrestling with the implications of bipolarity for its own interests, followed a tortuous path, leaning first one way, and then—after a period of deep isolation—the other, until finally pursuing an independent line while taking highly consequential steps toward opening up to the global economy.

These divergent strategies reckoned the benefits of security and economic cooperation through alignment with one of the competing superpowers against the costs to hard-won sovereignty, independence, and legitimacy, both at home and in each state's foreign entanglements. As a result, the foreign and domestic policies of the new Asian states were thoroughly intertwined. Most of the regimes in the new states were relatively weak and in need of external economic and military support at the outset. At the same time, in many cases, leaders of the new states faced political opposition that complicated and at times even threatened their hold on power. In such circumstances, the nationalist sentiments that fueled their independence struggles became potent political instruments in the hands of both the leaders and their opponents, and foreign policy issues played easily into domestic political struggles.

Nor could the two superpowers discount the political agendas of the elites they dealt with in Asia and the implications that their competition had in the domestic politics within the new states. Both Washington and Moscow shaped their strategies in Asia with these regional and local realities in mind. As a consequence, as much as the Cold War strongly affected the international politics of the Asian region, it is fair to say that the priorities and politics of the Asian states themselves also skewed, sometimes radically, the strategic competition of the two superpowers.

For no states were these calculations more complex than for the divided states that World War II and the early Cold War years produced in Asia—in Korea, China, and Vietnam. In these cases, in order to maximize its influence, each superpower helped to create and support a contender for national power from among the indigenous nationalist elites. The indigenous parties sought to maximize support from their respective patrons, all the while seeking to retain as much independence as possible to sustain their nationalist credentials and eliminate their rivals. As a result, the struggles for power and civil wars between the indigenous contenders in these three countries took on the complicating priorities of the Cold War, and vice versa.

All three divided countries emerged quickly as major flash points in the Cold War. In Korea and Vietnam, civil wars erupted into brutal and debilitating international conflicts with heavy involvement by their superpower patrons. In China, a civil war struggle whose roots antedated World War II was frozen short of completion by being pulled into the gravitational force of the global bipolar contest. Two of these three struggles—in Korea and in the present-day China-Taiwan standoff—remained unresolved and among the most dangerous flash points long after the close of the Cold War. The Vietnamese conflict was resolved, in 1975, with unification under a Communist regime, but only after a long struggle at enormous cost.

The end of the Cold War and the dissolution of the Soviet Union in 1991 closed the bipolar struggle and thus removed the powerful external dynamic that had shaped Asian international relations over the preceding decades. Among the changes that had taken place were the watershed 1968–72 transition marked most prominently by the U.S.-PRC rapprochement; the rise of Japan and an increasingly united Europe as emerging centers of power in what had been primarily a bipolar global structure; the end of the Vietnam War; the economic takeoff of South Korea, Taiwan, and the Southeast Asian "tigers"; and the rise of China under Deng Xiaoping and his successors.

Nevertheless, trends set in motion in Asia during the Cold War continue to shape the region's international relations in unmistakable ways. In addition to the remaining divided-country conflicts on the Korean peninsula and across the Taiwan Strait, other issues on the region's international relations agenda are unintelligible without reference to the Cold War. The deep disparity in economic fortunes and overall prospects between North and South Korea registers with dramatic clarity the superiority of the market-based approaches to national development over the variations of Soviet-style planned economies adopted—and to varying degrees abandoned—by other states in the Cold War era. At the same time, many of the ongoing dilemmas regarding trade—apparent most clearly in the perennial American bilateral trade deficits with Asian economies—trace their roots to the export-led development strategies adopted by the Asian market-based economies. Meanwhile, the structure of security alliances constructed by Washington against the Communist countries in Asia survived the end of bipolarity, seeking new rationales but still shaped in fundamental ways by Cold War circumstances.

Trends that matured in the region during the Cold War also made possible some of the new features of post–Cold War Asia. Emerging gradually across the period has been a stronger sense of solidarity among Asia's nation-states, where little had existed previously. It is true that Japan's rise—and its defeat of Russia in 1905—sparked a sense of common circumstance at the hands of Western imperialism that had been reflected in the pan-Asian sentiments among many politically active intellectual elites by the end of the nineteenth century. A sense of Asian solidarity based on Marxist-Leninist anti-imperialist internationalism was also galvanized by the electrifying success of the Bolshevik Revolution in 1917 and the creation of Communist parties in the region after the establishment of the Comintern (Communist International, the Moscow-directed international coordinating agency) in 1919. But through the pre–World War II decades and in the early postwar years, there was little perception among the subregions of Asia that their destinies were linked and no institutional expression of such solidarity.

In the post–Cold War period, however, there has been a gradual but steady advance of Asian multilateralism on regional and broader issues, despite persistent predictions of failure. Whether an outgrowth of common suspicions of both Cold War superpowers among the region's nonaligned countries, a result of solidarity in the face of regional threats—as in the case of the Association of Southeast Asian Nations (ASEAN)—or a consequence of accelerating interdependence attending the takeoff of many of the region's economies, a sense of solidarity among the Asian states is reflected in the creation of the ASEAN Regional Forum, the ASEAN Plus Three linkages with China, South Korea, and Japan, and other emerging regional groupings. In an era of presumed American hegemony in Asia, Washington nevertheless needed to adapt its agenda in the region to address complications posed by regional groupings that took their impetus in part from reaction to preponderant American power and in some cases have self-consciously excluded the United States.

The central themes of this history of Asia's international relations since World War II, then, derive from the intricate interplay between the United States and the Soviet Union for influence and power in the region, on one hand, and the struggles of the region's new nation-states to consolidate and sustain their newly gained sovereignty, on the other. Out of this interaction emerged secondary themes—the success of new varieties of market-based political economies and the failure of planned-economy approaches, the slow emergence of Asian solidarity and multilateralism, and others—that thread through the period and feature prominently in the Cold War's aftermath.

## PERSPECTIVES ON THE ORIGINS OF WORLD WAR II IN ASIA

World War II was by far the most destructive and, from both a regional and a global perspective, most transformative war in modern world history. For that reason alone, it is useful for the purposes of this history to gain some appreciation of the war's origins in Asia.

The origins of World War II in Asia may be understood from a variety of perspectives. One approach, for example, might be to see the origins of the war as a consequence of Japanese aggression. Japan's efforts to construct an Asian empire may be traced back into the nineteenth century, coincident with its transformation since the 1868 Meiji Restoration into an increasingly modern great power. In this view, Japan's imperialism was registered in its incorporation of the Ryukyu Islands in 1879, the defeat of China in 1895 and Russia in 1905 in wars for predominance on the Korean peninsula, and the resulting annexation of Taiwan and Korea. It continued with the effort to establish a predominating influence in Northeast Asia and North China, including stringent demands on China during World War I and its Siberian expedition during the Russian civil war.

More proximately, Japan's advance into China—beginning with the severing of Manchuria in 1931 and full-scale invasion in 1937—moved the region well down the path to wider war. By this time, Japan's expansionism, as depicted by wartime Allied propaganda, was increasingly guided by militarist fanatics who had hijacked the nation's foreign policy. Japan's empire building began to acquire broader implications with its advance into the Asian colonies of the Western empires. This began with its move into northern Indochina following the fall of France to Nazi Germany in May 1940, then its incursion into southern Indochina in the summer of 1941, and finally its attack on the American fleet at Pearl Harbor in December 1941 and its push into the Philippines and into British and Dutch Southeast Asia immediately thereafter.

From this perspective, the origins of the war may be understood as the consequence of Japanese aggression, whether one traces the roots of expansion deep into the early decades of the Meiji era or more immediately into the 1930s. The logic of expansion followed directly from the famous distinction, drawn by Meiji oligarch and founder of the Imperial Japanese Army Yamagata Aritomo in an 1890 memorandum, between Japan's "line of sovereignty" and its "line of advantage." The line of sovereignty demarcated the Japanese islands themselves. The line of advantage referred to adjacent areas, the disposition of which directly affected Japan's fundamental interests. By this logic, securing predominant influence on the Korean peninsula—the "dagger pointed at the heart of Japan," which in the 1890s fell within Japan's line of advantage—was necessary to preserve its line of sovereignty, the Japanese homeland. Once Korea was made a colony outright in the Japanese Empire, the line of advantage moved outward to include areas of eastern Russia, Mongolia, and North China. Securing predominant influence over territories within this new line of advantage was critical to sustaining Japan's new line of sovereignty. By this logic, Japan's imperialism followed a step-by-step calculus of expansion.

This approach, however, has its limitations as a framework for analysis. In locating the causes of the war in the behavior of only one of its antagonists, it not only lends itself to the moralism of wartime propaganda but also ignores the impact of broader trends and the actions of other states that make more intelligible the reasons for Japan's expansion and contributed to the outbreak of the war. A more interactive perspective tries to understand the origins of the war in Asia as a collision between two rising Asian-Pacific powers—Japan and the United States—as the relative power of the region's traditional hegemon—Britain—slowly declined. From this perspective, the outbreak of the war reflected the failure of these contestants to accommodate each other's interests.

Viewed in this framework, the United States and Japan embarked on a collision course at the beginning of the twentieth century, when Japan acquired special rights in southern Manchuria as a consequence of its victory over Russia in 1905. From an American viewpoint, this violated Washington's Open Door policy in China, enunciated at the turn of the century, which sought to ensure equal access to China's markets and resources among all great powers active in China. Washington and Tokyo clashed again in 1915, when Japan's Twenty-one Demands levied five groups of special economic, political, and security rights on the weak Republican regime of Yüan Shih-k'ai that effectively made China a protectorate of Japan. U.S. diplomacy succeeded in rolling back one group of demands (which required Chinese employment of Japanese advisers and joint police arrangements) but not the other four. In 1917, the Lansing-Ishii Agreement papered over the emerging clash of interests, exchanging Washington's acceptance of Japan's "special rights in China" for Tokyo's declaration of adherence to the Open Door policy and respect for China's territorial integrity.

These conflicts of interest between Japan on one side and the United States and Britain on the other continued into the 1930s. Ultimately, talks in Washington between Secretary of State Cordell Hull and Japanese Ambassador Nomura Kichisaburō, which ended in failure as Japan's forces advanced into southern Indochina in the summer and fall of 1941, and the ultimatum Washington delivered to Tokyo thereafter marked the last attempts to avert a collision between the two. Faced with equally unacceptable alternatives of disastrous American economic sanctions and loss of most of its empire, Tokyo resorted to force.

This essentially bilateral approach to analyzing the genesis of World War II in Asia is more effective than the one locating the origins of the war solely in Japanese aggression. But it still falls short of a satisfactory account that adequately encompasses all of the actors and events that led to the war. For that, a more comprehensive, systemic approach is necessary. That approach must focus on the rise and decline of the Washington treaty system in the 1920s and 1930s.

## THE WASHINGTON CONFERENCE TREATIES

From November 1921 to the following February, delegations from eight countries gathered in Washington to address common interests in East Asia and the western Pacific with Secretary of State Charles Evans Hughes. The Washington Conference produced three treaties that together addressed the central issues in a post–World War I order in the region: security, the balance of naval power, and the powers' approach to China, the most important interest they shared in the region. Taken together, the treaties embodied a system of relationships and expectations that was intended to guide and stabilize the great powers' interaction in the region indefinitely.

The need for a new treaty system for the East Asian–Pacific region was a consequence of World War I. Although the war had not spread directly to the region, it nevertheless significantly altered the cast of great powers that had interacted there before 1914. Germany lost its possessions on China's Shandong Peninsula and among the South Pacific island groups early in the war to Japan, which had moved quickly to seize them after declaring war on the side of the Allies soon after the war began. The war also weakened Britain and France, the two leading colonial powers in the region when the war began. Although their hold on their colonial possessions in the region was not in doubt as a consequence of the war, their colonial administrations now confronted emerging nationalist sentiments among the indigenous and often metropolitan-educated elites in their colonies, and their capacity to project power in the manner they had through the nineteenth century up to 1914 was diminished.

The United States emerged from World War I stronger in international affairs. Its late entry into the war tipped the conflict against Germany, and President Woodrow Wilson's voice on behalf of a new approach to world affairs spoke with enhanced authority in postwar peace deliberations. Wilson's internationalist agenda was inherited and extended by Hughes, who served in the administration of Wilson's successor, Warren G. Harding, a man who took little interest in foreign affairs.

Finally, in 1917, the Bolsheviks seized power with the October Revolution, taking Russia out of the war and radically transforming its place in world affairs. Moscow eventually resumed an active role in the international affairs of Asia, but for several years after 1917 the new Bolshevik regime was effectively isolated by the Western great powers and Japan as a pariah in international politics.

A new international order in East Asia and the Pacific was thus needed to address these changes, paralleling the agreements made for Europe at Paris in 1919. In that sense, the Washington Conference treaties extended the postwar settlement to East Asia and the Pacific, and the same approach to international relations incorporated in the Paris treaties informed the agreements arrived at in Washington three years later.

A four-power treaty, concluded by the United States, Britain, France, and Japan, was designed to provide a mechanism by which the four strongest powers in East Asia and the Pacific would address disputes in the region that might result in conflict. The treaty stipulated that any "controversy arising out of any Pacific question" among the four powers that could not be resolved through direct bilateral diplomacy would be referred to a conference of all for "consideration and adjustment." Further, if any other power in the region resorted to "aggression" affecting the rights of the four in the region, the four would "communicate with one another fully and frankly in order to arrive at an understanding as to the most efficient measures to be taken, jointly or separately," to deal with the situation. Finally, the Anglo-Japanese alliance, concluded in 1902 and renewed in 1911, would be abrogated upon ratification of the treaty.

Next, a five-power treaty, concluded by the same four plus Italy, limited the size of navies that each power would maintain. The treaty limited the total tonnage for "capital" ships (mainly battleships and aircraft carriers) to ratios of 5 (each, Britain and the United States) to 3 (Japan) to 1.75 (each, France and Italy). It also froze construction of new fortifications and naval bases by Britain, the United States, and Japan in the territories each held in the region.

A nine-power treaty, concluded between China and eight powers having interests in China, formalized the "principles" of the Open Door policy toward China that had been enunciated by Secretary of State John Hay in 1899 and 1900. The eight agreed to "respect the sovereignty, the independence, and the territorial and administrative integrity" of the ninth, China, and to aid it in establishing "effective and stable government." The treaty also obligated the eight to refrain from seeking exclusive rights and privileges and so to maintain equal access for all to commerce and industry in China.

Taken together, the Washington Conference treaties reflected the attending powers' efforts to arrange a stable structure of relationships and commitments in East Asia through which to address their interests for the future.[1] The three treaties incorporated new concepts of international relations that became prominent in world politics as a consequence of the war's devastation and in response to what were perceived to have been the war's causes. For Europeans and Americans, World War I had been the most destructive in their history. Although the American Civil War had earlier demonstrated the potential of the Industrial Revolution for mechanizing warfare, World War I reflected the maturation of this potential, deploying the full panoply of increasingly devastating weapons of modern war, including tanks, chemical weapons, aircraft, and submarines. The war resulted in an appalling total of more than twenty million dead, and it left horrific devastation of large areas that had served as battlegrounds, especially in France. For these reasons, the war had to be "the war to end all wars," and a new approach to international affairs, different from that preceding the war, had to be established that would end war and the devastating weapons that nations now had in their arsenals.

The causes of World War I were thought at the time to have been inherent in realpolitik, or realism, the outlook that had characterized the statecraft of the European powers.[2] In a realist outlook, states address conditions of perpetual international anarchy in which they engage in an unending competition for power in pursuit of narrow national interest, leading inevitably to conflict and war. Realist views of international politics complement a pessimistic, conservative analysis of human society such as that of the seventeenth-century English political philosopher Thomas Hobbes, whose *Leviathan* depicted human nature as intrinsically selfish and human society as a ruthless competition among individuals in pursuit of narrow self-interest—"a war of all against all," making lives "nasty, brutish, and short." Hobbes argued on behalf of an authoritarian political regime—an absolute monarchy—to contain English society's self-destructive impulses.[3]

In international politics, according to realists, no such overarching authority is possible. The best that can be achieved is a temporary peace, created and sustained by states' efforts to maintain a balance among all competitors for power that inhibits any one state from gaining hegemony over the others. Skillful practice of these precepts sustained the long European peace from the 1815 Congress of Vienna to 1914. But in the wake of World War I, reliance on balance-of-power tactics by means of alliances, ententes, and secret pacts—usually arrived at among aristocratic elites who were unresponsive to the peoples they governed and manipulated by arms merchants and international bankers—was blamed for the onset of general war in August 1914. It took only the assassination of an Austro-Hungarian prince to trigger the cascading entry of all of the European powers, linked in intricate webs of alliance commitments, into the war.

Based on these perceptions of realism's failure, an alternative approach to securing peace—usually referred to as idealism or liberalism—gained currency in the wake of the war and informed many of the postwar agreements, including those adopted at the Washington Conference. Following another seventeenth-century English philosopher, John Locke, idealists argue that conflict can be resolved and peace established through collective assent to a "social contract," by which individuals surrender some measure of autonomy in exchange for assurance of some fundamental level of security. At the level of international relations, idealists posit that an analogous process of collective assent to overarching norms, laws, and ultimately institutions may permanently ensure international peace. The narrow causes of war may be redressed through mechanisms of open and collective deliberation, in which disputes and grievances in international relations that might lead individual states to war may be resolved fairly by statesmen reasoning together. More broadly, the impulse toward war and hegemony on the part of any individual state may be deterred by the collective commitment of all states to oppose it together, based on the logic that the power of the whole is always greater than the power of any single state. States therefore agree to surrender some measure of sovereignty—the right to go to war to pursue some national interest—in exchange for collective security.

In contrast to realists' preference for mercantilist policies with respect to international economic relations, idealists espouse free trade. They do so not only because, as Adam Smith and David Ricardo argued, foreign trade is a positive-sum interaction in which all partners may profit through comparative advantage. Idealists also argue that free trade enhances the prospects for peace over war by giving states whose prosperity is sustained through economic interdependence an interest in enduring stability.

In the post–World War I era, the man whose views most vividly reflected this outlook was Woodrow Wilson, whose January 1918 address to Congress justifying the American entry into the war and projecting the terms of peace—the Fourteen Points—incorporated several of its essential elements. After declaring over "the day of secret covenants entered into in the interest of particular governments," Wilson made as his first point an insistence on "open covenants openly arrived at" through which "diplomacy shall proceed always frankly and in the public view." The second and third points—positing "absolute freedom of navigation upon the seas" and "removal . . . of all economic barriers and the establishment of an equality of trade conditions among all the nations assenting to peace"—endorsed the idealist commitment to free trade. The fourth point called for steps to reduce "national arms," resting on the belief that smaller arsenals reduce the capacity of states to wage war, provide assurance to states committed to collective security, and undercut the ability of arms merchants and bankers to manipulate states and profit from war. The fifth point endorsed the principle of popular sovereignty in resolution of "colonial claims," which Wilson intended to be applied to the disposition of Austro-Hungarian imperial claims in the Balkans, where nationalistic sentiments had fueled the outbreak of the war. But, more broadly, it also registered the belief that representative, democratic governments go to war less easily because they must be more responsive to the desires of their citizens than must autocratic regimes, which can pursue foreign policy agendas unencumbered by popular opinion. Finally, the fourteenth point addressed the core idealist notion of collective security, calling for "a general association of nations" that would be "formed under specific covenants for the purpose of affording mutual guarantees of political independence and territorial integrity to great and small states alike." The establishment of the League of Nations in 1919 reflected this outlook, though Wilson lacked the domestic backing to bring the United States into the organization that he had espoused. Similarly, the Washington Conference treaties embraced a collective security pact, an arms-limitation agreement that was the first of its kind in the Asia-Pacific region, and an agreement formalizing free trade principles.

## Weakness of the Washington Conference Treaties

The Washington treaties thus reflected a new, idealist departure in the great powers' approach to securing their interests in East Asia and the Pacific. As historian Akira Iriye pointed out, the treaties composed a system intended to provide a foundation for enduring stability in the region and a mechanism for resolution of disputes that might disturb the equilibrium.[4] The signatories did not intend a perpetual status quo. Thus, the nine-power treaty provided for revision of China's less than fully sovereign status over time, calling on the powers to aid reform in China, which might eventually lead to restoration of tariff autonomy and revocation of extraterritoriality once China established a stable, modern regime according to contemporary Western standards. In addition, the entire treaty system, as Iriye noted, also rested on the commitment of all of the major powers to the gold standard in foreign exchange.

Although the treaties were intended to provide a comprehensive system to ensure stable relations among the great powers interacting in the Asia-Pacific region, the treaty system suffered from weaknesses that figured in its demise in the 1930s. First, the treaty system was not in fact comprehensive. Although the United States was a signatory to the three Washington treaties, it was not a member of the overarching institution intended to provide a forum to resolve disputes, the League of Nations. The consequences for the Asia-Pacific region were made apparent in Western diplomacy following the 1931 Manchurian Incident, which led to the Japanese puppet state of Manzhouguo (Manchukuo). When Washington proposed collaboration with London to press Japan to reverse its course in Manchuria, London rejected a bilateral initiative, arguing that to proceed on that basis would undermine the effectiveness of working through the League to address the affair.

The Washington Conference system was also incomplete in not including Bolshevik Russia. Wilson, like other Western leaders, expected that the Bolshevik regime would quickly collapse as a result of its own internal contradictions and at the hands of its domestic resistance, and in 1918 he twice sent American troops to participate in the Allied intervention in the Russian civil war. No major Western government recognized the Moscow regime until 1922, and Washington did not do so until 1933. Under these circumstances of diplomatic isolation in its early years, the Bolshevik government was not invited to participate in the Paris Peace Conference or the Washington Conference. Its exclusion from the Washington Conference system was reflected in 1929, after Soviet and Chinese forces clashed over control of the China Eastern Railway, which traversed northern Manchuria. After Washington enjoined Moscow to cease hostilities and honor the provisions of the nine-power treaty, Moscow replied that since it had not been invited to participate in the Washington Conference, it felt no obligation to observe the terms of its treaties.

The Washington treaty system was also weak because it lacked effective mechanisms for enforcement. The four-power treaty called upon its signatories only to consult in the event of a dispute among the powers in the region. The 1902 Anglo-Japanese alliance that the treaty replaced did have real consequences—joint British-Japanese military cooperation—in the event of a widening conflict involving either of its signatories. Japan's seizure of Manchuria in 1931–32 provoked consultation among the powers, both on the basis of the Washington treaties and through the League, which appointed the Lytton Commission to investigate the affair. In the end it resulted only in Tokyo's decisions to leave the League and to renounce the Washington treaties.

## Breakdown of the Washington Conference Treaty System

Despite these flaws, the Washington treaty system worked well for most of the 1920s. Two events at the end of the decade, however, set in motion trends that undermined the system and led to its breakdown. The first of these was the reunification of China under Chiang Kai-shek and the Chinese Nationalist Party (the Kuomintang [KMT]). The KMT rose to power in part by drawing on a mass nationalism new to China and aroused by the failure of the Republican government after the 1911 Revolution, which ended the Qing dynasty's long reign, and by the continued great-power encroachments on Chinese sovereignty after the creation of the Republic of China. This mass nationalism was expressed most spectacularly in the 1919 May Fourth protests in Chinese cities upon the Paris conference's award of Germany's concessions in Shandong Province to Japan, and in the series of antiforeign boycotts and demonstrations that erupted through the 1920s.

In addition, the KMT succeeded in establishing a reunified Republican regime thanks to its raising, with Soviet assistance, a military force that enabled it to overcome the regional warlords as well as crack down on the Chinese Communists, previously its allies.

Under Chiang Kai-shek's leadership, this force embarked on the Northern Expedition in July 1926, conquering most of China's south, designating Nanjing as the new capital, and asserting the new regime's sovereignty over the north within two years.

The Nanjing regime's nationalistic agenda was evident from the outset. In July 1928 the government declared its ambition to revise all of the "unequal" treaties on which the treaty-port system rested in China. This ambition was not necessarily out of step with the provisions of the Washington Conference treaties—conferences on tariff revision had convened, for example, in 1925–26. Nor did the Nanjing regime seek the immediate renunciation of the treaty-port system that the nine-power treaty sustained; rather, seeking international recognition and assistance in China's development, it pursued its goals with respect to the treaty-port system through negotiation, not outright rejection. In response to the Nanjing regime's call for treaty revision, the treaty powers might have responded in concert through multilateral negotiations, in keeping with the spirit if not the letter of the Washington treaties. They responded unilaterally, however, led by Washington itself, which signed a new bilateral tariff treaty with Nanjing later in July; most of the other treaty powers followed suit in the following months.

In addition, the reunification of China presented problems for Japan's special position in Manchuria. Until 1928, Japan's interests in Manchuria were secured through its rights to the South Manchuria Railway and the ports on the Liaodong Peninsula, won from Russia in the 1904–5 war, and through its patronage of the Manchurian warlord Zhang Zuolin. Zhang had consolidated his position in the 1920s by playing off Japanese backing against the weak regime in Beijing, which he sought to take over himself, and succeeded in doing in April 1926. When Chiang Kai-shek's armies moved north against Zhang in Beijing in the spring of 1928, Japan faced a dilemma regarding its position in Manchuria: either support Zhang in north China or deny him support at the risk of spreading the Chiang-Zhang struggle to Manchuria itself. When Zhang abandoned Beijing to Chiang and retreated to his Manchurian home base, he was assassinated by officers of Japan's Kwantung (Guandong) Army. His son, Zhang Xueliang, who immediately succeeded him, consolidated his hold over his father's position in Manchuria and at the end of 1928 brokered Nanjing's recognition of his role in Manchuria in exchange for his declaration of allegiance to the Nanjing regime. As a consequence, Manchuria lay open to Nanjing's authority and to penetration by KMT agitators for revocation of Japan's rights in the region. The reunification of China by Chiang Kai-shek's regime thus posed a particular challenge to Japan's interests.

The second event that set in motion trends that undermined the Washington treaty system was the onset of the world Great Depression in 1929. Rather than pushing free trade to stimulate growth, the principal Western trading states responded to the Depression by seeking to protect their domestic markets by raising high tariff barriers to foreign imports and by going off the gold standard in foreign exchange transactions. This resort to protectionism dramatically undermined the idealist free trade outlook that underlay the Washington treaties and, in the opinion of many economic historians, made the Depression worse and harder to overcome.

The resorting by major Western nations to strongly protectionist trading blocs—the 1930 American Smoot-Hawley tariffs were representative—affected Japan severely, particularly as it decided in November 1929 to return to the gold standard as most Western nations were about to abandon it. As Japanese exports dwindled, unemployment in the export sector of the Japanese economy—especially textiles—rose, generating political dissatisfaction with the succession of liberal party governments. As economic conditions declined, extremist voices found a larger hearing in Japanese politics. Some right-wing extremist groups in the military resorted to violence in pursuit of a revolutionary change of regime, launching a string of assassinations of government officials beginning with the murder of the prime minister in 1931 and culminating in an attempted coup in 1936 by a group of army officers seeking to "restore" real power to Emperor Hirohito by assassinating the members of the cabinet. As the Depression wore on, discrediting cabinets of parties committed to liberalism, and as extremist right-wing groups resorted to political violence, conditions were set for conservative cabinets to take over in the name of imposing order. These cabinets were composed mostly of military men and bureaucrats from the government ministries rather than party politicians; by the mid-1930s, military-bureaucrat cabinets were the rule and liberal party government was at an end.

The impact of the Depression on Japan's domestic politics had consequences for its foreign policies, especially in China. As one scholar has observed, until 1930 two alternative approaches to securing Japan's interests in China had coexisted, each represented by distinct clusters of constituencies and government institutions.[5] One approach addressed Japan's interests in the treaty ports in China, interests best secured through the idealist internationalist logic of the Washington Conference treaties that served the treaty-port interests of all the signatory nations. The Japanese constituencies and government bureaucracies engaged in this approach included the export business sector, especially textiles, and the government's foreign and light-industry ministries. Idealist multilateral diplomacy in conjunction with the two major maritime trading nations—Britain and the United States—in the 1920s reflected these economic interests and rested on a distinct base of institutional interests in Tokyo.

Meanwhile, another approach addressed Japan's interests in Manchuria, where over the decades since the Russo-Japanese War it had secured an ambiguous recognition from the other powers of its "special" interests. Because Manchuria was important as a source of iron and coal for Japan's heavy industries, which in turn served Japan's military, a coalition of powerful interests developed among the Japanese military, the heavy-industry ministries, and large industries that consumed Manchurian resources. These interests were not well served by the multilateralism of the Washington system and, in view of perennial concerns about Russian interest in the region, were best served by more direct and at least informal if not outright control.

The impact of the 1929 Depression undermined the multilateralism of the Washington treaty system in Japan economically and politically, discrediting the liberal party governments that had pursued it through the 1920s. At the same time, it made resorting to unilateralist courses to secure interests in Manchuria and in other locations deemed critical to Japan's security all the more inviting. These economic, political, and foreign policy trends set the stage for the Manchurian crisis in September 1931.

The events of September 1931 in Mukden (Shenyang), in which Kwantung Army officers engineered a pretext for a takeover of all of Manchuria and creation of the puppet state of Manchukuo, under the last Qing emperor, forced Tokyo to decide between multilateral internationalism and unilateral pursuit of exclusive control in this critical area. Weak cabinets eventually acceded to occupation of all of Manchuria in January 1932 and the creation of the puppet regime thereafter.

The weak international response only solidified Tokyo's decision on behalf of unilateralism in Manchuria. In January 1932 Washington enunciated a "nonrecognition doctrine" according to which it would not recognize any step that violated the 1928 Kellogg-Briand Pact's outlawing of war as a means of foreign policy, but it did little more. In the same month, the League of Nations appointed a commission under Britain's Lord Lytton to investigate the course of events in Manchuria. After the League's February 1933 endorsement of the commission's report censuring Japanese actions in Manchuria, Tokyo responded the next month by withdrawing from the League. By January 1936 it had withdrawn from all of the Washington Conference treaties. With these steps, Tokyo had decided firmly on a unilateralist course toward autarky and exclusive control over resources in northeast Asia and China.

## THE ROAD TO WORLD WAR II IN THE ASIA-PACIFIC REGION

Over the next several years, Japan's expansion into north China followed the logic inherent in the aforementioned 1890 doctrine demarcating Japanese lines of "sovereignty" and "advantage." As each new area was secured within Tokyo's line of sovereignty, a new line of advantage necessary to buffer the broadened territory was created. Step by step and without a grand master plan of expansion, Japan's empire expanded incrementally and opportunistically. From Manchuria it sought to secure predominant influence in north China. After a clash between Japanese and local Chinese forces at Marco Polo bridge outside Beijing in July 1937 and Chiang Kai-shek's fateful decision to move Nationalist main forces into the area, Japan launched a full-scale military invasion into the heavily populated economic heartland of eastern and southeastern China, taking the major cities of Shanghai, Nanjing, Wuhan, and Canton by the end of 1938. With the fall of France in May 1940, Japan moved into northern Indochina the following September, an action that it justified as being required to sever supply lines to the Chinese. Finally, following the Nazi invasion of the Soviet Union in June 1941, Japanese forces moved into southern Indochina in July and seemed poised to expand deeper into Southeast Asia, thereby menacing British and Dutch possessions.

Japan's southward expansion into Southeast Asia reflected the resolution of differences in Tokyo over which powers—the Soviet Union or Britain and the United States—presented the greater danger to Japan's position in Asia. The Soviet Union had been the focus of Imperial Japanese Army planners' concern because of its proximity and perennial interest in Manchuria and, in the 1890s, Korea. Conclusion between Germany and Japan (and later Italy) of the Anti-Comintern Pact in 1936 was followed in 1937 by the Sino-Soviet Nonaggression Pact, setting the stage for a simmering confrontation between Japan and the

Soviet Union in northeast Asia over the next three years. However, heavy losses suffered by the Imperial Japanese Army in clashes with Soviet forces, first along the Soviet frontier with Manchuria at Zhanggufeng (near Vladivostok) in July 1938, then the following summer along the Mongolian frontier at Nomohan, surprised Tokyo with the strength of the Red Army's capacities under Joseph Stalin's accelerated program of military preparation since the early 1930s. Finally, the conclusion of the Nazi-Soviet Pact in August 1939 (as the Nomohan clashes were coming to an end), of the Tripartite Pact with Berlin and Rome in September 1940, and finally of the Soviet-Japanese Neutrality Pact in April 1941 stabilized the Japanese-Soviet confrontation in continental northeast Asia.

The United States and Britain had been the particular focus of Imperial Japanese Navy planners as far back as the Soviet Union had been for their army counterparts. The U.S. Navy represented the principal challenge to the Japanese Navy's supremacy in the western Pacific, but at the same time Japan's dependence on imported oil, scrap iron, and cotton from America posed a long-term dilemma for Tokyo. The navy brass had grumbled at Tokyo's accession to the 1922 five-power treaty limiting naval forces, and they fumed over the acceptance at the 1930 London Naval Conference of a revision of Japan's ratio of capital ships to those of the United States and Britain, even though the new ratio fell only slightly short of what they had sought. Tokyo's renunciation of the five-power and London naval treaties in 1934 had come under the administration of a former admiral, Prime Minister Okada Keisuke.

In July 1939, Washington informed Tokyo of its intention to allow a bilateral commercial treaty to lapse in 1940 as part of an emerging program of economic sanctions against Japan's expansionism in China. Thereafter, Tokyo's dilemma steadily sharpened into a fateful choice. Either it could pursue further expansion in East Asia to secure the means of autarkic economic development that would free it from dependence on American imports at the risk of conflict with the United States, or it could acquiesce in Washington's pressures and continue its economic interdependence with America.

Events in 1940 and 1941—the fall of France and the conclusion of the Tripartite Pact—inclined Tokyo to the first alternative. After the Japanese thrust into northern Indochina, which had the assent of Vichy France's collaborationist regime, Washington responded with new sanctions embargoing the sale of scrap iron to Japan, following an embargo on the sale of aviation fuel. With the conclusion of the Soviet-Japanese Neutrality Pact in April 1941 and then the Nazi invasion of the Soviet Union in June, Japanese forces moved into southern Indochina. Washington responded by freezing Japanese assets in the United States and suspending oil shipments. In negotiations with Japanese Ambassador Nomura Kichisaburō (an admiral and former foreign minister) in the fall of 1941, Secretary of State Cordell Hull sharply increased American pressure by demanding Japan's pullback not only from southern Indochina but from all of its advances in China since 1931.

The convergence of widening opportunities for expansion into Dutch and British Southeast Asia and escalating American sanctions brought Tokyo's dilemma regarding the United States to a strategic crossroad. Either it could acquiesce in Washington's pressures and accept retreat to the position of a secondary power in East Asia, or it could continue its unilateral advance to ensure economic autonomy at the risk of war with America,

Britain, and the Netherlands. In December it chose the latter course, attempting to cripple American naval power in the Pacific at Pearl Harbor and moving immediately into the Philippines and British and Dutch possessions in Southeast Asia.

More forceful British and especially American steps earlier in the 1930s might have deterred Japan's aggression in Manchuria and north China and so its advance to this critical point. Or, as late as the fall of 1941, had Hull presented Tokyo with less sweeping demands, Tokyo might have regarded them less as an all-or-nothing ultimatum and more as an opening for a negotiated political outcome. But continued American reliance in the 1930s on the diplomatic assumptions of idealism that framed the Washington Conference system while departing from its economic tenets and resorting to economic sanctions contributed to this outcome. President Hoover's belief that the United States could not be the policeman of Asia and the doctrine of "nonrecognition" in 1931 did little to deter a Japan that was itself facing increasingly difficult choices between continued reliance on the idealist internationalism it practiced in the 1920s and unilaterally securing direct control over the critical economic resources it needed. The U.S. Neutrality Acts of 1935, 1936, and 1937 were also ineffective and may have harmed China more than Japan. After the full-scale Japanese invasion of China in July 1937, President Franklin D. Roosevelt may have desired stronger steps in response, but domestic sentiment favoring isolationism constrained his options politically, despite a growing sympathy for China with the 1938 release of an emotionally stirring movie based on Pearl Buck's 1933 novel *The Good Earth*. His "quarantine" speech in Chicago in October 1937 offered no real deterrent to Japan's advance in China. His resort to economic sanctions in 1939, on the eve of the German invasion of Poland, and in 1940 and 1941 only sharpened the alternatives Tokyo faced.

## THE IMPACT OF WORLD WAR II IN ASIA

The war in Asia had lasting consequences for the structure of power in the region and invited conclusions that impressed postwar statesmen in designing a new international order in the region and in responding to events for a long time after. With respect to the war's impact on the international structure of power, Japan itself suffered two million dead in the war and became an occupied country at the war's conclusion. Japan's empire was dissolved, offering Koreans an opportunity to turn a promise of independence into a reality after thirty-five years as a Japanese colony. In China, the war dead totaled upward of thirteen million. Chiang Kai-shek's Republican government spent the later years of the war bottled up in China's southwest, cut off from its base of power in the wealthy cities of eastern China. Meanwhile, the war had given the Chinese Communists, on the verge of extinction in 1936, an opportunity to rebuild. By the end of the war, their strength presented a significant challenge to the ambitions of the Chiang regime to reestablish itself and restore national unity. China loomed as the greatest power vacuum in Asia after the war.

In South and Southeast Asia, the war kindled nationalistic sentiments among the indigenous peoples who had seen Japan rout the Western colonial powers in the region and animated their attempts in the postwar years to resist the reestablishment of colonial regimes. The rise of nationalistic movements for independence in the broad band of Asian colonies that existed before the war was abetted by the war's weakening of the colonial powers themselves. France and the Netherlands had been occupied countries themselves under the Nazis, and it was left to the British to attempt to reimpose colonial order on their behalf in the East Indies and Indochina.

Only the United States stood strengthened by the war, which confirmed overarching American dominance in the global order, replacing Britain's position before the war. The United States emerged from the war with its economy strengthened though distorted by war spending priorities, in possession—with the Soviet Union—of one of the two largest military forces in the world, and in sole possession of nuclear weapons.

The war thus provided Washington with new opportunities to recast the world order. To this task American leaders applied conclusions drawn from their understanding of the causes of the war to designing a postwar peace. Among these were the injunction "no more Munichs" and an appreciation of the weaknesses of idealist approaches to peace. The war evoked powerful critiques of idealist ideas in international relations—embodied at the onset of the war in E.H. Carr's classic *The Twenty Years Crisis, 1919–1939* and in the early postwar years in Hans Morgenthau's text *Politics Among Nations*. But the war did not altogether discredit idealist ideas, and American leaders in particular continued to apply them, now tempered by elements of realism. To these efforts we now turn.

# 2 PLANNING THE POSTWAR WORLD

Even before the United States entered the war, the future Allies enunciated their war aims in a manner redolent of the idealism President Woodrow Wilson expressed during World War I. Thus, the Atlantic Charter, issued after a meeting between President Franklin D. Roosevelt and Prime Minister Winston Churchill off Newfoundland in August 1941, declared that there would be no territorial changes without the "freely expressed wishes of the people concerned," and that all peoples had the right to choose their governments. The statement said that sovereignty would be restored to those "who have been forcibly deprived" of this status. It prefigured future arrangements by pledging equal access to the world's trade and resources and by favoring establishment of "a wider and more permanent system of general security." It is instructive to trace how these principles fared, in interpretation and application, as they were subjected to the exigencies of war and to the conflicts of interest and mutual suspicions that produced the Cold War in the ruins of the hot one.

The principle of self-determination was particularly vulnerable to challenge. After all, Churchill himself, a leader who said he did not become prime minister in order to preside over the dissolution of the British Empire, craftily sought to limit the use of the principle as an instrument of decolonization. Joseph Stalin, for his part, was loath to turn over his territorial gains from the hugely costly struggle against Nazi Germany, though he of course supported decolonization elsewhere. The other European colonial powers were also resistant to the loss of their far-flung possessions, notably the French and Dutch as well as British colonies in Asia.

## EARLY WARTIME CONFERENCES

The Wilsonian principles reflected in the Atlantic Charter continued to find expression as the Allied leaders began to grapple with the prospects and plans for the postwar world. The Moscow meeting of foreign ministers in October 1943 adopted a declaration embracing a framework of principles, including a call for establishment of a universal international organization based on the principle of the equal sovereignty of all states. Interestingly, notwithstanding Soviet hesitations, the declaration was open to signature by the Chinese foreign minister as well as his American, British, and Soviet counterparts. This foreshadowed the role China was to be accorded in planning and, it was expected, in executing the plans for the postwar arrangement, including status as a permanent member of what became the United Nations Security Council.[1] Secretary of State Cordell Hull, addressing a joint session of Congress upon his return from Moscow, exulted that as the provisions of the declaration were put into effect, there would "no longer be need for spheres of influence, for alliances, for balance of power."[2] This repudiation of the realist worldview harked back to American goals for the post–World War I world, but it proved to be sadly lacking in prescience regarding the geopolitical realities soon to envelop the planners. Indeed, the high-flown principles of the Moscow declaration were accepted by the foreign ministers only by removing elements that addressed more directly the hard issues that the Allies would face. Notably, the final document committed them to employ their forces in other states only after joint consultation, but the original American proposal had called for "joint consultation *and agreement*."[3]

In addition to China's being one of the signatories of the declaration, Asia began to figure in Allied deliberations in another significant way: Moscow's secret promise to enter the war against Japan after the defeat of Germany. Secrecy was required by Moscow's neutrality treaty with Japan, which served the Soviets' concern that they not be faced with a second front while the battle with the Nazis raged on. The commitment to enter the war did not, of course, come without a price, and this part of the Soviet agenda for the postwar world began to emerge at the first summit of the Big Three, held in Tehran a few weeks after the foreign ministers had met in Moscow. The Tehran conference was sandwiched between two meetings held in Cairo that were attended by Roosevelt, Churchill, and Chinese leader Chiang Kai-shek, which afforded the main participants in the Pacific theater an opportunity to concert their plans and to issue an important statement that could be shown to Stalin for his approval.

The United States was concerned about the prospect of the Chinese dropping out of the war, and it wished to bolster the war effort in China by removing the Japanese from Burma in order to provide a land line of communication to China—the Burma Road. The British, however, were resistant to the role intended for them, naval operations in the waters adjacent to Burma, and were skeptical of what they viewed as an American obsession with China and its future role in the region and the world. Moreover, the British had their own geopolitical reasons to concentrate on naval operations in the western Pacific: to regain control over their valuable colonial possessions in the Malay Peninsula and Hong Kong. The China-Burma-India theater remained a secondary or tertiary area of operations in terms of grand strategy, and the Chinese, who reeled from a Japanese offensive late in the war, played a minor role in the largely sea-based American offensive in which islands large and small were recaptured in the drive toward the main islands of Japan. This island-hopping campaign, in the era before intercontinental bombers and missiles, served to choke off Japan's access to food and raw materials along the East Asian sea-lanes and to establish platforms for air attacks on the Japanese homeland.

**THE ALLIES' PLAN FOR POSTWAR ASIA: THE CAIRO DECLARATION**

It is their [the United States, China, the United Kingdom] purpose that Japan shall be stripped of all the islands in the Pacific which she has seized or occupied since the beginning of the World War in 1914, and that all the territories Japan has stolen from the Chinese, such as Manchuria, Formosa, and the Pescadores, shall be restored to the Republic of China.... The aforesaid three powers, mindful of the enslavement of the people of Korea, are determined that in due course Korea shall become free and independent.

Cairo Declaration, 1 December 1943, in U.S. Department of State, *Foreign Relations of the United States 1943: The Conferences at Cairo and Tehran* (Washington, DC: U.S. Government Printing Office, 1961), 448–49.

On the political front, the Cairo Declaration[4] registered the Allies' demand for Japan's "unconditional surrender." It also put their postwar aims in Asia on public record (except for Stalin's endorsement at Tehran), calling for dissolution of the Japanese Empire by stripping Japan of all territories it had occupied since the beginning of World War II. It said that all territories "stolen" from China, such as Formosa (Taiwan) and Manchuria, "shall be restored" to the Republic of China. Note that the three Allies declared these aims to be "their purpose," a phrasing that would figure in diplomatic parsings of the juridical status of Taiwan as that island's future became a political and strategic issue after the war. Another issue addressed, albeit sketchily, proved also to be intractable: Korea, which was promised independence "in due course."

During this period, as the Allies groped for formulas to shape the postwar world, the major role envisaged by Roosevelt for China was reflected in its identification as one of "the four policemen"—along with the United States, Britain, and the Soviet Union—that would enforce the peace as part of a new international security organization. Such a role presupposed that China would become a strong and unified state capable of discharging this responsibility. Moreover, from the perspective of the Western Allies, it assumed that such a China would be friendly to their interests and a reliable partner in pursuing their agenda. These assumptions would rest on shaky foundations; to the extent the first goal was realized, the second one was overturned by the results of the Chinese civil war.

Soviet goals for postwar Asia were broached at Tehran.[5] While confirming Moscow's intention to enter the war against Japan after Germany's defeat, Stalin asked what the rewards were to be for the Soviet Union. Stalin's interests conformed to realist expectations: age-old Russian aspirations for year-round ice-free ports and recovery of territories previously lost to Japan, such as the southern half of Sakhalin Island. There was talk about Dairen (now Dalian) becoming a free port (Roosevelt's preference) or being leased by the Soviet Union (Stalin's desire), giving the Soviets access to warm waters through the use of the Manchurian railways. This agenda would shape Moscow's maneuvering as the postwar Asian settlement began to emerge.

In the wake of the Cairo and Tehran conferences, and of the U.S.-British invasion across the English Channel in June 1944 to open the second front long demanded by Moscow, steps were taken toward creating international institutions that would become significant features of the postwar world. In July 1944, at Bretton Woods in New Hampshire, forty-four nations (not including the Soviet Union) agreed to establish the International Monetary Fund and the World Bank (the International Bank for Reconstruction and Development) in an effort to avoid the post–World War I financial crises that contributed to the successor war and to fight the economic backwardness thought to spawn instability. The U.S. dollar, convertible to gold at a fixed rate, would serve as the world's reserve currency and the basis for international exchange. Together with GATT (General Agreement on Tariffs and Trade, formed in 1947), these multilateral institutions were intended to avert the trade wars, competitive devaluations, liquidity crises, and other economic challenges that had bedeviled the interwar era.

A couple of months later, at Dumbarton Oaks in Washington, D.C., representatives of the Allied powers met to prepare proposals regarding the structure and functions of the international security organization discussed by their leaders the previous year. The new organization, which was established the following year in San Francisco, was to supplant the ineffectual League of Nations and to overcome the power politics and alliance rivalries that had produced wars and misery in an anarchic international environment. The framers of the new body, one might say, intended to repeal the realist laws of international behavior. If so, they hedged their bets by creating both the General Assembly—an idealist institution with universality of membership and equality of vote—and a Security Council of limited numbers, five of which (China, France, and the Big Three) were accorded permanent membership with a right of veto. (In practice, the exercise of this power has not comported with the literal terms of the charter, which stipulates that Security Council decisions require "the concurring votes" of the permanent members. Parties to a dispute "shall abstain" from voting, but permanent members that were not parties to the dispute have abstained from voting rather than casting a concurring vote, and in an implicit revision of the charter, this has not been treated as a veto.) Thus, the Security Council, according special status to the major powers, represented a bow to the realist worldview. As an incentive to these powers to form an organization dedicated to collective security, they were handed an instrument for protecting their own vital interests against encroachments by the collective body.

For a real demonstration of the realist worldview, there may be no better example than what occurred during Churchill's visit to Moscow in October 1944. In addition to a discussion of military plans for the Soviet role in Asia, to be undertaken within three months of the defeat of Germany, Stalin and his visitor took up the question of Eastern Europe. As Churchill related the story, he jotted down on a sheet of paper the percentage of control each side would exercise in the territories liberated from the enemy: Romania, 90 percent Soviet control; Greece, 90 percent for the Western allies; Yugoslavia, fifty-fifty, and so on. Stalin signaled his assent with a tick mark.[6] This proposal of what amounted to spheres of influence, it should be noted, originated with a cosignatory of the Atlantic Charter.

To be fair, this agreement lends itself to a more benign interpretation than that of raw realpolitik. Churchill's motivation may have been concern over forestalling civil strife and collisions with local Communist forces in areas liberated from German occupation. It may also have been an effort to postpone a political settlement in these areas in order to ensure maximum harmony among the Allies in pursuing the military campaign. A pattern of Soviet behavior was emerging, however, that began to cloud the prospects of continuing accord, namely, a tendency to assert political goals and to extract commitments to pay Moscow's price for its military contributions. The Western Allies, particularly Roosevelt, had resisted this tendency to have political ends prefigured in military means. (Churchill, for his part, recognized the importance of a military presence as the basis for political demands—witness his advocacy of a military campaign by the Western Allies in the Balkans in order to establish a presence in Central Europe before the arrival of the Red Army gave the Soviets a free hand.) As the war in Europe entered its final phases and a massive undertaking to subdue Japan loomed on the horizon, however, military and political aims began to be intermeshed, and military "facts on the ground" acquired a forcefulness that the language of diplomacy would find hard to match.

## THE BIG THREE AT YALTA

This pattern asserted itself most notably at the Yalta Conference in February 1945, an event that was destined to be the subject of bitter historiographical contention for decades (and still is).[7] Discussion of the Pacific theater was left mainly to the United States and the Soviet Union, with Churchill remaining in the background. American representatives told of plans to liberate the Philippines and Okinawa, thereby providing air and naval bases near Japan to intensify the crippling attacks on the enemy's military and economic resources, including its maritime lifelines, that the island-hopping campaign had supported—the strategy of a systematic island-by-island rollback of the Japanese presence in the western Pacific. There was no mention of the favorable prognosis for the atomic bomb, and the Americans indicated their interest in Soviet participation in what was projected as a protracted, casualty-laden offensive to subdue Japan. (Indeed, U.S. planners underestimated the power of the new weapon and foresaw Japanese resistance extending

### STALIN GAINS REWARDS FOR ENTERING WAR VERSUS JAPAN: THE YALTA SECRET PROTOCOL

The leaders of the three Great Powers—the Soviet Union, the United States of America and Great Britain—have agreed that in two or three months after Germany has surrendered and the war in Europe has terminated the Soviet Union shall enter into the war against Japan on the side of the Allies on condition that:

1. The status quo in Outer-Mongolia (The Mongolian People's Republic) shall be preserved;
2. The former rights of Russia violated by the treacherous attack of Japan in 1904 be restored, viz:
   (a) the southern part of Sakhalin as well as all the islands adjacent to it shall be returned to the Soviet Union,
   (b) the commercial port of Dairen shall be internationalized, the preeminent interests of the Soviet Union in this port being safeguarded, and the lease of Port Arthur as a naval base of the USSR restored,
   (c) the Chinese-Eastern Railroad and the South-Manchurian Railroad which provides an outlet to Dairen shall be jointly operated by the establishment of a joint Soviet-Chinese Company it being understood that the preeminent interests of the Soviet Union shall be safeguarded and that China shall retain full sovereignty in Manchuria;
3. The Kuril islands shall be handed over to the Soviet Union. . . .

Yalta Conference secret protocol, 11 February 1945, in U.S. Department of State, *Foreign Relations of the United States, 1945*, vol. 3, part 2 (Washington, DC: U.S. Government Printing Office, 1955), 984.

eighteen months after Germany's defeat.) Stalin offered to enter the war against Japan two or three months after Germany's defeat, thus providing time for necessary logistical efforts to shift the Red Army's might to the east. The Soviets presented their bill for this offer, to which after some haggling Roosevelt acceded.

The secret agreement on East Asia[8] (secrecy was needed so as not to give Japan cause to attack the Soviet Union before the latter's troop transfers to the east after the end of the war against Germany) assigned gains to Moscow that served to reverse Russian losses from the tsarist era; according to one provision, "the former rights of Russia violated by the treacherous attack of Japan in 1904 shall be restored." These "rights" were the return of the southern half of Sakhalin Island, internationalization of the commercial port of Dairen and Soviet leasing of the naval base of Port Arthur, and access to these ports in Liaodong Peninsula by use of the railways in Manchuria to be operated "jointly" by a Sino-Soviet company. The Soviets added phrasing to a previously agreed text of the agreement that toughened their claims, namely that "the preeminent interests" of the Soviet Union were to be "safeguarded" as regards Dairen and the railways.[9] Though China's sovereignty in Manchuria was confirmed, it was also compromised by these reversions to tsarist special interests in the region. Further, since no representative of China participated in the discussions, Roosevelt agreed to obtain Chiang Kai-shek's "concurrence" in these arrangements.

In addition to these "restored" rights, a separate clause "handed over" the Kuril Islands to the Soviet Union, though ethnographic and historical arguments could be adduced in favor of Japan's retention of the southernmost islands. An 1855 boundary agreement had assigned the latter to Japan, and in 1875 Russia relinquished its claims to the central and northern Kurils in exchange for Japan's ceding of its interests in Sakhalin. Japan's claim to the southern islands, which it calls the "Northern Territories," would continue to block attempts to close the books on World War II by conclusion of a Soviet/Russian-Japanese peace treaty.

Stalin also gained acceptance at Yalta of the status quo of Outer Mongolia (which had broken from the new Republic of China in 1912 and fallen into the Soviet orbit as the Mongolian People's Republic), thereby securing that satellite's subordination to Moscow and blocking any claim of Chinese sovereignty. Like the special Soviet rights in Manchuria, this was an irritant to Chinese nationalism, the Nationalists and Communists alike harboring an irredentist claim to that land. (Deference to Chinese sensitivities led Washington to delay diplomatic recognition of the Mongolian People's Republic in the 1970s.)

Stalin's goals were realist in nature, being strategic and economic, not ideological, in motivation. He was reprising traditional tsarist impulses in the region, as reflected in the goals of regaining prized areas lost earlier in the century to Japan and seeking broader outlets to the Pacific—while blocking others' access from the Pacific—by gaining the Kurils. (Likewise, Moscow regained territory in Eastern Europe that had been within the tsarist ambit, though this time Poland was not partitioned but moved westward at Germany's expense.) The Soviets were opportunistic in seizing war booty as it became available (as it did in Manchuria and North Korea as well as Eastern Europe). There was a difference, however, between the drive to establish buffer zones in the Asia-Pacific area and the drive to establish one on the European front. Where the Soviet despot had the advantage in Eastern

Europe of military occupation as the means of securing geopolitical gains, in Asia he was acutely sensitive about showing his hand to the Japanese lest a second front be opened prematurely. Moreover, even after Soviet entry into the war against Japan, Stalin cautiously limited his geopolitical reach out of concern over a possible collision with the United States, in contrast to his moves in Eastern Europe to establish a broad glacis far exceeding Russia's historical domination. Given these constraints, his bargaining leverage lay in offering military cooperation at a price of the political awards enumerated previously. How strong was that leverage, and did Roosevelt need to pay the price?

The answer turns, first of all, on the military prospects in the Pacific theater in early 1945. If it was anticipated that the drive to subdue the Japanese and conquer their home islands would follow the bloody, arduous pattern prevailing at the time—an expectation confirmed by the more than fifty thousand American casualties suffered in the battle for Okinawa that spring—Washington had a strong incentive to meet Stalin's price for entering the war. Military planning envisioned a significant Soviet role in taking on the huge concentrations of Japanese troops in Manchuria. China's contribution to combating the Japanese presence had been a big disappointment, crippled as it was by incompetence, corruption, and the priority the Nationalists attached to overcoming their domestic rivals, the Chinese Communists. Moreover, as has been noted, the United States, concentrating resources on the island campaign in the Pacific, played a limited role on the mainland.

This answer prompts other questions, however. Roosevelt was aware by the time of the Yalta Conference that a powerful new weapon was expected to be available in the middle of the year, or around the time when Germany would be subjugated and the Soviets would be preparing to enter the war against Japan. If the American campaign, already highly effective in advancing toward Japan proper and severely degrading its naval, air, and merchant marine capabilities, was to be further fortified by the atomic bomb, then Soviet help may have been of only marginal value. If anything, in this view, Moscow should have had to pay a political price to enter the war rather than the other way around.[10]

Roosevelt and his advisers may well have concluded at the time that the prospects for a long and costly final campaign were more compelling than speculation about the decisive effects of the air and naval war even if augmented by an awesome new weapon. In that case Soviet participation and the attendant political extractions were the price paid for saving enormous amounts of blood and treasure. Some scholars have argued that the Soviet entry, following a vain effort by the Japanese to have Moscow mediate a settlement of the war short of unconditional surrender, was in fact the decisive determinant of Tokyo's capitulation in mid-August a few days after the atomic attacks and the Soviet declaration of war.[11] Moreover, given the likelihood of civil conflict in China and the temptations that supporting the Chinese Communists may have presented to Moscow, Roosevelt may have been willing to accept Stalin's bargain up front as a way of enticing Soviet cooperation in efforts for China to play the role envisioned by the United States: a strong, unified country filling the vacuum in Asia left by Japan's defeat and responsive to American influence. In this regard, the Soviets expressed readiness in the Yalta agreement to conclude a treaty of friendship and alliance with Nationalist China. The alternative feared by the West was unequivocal Soviet support for the Chinese Communists and an effort to fill the vacuum with Soviet power.

Assuming that a bargain on Soviet entry was justified, was the price right? Moscow's insistence on its "preeminent rights" regarding Dairen and the Manchurian railways was ominous, clouding its profession of respect for China's sovereignty.[12] Within a week of declaring war against Japan, it honored its pledge to form an alliance with the Chinese Nationalists but insisted on incorporating in the treaty the geopolitical gains it extracted at Yalta. In an ambiguous situation, Moscow was keeping its options open for the postwar era while strengthening its hand for realizing its security and economic interests in northeast Asia. In Washington's calculations, the ambiguities were resolved in favor of enlisting Soviet support for the war effort against Japan and for cooperation in bolstering China for the role assigned to it in the postwar world. Washington also was determined to thwart Moscow's interest in a role in the occupation of Japan, an interest that may well have induced Stalin to take what gains he could without overextending his reach.

## POTSDAM AND AFTER

The composition of the Big Three changed by two-thirds after Yalta: Roosevelt died in April and Churchill's Tories were defeated in elections in July. At the next summit meeting, held at Potsdam (outside Berlin) in late July, the Big Three consisted of Stalin, President Harry S. Truman, and new Prime Minister Clement Attlee (who replaced Churchill while the conference was in progress). The United States, Britain, and China issued a proclamation on 26 July reiterating the Cairo Declaration's demand for Japan's "unconditional surrender."[13] At this time Truman informed Stalin that the United States was developing a powerful new weapon, something the dictator would have known about from espionage. In fact, the world entered the nuclear era a few days after the end of the Potsdam Conference with the atomic bombing of Hiroshima on 6 August, followed three days later by a similar devastation of Nagasaki. Between those two attacks—and three months after Germany's surrender—the Soviet Union declared war on Japan as it had promised, and by the fifteenth Tokyo had accepted the terms of surrender (the formal surrender coming on 2 September). The plans for a postwar world were now to be put to the test.

Revisionist historians have propounded the thesis that the United States exploited the atom bomb as an instrument in the Cold War contest with the Soviet Union.[14] To be sure, Washington saw the broader advantages of possession of such a weapon, and it was acutely concerned when the Soviets broke the atomic monopoly in 1949. Still, the momentum driving the uses of the bomb derived from the military imperatives of compelling Japan's surrender without incurring the

### ALLIES DEMAND UNCONDITIONAL JAPANESE SURRENDER: THE POTSDAM PROCLAMATION

The terms of the Cairo Declaration shall be carried out and Japanese sovereignty shall be limited to the islands of Honshu, Hokkaido, Kyushu, Shikoku and such minor islands as we determine....

We call upon the Government of Japan to proclaim now the unconditional surrender of all the Japanese armed forces, and to provide proper and adequate assurances of their good faith in such action. The alternative for Japan is prompt and utter destruction.

Potsdam Proclamation, 26 July 1945, in U.S. Department of State, *Foreign Relations of the United States 1945*, vol. 2, part 2 (Washington, DC: U.S. Government Printing Office, 1960), 1474–76.

extremely high costs of an invasion. The second bombing, which came a few hours after the Soviet entry into the war, was deemed necessary to bludgeon a divided Japanese leadership into acceptance of the unconditional surrender terms. (There was not enough time between the two events for the Soviet entry to be factored into the decision to carry out the bombing of Nagasaki.[15]) It may have been the case that by the time of the Potsdam Conference, Truman had resisted counsels to qualify the demand for unconditional surrender in order to make use of the bombs in a move to end the war before the Soviets could make their planned entry.[16] Contrary to previous expectations, the president also excluded Stalin from being a signatory to the proclamation. But as we have seen, Washington had awarded geopolitical gains to the Soviet Union in the postwar Asian settlement for the purpose of ending the war expeditiously. Though that result may have limited the time available to the Soviets for expanding their presence in the region, they nonetheless realized the awards they had been offered at Yalta to secure their participation in the climactic offensive against Japan. By and large, Washington could be faulted more for using military means for strictly military goals than for shaping military decisions with an eye to their geopolitical consequences.

The dominant influence of military exigency was reflected in the steady erosion in the course of the war of the idealist principles animating the Atlantic Charter, a process whose milestones included the casual division of spheres of influence in Eastern Europe by Churchill and Stalin, and then the awards given to Stalin at Yalta to obtain Soviet entry into the war against Japan. The San Francisco conference in 1945 establishing the United Nations combined idealism and realism by offering universality of membership in the General Assembly while in the Security Council effectively reserving enforcement power to the major nations. The composition of the five permanent members looked much like the core powers of the prewar multipolar system, omitting the defeated Axis powers and substituting China for Japan. Like many of the plans for the postwar world, as we examine in subsequent chapters, the workings of the United Nations became subject to the overarching force of bipolarity; in the case of the world organization, this meant that the veto power severely circumscribed the exercise of its enforcement machinery. The wartime cooperation dissolved into mutual mistrust and recrimination, and much of what happened in the world was determined or at least shaped in considerable measure by the calculations of the two superpowers in pursuing their zero-sum game for global influence and preponderance.

Moreover, expectations that the Allies might be able to pursue collaboration in the postwar period as they had during the war dimmed with the sudden departure of two of the original Big Three leaders—Roosevelt and Churchill—and their replacement by men of different temperaments and perspectives—Truman and Atlee. Stalin may well have wondered how committed the two new leaders would be to the agreements their predecessors had entered into, and so he may have had incentive to hedge against the possibility that they were not.

Bipolarity was more pronounced and clear-cut in Europe, its original arena, as symbolized by Churchill's vivid image of an Iron Curtain separating the Soviet sphere from the West, and in the stark two-camp thesis propounded in 1947 by Stalin's lieutenant Andrey A. Zhdanov at the founding of the Cominform (see Chapter 8). In contrast to

Europe, the limited role of the Red Army in the war against Japan meant that Moscow's writ did not extend much beyond its borders in the east. Outer Mongolia was an exception (in fact, its status was not affected by the war), and Korea fell almost accidentally into the same category as Germany by being divided along the lines of the occupying forces. As in the case of Korea, nothing came of Roosevelt's vague proposal of trusteeship status for the colonial areas of Southeast Asia. There the newly assertive forces of nationalism and Communist insurgency, overlaid by the impact of bipolarity, interacted in complex ways (see Chapter 6).

The bedrock fact was that the planning for the postwar era was strongly constrained and largely determined by military exigency. German aggression posed a mortal threat to the Soviet Union and Britain—and even more to other countries such as Poland and France; political questions were subordinated to the demands of the war effort and the need to maintain coalition unity. Military exigency during the war was translated into demands for buffer zones and spheres of influence in the postwar settlement. Another dimension was the ideological rivalry dating from the Bolshevik Revolution in Russia, which the West and Japan tried to suppress in its infancy. The ideological conflict sharpened what international relations theorists call the "security dilemma," in which a move by one side to enhance its security, made for what it may regard as purely defensive reasons, is interpreted by an adversary as a threat to that side's security, and thus a spiral of mistrust and ever-heightening tension is produced. That is a recipe for a Cold War.[17]

It may be worth taking stock at this point of the gains and losses emerging from World War II and at the onset of the Cold War. To be illustrative rather than comprehensive, note that Moscow got Bulgaria; the West won Italy. Poland was Moscow's; France remained a part of the West. Moscow gained concessions in Manchuria and half of Korea; the United States occupied Japan and the other half of Korea. The ledger looks overwhelmingly in favor of the West. There were areas in Asia fraught with ambiguity and uncertainty, however: How would the Chinese civil war resolve itself; what would become of a divided Korea; would the colonial powers be able to reassert their authority in the southern arc of Asia; how would these developments play into the bipolar conflict? We look at these questions in coming chapters.

# 3 THE CHINESE CIVIL WAR

In the summer of 1946, less than a year after the surrender of Japan, all-out civil war erupted in China. Wartime planning by the Allies had sought the establishment of postwar political unity and stability in China through the creation of a coalition government. The coalition would broaden the reigning Republic of China government led by Chiang Kai-shek and the Nationalist Party (Kuomintang [KMT]) by incorporating the resurgent Communist Party of China (CPC) and various "third force" parties and personalities that offered an alternative to the KMT and the CPC. The outbreak of full-scale civil war in 1946 meant the failure of American mediation through the last year of the war and immediately after the war to bring about a stable, unified coalition government.

In three short years, by the last months of 1949, Communist armies led by CPC Chairman Mao Zedong swept Chiang's KMT-led regime off the Chinese mainland and onto the island of Taiwan. On 1 October 1949, Mao proclaimed the establishment of the People's Republic of China (PRC), while Chiang Kai-shek reestablished the Republic of China (ROC) in Taipei, which he hoped to be a temporary stopover. Each regime claimed to be the sole legitimate government of China, launching a contest over national sovereignty that persisted until the 1990s (see Chapter 12).

The eruption of the Chinese civil war in the summer of 1946 coincided with the surfacing of Soviet-Western tensions that rapidly intensified into the hostilities of the Cold War. As these tensions played out in Asia, the early postwar years saw the division of three countries within which rival claimants contested sovereignty with the backing of one or the other side in the increasingly global Cold War. Korea's temporary division after Japan's surrender into a Soviet-administered zone north of the thirty-eighth parallel and an American-administered zone south of it gave way in 1948 to two rival Korean regimes, each claiming to represent all of Korea and each backed by a great-power patron (see Chapter 5). In Vietnam, the dissolution at the 1954 Geneva Conference of French claims to a colonial empire in Indochina produced a division at the seventeenth parallel, with a Democratic Republic of Vietnam in the north and, in 1955, under unilateral American initiative, a Republic of South Vietnam in the south (see Chapter 6). In both Korea and

Vietnam, brutal civil wars were fought in which both the United States and the Soviet Union saw significant stakes in their contest for global power and in which both intervened—either indirectly (the Soviet Union) or directly (the United States). (Later, in Afghanistan, the superpowers' roles were reversed, with the Soviet Union intervening directly; see Chapter 10.)

In the case of China's civil war, neither the United States nor the Soviet Union intervened by sending forces of its own. But each power was significantly engaged in the Chinese contest, and each saw major consequences from the Communist victory in 1949 for its own approach to the Cold War. In many respects, the Chinese civil war became the template by which the stakes were thereafter judged in Korea and Vietnam, as well as in other independence struggles in Asia. In this respect, the lessons that were drawn from the Chinese civil war—added to those drawn from World War II—shaped the framework and fueled the dynamic of the Cold War in Asia for the following two decades.

## PROBLEMS OF INTERPRETATION

Interpretation of the Chinese civil war and its outcome has long been contested on all sides. In the PRC and Soviet Union through the 1980s, accounts of the Chinese civil war were strongly skewed by the ups and downs of Sino-Soviet relations and by the cult of personality erected around Mao Zedong in the midst of a widening Chinese leadership split in the 1960s. During the heyday of solidarity between Beijing and Moscow in the 1950s, Chinese accounts routinely credited the critical assistance the USSR provided the CPC during the civil war. A highly authoritative short history of the party's revolutionary struggle proclaimed, for example, that

> the thirty years' history of the CPC has proved that without the great and unfailing assistance of the Soviet Union and the international proletariat, and particularly the aid given to the CPC and the Chinese people during the First Revolutionary Civil War [1921–27] by the Comintern under the leadership of Lenin and Stalin, and without the aid given by the Soviet Army destroying Hitler in the west and annihilating the Japanese Guandong Army in northeast China . . . the present victory of the Chinese revolution could never have been achieved.[1]

As the Sino-Soviet split emerged in the late 1950s and with the rise of the cult of personality around Mao, however, Chinese accounts began to play up Mao's strategic genius in pioneering a path of revolution not only responsible for the Communist victory in China without—and sometimes in spite of—Soviet aid and advice, but also relevant to the liberation struggles of peoples throughout the third world.

Conversely, Soviet renditions of the Chinese civil war in the 1950s heralded the successful strategy pursued by the CPC and its leader, Mao Zedong. After Sino-Soviet relations soured, however, Soviet accounts criticized Mao's leadership as "obsessed with 'revolutionary impatience'" in the early stages of the civil war but also as given to "defeatist" moods in later stages, when victory was imminent. One standard history of Sino-Soviet relations, for example, recalled that in the civil war years "Mao Zedong's political waverings revealed his petty bourgeois outlook, his proneness to change to one extreme or another: from efforts to spur on the revolution in 1945–1946 to lack of confidence in 1948–1949 in an early victory of the Chinese revolution."[2]

China and the Soviet Union were not the only countries whose accounts of the Chinese civil war were warped by the vagaries of contemporary international and domestic politics. American historiography of the Chinese civil war up until the late 1980s was decisively shaped by domestic political controversy in the early stages of the Cold War. Once the tide of the Chinese civil war began to turn in favor of the Communists in 1948, the Republicans, who had gained control in Congress in the midterm election of 1946, seized on President Truman's handling of China policy as a potent political weapon with which to attack the Democrats, who had controlled the executive branch since 1933, for being "soft on Communism." As political controversy escalated over American postwar China policy, clashing accounts of the Chinese civil war and the American role in it rapidly emerged to address the question of "who lost China." In this context, two politics-driven narratives took shape, each arguing diametrically opposite interpretations, and each elaborated on by political hacks, policy officials, and politically attuned academics. The academic field of China studies in the United States was born in this setting, and the questions posed in this debate dominated the field for the next four decades.

One line of interpretation, which implicitly defended the Truman administration's China policy and which predominated in academic writings, argued that the United States did not "lose China" because it did not have China to lose. Coinciding with the eruption of nationalistic struggles for independence throughout the European colonial empires in Asia in the wake of World War II, the Chinese civil war was essentially a contest between indigenous political movements to speak legitimately for a Chinese nationalism aroused by the Japanese invasion and occupation of much of China. Originally the legitimate vehicle of anti-imperialist Chinese nationalism in the 1920s and 1930s, the Kuomintang regime under Chiang lost that role by failing to stand up to Japanese aggression and by withdrawing to Chongqing, deep in China's southwestern interior, where it bided its time and fought the Chinese Communists rather than the Japanese invaders. For its part, the CPC under Mao's leadership seized the role as legitimate spokesman for Chinese nationalism by harnessing China's vast peasantry to fight the Japanese.

In this line of interpretation, neither the United States nor the Soviet Union could do much to shape the outcome of the civil war that inevitably followed Japan's surrender. Stalin and the Soviets disowned the CPC, believing that it was militarily too weak to matter in the war against Japan and too weak to displace Chiang's regime after the war, and dismissing Mao and his approach to revolution based on the peasantry rather than the worker proletariat as heretical in the international Communist movement. The USSR was therefore irrelevant to the ensuing Chinese civil war, and the CPC achieved its victory without Soviet aid and advice. For its part, with the exception of a few Foreign Service officers in Chongqing, Washington failed to recognize the CPC's strength at the end of the war and the legitimacy of its pronouncements. In the postwar years, it continued to support a KMT regime delegitimized by its failure to fight the Japanese, its corruption and incompetent economic policies, its alienation of critical urban constituencies, and its military leaders' ineptitude.

In these circumstances, according to this line of interpretation, the victory of the Chinese Communists was a matter of time. Mao won the civil war because he perceived that the Japanese invasion afforded the opportunity to rebuild a nearly exterminated Communist movement in the countryside on the basis of peasant nationalism. The CPC victory in 1949 therefore resulted from its rise as an indigenous, agrarian-oriented, nationalistic movement independent of foreign allegiance or aid. The ability of either of the major foreign powers to influence the outcome was negligible. As the popular historian Barbara Tuchman concluded in the closing lines of her study of Joseph Stilwell, the American general sent to China to reform the ROC army during World War II, "China was a problem for which there was no American solution. The American effort to sustain the status quo could not supply an outworn government with strength and stability or popular support. It could not hold up a husk nor long delay the cyclical passing of the mandate of heaven. In the end China went her own way as if the Americans had never come."[3]

The second line of interpretation, critical of the Truman administration's handling of China policy, argued that the ability of the external great powers to manipulate China's domestic politics was at a maximum, not a minimum, at the end of World War II. The outbreak of the civil war reflected the inability of the two major powers to arrange a stable balance of power in China. In this line of interpretation, Washington pursued an excessively idealistic policy of attempting, with the presumed collaboration of Moscow, to unite the KMT and the CPC into a stable coalition government. Admittedly, Moscow lived up to the commitments it undertook at the Yalta Conference in February 1945 in support of this effort, but Moscow also took steps to undermine these arrangements, supporting the Chinese Communists clandestinely in Manchuria by aiding the CPC effort to establish a base area in the northeast countryside and by turning over to Communist forces large numbers of Japanese weapons.

Once full-scale civil war broke out in the summer of 1946, Washington and Moscow responded differently. Washington first persisted in what in this interpretation was an unrealistic policy of pursuing a coalition government by pressuring Nanjing diplomatically and through an arms embargo to reopen negotiations with the CPC, and then, as the tide began to turn against the Nationalists in 1947, by effectively abandoning the KMT—its natural ally in China. Moscow continued to play its double game, overtly working with Nanjing through official channels, all the while continuing to support the CPC. Over the ensuing two years, limited by Washington's self-imposed constraints and suffering the consequences of overextension and its own strategic mistakes, the KMT regime collapsed on the mainland, while the Communists conquered the mainland and established the People's Republic. Moscow, sustaining official relations with the ROC until the very end to live up to the letter of the Yalta accords if not their substance, established diplomatic relations with the new PRC regime in Beijing the day after its proclamation.

The tenets of this line of interpretation are that the outcome of the Chinese civil war was substantially affected by the interests and purposes of the two major external powers. In that respect, the Chinese Communists were not an independent political force in China, and their victory was a victory for Moscow. The CPC won not only because of its own efforts, but also because Moscow correctly identified its own interests and pursued them successfully. For its part, the United States "lost China" because it did not follow the intrinsic logic of its own hard interests in China and pursued an unrealistic, idealist policy in the face of harsher realities in East Asia. This perspective is summed up by Hans Morgenthau in his preface to the most judiciously balanced analysis of the Chinese civil war and American China policy, Tang Tsou's *America's Failure in China, 1941–1950*:

> Underlying our analysis is a belief that one factor stands out as the decisive factor in determining the success and failure of the China policy of the United States from the dispatch of the Open Door notes to the eve of the North Korean aggression. This is the imbalance between ends and means. From one point of view, this imbalance takes the form of an unwillingness and inability to use military power purposefully to achieve political objectives. From another point of view, it appears as an unwillingness to abandon unattainable goals in order to avoid entanglement in a hopeless cause. The first aspect of the imbalance emerges most clearly in American policy up to 1947, while the second aspect looms large from 1947 to June 1950. Yet both unwillingness to use military power and espousal of idealistic objectives were integral parts of America's China policy. Together, they turned China into America's dilemma and compelled the United States alternately to advance and retreat in the Far East. Together, they denied the United States any chance for lasting success, while magnifying the consequences of America's ultimate failure. Together, they formed the source of such American illusions as the belief that China under the Nationalists would become a great power, that the Nationalists and Communists could establish a coalition government, and that a Communist China would not pose a serious threat to the United States.[4]

In his own conclusion, Tsou echoed the same judgment: "One could hardly find a more sobering example of the tragic results produced by a policy of good intentions and high ideals which lacked the foundation of a correlative estimate of self-interest and which was not supported by military power equal to the noble tasks."[5]

Variations of these two lines of interpretation dominated among the polarized American views on the Chinese civil war and its implications for American foreign policy through the 1980s. Direct American engagement in Vietnam after 1965 only intensified and extended the politicized debates on the significance of the Chinese civil war. Thus, in the same way that Washington failed to recognize the nationalist credentials of Mao Zedong and the Chinese Communists in the Chinese civil war, it failed to see that Vietnamese Communism was rooted in a powerful anticolonial Vietnamese nationalism under Ho Chi Minh's leadership. Conversely, just as Washington lost China to Soviet and Communist expansionism in 1949, it was in danger of losing Vietnam by failing to draw the line against Chinese Communist expansionism in Indochina.

Each of these lines of interpretation has strong points, but neither is satisfying. The first interpretation, focusing on "peasant nationalism," blatantly excludes external factors, ignoring the degree to which both Chiang and Mao were forced to bend their domestic agendas to those of Washington and Moscow, particularly with respect to the plan of establishing a postwar coalition government. The second line of interpretation is comparably blatant in ignoring the impact of Chinese domestic factors on the agendas of Moscow and Washington. In particular, it offers no explanation for the KMT's dramatic loss of support in the early postwar years. Moreover, neither explanation puts forward a persuasive explanation for the Communists' ability to mobilize large numbers of recruits to fight for their cause. The argument that the CPC mobilized China's peasantry through appeals to anti-Japanese nationalism has not stood up well, nor has an alternative explanation based on Communist implementation of land reform.

In view of the shortcomings and biases of these traditional lines of interpretation, the most effective approach to explaining the Chinese civil war is to combine both external and domestic factors, taking due account of the goals and actions of all four actors, not just those of the two domestic antagonists or those of the two external powers. In this approach, the strengths of the two long-standing lines of interpretation may be incorporated and their inherent weaknesses and polemical biases discarded. Accounts since the 1980s have begun to do this, building on access to newly available sources. The serial compendium of American diplomacy and foreign policy decision making, the official *Foreign Relations of the United States*, published by the Department of State, continued until the last years of the Chinese civil war in the 1970s. In the 1980s, Beijing began to publish its own accounts of CPC decision making and actions through the revolutionary period and in the early years of the PRC. Finally, with the fall of the USSR in 1991, Soviet archives became accessible to researchers, making possible more accurate accounts of Moscow's motives and behavior during the civil war period. By virtue of these sources and with the advantage of increasing distance from the politics of interpretation, a more comprehensive and well-grounded account of the Chinese civil war incorporating the complex interactions of all four major actors is feasible.

## CHIANG AND MAO

At the end of World War II, Chiang's Nationalist Party looked forward to completing a national agenda that it had pursued since the 1920s. The foremost of these goals was completing the task of establishing Chinese sovereignty by overturning the treaty-port system that had encumbered Chinese sovereignty and by recovering territories lost to various foreign powers since the mid-nineteenth century. The Nationalists had made initial progress in this task soon after reestablishing the republic in Nanjing in 1928, and during the war it had achieved a critical breakthrough by gaining American and British agreement to end the extraterritoriality provision of the 1842–44 Opium War treaties, which established the legal foundations for the treaty ports. Chiang won agreement at the Cairo Conference in 1943 that upon defeat of Japan, all territories that had been lost to Japanese expansion since 1895 would be restored to Chinese sovereignty. Those territories included Taiwan and the Pescadores in the Taiwan Strait, lost in the 1894–95 Sino-Japanese War, and, most critically, Manchuria, whose severance Japan had engineered in 1931 (see Chapter 2).

The second item of Chiang and the KMT's agenda was establishing international recognition of China as a great power. For reasons of his own, Roosevelt had acceded to and gained British acceptance of this ambition in Quebec in August 1943. Soviet acquiescence, after initial rejection, came the following October. By the resulting Four-Power Declaration on General Security, the ROC was recognized as a member of the Big Four allies and started on a path to status as one of the four great powers that would enforce security in a postwar peace.[6] With this status assured, Chiang believed, continued American support would follow, enabling the ROC to secure its immediate postwar environment and to emerge as an important player in world politics.

Finally, Chiang and the KMT hoped to consolidate sovereignty internally in China, a process that was begun in 1928 but that was disrupted by the Japanese invasion in 1937. In particular, Chiang hoped to extinguish the threat to the ROC posed by the Chinese Communists. Chiang had nearly exterminated the CPC by 1936, reducing its number to several thousand members and forcing its retreat to a base area centered on the rustic northern Shaanxi town of Yan'an. But a forced negotiation in December 1936 on forming a united front against Japan—during the famous "Xi'an Incident" (discussed later in this chapter)—and then the Marco Polo Bridge skirmish between Chinese and Japanese troops that triggered the full-scale Japanese invasion of north China in July 1937 gave the Communists a respite from Chiang's suppression campaigns and an opportunity to regroup and grow. By the end of the war against Japan, the CPC had more than recovered. It counted 1.2 million members, fielded a guerrilla-based military force of 860,000, and lay claim to large areas of rural north China inhabited by one hundred million Chinese.

The KMT conflict with the CPC went back to the very roots of both parties in the early 1920s. Both owed their effectiveness in part to organizational assistance according to Leninist principles from the Soviet-dominated Comintern. The KMT was founded in 1912, the year after the fall of the Manchu Qing dynasty, and won the first parliamentary elections later that year but was hobbled by fragmentation and lack of resources until Sun Yat-sen concluded an agreement for Soviet assistance in 1923. With Comintern assistance, the KMT was relaunched as a much more disciplined and efficiently organized political movement.

The price of Comintern assistance was that Sun admitted members of the CPC into the KMT, creating a united front movement to overcome the warlords who controlled different regions in China and reunite the country under a renewed Republican regime. To achieve these goals, the Comintern also agreed to provide the united front with assistance in organizing and arming the military force—the Revolutionary Army—that could defeat the warlords and seize national power. Comintern military advisers helped establish an effective officer corps schooled at the Whampoa Military Academy, established in Guangzhou (Canton) in 1925, whose first commandant was Sun's professional military protégé Chiang Kai-shek; its first political commissar was Zhou Enlai, who became the PRC's first premier in 1949.

The CPC itself was also a creation of the Comintern. Although several Marxist study groups sprang up among Chinese intellectuals after the 1917 Bolshevik Revolution, there was no party until the Comintern aided the creation of the CPC at its First Congress in Shanghai in July 1921. For its first two years, the party operated underground, organizing workers in China's cities and mining enterprises. In 1923, in accordance with Sun's agreement with the Comintern, CPC members, despite their misgivings about working with what they regarded as a bourgeois political party, joined the KMT. For the next four years, they collaborated in a Comintern-backed united front with Sun's party to defeat the warlords and to reunify the country under a coalition Republican regime.

Soviet strategy in China, as in other colonies in Asia, operated on three levels. First, Moscow sought to establish formal diplomatic relations with the prevailing warlord government in Beijing to help overcome the USSR's isolation in the broader international system. This goal was achieved in 1924. Second, Moscow sought to encourage and aid nationalistic anti-imperialist movements—in particular, the KMT—seeking to overturn the Western and Japanese powers in China, expecting that once in power, Sun would remain favorably disposed toward Moscow. Finally, it pressed the CPC to work in a united front with the KMT, believing that after the KMT rose to power, the Communists could overthrow it from within and establish a pro-Soviet socialist regime in China. As Lenin put it, the Communists could then discard the KMT "as one discards the husk of a squeezed lemon." Moscow's calculation in aiding the KMT-CPC united front therefore called for strengthening it to the point that the KMT could seize power in Beijing but not become so strong that it could discard the CPC from within.

Sun Yat-sen and the leaders of the KMT's main factions were not blind to Moscow's goals in accepting Soviet aid. Their calculation was to maximize Soviet assistance to their movement while minimizing the power of the CPC's cadres within their ranks. Therefore, as the Comintern helped to reorganize the KMT and build the Revolutionary Army, there was constant infighting between the KMT and CPC members to control key positions in the provisional government, which was declared in July 1925, and in the army.

After Sun's death in 1925 and once the campaign to reunify the Republic of China—the Northern Expedition—began in July 1926, Chiang emerged as the most powerful leader. After entering the lower reaches of the Yangzi (Yangtze) valley in the spring of 1927, the KMT faced a strategic decision: whether to move northward toward Beijing or down the Yangzi to take Shanghai, the biggest treaty port and international financial center. Chiang decided on the latter, taking Shanghai and Nanjing in March 1927. Having gained access to the financial resources of Shanghai and the military provisions of an important arsenal, Chiang recognized that he no longer needed the support of the Comintern and the Soviet Union. In the following weeks, thousands of Communists in provinces under Nationalist control were executed and purged from within the ranks of the KMT, an event recalled by CPC historians as the "white terror."

Ejected from the united front with the KMT, the CPC had now to survive as an independent, underground movement. After a series of abortive uprisings in the south in the fall of 1927, the party was in full retreat and in need of a new strategy. That strategy emerged in June 1928 at the CPC's Sixth Congress, convened in Moscow under Comintern supervision. The congress's resolutions called for a two-pronged effort to rebuild the movement in opposition to the Nationalist regime. On one hand, the party would rebuild its underground urban base among workers in China's cities. On the other, it would create political and military power in the countryside by building what were called soviet base areas through appeals to the rural proletariat and lower tiers of the peasantry by way of land reform and by deploying guerrilla tactics. Some base areas had already been forming in the south before and after the defeats of the 1927 uprisings, including one in Jiangxi under Mao. Following the Sixth Congress, the number of rural soviet areas expanded in the south and northwest to more than a dozen.

The Nationalists meanwhile completed the unification of China. In April 1927, after taking Shanghai and Nanjing, Chiang declared Nanjing the capital of a new Nationalist-dominated Republican regime, claiming fulfillment of Sun Yat-sen's goals as a mantle of legitimacy. Over the next year, Nationalist armies subdued the remaining warlord armies, through either military defeat or negotiated subordination, and they finally took Beijing in June 1928. Now that Nanjing was the republic's capital, the Nationalists renamed Beijing—the "Northern Capital"—Beiping (or Peiping), meaning "Northern Peace." In step with its nationalistic foreign policy agenda, in July 1928 Nanjing declared its ambition to revise the "unequal treaties" by which the foreign powers had encumbered Chinese sovereignty since the nineteenth century. The first step in this revision was the restoration of tariff autonomy, and the first countries to respond to Nanjing's demand were the two foremost commercial powers—the United States and Britain.

In its early years, the Nanjing regime nevertheless faced repeated challenges to its sovereignty. In 1929, Nanjing's armies clashed with Soviet forces for control over the China Eastern Railway, a line that Russia had built across Manchuria in the late 1890s to link its Trans-Siberian Railroad—built in the same era—with its far eastern port Vladivostok. The conflict ended in December 1929 with restoration of the status quo. Nanjing also had to contend with Japan—with military encroachments in Shandong in 1928–29, and then with the annexation of Manchuria in September 1931, a watershed moment in East Asian international relations. After consolidating its puppet Manchu regime in Mukden (Shenyang) in 1932, Tokyo pressed through the early 1930s for new concessions in north China to buffer its position in Manchuria.

Domestically, the Nanjing regime also faced challenges to its authority as sovereign government of China, requiring a sixteen-month civil war against northern warlords before finally overcoming them in October 1930. Control over the broad coalition of political factions that composed the KMT and the military leaders who acquiesced in KMT rule during the Northern Expedition was at times tenuous, initiating the long, intricate balance of power played by Chiang among the regime's true adherents and its nominal supporters. Republican sovereignty in the far northwestern region of Xinjiang was contested, and, as had the early republic in 1912, the Nanjing regime declared but could not assert sovereignty over Mongolia and Tibet, which had declared independence in 1912–13.

In this context, Chiang also moved to suppress the Chinese Communists' challenge to the Nanjing regime. On 1 December 1930, the CPC declared the Chinese Soviet Republic, with its capital in Mao's Jiangxi base area, the largest of several developing in the rural south. The growth of soviet base areas presented an increasing challenge to the Nanjing regime, and in late 1930 Chiang launched the first of six "encirclement campaigns" to suppress the Communist movement in the countryside. The first four of these campaigns failed, but the fifth succeeded in dislodging the Communists from their biggest base area and the seat of the CPC central leadership and its competing regime, the soviet founded by Mao in eastern Jiangxi. Evicted by Chiang, the CPC leadership and its adherents were forced on a prolonged retreat—the Long March—through southeast and southwest China en route to a northwestern base area in Shaanxi, at Yan'an. Along the way, at an ad hoc meeting in the Guangxi village of Zunyi, Mao and his allies attacked the CPC's top leadership for mistaken political and military policies that led the party into disaster; Mao gained leadership over the CPC's military forces, a critical first step in his rise to overall party leadership. By the time the Long March columns reached Yan'an in the fall of 1936, Communist forces, which had numbered three hundred thousand at the beginning of the fifth encirclement campaign, were reduced to thirty thousand. Though Communist historians recall the Long March as a "great triumph," the CPC's prospects were at a nadir.

Meanwhile, the broader international and domestic context of Chiang's efforts to exterminate the Communists was changing. In a major policy shift in July 1935, the Comintern's Seventh Congress called for alliances of Communist parties in various countries with nationalistic parties in new "antifascist" united fronts. In step with this, the CPC altered its overall strategy, subordinating the domestic civil war against the Nanjing regime to resistance to Japanese aggression and calling for a national united front. In addition, in the wake of protests against new Japanese encroachments in Hebei, nationalistic public opinion was swinging against Chiang's priority on setting China's internal house in order while preparing for war with Japan and in favor of a unified, active resistance to Japan.

In this setting, in December 1936, as Chiang was preparing personally to lead a sixth campaign from Xi'an against the CPC's Yan'an redoubt, he was put under house arrest by Zhang Xueliang, one of his generals and son of the Manchurian warlord Zhang Zuolin. As a result, Chiang was forced to accede to broader political opinion to negotiate a second united front with the CPC, this time against Japan. Chiang called off the sixth campaign but attempted to maintain the quarantine on access into Yan'an. Out of the Xi'an Incident emerged principles of collaboration against Japan that were eventually formalized over the next several months. In February 1937, the CPC committed itself to ending the civil war, abolishing its soviet republic, subordinating its forces to the National Revolutionary Army, and accepting the leadership of the Nanjing government. Nanjing signaled its acceptance of the CPC pledge only in September, after the outbreak of full-scale war with Japan in July. Communist forces were reorganized, nominally under Nanjing command, and the following April a political council was established that was led by Chiang and the KMT but also incorporated the CPC and other political groups.

The establishment of the new united front and the onset of all-out war with Japan gave the CPC initial respite from the Nanjing regime's active efforts to exterminate it and the opportunity to regroup and rebuild. Over the next several years of the war, the Communists worked to expand areas of direct control—the "red areas"—beyond the regions administered by Japan—the "white areas"—and to recruit new party members and soldiers in the Red Army. In the early years of the war, the Communists established border governments to consolidate political control over the area they controlled in Shaanxi-Gansu-Ningxia (Shen-Gan-Ning) and in northern Shanxi, Chahar, and Hebei.

In these areas and others, the CPC rapidly rebuilt its military forces. By 1939 they numbered 181,700; they had expanded to half a million by 1940.[7] Mao's military strategy called for a three-stage approach to building the party's military forces and fighting the Japanese. In an initial stage of "strategic defensive," Communist forces would use guerrilla tactics that focused on avoiding direct engagement with the enemy and on steady attrition of the enemy's forces. When Communist forces using these tactics achieved a second stage of "strategic stalemate" with Japanese forces, they would begin to deploy mobile warfare tactics that dispersed larger-scale units into the enemy's rear for coordinated attacks. Finally, in the period of "strategic counterattack," full-scale positional warfare would be possible involving force-on-force engagements of conventional units.[8] Over the course of the war, Communist forces attempted to move beyond guerrilla tactics only once—during the "hundred regiments" campaign of August and September 1940. Although Communist forces succeeded in disrupting rail links in Hebei and Shanxi for a time, they took such heavy casualties in frontal attacks on Japanese forces that thereafter they reverted to guerrilla warfare and did not attempt engagements of this scale again for the remainder of the war.

Politically, the war years allowed the CPC to rebuild its membership and Mao to consolidate his leadership. Party membership in 1936, at low ebb on the eve of the war, numbered some 20,000. In 1937, as the war began, it grew to 40,000 members and in 1938 to 200,000. By 1940 it reached 400,000, and by the spring of 1945, as the war's end neared, it rose to 1.2 million. The reasons for the party's ability to recruit and mobilize such numbers have long been debated, but their success likely resulted from a combination of factors. Communist land reform—though gradualist and effectively based on the ROC's unimplemented land law of 1936—may have stimulated recruitment of peasants in the north China countryside, especially in a context in which the Japanese forced collaboration of the rural gentry. Appeals to nationalism may also have motivated some—especially urban intellectuals who made their way to Yan'an—to support the CPC. Perhaps the most compelling explanation for this mobilization may be the party's ability to fill a vacuum in governance in those areas where the traditional social order had dissolved and the KMT regime had not moved to extend its roots, and where the CPC managed to sustain a long presence during the war.[9]

The war years also provided Mao with the opportunity to consolidate his leadership over the CPC as a whole. The party's rapid expansion in the war years had brought in intellectuals whose commitment rested on nationalism rather than Marxist-Leninist doctrine. Meanwhile, Mao's dominance, resting on his role as the party's supreme strategist and commander since 1935, faced challenges from other senior leaders, particularly the Soviet-trained "International" faction around Wang Ming. Mao's 1942–43 "rectification" campaign at once tightened ideological discipline among the intellectuals, indoctrinated the burgeoning party membership, and undercut the credentials and power of the Wang Ming group. With respect to Wang and his cohorts, Mao argued that their rigid adherence to the letter of Marxist-Leninist orthodoxy meant that they were divorced from the social realities of the Chinese revolution and the anti-Japanese cause; to achieve victory, Mao asserted, the party would have to "seek truth from facts" in adapting the universal principles of Marxism-Leninism to Chinese realities and not rely on blind "book worship." Mao's supreme leadership over the Chinese Communist movement was consolidated in 1943 when he took the post of party chairman, a newly created position; this was endorsed at the CPC's Seventh Congress in April 1945.

For Chiang and the KMT, the war years militarily and politically undercut the ROC regime's strength severely. Chiang had begun to prepare for eventual war with Japan in

1932; his concerted program to modernize his military forces, launched in 1935 with German assistance, had made some progress by the time of the Marco Polo Bridge clashes of July 1937.[10] ROC forces took the brunt of the ensuing Japanese onslaught, losing a quarter of a million soldiers—and some of the core divisions of Chiang's modernized forces—in the battle for Shanghai in the fall of 1937. After retreating from the ROC capital in Nanjing in December 1937 (leading to the infamous atrocities by Japanese forces there), Chiang and his surviving forces moved their capital first to Wuhan and then in October 1938 to Chongqing, deep in the country's southwest basin. By the end of 1938, the war settled into a long stalemate. The Japanese controlled the heavily populated economic centers of eastern China from Beijing and Tianjin in the north to Canton in the far southeast, consolidating their occupation through two puppet "autonomous" provisional administrations in Beijing and Nanjing. Chiang and the ROC regime were isolated in southwest China, buffered by the neighboring provinces of Yunnan, Guizhou, Guangxi, and Hunan and with limited reach into areas in the eastern provinces, such as Fujian and Zhejiang, not occupied by the Japanese.

The impact of these circumstances on the ROC politically was debilitating. The regime was severed from its revenue base in the lower Yangzi region around Nanjing and Shanghai, forcing it to rely on resources and revenue from provincial administrations over which it had not established firm authority. As the war dragged on and its costs escalated, the regime compensated with its only recourse, printing currency, which triggered rampant inflation and facilitated the growth of a huge black market. The ROC's only supply line for military and other assistance was the Burma Road, which opened at the end of 1938 and connected Kunming in the neighboring province of Yunnan with Rangoon in British Burma. In addition, the battles against the Japanese during the first year of the war had destroyed the core units of the ROC army under Chiang's direct command, requiring reliance on forces commanded by regional and local leaders on whose loyalty Chiang could not count. Centralized command by Chiang of the remaining ROC armies—on paper, a sizable force of nearly three hundred divisions—consequently had to take into account the political necessity of balancing allegiances with the objective tasks of strategy and tactics.

Diplomatically, in the early years of the war the ROC fought the Japanese in near isolation. The last German advisers withdrew in 1938. From the beginning of the war, the ROC's sole source of material assistance was the Soviet Union, which was ready to aid Chongqing against Japan for its own strategic reasons. But the conclusion of the Soviet-Japanese Neutrality Pact in April 1941 and the German invasion of the USSR the following June meant an end to Soviet aid. Britain was preoccupied with the German conquest of Europe after 1939 and attacks on Britain itself in 1940, and the United States did little more than extend loans to the ROC and in 1940 sell it a hundred fighter aircraft that were piloted by an unofficial volunteer force of American pilots.

The Japanese attack on Pearl Harbor in December 1941 brought America officially into the war against Japan and so alleviated Chongqing's isolation. Now joined by Washington and London, Chongqing was one of the major Allies in World War II, a status that brought direct American assistance and advice to the ROC cause. The alliance, however, was not a comfortable one, as American advisers—mostly famously "Vinegar Joe" Stilwell, the general Roosevelt sent to help train ROC forces and coordinate Lend-Lease aid—repeatedly differed with Chiang over strategy and command issues. In addition, by 1943 it was clear that the American strategy to defeat Japan would rest principally on the island-hopping campaign that would enable American bombers to strike the Japanese home islands directly. This reduced prospects of American landings on the Chinese coast to engage Japanese forces on the continent and meant that the principal value of the ROC as an ally was to tie down Japanese forces on the continent. Finally, in the summer of 1944, in response to American bombing raids against the southernmost main Japanese island of Kyushu, Tokyo launched the "Ichigo" offensive to eliminate ROC airfields in south China, crushing Chinese forces and effectively damping both ROC morale and the regard of their American advisers. For a brief interval in 1944, Washington explored opening contacts with the CPC and arming its forces as a complement to American aid to Chongqing, but it had dropped the idea by early 1945.

On the eve of the war's end, the circumstances of the KMT and the CPC were dramatically revised from where they had been when the war began. The seven-year war had weakened the KMT-led ROC regime and at the same time had given the CPC the opportunity to rebuild itself into a contender for national power. Chiang's government had survived the war and still fielded an army of 2.5 million soldiers in 290 divisions. Some 39 of those divisions had been trained during the last year of the war under the direction of General Albert Wedemeyer, who replaced Stilwell in September 1944, but the remaining troops were of uncertain quality and political reliability. The Communists meanwhile emerged from the war with a force of 860,000 soldiers, backed by local militias in north China numbering some two million.

Under these circumstances and given their hostility over the previous two decades, both Chiang and Mao looked ahead to what each viewed as an inevitable struggle for national power. Each man nevertheless skewed his agenda to accommodate the priorities of the main external powers, the United States and the Soviet Union.

## WASHINGTON AND MOSCOW

American interests in China from the birth of the United States until just before the war had been overwhelmingly commercial. For a century and a half, these interests had never warranted the use of military force. American participation in the Asia-Pacific theater of World War II prompted by the Japanese attack on Pearl Harbor changed that. Given the significance of the China theater in tying down the massive concentration of Japanese soldiers, it became a priority interest in American strategic planning to keep the ROC in the war on the side of the Allies and to foster the effectiveness of its armies. (As discussed in Chapter 2, this was a principal goal of the Cairo Conference.)

As Washington looked ahead to the postwar period, American interests in China, like Britain's, would continue to be commercial. But they would include a new strategic dimension. With the anticipated defeat of Japan would emerge a huge power vacuum in Asia that Roosevelt hoped a strong China would help to fill. In that role, the ROC would partner with Britain, the USSR, and the United States to become the "four policemen" who worked together to maintain stability in world affairs. Both Churchill and Stalin were skeptical of this expectation, and in the last two years of the war, as the prospects for postwar civil war in China increased, Roosevelt grew to share this skepticism.

That gave way to the related U.S. concern that a China divided between a weakened ROC and a resurgent CPC would become a power vacuum itself and possibly an arena of contention between America and Britain on one hand and the Soviet Union on the other. Civil conflict in China between Chiang's ROC and a CPC with links to Moscow might force Washington to contemplate military intervention in China itself, a prospect that historically Washington had deliberately avoided. Arranging a stable postwar China—in the words of American official statements of the time, a "strong, united, and democratic China"—therefore became the dominant priority in American China policy as the end of the war approached. A "strong" China could play the stabilizing role envisioned for it in the postwar international security structure and also sustain its sovereignty against potential Soviet encroachment. A "united" China would be sufficiently stable to permit it to play its broader regional and international role, and a "democratic" China would presumably be friendly to the Western democracies, especially the United States, and so also to American commercial interests.

Washington's efforts to head off the prospect of postwar civil war in China grew directly out of its efforts during the war years to enhance unity between the KMT and the CPC against Japan. After the January 1941 New Fourth Army Incident—in which Communist and KMT forces clashed in central China—and after Chiang imposed an economic blockade against the Shen-Gan-Ning border region, the KMT-CPC united front existed in name only, as each side increasingly looked ahead to the conflict for national power that they believed would inevitably follow the defeat of Japan. Washington's exploration of the option of arming CPC forces with the Dixie Mission led by Colonel David Barrett to Yan'an in July 1944 was undertaken not only to complement American efforts to aid the ROC against Japan, but also to spur renewed unity between Chongqing and Yan'an. A visit to Chongqing in June 1944 by Vice President Henry Wallace had prepared the way for the Barrett mission, and it was followed that November by the visit to Yan'an of Roosevelt's new ambassador to Chongqing, Patrick Hurley, for the same purpose.

Soviet interests in postwar China concerned security foremost. As everywhere else on the USSR's periphery, Stalin sought the establishment of a buffer zone in China. Stalin undoubtedly recognized that the United States and Britain would seek to renew their commercial and political influence in postwar China, which Moscow could not easily oppose. Presumably, therefore, Stalin at a minimum sought a neutralized north China; at a maximum he sought to make north China a zone of predominant Soviet interest. Constraining these objectives was his desire not to provoke a prolonged American military presence in China.

In addition, the USSR had abiding special interests in China, primarily in Manchuria but also in Xinjiang. In Manchuria, Moscow sought sure access to the China Eastern and South Manchuria railways and to the major ports on the Liaodong Peninsula, Dairen (Dalian) and Port Arthur (Luda). The tsarist Russian regime had won agreement from the

Qing Empire in 1896 to build the Chinese Eastern Railway, linking Chita and Vladivostok across northern Manchuria as the last leg of the Trans-Siberian Railroad, and two years later to build the South Manchuria Railway, linking the China Eastern Railway at Harbin with the Liaodong ports. Over the succeeding decades, and on into the Soviet era, control over the railroads and the Liaodong Peninsula ports had been the object of perennial conflict among Beijing, Moscow, and Tokyo. The railways and ports remained an abiding Soviet interest, and Stalin persistently sought to reassert Soviet interest in them in postwar planning (see Chapter 2).

During the early years of the war, acting on its own strategic interests in deterring Japanese expansion into the USSR, Moscow had been the ROC's virtually sole source of foreign support. Even though the April 1941 Soviet-Japanese Neutrality Pact ended that assistance to Chongqing, Chiang nevertheless continued to hope for Moscow's eventual entry into the war against Japan. By late 1943, however, as Moscow began at Tehran to explore its Western allies' receptivity to acceptance of postwar Soviet interests in Manchuria and elsewhere, Chiang began to seek to prevent Soviet entry into the war, hoping to weaken Soviet postwar claims that might perforate full ROC sovereignty in Manchuria, as promised at Cairo. By 1944, Chiang's resistance to Soviet entry into the war against Japan ended after months of diplomatic pressure from Moscow and as American efforts escalated to bring about a postwar unity government that incorporated the CPC under the ROC umbrella. These events strengthened Moscow's prospects of addressing its interests in China by working with the ROC.[11] In January 1944, Moscow appeared to convey to Yan'an its wish that the CPC join a coalition regime with the KMT.[12]

Moscow could also expect to address its interests in China through the Chinese Communists. It is true that Stalin played down Soviet links to the CPC and that after the dissolution of the Comintern in 1943 no formal relationship existed. It is also true that Stalin expressed doubt about the ideological credentials of the CPC, remarking famously to Averell Harriman in 1943 that the Chinese Communists were "margarine communists." Finally, it is also true that after the establishment of the PRC and during Mao's December 1949–February 1950 visit to Moscow, Stalin acknowledged that at the end of World War II he had doubted that the CPC could win a contest for national power with the KMT. However, it is also clear that Moscow regarded the CPC as an important asset, though not an unquestioning tool, in securing Soviet interests in China. Throughout the war and after, Moscow retained communication links with Yan'an, and Stalin's advisers there both monitored developments in the CPC under Mao and passed on his advice. Moreover, however much Stalin may have distrusted the implications of the rise of Mao over Wang Ming's International group in the CPC leadership, he also could observe that Mao was ever careful to frame his own policies within the context of broader Soviet priorities. By 1944, paralleling the Soviet approach to recommending coalition arrangements in some areas of postwar Europe, Moscow had opted to pursue its interests in China through a Soviet-American condominium of interests in the form of a U.S.-fostered coalition government broadened to incorporate the CPC; therefore, Stalin had every reason to play down links between Moscow and the Chinese Communists.[13] Should the coalition government fail (as probably seemed likely to Stalin), the Chinese Communists would become a critical asset in the

Soviet effort to secure a buffer in north China, where CPC power predominated, and in Manchuria.

From both the American and Soviet perspectives, therefore, a national unity government resting on a coalition of the KMT, CPC, and "third force" parties seemed to offer the best chance of stabilizing the situation in face of a looming Chinese power vacuum and civil war. Chiang and the KMT would dominate the coalition. The KMT, certain to depend on American aid in the postwar era, would be sympathetic to American interests, commercial and otherwise, and so would satisfy American goals in postwar China. The Communists, as the lesser faction in the coalition, could be expected to hew to Soviet interests.

These calculations were the core of the arrangements regarding China arrived at by Roosevelt, Churchill, and Stalin at Yalta in February 1945. As discussed in the previous chapter, in the secret protocol negotiated at Yalta, Roosevelt and Churchill acceded to several Soviet demands that satisfied Moscow's special interests in China, including lease arrangements for the Manchurian railroads and the ports of Dairen and Port Arthur. In exchange, in addition to agreeing to enter the war against Japan, Moscow agreed to recognize the ROC regime as the legitimate government of China and to sign a treaty of alliance with it that respected Chinese sovereignty. These arrangements were expected to reinforce joint U.S.-Soviet efforts to bring about a coalition government in China that broadened the ROC to end the KMT's era of "tutelary" dictatorship, incorporate the CPC and "third force" elements, and stabilize China under a U.S.-Soviet condominium of interests.

However, in addition to offending Chinese nationalistic sentiments both in the KMT and in the CPC, these arrangements papered over a fundamental contradiction in American and Soviet goals for the resulting condominium. In pressing for a "strong, united, and democratic" Chinese regime, Washington sought a China strong enough to play its role as a guarantor of postwar peace and stability in regional and world politics and strong enough to counter CPC efforts to destabilize the regime and resist Soviet pressures in it. Moscow sought a regime stable enough to uphold the concessions to Soviet interests in Manchuria and Xinjiang, but not strong enough to overthrow them. In addition, should the coalition arrangement fail, Soviet interests could still be pursued through its connections to the Chinese Communists. Washington entertained no real prospect of direct intervention in China should the coalition government break down.

## FROM YALTA TO BEIJING

As the war against Japan ended, both Moscow and Washington moved immediately to follow through on the Yalta arrangements for China. Moscow had already notified Tokyo in April that it would not renew the 1941 Neutrality Pact. On 8 August 1945, just meeting the deadline by which Stalin had agreed to enter the war against Japan, Moscow declared war and sent Soviet forces into Manchuria. By 22 August—a week after Tokyo's agreement to unconditional surrender—Soviet forces had occupied the whole of Manchuria as well as the neighboring north China provinces of Chahar and Jehol.

Moscow also pressed to conclude the Sino-Soviet treaty promised in the Yalta protocol, negotiations for which had begun in June. The resulting Treaty of Friendship and Alliance was signed on 14 August and conveyed Soviet recognition of the ROC as the legitimate government of China, thus registering Stalin's acceptance of the planned incorporation of the Chinese Communists under the ROC umbrella. The treaty was formally an alliance against Japan, committing both sides to "take jointly all measures in their power to render impossible a repetition of aggression and violation by Japan" once it was defeated and to come to the aid of each other in the event of attack by a resurgent Japan.

American Ambassador Hurley pressed ahead with the effort to negotiate the coalition government uniting the KMT and CPC. Chiang cabled Yan'an three times—on 16, 22, and 24 August—inviting Mao to come to Chongqing for negotiations. Mao demurred twice, but on the twenty-fourth he finally accepted, following receipt of two cables from Stalin pressuring him to accept and receiving assurances from Hurley that he would escort him to Chongqing. Mao and Chiang negotiated for six weeks, finally arriving on 10 October at a limited agreement to convene a Political Consultative Conference to work out a coalition regime, but little more.

Meanwhile, the war's end triggered an intense scramble by the KMT and CPC to assert control over areas under Japanese control in north and eastern China. The Communists launched a general offensive on 10 August to seize cities and communications centers held by the Japanese. President Truman's General Order No. 1, complemented by orders from Chiang, however, ordered Japanese troops to surrender only to ROC authority and to maintain their positions until ROC or Allied forces arrived; as a result, the CPC's moves met with resistance. Meanwhile, fifty thousand U.S. Marines landed in several Chinese ports to accept the surrender of Japanese forces on behalf of Chongqing, and the U.S. Army airlifted ROC garrisons to Beijing, Tianjin, Shanghai, and Nanjing and aided the transport of ROC forces to other areas.

In Manchuria, where Moscow had a critical interest in maximizing its hold, occupying Soviet forces in September welcomed some hundred thousand CPC forces under the leadership of Lin Biao and turned over large stores of captured Japanese weapons to them. By the end of 1945, under Soviet cover, Lin's forces in Manchuria grew to four hundred thousand and the CPC began the work of establishing a key base area in the region. Meanwhile, Soviet forces in Manchuria slowed the entry into the region of ROC forces transported in American ships in November, refusing them permission to land at several ports. With Soviet acquiescence, ROC forces eventually arrived and moved to assert control of Manchurian cities, taking Shenyang on 15 January 1946. Through these months until the final withdrawal of Soviet forces in the spring of 1946, Moscow had to take special care in managing events in Manchuria, seeking to establish the appearance of cooperation in the ROC's effort to assert sovereignty in the region and avoiding the appearance of aiding the expansion of CPC power there.

As these events unfolded and as clashes between KMT and CPC forces escalated, Washington's approach began to underscore the limits of its support to the ROC. Specifically, over Hurley's protest and resignation in November 1945, Washington rejected any prospect of direct military intervention on behalf of the KMT and instead renewed the effort to arrange a peace based on a coalition regime. For this purpose, President Truman appointed General George Marshall as his special representative to China.[14] The president's public statement on China policy of 15 December underscored the limits of the American commitment. Washington, the statement said, would continue to recognize the ROC as the legitimate government of China and "as the instrument to achieve the objective of a unified China." American troops had been introduced into China solely to aid in the surrender of Japanese forces in China, but the role of American forces would not extend to "military intervention to influence the course of any Chinese internal strife."

Under Marshall's mediation, the KMT and CPC agreed on 10 January 1946 to an immediate cease-fire and to convene the Political Consultative Conference called for in the agreement negotiated by Hurley the previous October. The conference then met and by 25 February had reached agreements on formation of a coalition cabinet pending convocation of an elected National Assembly and on the merger and reduction of ROC and CPC forces into a national army. With these agreements, Washington announced plans for a military mission under the direction of General Wedemeyer to train the proposed unified Chinese army, and Marshall returned home to negotiate loans for the pending coalition regime. In June, Washington further agreed to turn over to the ROC nearly a billion dollars' worth of Lend-Lease military equipment already in China.

While Marshall was in Washington, however, the cease-fire broke down and clashes between ROC and CPC forces broke out in east China and particularly in Manchuria. Marshall returned to negotiate a fifteen-day cease-fire in June, but soon thereafter both Chiang and Mao opted for all-out civil war. Chiang believed he could deliver a quick and decisive blow to Communist power and establish the ROC's hold over the key urban and economic centers, and he counseled Marshall that a hard line toward the CPC would result in a more accommodating stance later. Mao believed that the Communists were building a position from which eventual overall victory was possible. As the conflict escalated, Truman imposed an embargo in July on further transfers of American military equipment to China, a ban that was sustained until the following summer.

Over the next several months, Chiang's forces won a series of significant victories, in Manchuria and elsewhere. These culminated in the capture of Yan'an in March 1947, perhaps the high tide of ROC strength. Nanjing now controlled the major cities in east and north China as well as most of those in Manchuria, all linked by the major north-south (Beijing-Hankou and Tianjin-Pukou) and east-west (Beijing-Shenyang,Shanghai-Nanjing, and Xuzhou-Kaifeng) rail lines. As ROC armies advanced against the Communists, Chiang announced unilaterally that elections would be held for the proposed National Assembly, which the CCP boycotted. The resulting National Assembly convened in November 1946 and adopted a new constitution in December, which the Communists rejected as a violation of the agreements concluded in February.

In frustration and disgust at both the KMT and the CPC, Marshall returned home in December, ending his mediation effort. Truman issued a second public statement on China policy on 18 December 1946, in which he defended American goals and policy during Marshall's mediation and reiterated Washington's desire for a broadened ROC government on the basis of the February 1946 agreements that Marshall had negotiated. Marshall issued a supplementary statement on 7 January 1947 lamenting the "almost complete, overwhelming suspicion" with which the KMT and CPC regarded each other, making mediation difficult, and blamed elements in each party for the breakdown of the mediation effort.

By the fall of 1947, however, Communist forces under Lin Biao began to turn the tide against the overextended ROC forces in Manchuria and elsewhere. The dependence of the ROC forces on control of the railroads for logistics meant that the Communists could strangle them in isolated cities and wipe them out one by one. In 1948 Lin won a string of such victories and finally defeated ROC forces in Manchuria, taking Changchun and Shenyang in October and November 1948, respectively. Recalling the disastrous impact of the Japanese annexation of Manchuria and fearing the comparable danger of a Soviet-CPC hold on the region, and contradicting American advice that he withdraw, Chiang had attempted to hold on to Manchuria. In doing so, he lost half a million troops. In east China in 1948, Communist forces began to make comparable advances, as Shandong fell in September. In perhaps the decisive battle of the civil war, massive CPC forces engaged and finally defeated comparably large ROC forces for control of the strategic rail junction at Xuzhou, where the Tianjin-Pukou and Long-Hai rail lines crossed, in the Huai-Hai campaign of October. From that point forward, major cities fell to the Communists. Tianjin and Beijing surrendered in January 1949. In April they took the ROC capital at Nanjing, and in the next month they conquered Wuhan and Shanghai.

As the Communists' tide swelled in the wake of the Huai-Hai campaign, Chiang resigned as president of the ROC in January 1949 in favor of his vice president, Li Zongren (Li Tsung-jen). In early April, Li renewed negotiations with the CPC to no avail, and with the advance of the Communists on Nanjing, Li moved the ROC capital to Guangzhou. With the CPC conquest of that city in October, the ROC transferred its capital to Taiwan, where it was destined to remain.

Washington's China policy after the end of the Marshall mediation continued to urge political accommodation but stopped short of any prospect of more direct and forceful intervention. Recommendations by Wedemeyer in the summer of 1947 for renewed military aid to the ROC were dropped, although a package of economic assistance was extended in 1948. Meanwhile, a policy review concluded in September 1948 began to consider options in the event of the likely conquest of China by the Communists. Drafted under the auspices of the State Department's Policy Planning Staff under George Kennan and reflecting his hard-nosed realist policy outlook, it concluded that the KMT was on the verge of losing the civil war and that an American attempt to intervene would be "a course of action of huge, indefinite and hazardous proportions" that would "gamble thus with American prestige and resources" with uncertain success.[15] The estimate projected that a Chinese Communist regime would be tightly linked to Moscow and Soviet goals in Asia, but it also predicted that an impoverished Communist China would be a drain on Soviet resources, not an asset. In the long term, it concluded, the intrinsic nationalism of Mao and the Chinese Communists would divide them from Moscow. "The possibilities which such a situation would present us," the document noted dryly, "provided we have regained freedom of action, need scarcely be spelled out."

As the Communists began their advances in late 1947, Moscow quietly stepped up its aid to the CPC, turning over large stores of Japanese heavy weapons, including tanks and artillery, in Manchuria. Even so, as Communist forces won victory after victory in 1948, Moscow remained careful not to provoke American consideration of military intervention, especially as Communist forces advanced into the Yangzi valley—an area of traditional American and British commercial interest—and in the context of the hotly contested American presidential election of November 1948. Consistent with this priority, in 1949 Moscow maintained recognition of the ROC regime (there was no Communist national regime to recognize yet) and moved its embassy in tandem with the transfer of the ROC capital to Guangzhou.

As the CPC moved to complete and consolidate its defeat of the KMT, Mao in late September convened a new Political Consultative Conference in Beijing, which drafted the Organic Law establishing the People's Republic of China on 1 October 1949, with its capital at Beijing. Moscow recognized the new regime the next day. Over the next six weeks, Beijing was recognized in turn by the fraternal socialist states of the Soviet bloc.

Beijing's readiness to "lean to one side"—toward the Soviet Union against the United States—was embodied in the conclusion of a security alliance in February 1950 (see Chapter 8). Mao had considered an alliance in April 1949—as the CPC took the ROC capital at Nanjing—in proposing a summit with Stalin to discuss the formation of the PRC. The CPC's second-ranking leader, Liu Shaoqi, visited Moscow from 29 June to 14 August to discuss, among many things, the possibility of a Sino-Soviet alliance. While Liu was in Moscow, Mao published his famous work "On the People's Democratic Dictatorship" on 30 June, marking the twenty-eighth founding anniversary of the CPC. Mao proclaimed that "all Chinese without exception must lean either to the side of imperialism or to the side of socialism" and that the forthcoming Chinese Communist regime would "ally ourselves with the Soviet Union, with the people's democracies and with the proletariat and the broad masses of the people in all other countries, and form an international united front." Following the establishment of the PRC, Mao boarded the Trans-Siberian Railway on 6 December for treaty negotiations with Stalin.

### U.S. AID TO CHINESE NATIONALISTS WOULD BE "HAZARDOUS": PPS 39

The question naturally arises: late as it is, might not the Kuomintang and National Government as now constituted yet save themselves and might not American aid reverse the course of the civil war? The answer to the first half of the question is, "No"; it began to be evident ten years ago and is now abundantly clear that the Chiang-Kuomintang-National Government combination lacks the political dynamism to win out. The answer to the second half of the question is "It might, but only if the U.S. would provide as much aid as was necessary for as long as necessary." . . .

Open U.S. intervention would, as it militarily strengthened Chiang, tend politically to strengthen the Communists. . . .

"All-out aid" to the National Government is therefore a course of action of huge, indefinite and hazardous proportions. The American Government cannot rightly gamble thus with American prestige and resources.

U.S. Department of State Policy Planning Staff, PPS39, 7 September 1948, in U.S. Department of State, *Foreign Relations of the United States, 1948*, vol. 8, 146–55 (Washington, DC: U.S. Government Printing Office, 1973).

## INTERNATIONAL CONSEQUENCES OF THE COMMUNIST VICTORY

The "loss of China" became a subject of bitter political debate in the United States and one of the enduring topics of Cold War historiography. The Republican Party, having gained control of Congress during the midterm elections of 1946, used the issue as a political weapon to charge the Truman administration with malfeasance, ranging from misjudgment of the Communists' nature to treasonous abetting of the Communist cause. Under political pressure in 1947–48, the administration continued limited aid to the ROC but steadfastly refused to reverse the policy of military nonintervention. In August 1949, in the face of continuing Republican attacks, the administration published a white paper to rebut the charges, together with a huge volume of internal documents and correspondence on China policy.[16]

After the failure of mediation efforts, American policy rested on the hope that the force of Chinese nationalism, as predicted in Kennan's 1948 estimate, would eventually produce tensions and conflict with Moscow. There had been tentative feelers between the Americans and the Chinese Communists in the spring of 1949, and even after Mao's declaration in June that the CPC would "lean to one side" and the proclamation of the PRC in October 1949, Washington had not decided whether to recognize Beijing. But the outbreak of the Korean War on 25 June 1950 rendered the prospect of an accommodation moot for the foreseeable future. Instead, the meaning of the North Korean attack transformed the American mind-set toward Asian developments, particularly regarding nationalism. Where nationalism had been seen as a potential source of Sino-Soviet conflict, now nationalism intertwined with revolution—the national liberation movement—was regarded as a potential opportunity for the Kremlin to pursue its goals of expansion and global hegemony. This perception and its implications are explored in later chapters.

# 4 JAPAN: OCCUPATION AND RECOVERY

It is difficult to offer a net assessment of the treatment the victorious Allies meted out to the Japanese after their surrender in August 1945. There were aspects of leniency and moderation, but the sovereignty that the country regained was a conditional one, subject to American Cold War demands. During the closing months of the war, Japan's hopes for Soviet mediation to obtain more favorable surrender terms were dashed by Moscow's decision to enter the war in violation of its neutrality treaty with Tokyo. Emperor Hirohito, saying "the unendurable must be endured," broke the deadlock among his top advisers by accepting the unconditional surrender terms conveyed in the Potsdam Proclamation. As it turned out, however, the Americans—who all but formally ran the occupation unilaterally—for prudential reasons satisfied Japan's hopes for retaining the imperial institution and shielding the emperor from the war crimes trials that led to the execution of the wartime prime minister, Tojo Hideki, and other leaders.[1] Moreover, the exclusion of the Soviets from the occupation meant that Japan was spared Germany's fate of being divided among the victors. In still another difference from Germany, rather than administering the defeated foe directly, the occupiers used a civil service left largely intact in Japan to implement occupation policies.

Yet the constitution that the United States imposed on the Japanese severely attenuated the authority that had been vested in the emperor, and a sweeping reform program—described as a Japanese version of President Franklin Roosevelt's New Deal[2]—sought to transform Japan into a democratic state purged of the militarism and concentration of power that the Americans believed had spawned Japanese aggression. As in the case of Germany, there were those among the occupiers who believed that only a deep-going eradication of the sources of Japanese militarism and authoritarianism would suffice to prevent a recurrence. Here again, however, the Americans perceived a reality, in this case the emerging Cold War, that led them to take steps that would restore much of the institutional structure and polity that the reform measures were designed to eliminate or diminish. Reform was reversed or abated to various degrees, and under the impact of the outbreak of war on the Korean peninsula, an impasse over a peace settlement with Japan was broken and a treaty fashioned that was marked by notably lenient terms.

It would thus appear that at its conclusion the occupation was on balance a moderate if not generous affair, at least from the perspective of the traditional elites, who had largely regained their grip on power and now would lead a nation that had recovered its sovereignty. Such a judgment requires some qualification, however, inasmuch as the recovery of sovereignty in a lenient peace treaty was conditioned by U.S. demands for a continuing military presence and subordination of Japan's security policy to America's Cold War imperatives. It was effectively a limited sovereignty, much more benign, to be sure, than the Brezhnev Doctrine of limited sovereignty (according to which Moscow reserved the right to intervene by force in other states to preserve Communist systems), but one that produced strains and resentment within the Japanese body politic. To assuage these strains, in 1960 the two sides renegotiated the terms of their security treaty to remove, at least notionally, some of the more demeaning provisions. (The two bilateral treaties are discussed in Chapter 7.)

Out of this complex background of occupation policy and politics, with its interplay of surrender and restoration, reform and recovery, sovereignty and subordination, two notable developments were to emerge: The U.S.-Japanese security relationship, while undergoing trials and tribulations over the years, proved to be remarkably durable, outlasting the Cold War from which it arose; and Japan embarked on a path of economic development that would propel it to the status of the world's second-largest economy.

## SURRENDER AND OCCUPATION

Emperor Hirohito's radio broadcast on 15 August 1945—the first time his voice had been heard by his people—called on the Japanese to bow to the Allies' unconditional surrender terms, thus averting a final climactic invasion. Though the nation was prepared to carry on the fight to the end, it proved amenable, though often grudgingly, to occupation policies that in the first three years were radical in scope and depth.

In theory the occupation was directed by a thirteen-nation Far Eastern Commission based in Washington and a four-power Allied Council for Japan based in Tokyo (analogous to the one in Germany, with China in place of France). This was reflected in the title given to America's proconsul, General Douglas MacArthur, who was named Supreme Commander for the Allied Powers (SCAP). In practice, however, occupation policies not only were determined by the Americans but to a large extent were formulated by MacArthur—whom the Japanese regarded as the "blue-eyed shogun"—and his SCAP staff. (The imperious commander, ever vigilant about protecting his honor and prerogatives, was not above citing his formal role as a representative of the international bodies—which he otherwise ignored—in trying to deflect directions from superiors in Washington.) SCAP "sections" formed a kind of supercabinet that supervised the Japanese administration's implementation of its policies.[3]

The Potsdam Proclamation (26 July 1945), issued by the United States, Britain, and China—the Soviet Union still pretending to observe its neutrality pact with Japan—had demanded Japan's unconditional surrender, the alternative being its "prompt and utter destruction," an allusion to the recently tested atomic bomb. Though some within the Truman administration had urged surrender terms that would have offered retention of the imperial institution, the proclamation made no mention of the emperor, a fact that severely complicated some Japanese leaders' efforts to gain acceptance of the surrender terms.[4] Once surrender had occurred, however, MacArthur and others saw an advantage in retaining the emperor in order to legitimize and facilitate the occupation regime.

The broad objectives of the American occupation program were set forth in a September 1945 document drafted by the interagency body charged with coordinating postwar reconstruction.[5] The document reiterated the "terms" stipulated in the Potsdam Proclamation as the occupation's essential goals for Japan: loss of its empire, as called for in the Cairo Declaration; demilitarization; democratization; and an economy reconstructed to conform to Japan's "peacetime requirements." On this basis, the occupation's policies of its first three years focused on "remaking Japan."

The focus of the occupation's political reforms was a new constitution,[6] promulgated in November 1946 under close U.S. supervision and becoming effective the following May. In the new constitution, the imperial institution—already drastically reduced in authority, beginning with Hirohito's formal renunciation of his divinity at the beginning of 1946—was divested of "the rights of sovereignty" recognized by the 1889 constitution. Sovereignty now resided with the people, acting through an elected parliament as the highest organ of state. The emperor was thus reduced to being "the symbol of the state and of the unity of the people," deriving his position from "the will of the people."

The 1946 constitution also revised weaknesses in the structure of power provided for in the previous constitution and liberalized its provision for civil liberties. The Diet became the highest organ of the state, with the authority to appoint the prime minister and to pass budgets with a simple majority. The constitution also provided for an independent judiciary. Whereas civil liberties had previously been contingent—Japanese, for example, enjoyed freedom of religious belief "within limits not prejudicial to peace and order and not antagonistic to their duties as subjects"—such freedoms in the new constitution were absolute and without qualification. In addition, the new constitution for the first time extended suffrage to women.

More broadly, the occupation initiated an ambitious New Deal program of reforms to democratize Japanese society and eradicate the sources of the militarism that the United States perceived as causing the war and to encourage "liberal tendencies and processes." There was an extensive purge of "undesirable" military and political leaders (though as mentioned above, the civil service remained largely intact as the instrument through which occupation policies were implemented). Textbooks for Japan's schools were rewritten to excise the militarist and ultranationalist themes of the war years in favor of liberal ideals, and state support of Shinto was dismantled. In another move to overcome the repressive authoritarianism of the previous regime, the police were drastically decentralized.[7]

Meanwhile, dissident political leaders who had been imprisoned during the war years were released, and political parties of all stripes were encouraged. Although American military censorship continued, the occupation authority encouraged the reemergence of an opposition press. Unions gained collective bargaining rights, and their numbers expanded rapidly along with a rise in militancy and radicalism; the Communist Party, having now been legalized, also enjoyed a rapid rise in membership as well as political representation, garnering nearly 10 percent of the vote in 1949.

With regard to reform of the economy, two significant items, land reform and dismantling of the industrial and financial conglomerates (*zaibatsu*), had very opposite results from one another. Land reform proved enduring, with an extensive transfer of land ownership to tenant farmers. The rural electorate became a stronghold of the Liberal Democratic Party (LDP), destined to rule almost uninterrupted into the next century. In contrast, many of the *zaibatsu* escaped the dismantling fate that had threatened their power in the early years of the occupation.

## ARTICLE 9

Among steps toward the disarmament and demilitarization of Japan, some six million Imperial Army soldiers were demobilized. An International Military Tribunal tried twenty-five Japanese military leaders of war crimes, executing seven and passing long terms of imprisonment on the rest. The broader purge removed leaders in military, political, and business circles who were regarded as complicit with the wartime regime.[8]

The most consequential step, however, was the new constitution's Article 9, which "forever" renounced war as a sovereign right and committed Japan "never" to maintain armed forces or "other war potential." This constitutional constraint, along with the pervasive pacifism marking the Japanese mood in the postwar era, thereafter complicated Japan's security policy making and inhibited its reemergence as a "normal" member of the nation-state system.

Later efforts to parse the language of Article 9 in the interests of a more expansive security role for Japan were foreshadowed in the Diet's deliberations during the drafting of the constitution. Thus, regarding the first paragraph of Article 9, which renounced war or the use or threat of force as "means of settling international disputes," it was suggested that recourse to war or use of force was excluded only with respect to settling disputes with other states but not in matters of self-defense. This logic was extended to the second paragraph, forswearing armed forces, to which a prefatory clause was added—"In order to accomplish the aim of the preceding paragraph"—that similarly could be interpreted as limiting the ban on armed forces only to dispute resolution and not to self-defense. Indeed, the reconstituted armed services went under the euphemistic name of "self-defense" forces.[9]

### JAPANESE CONSTITUTION RENOUNCES WAR "FOREVER"

Article 9. Aspiring sincerely to an international peace based on justice and order, the Japanese people forever renounce war as a sovereign right of the nation and the threat or use of force as means of settling international disputes.

In order to accomplish the aim of the preceding paragraph, land, sea, and air forces, as well as other war potential, will never be maintained. The right of belligerency of the state will not be recognized.

Constitution of Japan, November 1946 (effective May 1947), in Hugh Borton, *Japan's Modern Century* (New York: Ronald Press, 1955), 490–507.

## COURSE REVERSAL AND THE REBUILDING OF JAPAN

By 1948, the reform period of the early postwar years had given way to an emphasis on Japan's economic recovery as the darkening clouds of the Cold War cast their shadows far beyond Europe. Reform policies were relaxed or discarded, the *zaibatsu* regained their dominance as economic deconcentration was abandoned, and policies were adopted to promote Japan's reentry into the international economy. The occupation authority reversed the direction of the purge, with the Communists now a target and those who had been purged for their role in the military machine now brought back to manage the economic recovery.[10] Where the thrust of initial occupation policies had been on remaking, reforming, and rehabilitating Japan, later policies aimed at Japan's recovery, revival, and rebuilding.

The reversal of course followed a Tokyo visit in February 1948 by George Kennan, director of the Department of State's Policy Planning Staff and author of the containment doctrine, and was registered in a policy review (NSC-13/2 of October 1948[11]) that put emphasis on "assimilating" the reform program. Not only was a brake applied to further reforms, but the new policy instructed the occupation authorities to relax implementation of existing ones. SCAP was advised to take a backseat, ceding initiative to the Japanese authorities. The policy called for steps to minimize strikes and strengthen the police, and it authorized preparations for establishment of a coast guard—the forerunner of the Japan Maritime Self-Defense Force, Japan's navy today. The gathering presence of the Cold War was reflected in the decision to defer consideration of a peace treaty in view of the menace of "aggressive Communist expansion."

What prompted the change of course? As one scholar wryly put it, how can an occupation be explained that "liberated the communists and then purged them, purged the prewar leaders and then liberated them, encouraged labor and then stopped its strikes, disarmed Japan constitutionally and then promoted rearmament in the euphemistic name of self-defense?"[12] One interpretation is that the impact of the Cold War dislodged U.S. occupation policy from the reformist path out of a perceived need to resist Soviet expansionism evident in ominous developments of the late 1940s. Alternatively, from a revisionist perspective, Washington wanted to harness Japan to its interests in preserving global predominance in order to make the world safe for American capitalism and free trade. A more benign view would be simply that the policy shift was responsive to Japanese internal developments, and that it represented a natural evolution from reform to consolidation.

Other factors may have played a role. The policy shift may have reflected in part an effort by Kennan and the State Department to wrest control from the Pentagon over policy toward a critical element in Kennan's conception of containment. In addition, 1948 was a presidential election year, and with the civil war in China favoring the Chinese Communists, the Truman administration sought not to be open to charges of weakness in the face of Communist expansion. Finally, in some measure the shift in occupation priorities may have reflected Japanese officials' success in capturing initiative in their interaction with their American counterparts. In any case, Japan was now being readied for reintegration

### UNITED STATES CHANGES COURSE OF OCCUPATION OF JAPAN: NSC-13/2

Henceforth emphasis should be given to Japanese assimilation of the reform programs. To this end, while SCAP [the Supreme Commander for the Allied Powers, General Douglas MacArthur] should not stand in the way of reform measures initiated by the Japanese if he finds them consistent with the overall objectives of the occupation, he should be advised not to press upon the Japanese Government any further reform legislation. As for reform measures already taken or in process of preparation by the Japanese authorities, SCAP should be advised to relax pressure steadily but unobtrusively on the Japanese Government in connection with these reforms. . . .

Second only to U.S. security interests, economic recovery should be made the primary objective of United States policy in Japan for the coming period.

National Security Council, document NSC-13/2, 7 October 1948, in U.S. Department of State, *Foreign Relations of the United States, 1948*, vol. 6 (Washington, DC: U.S. Government Printing Office, 1974), 858–62.

into the international system, and its traditional elites were regaining control over the nation's affairs.

## THE PEACE TREATY OF 1951

The peace treaty Japan signed with forty-eight countries in September 1951 reflected the growing force of bipolarity in the region, the outbreak of hostilities in Korea having deeply implanted the Cold War in Asia (see Chapter 5). The peace treaty and the simultaneously signed U.S.-Japanese security treaty[13] were interdependent developments: Japan's acceding to the latter was the price for ending the occupation. While the United States thus arranged to satisfy its security interests by harnessing Japan to its side in the Cold War rivalry, the other side of the coin was that it was a partial and incomplete peace. The Soviets attended the San Francisco conference, but they refused to accept what they perceived as a stage-managed result that was linked to the security tie the United States had forged with Japan. Neither China—the ROC or the PRC—was represented at the conference, the United States and its close ally Britain being at odds over which party to the Chinese civil war should be recognized. Neutralist India avoided the conference, preferring instead to negotiate a peace with Japan the following summer. It was not until 1978 that Japan and China finally signed a peace treaty; one with the Soviet Union and its successor state Russia remained out of reach even with the end of the Cold War.

The trade-off represented by the peace treaty and the security alliance with the United States met with some resistance in Japan. The Yoshida Doctrine (named after Prime Minister Yoshida Shigeru), guiding Japanese policy at the time, signified acceptance of a conditional independence and sovereignty in exchange for an American strategic shield under which Japan could pursue the economic development that brought it to number two status in the world economy. Opponents on the left decried the Cold War alignment, preferring a more comprehensive peace treaty and neutrality between the contending camps. There was also opposition from the right, which was uneasy over the limitations on rearmament and the emperor's role. Under U.S. pressure, and with the traditional elites returning to power after the reversal of course during the occupation, the conservative leader Yoshida was able to impose his will to set a course that would prove to be remarkably durable.[14]

The Korean conflict broke an impasse in U.S. policy making on Japan. Some officials, particularly in the State Department, feared that a prolonged occupation might alienate the Japanese and thus undermine Kennan's containment doctrine with its focus on promoting recovery in Western Europe and Japan as bulwarks against Soviet expansion. Pentagon officials interpreted the implications of the Cold War differently, perceiving a need to continue the occupation in the face of rising Communist pressures in the region. MacArthur complicated the picture by playing at times with the notion of a neutral Japan, paradoxically putting him on the side of the Japanese left.[15] But in September 1950 Truman authorized John Foster Dulles, recently an interim senator who lost an election to retain his seat, to arrange a peace treaty that would end the occupation, provide basing rights for the U.S. military, and continue the exclusion of the Soviets from a role in Japan.

By the terms of the treaty, Japan was confined to the four major islands and some minor ones, and it recognized Korea's independence and renounced claims to Taiwan, the Kuril Islands, the southern half of Sakhalin Island, and the Mandate islands in the Pacific awarded to Japan after World War I. The United States was assigned "the sole administering authority" over Okinawa, scene of bitter fighting in the spring of 1945. The U.S. military regarded use of that island as essential, and it became the site of major concentrations of American forces thereafter. The concept of Tokyo's "residual sovereignty" over Okinawa was crafted to assuage Japanese unease over this arrangement, buying time until its reversion to Japan's explicit sovereignty in 1972 (though resentment among Okinawans toward the American presence would persist and remain an irritant in U.S.-Japanese relations). The treaty left the disposition of other islands ambiguous or unresolved, a legacy for the next century. Japan contested the Soviet claim to all of the Kuril chain, specifically four islets and islands just above the northernmost main island of Hokkaido, which it regarded as its "Northern Territories" and which impeded conclusion of a peace treaty with Moscow. Tokyo also disputed sovereignty over Takeshima/Tokdo, a small group of islets between South Korea and Japan, and over the Senkaku/Diaoyutai, a group of islands located between Okinawa and Taiwan. Most notably, of course, the peace settlement only dispossessed Japan of Taiwan without juridically transferring sovereignty over the island to a successor, the most fateful part of the legacy of unfinished business. (Formally, the treaty itself did not transfer the Kurils and southern Sakhalin to the Soviet Union, but these dispositions were understood and broadly accepted at the time.)

## CHINA ISSUES

As discussed in the following chapter, the outbreak of the Korean War brought the United States back into the Chinese civil war with President Truman's order for the interdiction of the Taiwan Strait by the Seventh Fleet, intended to deter both sides from renewing the conflict. This also deeply enmeshed the Taiwan issue in the Cold War. One result was that the impasse on this issue, complicated further by U.S.-British differences over recognition of the PRC, precluded a full disposition of Taiwan's status in the Japanese peace treaty. Truman said Taiwan's status remained undetermined pending further developments.

Japan's China policy became a source of tension with the United States, which put pressure on Tokyo to disavow any interests in developing ties with Beijing and instead to establish formal relations with the ROC on Taiwan. The result was the Yoshida Letter of December 1951, ghostwritten by Dulles, in which Japan pledged to establish relations with Taipei and offered an assurance that Japan would not conclude a treaty with the Communist regime on the mainland. A peace treaty and diplomatic relations were duly completed the following year.[16]

Likewise, Washington's Cold War imperatives thwarted Japanese interest in economic relations with mainland China. Chinese entry into the Korean War prompted Washington to impose an economic blockade on the mainland, and Japan had no alternative but to fall in line, although these restrictions were skirted in the mid-1950s' and early 1960s' "memorandum trade" with the PRC. Thus were Japan's options on relations with China foreclosed and its foreign relations tightly circumscribed by overriding American interests.

## THE KOREAN WAR AS A "GIFT OF THE GODS"

The Korean War did, however, have a significant positive impact by imparting a powerful momentum to the economic recovery of Japan that the reverse course had been designed to promote. Japan became a crucial logistical base for the American war effort in Korea, providing a jump start to Japan's economic recovery by the injection of hundreds of millions of dollars in military procurement. In 1952, for instance, these procurements represented nearly 40 percent of the country's foreign earnings.[17] Yoshida called the Korean War's contribution to his country's economic revival a "gift of the gods." A similar sentiment was voiced by the Toyota corporation's president, who had arrived in the United States on the day of the war's onset to seek a link with the Ford Motor Company in an effort to rescue his faltering business. The orders for Toyota trucks for the war effort represented "Toyota's salvation" and set his company on a trajectory that would thrust it into global leadership in automobile production.[18]

The impetus to Japan's recovery supplied by the Korean War was an unanticipated but significant element in realizing the U.S. strategy for conducting the Cold War in Asia. As one scholar has put it, Japan "arose from the ashes of the Second World War largely on the crest of an expanded American military crusade in Asia."[19] To compensate for Japan's loss of the China market because of the embargo on trade with the mainland—the China subcommittee of CoCom (Coordinating Committee for Multilateral Export Controls) placed even tighter restrictions on China than on the Soviet Union—Washington looked to Southeast Asia as a source of resources and markets for the newly stimulated Japanese economy. With America as a market and source of capital, a triangular relationship linking the United States, Japan, and Southeast Asia was expected to be a key dimension of the containment policy through promotion of economic growth as a defense against Communist inroads. This prospect was slow to be realized, particularly given Southeast Asia's impoverished conditions as well as the region's memories of Japanese brutality. That it eventually did materialize owed much to yet another conflict, the Vietnam War, which supplied a new catalyst for Japan's economic development and put it on a trajectory—the Toyota experience writ large—to becoming an economic superpower.

Though Yoshida hailed the catalytic effect of the Korean War on the Japanese economy as a "gift of the gods," the other—and unwelcome—side of the coin was that the deepening of the Cold War impelled the Americans to erect the barrier impeding trade with the Chinese mainland. This was the economic counterpart of Washington's demand that Tokyo maintain diplomatic relations with the ROC on Taiwan instead of the PRC. As we will see (Chapter 10), it was not until the 1970s that Japan was able to resume full-scale diplomatic and economic relations with China.

## JAPAN IN THE SAN FRANCISCO SYSTEM

The "San Francisco system"[20]—the partial peace that aligned Japan with the emerging U.S. alliance system at the expense of estrangement from China—and the Yoshida Doctrine—subordinating Japan's security and foreign policies to American interests while concentrating on economic development—proved to be a highly successful recipe for Japan's recovery and ascent to economic superpower. The U.S. strategic shield relieved Japan of heavy military expenditures as well as alleviating trading partners' concerns about a revival of the militarism from which many of them had suffered. Japan's acceptance in the international community was registered in its accession to GATT and the UN in the mid-1950s. The loss of the China market was a small price to pay for Japan's integration into the global economy, greatly abetted by generous access to American markets and investment (not to mention Japanese protectionism). By the time the China market became potentially attractive, the tectonic geopolitical changes in the 1970s transforming Sino-American relations had freed Japan to enter a relationship with its neighbor that would make China its number one trade partner. Japan had profited handsomely from the Cold War, and then—after absorbing the "Nixon shock" of the American president's trip to China—found itself in a position to capitalize on the dramatic shifts in the international landscape.

From the start, the American-Japanese security framework established by the two treaties and the associated Yoshida focus on Japan's economic recovery and development played strongly into postoccupation Japanese politics. In turn, over time, the evolution of Japanese domestic politics reinforced the framework and extended its application for four decades. The encumbrance of Japan's sovereignty by the dependence on the United States for security, the linking of Japan into the American Cold War architecture, and the presence of U.S. bases on Japanese soil evoked perennial criticism from both the right and the left. Regardless, the logic of the framework and the persistent focus on Japan's economic growth ultimately proved to be effective counters to alternatives advanced by both the left and the right to modify the tenets of the San Francisco system and the Yoshida Doctrine.

The signing of the San Francisco treaties fed immediately into competition among Japan's reborn political parties and led quickly to the domination of Japanese politics by a single party—the Liberal Democratic Party—for nearly four decades.[21] On the left, the Japan Socialist Party (JSP), formed in 1945 from several left-wing groups, split in October 1951 in reaction to the San Francisco treaties. The JSP left held fast to broadly popular pacifist ideals, calling for the rejection of both treaties in favor of neutrality in the escalating

Cold War. The JSP right accepted the peace treaty but endorsed the security treaty only with ambivalence, though it nevertheless favored Japan's tilt toward the United States and the West. On the right, Yoshida's leadership of the Liberal Party was challenged by the political rehabilitation in 1951 of Hatoyama Ichiro, a conservative party politician who had been purged as an "undesirable" early in the American occupation (paving the way for Yoshida's first term as prime minister in 1946). Hatoyama, whose faction included Kishi Nobusuke and other politicians whose postwar careers had been similarly disrupted because of their involvement in the wartime regime, favored maintenance of solid relations with Washington but also stronger steps toward rearmament and toward establishing the autonomous authority to set foreign and security policies than Yoshida had been willing to take. In November 1954, following a disappointing showing by the Yoshida-led Liberal Party in Diet elections, Hatoyama broke ranks and formed a new Japan Democratic Party by combining with another conservative group, the Japan Reform Party. This combination, together with support for different reasons from the left, was effective in delivering a no-confidence vote in the Diet in December 1954, ending Yoshida's tenure as prime minister. As a result, Hatoyama became prime minister in early 1955.

In October 1955, however, the two JSP factions reunited, giving them together a third of the seats in the Diet and so making them a rising power in Japan's politics. In reaction, in November 1955, Hatoyama's Democrats and Yoshida's Liberals united to form the Liberal Democratic Party. Beginning with Hatoyama's 1955–56 tenure as prime minister, fifteen LDP cabinets in succession presided over Japan's domestic politics and foreign policy, until the Miyazawa cabinet fell as a result of a Diet vote of no confidence over corruption charges in 1993. This enduring structure of Japanese politics, in which no other party, including the JSP, or coalition of opposition parties was able to mount a significant challenge to LDP dominance, became known as the "1955 system."

As prime minister, Hatoyama set out to modify Yoshida's foreign policy and security framework in favor of a more autonomous though still pro-Western foreign policy and a more extensive rearmament. With respect to the former, in particular, he sought normalized relations with the Soviet Union, a goal that would require conclusion of a separate peace treaty (since Moscow had not signed the San Francisco treaty) and resolution of the question of sovereignty over the four southernmost Kuril Islands (Tokyo's Northern Territories).[22] Moscow, in the midst of a post-Stalin thaw in its foreign policy, was receptive. Moscow offered to conclude a peace treaty with Tokyo, to cede to Japan two of the four islands in the Northern Territories dispute, and to agree to Tokyo's admission to the United Nations. In the end, the territorial settlement succumbed to domestic pressure from Yoshida's cronies in the Foreign Ministry and external pressure from Washington—Secretary of State Dulles declared that the United States would have to forswear return of Okinawa to Japan were Tokyo to agree to the Soviet compromise on the Northern Territories. Forced to defer resolution of the territorial dispute and conclusion of a peace treaty indefinitely (both issues remain unresolved today), Hatoyama nevertheless established diplomatic relations with Moscow, and Japan entered the UN at the end of 1956.

With respect to expanding Japan's military, Hatoyama sought revision of Article 9 to permit more extensive rearmament. To that end, the Diet adopted a bill in 1956 establishing a commission to assess revision of the constitution. To achieve the two-thirds majority required in the Diet's lower house required to amend the constitution, Hatoyama concurrently sought revision of the electoral system. That effort, however, engendered opposition from the left and from factions within the LDP, all of which recognized that the revision would undercut their strength in the Diet. As the opposition solidified over the next two years, the attempt to modify the constitution dissolved.

The last major challenge to the San Francisco system and the Yoshida Doctrine was the massive protests of the revised U.S.-Japanese security treaty in 1960.[23] Efforts to undertake revision of the treaty began during the Hatoyama government and were continued under the administration of Kishi Nobusuke (1957–60). Kishi had served in the wartime regime, had been arrested as a war criminal in 1945, but had been among those released in the reverse course in 1948 and politically rehabilitated in 1951. An archconservative, he shared Hatoyama's priorities in foreign and security policy and sought in treaty revision the opportunity to recast the security relationship with Washington as a more equal partnership. The resultant treaty effectively normalized the U.S.-Japan security commitments in accord with those incorporated in the other American security treaties with allies in the western Pacific (see Chapter 7).

Opposition to the treaty revision grew immediately among the left, which feared that Japan would become even more strongly linked to Washington in the Cold War and, with an expanded military, play an increasingly active role in regional security, and came to a head as treaty negotiations finalized a draft. Students associated with the national student union Zengakuren attempted unsuccessfully to block Kishi's departure for Washington on 16 January 1960 to sign the treaty. Kishi's efforts to gain ratification of the new treaty before the Diet's normal session ended on 19 May 1960 and in anticipation of a scheduled visit by President Dwight D. Eisenhower in June were stymied by delaying tactics by the JSP and other left-wing parties. When Kishi extended the Diet session to ratify the treaty, huge protests attempted to block the proceedings. The treaty was ratified only after Kishi ordered the police to remove protesting JSP members from the Diet. Amid continuing protests over the treaty, the Eisenhower visit was canceled and Kishi resigned as prime minister. A new cabinet was formed in July around Prime Minister Ikeda Hayato, a Yoshida protégé.

Under Ikeda, the political turbulence attending the revision of the security treaty subsided and gave way to a much more stable pattern of politics.[24] In September 1959, the JSP split again over the growing strength of the left within the party and over differences in opposition to the treaty revision. The result was the creation by the JSP right of the Japan Democratic Socialist Party (JDSP) in January 1960, which splintered the power of heretofore the most important alternative to the LDP. Over the course of the 1960s, the emergence of new parties—in particular, the Komeito—fragmented the opposition further, as did the resurgence of the Japan Communist Party later in the context of opposition to American escalation of the Vietnam War. Consequently, the LDP enjoyed its most stable period in power, as only two cabinets presided over Japan after the 1960 crisis—Ikeda's (1960–64) and that of Eisaku Sato (1964–72), also a Yoshida protégé.

Stabilization in Japan's domestic politics was an outcome not only of the fragmentation of the LDP's opposition, but also of the dramatic economic growth Japan saw by the 1960s. In turn, its spectacular success in the 1950s and 1960s made Japan a rising force in international politics in ways that complicated—but did not overturn—the San Francisco framework in the 1970s and 1980s.[25] The economic development approach adopted by Japan's postoccupation leadership was both a return to the pattern of government-business interaction that had emerged in the Meiji period and had flourished in the decades before World War II and also an effective adaptation to the international context created by the San Francisco treaties. Sometimes described as the "developmental state" model or, alternatively, the "East Asian developmental model" (given the variations on the approach adopted by South Korea, Taiwan, Singapore, and eventually even the PRC), the Japanese approach incorporated several core elements, including active government intervention in a private market-based economy having a negligible state-owned sector; promotion of economic growth by minimizing competition and maximizing efficiency among corporations in key industrial sectors; promotion of exports through subsidies; and shielding of domestic industries from foreign competition through import and administrative barriers. Government intervention rested not on direct administrative command, as in the planned-economy approaches of the Soviet bloc economies, but rather on close collaboration among party politicians, permanent civil service officials, and business elites and on government use of incentives and persuasion. In addition, the government encouraged paternalistic patterns of corporate governance to minimize worker agitation and unrest and mandated universal education to provide opportunity throughout society for advancement. Confucian traditions—ironically, long vilified as an obstacle to modernization in China—undergirded the approach with values stressing high savings, literacy and education, a Calvinistic work ethic, and individual sacrifice for the larger social good.

Steps toward the deployment of this approach began during the occupation as part of the reverse course. SCAP had employed civil bureaucrats who had worked before the war for the Ministry of Commerce and Industry to manage Japan's foreign trade and foreign exchange on its behalf. In 1949, as part of the effort to bring Japan out of recession and onto a path of recovery, a new Ministry of International Trade and Industry (MITI) took over these roles, in addition to new authority over export-import licensing.[26] In 1951, MITI and the Ministry of Finance established the Japan Development Bank, with MITI in charge of supervising its lending operations. In 1952, the antimonopoly law, adopted early in the occupation as part of its anti-*zaibatsu* program, was modified to permit the merger and interlocking of corporations, giving rise to the business cartels (*keiretsu*) that dominated much of Japan's high-speed growth. These institutions gave the conservative leadership the tools to manage Japan's recovery and takeoff under the American security umbrella provided by the San Francisco system.

Washington abetted this approach. Apart from the steps taken during the occupation, it aided the effort to locate external markets and sources of raw materials for Japan's reindustrialization. In particular, given the constraints on Japanese trade with the PRC and the slowness of Southeast Asia to emerge as a complement to Japan's economic recovery, Washington sponsored Tokyo's accession to GATT in August 1955, locking in favorable tariff treatment and easy access for Japanese goods into the American market even while most of the European states maintained high tariff barriers against Japan.[27]

After the political turbulence attending the 1960 security treaty revision and under Prime Minister Ikeda's push for political consensus behind economic growth as the country's foremost priority, Japan accelerated its era of high-speed growth. From 1958 to 1965, Japan's gross domestic product (GDP) grew at an average annual rate of 10 percent; from 1965 to 1970, its GDP grew at an average annual rate of 11 percent. In 1960, Japan was already the fifth-largest economy in the world. By 1970, it ranked second, after the United States.

By the 1960s, the American-encouraged effort to link the Southeast Asian and Japanese economies bore fruit. Through the 1950s, the reparations issue in Japanese relations with the region had been largely resolved, beginning with Burma in 1954, mostly through ingenious mechanisms, such as the use of reparations to fund Japanese infrastructure projects in the region and to import Japanese products that served simultaneously to stimulate Japan's home economy. By the end of the 1960s, Japan was among the foremost traders in the region, and by the 1970s it was the region's foremost foreign investor.

The prodigious success of Japan's industrial policy in the context of the San Francisco system strengthened the dominating position of the LDP in Japanese politics and helped to solidify relations with Washington. In 1964, Tokyo hosted the Olympic Games, an event that Japan celebrated as symbolically marking its successful rehabilitation into the international community. In 1969, Prime Minister Sato and President Richard Nixon arrived at an agreement on the return of Okinawa to Japan in 1972, an event that Japan marked as the end of the last vestige of the occupation.

By the early 1970s, Japan's economic triumph also brought new complications and dilemmas, however. The international community—both in the Eastern bloc and the West—pondered how Tokyo might translate its burgeoning economic strength into political and military power.[28] Japan's return as a major economic power—along with the rise of the European Union economies—contributed to the demise of the Bretton Woods system and so to perceptions of American economic and strategic decline (see Chapter 10). The success of Japan's export-led growth triggered emergent trade frictions, especially with the United States, which by the late 1970s was beginning to see Japan as a neomercantilist power.

At home, economic progress brought new prosperity but also new social and economic constituencies that complicated the pork-barrel electoral politicking that sustained LDP dominance. Foreign competition in the heavy industries that had fueled Japan's high-speed growth in the 1950s and 1960s—especially from South Korea, which saw its own takeoff under the guided-capitalism variant of Japan's developmental state model promoted by Park Chung Hee—required that Japan move up the industrial cycle and focus increasingly on technology-intensive goods. As Japan's technological base attained the level of those of the Western economies, future economic progress would increasingly require indigenous innovation rather than continued reliance on imported technology. Growing agitation in Japanese society protesting environmental degradation and other consequences of the single-minded pursuit of economic growth contributed to these dilemmas and complicated LDP politics. The 1973–74 oil shock, stemming from the OPEC response to the 1973 Arab-Israeli War, blunted Japan's record of dramatic economic growth and underscored the fragility of Japan's economic miracle. All of these dilemmas introduced new strains and so required new adjustments in the postoccupation security system that had served both Tokyo and Washington well for two decades.

# 5 THE KOREAN WAR

The North Korean tanks rumbling across the thirty-eighth parallel on 25 June 1950 were set in motion by a train of events marked by miscalculation, misperception, and unintended consequences.[1] The division of the peninsula had been ad hoc and hasty, and neither of the superpowers involved in that impromptu action could have foreseen the high stakes that would come to be invested in the disposition of the former Japanese colony. Neither envisaged Korea as a major arena of the Cold War, yet the inexorable pressures from that global conflict became superimposed on a situation bristling with the potential for civil war. The result was that bipolarity became deeply implanted in Asia and spawned a new type of conflict known as a "limited war." The Cold War thus became hot in Asia, a phenomenon that would repeat itself in other parts of the continent in subsequent decades until the demise of the Soviet Union ended the superpower rivalry.

It was not that Korea had no experience as an arena of international conflict. Its geopolitical setting lent it a vulnerability like that of Poland's, making it a crossroads trampled by armies from east and west. It had been a tributary state of China-based empires for centuries, and then became a battleground in struggles for supremacy between China and a rapidly modernizing Japan (the Sino-Japanese War, 1894–95) and between Japan and Russia (the Russo-Japanese War, a decade later), marking Japan's rise to major-power status. Korea became a Japanese protectorate at the end of the latter war, 1905, and five years later was made into a colony, one of the early building blocks (along with Taiwan) of what would become the vast empire that was dismantled after Japan's defeat in World War II.

## EMERGENCE OF THE TWO KOREAS

As we have seen (Chapter 2), the wartime conferences agreed that "in due course" Korea would become "free and independent," but planning for the peninsula's postwar status was sketchy and left much unsaid. Paralleling his hopes for Southeast Asia, President Roosevelt spoke of placing Korea under trusteeship to provide a transition from colony to independence. Stalin did not challenge this approach and remained silent during the military discussions at the Potsdam Conference, held only days before Soviet entry into the war against Japan. After declaring war on 8 August, the Soviets entered Korea, though they did not try to occupy all of the peninsula even with U.S. forces otherwise occupied and unable to immediately contest control of the country (they arrived a month later). Instead, two days after Moscow's declaration of war, two American officers—including future Secretary of State Dean Rusk—were instructed to determine a line dividing the peninsula for the purpose of occupation by Soviet and American troops, respectively. In what has been described as "casual and arbitrary" and a "hasty improvisation,"[2] they unilaterally chose the thirty-eighth parallel, which landed the capital city, Seoul, in the U.S. zone. A cautious Stalin, intent on avoiding any action that would jeopardize the gains awarded at Yalta, acquiesced in their choice.

The trusteeship project was soon to be overtaken by the impatience of the Koreans—like other colonial subjects in Asia—to gain full independence immediately, and by the determination of the superpowers to protect their interests in an evolving situation for which planning had been inchoate. Washington feared the consequences of a power vacuum in the region, with Japan now defeated, China weak and disunited, and potential opportunities for the Soviets to expand their presence. Stalin hoped for a bigger role in the occupation of Japan, which may have contributed to his restraint in Korea, and meanwhile he saw in the northern half of the peninsula a buffer zone and a source of war booty, paralleling his approach to Eastern Europe. Both superpowers proceeded to strengthen their positions in their respective spheres, and within months of the end of the war, the dividing line had acquired a political character with the emergence of mutually antagonistic Korean leaders.

Moscow's client, Kim Il Sung, who had been a leader of anti-Japanese guerrillas and fought alongside the Chinese Communists before becoming a member of a Soviet unit during World War II, was taken to Korea in October 1945 to be installed as the leader of the northern half of the country. His opposite—very opposite—number in the South, Syngman Rhee, at seventy years old nearly four decades older than Kim, had long been an exile in the United States, had a PhD from Princeton, and was a Christian married to an Austrian. Thus a committed Communist and a longtime anti-Communist assumed leadership under the watchful eyes of their patrons in a rapidly polarizing peninsula.

A December meeting in Moscow of the Allied foreign ministers, the mechanism established at Potsdam for implementing postwar plans, formed a joint commission to submit proposals for a provisional Korean government and a four-power trusteeship (the United States, Britain, the USSR, and the ROC) to last five years. The Soviets craftily manipulated the trusteeship project in the face of massive demonstrations in the South opposing it; demonstrations favoring trusteeship were organized in the North, while the Communists did likewise in the South.[3] The Soviets insisted that only those groups favoring trusteeship should be consulted, an approach paralleling their tactics in Eastern Europe of dealing only with "democratic" elements. The anti-Communists were thus confronted with a choice between trusteeship and partition,[4] and they found the former an intolerable option. The joint commission adjourned the following May, not to reconvene for a year, and meanwhile the Soviet authorities proceeded to create a separate administration in the

North, for which they drafted a constitution.[5] The reconvening of the joint commission in mid-1947 confirmed the deadlock over trusteeship; reunification by means other than force was now no longer a possibility.

To move beyond this deadlock, the United States turned to the UN General Assembly, which passed a resolution over Soviet opposition calling for peninsula-wide elections for a national assembly and establishing a body to supervise them. The Soviets having denied the supervisory body entry into the North, elections were held in the South in May 1948. A national assembly, one hundred seats of which were reserved for representatives from above the thirty-eighth parallel as a demonstration of the body's claim to represent the whole country, adopted a constitution and chose Rhee as president. The Republic of Korea (ROK) was formally established on 15 August. Less than a month later, on 9 September, the Soviets established the Democratic People's Republic of (North) Korea (DPRK) with Kim Il Sung, who held the crucial position of general secretary of the Communist Party (officially the Korean Workers' Party), as premier (later president).

## THE ROAD TO WAR

The peninsula was now hopelessly polarized, a microcosm of the division of Europe as the Cold War deepened and the wartime alliance collapsed into mistrust and intransigence. Had the occupying powers remained in Korea, the situation may well have become frozen in place, neither side willing to make aggressive moves that could trigger a confrontation and a potential World War III. But here the parallels between Korea and Europe diverged, leaving a highly volatile situation in which two bitterly antagonistic Korean rivals were left without the constraining presence of their respective patrons. Moscow, outvoted in the UN General Assembly during this period, sought mutual withdrawal of Soviet and American forces from Korea in order to avert further moves by the UN to impose a settlement. Washington, on the other hand, regarded Korea as having limited strategic significance. This judgment was conveyed in classified National Security Council Korea policy reviews in April 1948 and reaffirmed in March 1949,[6] which concluded that Washington should do what it could to aid the South in defending itself against North Korean attack but not commit itself to the ROK's defense. It therefore preferred to keep it within the UN's purview rather than to tie down American troops on the peninsula. Acting out of different considerations, the Soviets withdrew at the end of 1948, the United States by the following June.

Thus, in contrast to Europe, where the presence of the opposing blocs' forces inhibited military actions that might destabilize a tense situation, the Koreans were left with a dangerous scope for aggressive maneuvering. Tensions along the border separating the two halves of the peninsula frequently boiled over into serious incidents.[7] Both Washington and Moscow had reason for concern over their clients' intentions, given each Korean side's claim to legitimacy as leader of the quest for reunification of the country. Washington was wary of Rhee's desire for security guarantees as a shield for potential attempts to achieve forcible reunification. This wariness extended through the Korean War and was reflected in the hedged commitment contained in the mutual security treaty eventually signed after the war (see Chapter 7).

For its part, Moscow fended off Kim's persistent importunities for approval of an invasion of the South. These appeals dated back at least to early 1949; at a meeting that March the two sides concluded economic and cultural agreements, but there was also a secret agreement on Soviet military aid. Sensitivity regarding the implications of Soviet support for Kim's ambitions was shown at that time when Pyongyang radio corrected a speech by the DPRK defense minister acclaiming "the fraternal assistance" of the Soviet Union.[8] That the correction was broadcast the day after the speech suggests strongly that the Soviets intervened to remove the provocative remark. That would have been consistent with Stalin's cautious approach and his warnings to the North Koreans to avoid provocations that could spark a war. Finally, though, after dozens of cables from Kim, Stalin invited the North Korean leader to Moscow in spring 1950 and acquiesced in the decision to invade the South. Stalin conditioned his approval on Kim's securing Beijing's support, which he did during a visit there in May.

Why did Stalin give Kim the green light? The Kremlin dictator began changing his mind at the beginning of the year, when Mao was in Moscow to negotiate a new Sino-Soviet treaty (see Chapter 8). (Ho Chi Minh was also in town to press for support of his drive to expel the French.) Stalin had been wary about a new treaty with Beijing, fearing that it could jeopardize the Yalta accords and his gains derived therefrom. He now made a turnaround, concluding a mutual defense treaty with Mao that could draw the Soviet Union into conflict with the United States as a result of a Sino-American collision. He also extended diplomatic recognition to Ho's government, and he agreed to receive Kim to concert plans for an invasion of South Korea. Stalin had concluded that the "international situation" had "sufficiently changed"[9] to permit the invasion. New conditions had arisen from the Chinese Communists' victory in their civil war, allowing them now to aid their Korean brethren, and the conclusion of the Sino-Soviet treaty, posing a deterrent to the Americans. The Soviets also had broken the U.S. monopoly on atomic weapons. Moreover, Moscow had been effectively frozen out of a role in Japan, removing the need Stalin felt earlier to temper his ambitions for Korea while seeking a role in Japan; instead, he now had an incentive to strengthen the Soviet position in the peninsula as a buffer against Japanese or American aggression.

### SOVIET ENVOY'S CABLE: KIM IL-SUNG DREAMS OF CONQUERING SOUTH KOREA

"Lately I [Kim Il-sung] do not sleep at night, thinking about how to resolve the question of the unification of the whole country." . . . He [Kim] thinks he needs again to visit Comrade Stalin and receive an order and permission for offensive action by the Peoples' Army for the purpose of the liberation of Southern Korea. Further Kim said that he himself cannot begin an attack, because he is a communist, a disciplined person and for him the order of Comrade Stalin is law.

Remarks to the Soviet ambassador, 19 January 1950, in *Cold War International History Project Bulletin*, no. 5 (Spring 1995), Woodrow Wilson International Center for Scholars, Washington, DC, 8.

Stalin's overriding concern was the risk of American intervention in a Korean war, and it was only when this concern was allayed that he assented to Kim's pleas. During his talks with Stalin, the North Korean leader assured him that the United States would not intervene and that in any case the DPRK, with superior military forces and with the assistance of uprisings in the South, would achieve a quick victory before the Americans had a chance to become involved.[10] The harsh dilemma facing Moscow, producing what one scholar has termed a tragic irony, was that the all-out blitzkrieg assault by the North Koreans required for a quick victory was just what would be most likely to trigger American intervention.[11] Kim's impatience prevented him from pursuing other options, such as waiting for a major move by the South Koreans that would trigger civil war but would not justify American intervention, or an uprising in the ROK against an unpopular Rhee that Washington would not try to suppress. "I do not sleep at night," Kim lamented, because of thinking about unification of the country and waiting for an offensive by South Korea that would afford him an opportunity to launch a full-scale counteroffensive.[12]

The Communists presumably were basing their calculations on signals from Washington indicating a policy of risk aversion in Asia. In a statement on 5 January 1950, based on secret assessments the previous month advising against overcommitting military resources to Asia, President Truman declared that the United States would not defend Taiwan, thus conceding final defeat in the Chinese civil war. A week later Secretary of State Dean Acheson, in an address to the National Press Club in Washington that evoked a storm of controversy, elaborated on the implications of this position.[13] His talk, billed as "Crisis in China—An Examination of United States Policy," was an attempt to propound the "wedge strategy" of prying Communist China from Moscow's embrace by appealing to Chinese nationalism (he warned that the Soviets wanted to detach Xinjiang, Mongolia, and Manchuria from China). That aspect of Acheson's presentation, however, was swamped by reaction to his drawing of a "defensive perimeter" that ran from the Aleutians to Japan to the Ryukyus (mainly Okinawa) to the Philippines, thus excluding Korea and Taiwan. After the outbreak of the Korean War, Acheson's detractors virulently accused him of effectively inviting an invasion by placing the peninsula outside the U.S. line of defense. (As Acheson noted in his memoirs, his detractors' great hero, General MacArthur, had drawn precisely the same line, though in the opposite direction.[14] By this time, however, MacArthur vigorously opposed abandonment of Taiwan.)

Acheson spoke vaguely about the possibility of armed attacks in areas outside the line he had drawn, remarking only that it would be up to those attacked to offer initial resistance and then to rely on international commitments under the UN Charter. In his specific reference to Korea, he spoke scornfully of congressional resistance to the administration's proposed legislation appropriating aid for South Korea. As it happened, Congress a week later delivered "a bitter and unexpected blow" by defeating a Korean aid appropriations bill, though the next month the aid was restored by being joined to a China aid

### ACHESON DELINEATES THE U.S. DEFENSE PERIMETER IN THE PACIFIC

This defensive perimeter runs along the Aleutians to Japan and then goes to the Ryukyus . . . [and] runs from the Ryukyus to the Philippine Islands. . . .

[Should an attack on other areas of the Pacific occur,] the initial reliance must be on the people attacked [and] . . . the Charter of the United Nations which so far has not proved a weak reed to lean on by any people who are determined to protect their independence against outside aggression. But it is a mistake, I think, in considering Pacific and Far Eastern problems to become obsessed with military considerations.

Secretary of State Dean Acheson, speech to National Press Club, 12 January 1950, in Thomas G. Paterson, *Major Problems in American Foreign Policy*, vol. 2: *Since 1914*, 3rd edition (Lexington, MA: D.C. Heath, 1989), 398–99.

bill—thereby adding "a little sweetening" for congressional supporters of Chiang Kai-shek, as Acheson noted wryly in his memoirs.[15]

Given these signals and the context in which they were delivered—America's concentration on defense of Europe as a priority matter (NATO and the Federal Republic of Germany were established in 1949 as the polarization of Europe deepened), aversion to military commitments in Asia, and a readiness to concede defeat (and Taiwan) to the Chinese Communists—there was some basis for discounting a strong American response to a North Korean invasion of the ROK. Obversely, while underestimating the U.S. reaction, the Communists were overconfident regarding the prospects of a swift triumph by the North Koreans. Though the number of combatants was comparable, the North enjoyed superiority in armor, artillery, and aircraft, and its forces were bolstered by thousands of battle-hardened Koreans who had fought in the Chinese civil war. By contrast, the United States had been wary of equipping the southerners with offensive potential out of concern that Rhee would seize an opportunity to attack first. Still, the most important consideration on the Communist side was the firm conviction that the Americans would not intervene in time to avoid a fait accompli.

In this calculus, not only would Stalin have appreciated the enhancement of Korea as a buffer zone that control of the whole peninsula would confer, but the age-old Russian quest for warm-water ports would make the ones in South Korea all the more inviting. In the immediate postwar era, the Soviets had raised the possibility of gaining use of such ports as part of the proposed trusteeship arrangements.[16] (This would have been effected under Article 83 of the UN Charter, which concerns "strategic areas" under trusteeship.) At that time, access to the ports would have enhanced the Soviet Union's sea communications between Korea and Port Arthur; in view of its exclusion from Japan and its commitment in the 1950 Sino-Soviet treaty to return Port Arthur to Chinese control, Moscow now would have perceived even more strategic value in the South Korean ports. During this period, Moscow made much of the danger of a revival of Japanese militarism, and control over the entire Korean peninsula must have been a compelling objective by improving the Soviet Union's strategic position and possibly inducing the Japanese to move toward a more neutral position. Not only the Japanese but possibly the Chinese Nationalists as well might see the benefits of accommodating the Communists if the latter controlled all of the northeast Asian mainland.

Stalin had not abandoned his customary caution, however, even after being convinced that U.S. intervention was unlikely. As only the dictator could do, he made brutally clear to Kim that the Soviets did not intend to become involved in the planned hostilities. Moreover, he made approval of an invasion by the North Koreans conditional on China's agreement to support them. If matters chanced to go badly, it would be up to the Chinese to pull the chestnuts out of the fire. But what was in it for the Chinese?

Having proclaimed establishment of the PRC in October 1949 and then negotiated the Sino-Soviet mutual defense treaty, Mao and his colleagues were in an aggressive mood. They not only were eager to complete the revolution—the large island of Hainan was seized in May 1950 and plans were being readied for an invasion of Taiwan—but they sensed that they were at the vanguard of a revolutionary wave sweeping over Asia. During their talks in

Moscow, Stalin had urged that Mao and the CPC take the lead in supporting insurgencies in South and Southeast Asia because the Chinese model of revolution was better suited there than the Bolshevik one. The Chinese provided aid to Ho Chi Minh's forces in Vietnam, fanned the flames of Communist insurrection across a wide arc of Southeast Asia, and undertook harsh actions against American diplomatic personnel in the PRC (who were withdrawn by May). Mao frequently invoked the likelihood of an eventual war with the Americans as if it were inevitable, and he could see that a conflict with the United States in the narrow, mountainous terrain of Korea, logistically accessible to the Chinese (and Soviets), would be the most favorable setting. Moreover, reunification of Korea under the Communists would provide an extended buffer for the industrially important Chinese Northeast.

Mao thus could find significant strategic gains in a successful North Korean offensive. He perceived an opportunity to puncture what he described as American arrogance, a result that would also be expected to foster an impression among Asians that Communism was on an irresistible march to victory throughout the region. He may have also felt an obligation to the Korean Communists because of the role they played in his civil war. As for Stalin's behest that the Chinese agree to back the North Koreans, a positive response would help remove any doubts the Kremlin autocrat still harbored about the Chinese Communists' reliability as an ally. At the same time, the newly signed mutual security treaty, coming a half year after the Soviet Union tested its first atom bomb, provided a strategic deterrent against an unduly aggressive U.S. response to hostilities in Korea. Nevertheless, when the crunch came and the Chinese were faced with an urgent decision regarding whether to intervene against the U.S.-led forces driving across the thirty-eighth parallel and menacing China's borders, Mao encountered problems not only with Stalin but also with his own colleagues.

## THE NORTH KOREAN OFFENSIVE

The conventional (or orthodox or traditional) American view of the origins of the Korean War was that it was planned and initiated by Stalin as a Cold War move on the global chessboard. In this view, Pyongyang acted willy-nilly as Moscow's proxy in the zero-sum contest between the two superpowers. A revisionist interpretation, however, paralleling the broader revisionist take on the Cold War in general, assigns blame more evenly to the two sides, and tends to see the conflict in Korea as essentially a civil war that acquired broader strategic significance when Washington misinterpreted the outbreak of hostilities as part of a concerted Kremlin-coordinated offensive to test American resolve and erode the U.S. position in the Cold War. In the revisionist view, given the highly combustible situation in a divided Korea, both parts ruled by leaders vowing to reunify the country on their own terms, it is largely a meaningless exercise to try to identify who started the war; it was virtually certain to erupt at some point, the triggering event as likely to be instigated by one side as the other.[17]

Archival and other material that became available after the end of the Cold War requires considerable qualification of both perspectives. As discussed earlier, Stalin was hardly disposed to engage America in conflict, his caution evidenced by his dismissals of Kim Il Sung's persistent importunities. It was only after becoming convinced that Korea presented a target of opportunity, with a minimal danger of U.S. intervention, that he flashed a green light to his protégé in Pyongyang. This would serve not only to consolidate but also to broaden his gains from entering the war against Japan, but it can be viewed as basically a defensive move taken in circumstances in which the United States was playing a largely unilateral role in Japan, a source of deep suspicion and apprehension for the Kremlin. In short, Stalin was making a move on the chessboard of northeast Asia.

The evidence is overwhelming, however, that the North Korean attack was carefully planned and went far beyond a reaction to provocations along the thirty-eighth parallel.[18] Once Stalin gave his assent to the offensive, the Soviets began to play a major role: A new team of military advisers was dispatched to North Korea and drafted the plan for the attack. Stalin agreed with Kim's idea of disguising which side initiated hostilities by first taking action on the volatile Ongjin Peninsula along the western coast, a site of persistent tension and incidents where sorting out who was the aggressor was particularly difficult, and then broadening the front and pressing forward to a speedy victory. But in their eagerness to get on with the job, the Communists even put aside this attempt at disguise and launched an offensive immediately across the entire front line.[19] Thus, while the United States was taking care to avoid having South Korea's Rhee possess the wherewithal to launch an offensive, Stalin and Kim were planning a full-scale assault designed to reunify the country by force. This was a planned offensive, not a tit-for-tat reaction to incidents along the dividing line, and there was nothing comparable in the American backing for Rhee's regime, whose aspirations toward the North were a subject of apprehension rather than encouragement.

The Truman administration's assessment of the North Korean attack comported with the conventional view mentioned earlier, interpreting it as one move in a global offensive and pondering where the Kremlin would strike next. This perspective shaped the administration's deliberations during the first days of hostilities, beginning with a meeting of the president and his advisers on 25 June (the North Korean offensive began on the twenty-fourth, Washington time) at which he agreed with the view voiced by General Omar Bradley, the chair of the Joint Chiefs of Staff, that "we must draw the line somewhere."[20] An intelligence estimate dated the twenty-fifth called the invasion a "Soviet move" as part of the Kremlin's "global strategy" designed to undermine U.S. prestige in Asia and Europe, intimidate the Japanese into moving toward a neutral position, and demoralize the Chinese Nationalists on Taiwan.[21] The result of these deliberations was encapsulated in a statement issued by the president on the twenty-seventh that put the North Korean invasion in a sweeping context: "The attack upon Korea makes it plain beyond all doubt that Communism has passed beyond the use of subversion to conquer independent nations and will now use armed invasion and war."[22] With this mind-set Washington was prepared to draw a long line indeed.

In addition to ordering U.S. air and naval forces to support the ROK troops—participation by ground forces was authorized a few days later—Truman's statement announced other decisions with far-reaching implications. He ordered the Seventh Fleet to

**TRUMAN: COMMUNISTS MOVING BEYOND SUBVERSION TO ARMED INVASION**

The attack upon Korea makes it plain beyond all doubt that Communism has passed beyond the use of subversion to conquer independent nations and will now use armed invasion and war. . . . In these circumstances the occupation of Formosa [Taiwan] by Communist forces would be a direct threat to the security of the Pacific area and to United States forces performing their lawful and necessary functions in that area.

Accordingly I have ordered the Seventh Fleet to prevent any attack on Formosa. . . . The determination of the future status of Formosa must await the restoration of security in the Pacific, a peace settlement with Japan, or consideration by the United Nations. . . .

[In addition to accelerated military aid to the Philippines] I have similarly directed acceleration in the furnishing of military assistance to the forces of France and the Associated States in Indo-China and the dispatch of *a military mission to provide close working relations* with those forces. (emphasis added)

"Statement by the President," 27 June 1950, in U.S. Department of State, *Foreign Relations of the United States, 1950*, vol. 7 (Washington, DC: U.S. Government Printing Office, 1976), 202–3.

be dispatched to the Taiwan Strait to prevent military action from either side, strengthened military assistance to the Philippines, and accelerated military assistance to the French and their allies in Indochina, including—fatefully—the assignment of an American military mission there. Washington had been providing economic and military assistance to the French, but now the presence of a military mission marked the first step toward replacing the French and direct involvement in Vietnam. Thus the impact of the surprise attack from North Korea resolved a range of issues in favor of hard-liners in the administration and transplanted the Cold War in a new form to Asia.

As mentioned earlier, MacArthur along with other officials had been pressing for a reversal of the administration's position that called for disengagement from Taiwan. He had submitted a memorandum in mid-June forcefully presenting his case, describing Taiwan as "an unsinkable aircraft carrier and submarine tender" that had historically served as a springboard for military action in the western Pacific. Loss of this territory, he warned in characteristically apocalyptic terms, would be "a disaster of utmost importance" to the United States. He renewed his request, already endorsed by the Joint Chiefs, to conduct a Taiwan survey to determine the military requirements for its defense.[23] Now with the North Korean invasion MacArthur and other advocates of this line (including the new assistant secretary of state for the region, Dean Rusk, who took a harder line than his boss, Acheson) received a more receptive hearing. Indeed, Bradley read aloud MacArthur's memo at the beginning of the 25 June meeting of the president and his advisers.[24]

At that meeting Acheson had managed to salvage his position on the Taiwan issue by suggesting that the Seventh Fleet's interdiction of the strait serve to prevent action by either side, that is, to neutralize the area rather than aligning with one side. (In May Rusk had recommended interposing the U.S. Navy in the strait to prevent military action from either direction.)[25] The secretary had been on the defensive even before the outbreak of hostilities in Korea; he was bitterly attacked by the so-called China Lobby (supporters of Chiang Kai-shek) and subjected especially to the fulminations of a hitherto obscure senator from Wisconsin, Joseph McCarthy, who charged that the State Department was infested with Communist sympathizers or dupes who had sold out the Chinese Nationalists. Moreover, Acheson's "wedge" strategy, waiting for the dust to settle in China while expecting Chinese nationalism to chafe under Soviet domination, had been dealt a serious blow by the conclusion of the Sino-Soviet mutual security treaty. In fact, Acheson had begun retreating from the position he had taken in January, notably in a speech in mid-March in which he accused China of "adventures beyond their borders" in Asia and extended the Truman Doctrine to cover the region.[26]

## THE TIDES OF WAR

The UN Security Council adopted a resolution on 25 June identifying North Korea as the aggressor and demanding that its troops be withdrawn behind the thirty-eighth parallel. On the twenty-seventh, the date the North Korean offensive captured Seoul, the Security Council approved a U.S.-sponsored resolution calling on UN members to provide the ROK with "all necessary aid to repel the aggressors" and "to restore international peace and security in the area," a formulation (drawn from the enforcement provision of the UN Charter, Article 42) open to a broad interpretation granting the United States and its allies latitude for extensive military action against the North.[27] Washington was able to push through these measures because at that time the UN was dominated by sympathetic members and in particular because of the absence of the Soviet representative to the Security Council, thus depriving Moscow of its veto power. The Soviet delegate had walked out of the council in mid-January, declaring that his country would not recognize the legality of Security Council actions until the PRC was given the seat occupied by the Chinese Nationalists. Though there has been Machiavellian speculation that Moscow took this step mainly to keep their Chinese brethren out of the UN, thus keeping them dependent on big brother, it bears noting that it took place while Stalin and Mao were progressing toward conclusion of their mutual security treaty and thus served Stalin's interest in cementing a relationship he had just decided to promote. Another question is why Stalin kept his representative out of the Security Council after the North Korean invasion—he did not return until early August—and thus was powerless to prevent the United States from wrapping itself with the UN mantle in responding to the outbreak of hostilities. One answer is that Stalin actually preferred the action in the name of the UN—which Washington termed a "police action" under the UN Charter rather than a war declared by the United States—in order to avoid triggering the Sino-Soviet treaty.[28]

The South Koreans and a UN force eventually comprising seventeen contributing nations, put under the command of General MacArthur, found themselves in the first weeks clinging to a foothold in the far southeastern corner of the ROK, known as the Pusan perimeter after the name of the port there. After a period of buildup in Japan, MacArthur made a daring move to capitalize on North Korea's rapid rampage through the South by counterattacking behind the enemy's overextended lines and trapping it below the thirty-eighth parallel. This was the audacious amphibious landing on the Inchon peninsula west of Seoul in mid-September, an operation whose precise timing required that it take place within a few hours of the one day of the month when the tides permitted use of landing craft. Before the end of the month the UN had regained Seoul and linked up with forces that had broken out of the Pusan perimeter, catching much of the North Korean force in a vise.

The situation may now have been ripe for a restoration of the status quo ante bellum.[29] Divided U.S. councils offered alternative courses ranging from that option to elimination of the DPRK and even to preventive war against the Soviet Union. If the North Korean invasion had been interpreted as an opportunistic move to gain ground in the Cold War in a place of marginal U.S. strategic significance, while the United States was consolidating its control over the much more consequential Japan, then stabilization of the confrontation along the thirty-eighth parallel would represent a proportionate response to a Communist probe, clarifying the lines of containment and contributing to overall stability. An interpretation of the invasion as part of a global Soviet design, on the other hand, invited a response along the more aggressive end of the spectrum. If the Kremlin contemplated probes like the North Korean action as a way of testing Western resolve and engaging in a war of attrition at low risk and at times and places of its choosing, a forceful U.S. reaction would send a sharp warning that the risks were in fact high and fraught with potentially grave consequences.

The more ominous interpretation would also pose a challenge to the administration's effort to remain disengaged from the Taiwan issue and to let the dust settle on the China question. MacArthur, with backing from the military hierarchy and the China Lobby, pressed this challenge in ways that sorely tested the administration's patience. His insistence on denying Taiwan to the Communists having been at least partially accepted in Truman's order for the interdiction of the strait, the headstrong commander tried to capitalize further by making an unauthorized visit to Taiwan at the end of July, occasioning a call by Chiang Kai-shek for military cooperation. The administration, buffeted from one side by domestic pressures for an aggressive approach while having to deal with foreign—notably British—counsels against overreacting, offered reassurances that the decision on the strait was a military expedient and left the question of Taiwan's political status still open. It also sought to rein in the commander's aggressive urges toward North Korea, and in the early weeks of the fighting had ordered him to "stay well clear" of Chinese and Soviet borders.[30] After the Inchon success, though, Washington authorized an offensive across the thirty-eighth parallel,[31] discounting the likelihood of Chinese intervention—warnings by the Indian ambassador in Beijing were ignored because he was regarded as an unreliable source. ROK troops crossed the parallel in early October, followed shortly by the Americans, an action backed this time by a UN General Assembly resolution, the return of the Soviets to the Security Council having removed recourse to the latter body as an option.

It was at this point that the Chinese were sending minatory signals that destruction of the North Korean buffer would not be tolerated. In a public statement and in a meeting with the Indian ambassador, Premier Zhou Enlai warned that the Chinese would not stand idly by in the face of the enemy's northward advance.[32] Kim Il Sung appealed to Mao for help, the situation having reached a perilous point at which Mao's previous pledge at Stalin's bequest to become the DPRK's guarantor now required redeeming. It was a contentious matter within the Chinese leadership, with some understandably concerned over the danger of American attacks and over the impact more warfare would have on the struggling Chinese economy, but Mao imposed his will and cabled Stalin to say the Chinese would intervene in the guise of "volunteers" (one implication being that this would not be an official war and thus potentially trigger the Sino-Soviet treaty). Mao explained that if the United States were allowed to occupy all of Korea, there would be an unfavorable impact on "the entire East."[33]

As happened during negotiations over their treaty earlier in the year, Mao and Stalin appeared to engage again in some maneuvering, in this case over Soviet supplies for the Chinese. Mao tried to extract Soviet support, including air support, by telling Stalin that the Chinese would undertake only defensive operations while awaiting Soviet deliveries, and by dispatching Zhou to Moscow in quest of Soviet aid.[34] Eventually, on 13 October, nearly two weeks after the original decision to intervene, Beijing felt sufficiently reassured over Soviet aid to reaffirm its intent, and in mid-month the Chinese People's Volunteers crossed the Yalu River boundary into North Korea. Though there were some limited engagements with ROK forces later in the month, it was not until the next month that the vast scope of the Chinese intervention began to emerge.

Before U.S. troops had crossed the thirty-eighth parallel on 9 October, two days after the General Assembly's authorizing resolution, MacArthur had broadcast an appeal to the DPRK to lay down its arms and cooperate with the UN in establishing a unified government for the peninsula. Kim, citing Soviet and Chinese support, rejected the demand to dismantle his regime. On the fifteenth, at a meeting with Truman on Wake Island in the Pacific, MacArthur belittled the likelihood of Chinese intervention and anticipated the end of resistance to his forces by Thanksgiving. He pressed ahead with his offensive, heedless of Washington's admonitions against provocative moves near the Chinese border. After a UN offensive in November, the Chinese mounted a massive counterattack later in the month that would drive the UN forces back below the thirty-eighth parallel. In early 1951 Seoul was retaken by the Communists, the third time the South Korean capital had changed hands, and the Chinese mirrored their enemy's march northward by penetrating deeply into the South until they too were vulnerable to counterattack. With the Chinese supply lines overextended and subject to superior UN air power, MacArthur's forces were able to push the Communists back out of the South.

MacArthur's defiance of Washington's restraining hand now reached a critical point. The Truman administration was prepared to acknowledge a military stalemate and to negotiate a settlement that would restore the line dividing the peninsula. The imperious MacArthur insisted on taking the war to China in quest of a decisive victory, an adventure the administration regarded as unacceptably raising the odds of a larger war involving the Soviet Union. (During the Korean fighting the Soviets provided air support to help counter devastating American air power, but it was kept well behind the lines to avoid losses of planes and personnel in enemy-held territory).[35] Truman's patience was finally broken in April when a congressional leader released a letter from MacArthur advocating all-out war and the use of Chinese Nationalist forces. The president promptly relieved MacArthur of his command, a move that combined with a failed Chinese offensive in the spring to set the stage for acceptance of a stalemate and negotiations to end the fighting.

The negotiations, which began in July 1951, were arduous and tortuous: It took months even to agree upon an armistice line and two years to sign a truce. The Communists may have been tempted to wage a war of attrition in the hope of outlasting the Americans, but this risked the escalation that the Truman administration had averted, at the cost of a severe domestic backlash, by ousting the charismatic MacArthur. Dwight Eisenhower, another war hero, visited Korea after winning the 1952 election and pledged to take action to break the stalemate. After his inauguration the new president announced that the Seventh Fleet would no longer prevent attacks on the mainland from Taiwan, the famous "unleashing" of Chiang Kai-shek, which went some way, at least symbolically, toward removing restraints applied by his predecessor. More ominously, the Eisenhower administration, like its predecessor, engaged in nuclear saber rattling during the negotiations, in an effort to induce the Communists to make the concessions required for an agreement.

## THE POW QUANDARY

The protracted negotiations got snagged on the issue of repatriation of prisoners of war.[36] According to the 1949 Geneva Convention, POWs "shall be released and repatriated without delay after the cessation of hostilities," but Washington found reasons to resist application of this principle in the Korean context. The UN held many more prisoners than did the Communists, which meant that in an exchange the UN would deliver substantially more combatants to replenish enemy ranks than it would receive. To reduce this imbalance, the UN wanted to reclassify some of the captured Koreans as southerners impressed into the North's army, and by giving the Chinese detainees the choice of repatriation to China or not. Beijing was adamantly opposed to such a choice, which would allow Chinese POWs to opt between the PRC and its Nationalist rivals—and thus smack of a two-Chinas solution. On the American side, negotiating latitude was circumscribed by Truman's determined insistence on the principle of nonforcible repatriation.

A breakthrough occurred after the United States proposed concessions in May 1953 calling for screenings of POWs before a neutral commission. The process included a period when the opposing sides had access to their captured troops and so had the opportunity to entice repatriation. Eventually, remaining nonrepatriates would be turned over to the General Assembly for disposition. The Communists accepted this procedure, in effect conceding the principle of nonforcible repatriation and political asylum, a sign of the flexibility emerging in the post-Stalin era; they did not take up the offer of a General Assembly role, doubtless aware that they would not prevail in this forum and that it would only highlight the embarrassment of being rejected by their own troops.

The way was now cleared for concluding the negotiation of an armistice, which was signed on 27 July 1953. Syngman Rhee played an obstructionist role during this time, for example, unilaterally releasing a large number of anti-Communist POWs from camps in South Korea. His government was also a no-show at the armistice signing. It was in these circumstances that Washington sought to mollify and restrain him by beginning negotiations on the mutual defense treaty he desired.[37]

## LESSONS AND CONSEQUENCES OF THE WAR

Human conflicts typically are rife with misperception and miscalculation, but the Korean War stands out (along with World War I) in this respect. An assessment of this war raises the question of whether three years of carnage and destruction did nothing to resolve the underlying conflicts of interests, resulting only in the stalemate and confrontation present at the beginning. The armistice line largely followed the thirty-eighth parallel, though it drooped below the parallel in the west (in effect moving the most volatile area, the Ongjin Peninsula, farther from the line of confrontation) while more than compensating South Korea with territory above the parallel in the east that improved its defense positions. These seemed to be marginal changes that hardly justified the massive expenditure of lives and property: more than a million North Korean deaths and a comparable number of South Koreans, along with enormous destruction of the peninsula; huge Chinese casualties of several hundred thousands; and thirty-three thousand American combat deaths. The territorial changes being minimal, the real gains from the war came from the clarity of commitment and containment that emerged from the conflict. One consequence no side anticipated was a stalemate largely retaining the status quo ante on the Korean peninsula, and more broadly the full-scale transplantation of the Cold War to Asia. This introduced a measure of stability to the continent, though of course it did not preclude the outbreak of still more conflagrations and thereby presented a sharp contrast to developments in Europe (where the opposing blocs avoided hot wars, apart from the USSR's interventions within its own alliance system).

The enhanced clarity was won not only at the cost of massive death and destruction but also from the miscalculations that haunted the war. The Truman administration had sent what were at best ambiguous signals regarding U.S. commitments along the Pacific Rim. Washington's primary interest was in explaining its disengagement from the Chinese civil war, but the casual treatment of Korea—reflecting the peripheral interest American strategists had assigned to the peninsula—led Stalin to accede to his North Korean protégé's insistence that a blitzkrieg offensive would quickly conquer South Korea and leave Washington with a fait accompli. The North Koreans then found themselves overextended and vulnerable to MacArthur's Inchon landing behind their lines. But now came time for the United States to miscalculate, the UN armies driving deep into North Korea and misperceiving China's likely reaction to a threat approaching their border. This in turn left the Americans and their allies vulnerable to the Chinese counteroffensive; the Chinese, for their part, mirrored the American behavior by believing that they could translate a temporary military advantage into a drive that would reunify the peninsula under Communist control. The symmetries of miscalculation were striking.

Military stalemate had been reached by the end of the first year of fighting. Both the Communists and the West perceived adverse regional and global implications from being driven out of the Korean peninsula. At great cost they had avoided such an outcome and had to settle for maintenance of the status quo as the alternative. The rival Korean sides may have found this a bitter disappointment, but the outside powers needed to find a way to wrap up the fighting. Political developments elsewhere in 1953 facilitated this quest: Eisenhower came into office promising to end the attrition and frustration that inconclusive fighting and negotiating had yielded, including a threat to domestic tranquility from demagogic McCarthyism (the Eisenhower administration found itself in confrontation with Senator McCarthy, though he was mainly a scourge of the Democrats). Notwithstanding hints of recourse to nuclear arms in Korea and the "unleashing" of the Chinese Nationalists, the administration was more concerned with avoiding a wider conflict and restraining the impetuous Rhee. U.S. officials, including the hard-line anti-Communist Vice President Nixon, sternly warned him that he would not receive American support for a war against the North.

Meanwhile, the other superpower was undergoing an even more consequential succession: Stalin died in March 1953. His putative successor, Georgy M. Malenkov, propounded a "New Course," calling for relaxation of tensions at home and abroad. (Ironically, this policy line was challenged, at least in part, by another aspirant to the succession, Nikita S. Khrushchev, who outmaneuvered Malenkov in the leadership sweepstakes and then proceeded to co-opt his policies.) A month after Stalin's death, Eisenhower had seized the occasion to deliver a highly lauded speech looking toward a more peaceful world. (A decade later President John F. Kennedy similarly gave an acclaimed speech on détente that led to productive negotiations with Moscow.) The Chinese, who also by now had absorbed the painful lesson that neither side would allow itself to be driven off the Korean peninsula, needed to get on with their long-delayed economic development; 1953, in fact, was the first year of their initial five-year plan. Thus the environment had become propitious for achieving an armistice, which the Soviets and Chinese hailed as demonstrating the possibilities of negotiations. This achievement ushered in a period in the mid-1950s during which they pursued high-profile diplomatic approaches on the global scene. Moscow reconciled with Yugoslavia, withdrew its troops from Austria, participated in the first East-West summit since the wartime conferences, and established diplomatic relations with Japan. The Chinese, having earned prestige in the region from having fought the Americans to a standoff, now cut a major figure on the diplomatic stage, notably including Zhou Enlai's prominent role at the first Asian-African conference in Bandung, Indonesia, in 1955.

America was not accustomed to indecisive conclusions to war, and the Korean armistice was hardly an occasion for jubilation, but the intervention was justified as a demonstration of collective security action, that is, a UN "police action" to deal with a disturbance of the peace (and thus not requiring a formal U.S. declaration of war). It also had far-reaching consequences in both deepening and broadening the American involvement in the Cold War. An extensive agenda for remobilization to fight the Cold War (known as NSC-68, discussed in Chapter 7) was converted from a proposal languishing on Truman's shelves to an operational plan, including more than a threefold increase in defense expenditures. NATO was stiffened by additional American divisions and expanded by the addition of Turkey and Greece, and arrangements began to be pursued for integrating West Germany into the alliance structure. In Asia, where bipolarity would now take deeper root, Washington was spurred by the outbreak of war on the Korean peninsula to overcome its divided councils and produce a peace treaty with Japan along with a mutual defense pact that became the cornerstone of the U.S. security structure in the Asia-Pacific region (see Chapter 7). Meanwhile the American reentry into the uncompleted Chinese civil war froze the Sino-American relationship in a tense deadlock, including a U.S. diplomatic and economic embargo that persisted for two dangerous decades. Mao would cite Truman's order to interdict the Taiwan Strait as the beginning of the U.S. "occupation" of Taiwan, which for Beijing was the "crucial" issue between the two countries. Kissinger later told the Chinese leaders at the outset of Sino-American rapprochement that the confrontation would not have occurred except for the outbreak of the Korean War, "which we did not seek and you did not seek."

The Korean War had injected not only confrontation and tension but also stability and clarity into the Asian geopolitical environment. The U.S. line of containment that was now drawn removed much of the ambiguity that had invited the Communists' miscalculations in 1950. The vigorous American response must have served as a sobering check on Soviet opportunism; a lesson had been taught that the United States would react forcefully to piecemeal probes in order to avert a gradual erosion of its international position. (Perceived Soviet opportunism in exploiting third world upheavals in the 1970s became a major source of tension in superpower relations.) To be sure, the Americans interpreted that lesson in extremely broad and rigid terms—this was the significance of NSC-68. Truman's 27 June 1950 order, in addition to interposing the Seventh Fleet in the Taiwan Strait, dispatched an American military mission to Vietnam to assist in the accelerated supply of materiel to the forces fighting the Communists there, a fateful step—putting "boots on the ground"—toward the massive intervention of the 1960s. With the French defeat in 1954, the United States drew the line of containment along the military line of demarcation, thereby defining the global stakes in Vietnam as comparable to those in Korea or even Germany.

The Korean War's most significant contribution was that it ushered in a new type of war called *limited war* within the global Cold War. This kind of conflict exhibited several defining characteristics:

- In contrast to the "total war" of World War II, the participants did not draw on the whole arsenal of available weaponry but limited themselves to conventional arms and thus avoided escalating the level of fighting. This held despite occasional American hints of recourse to nuclear arms, and notwithstanding Chinese charges of U.S. use of bacteriological weapons. There was even less talk of possible use of unconventional arms in the Vietnam War (that is, the Second Indochina War, the one that arose in the 1960s with growing American involvement).
- Nor did the participants expand the conflict geographically beyond its peninsular origins, despite urgings from some U.S. circles for action against "sanctuaries" in China. Remembering the Korean experience, the United States even confined its ground operations in the Vietnam War to south of the seventeenth parallel (the demarcation line drawn by the 1954 Geneva accords) rather than risk a reprise of Chinese intervention.
- In the limited wars, one superpower became directly and deeply involved in a conflict that was kept geographically localized, the other one confining itself to

> largely rear area, logistical, and diplomatic roles, thereby avoiding a direct confrontation between the two that could escalate into a global conflagration.

Thus, the logic of the Cold War—zero-sum rivalry, containment and deterrence, and perceived global implications of local or regional conflicts—acquired a different expression when transplanted to Asia: recurrent outbreaks of hostilities with global implications but prudently limited in scope, or what might be called the Hot and Cold War in Asia. The Korean pattern (which one scholar suggests was a substitute for World War III[38]) was re-enacted in Vietnam, though of course with a dramatically different ending, and then in mirror image in Afghanistan, whose results contributed significantly to ending the Cold War itself. But to reach that point the Hot and Cold War in Asia would traverse a long and bloodstained road from the North Korean offensive across the thirty-eighth parallel in 1950 to the Soviet retreat across the Termiz bridge from Afghanistan in 1989.

# 6 DECOLONIZATION, NATIONALISM, AND REVOLUTION

World War I had a fatal impact on imperial regimes in Europe; similarly, Asia underwent profound changes as a result of World War II. The European colonial powers were severely weakened by the war effort, which sapped their capacity for reasserting authority over their Asian possessions. Moreover, the shattering effect of the Japanese occupation on the image of Western superiority dealt a grievous psychological blow to the Western powers' ability to exert control. This psychological effect was heightened by the West's own ideas about self-determination and the expectations raised across the globe as Wilsonian idealism was turned against imperialism. Consider, for example, the first sentence in Ho Chi Minh's declaration of independence in September 1945, lifted directly (with attribution) from the American Declaration of Independence in asserting that all men are created equal,[1] or the remark the previous month by Indonesian nationalist leader Mohammad Hatta that the Atlantic Charter "succeeded in holding all men's mind in thrall" with its "solemn assurance from the Big Powers that they recognize the right of all peoples to live under a government of their own choice."[2] "All" was no longer to denote only white males of European ancestry.

As in Europe, where the destruction of Germany's administrative and military apparatus had left a vacuum of authority, so also in Asia the smashing of Japan's vast machinery of control produced a vacuum that the colonial powers could not fill. Instead, a complex of competing and interacting forces swirled about the region: anticolonialism, the rise of nationalism and indigenous elites, revolutionary movements inspired by Marxist-Leninist ideology and the Communists' success in China, and the impact of Cold War bipolarity arising from the superpowers' global rivalry. It was in northeast Asia that the impact of bipolarity was particularly evident: Japan became solidly anchored in the American security structure and Korea was divided according to the spheres of influence established by the occupying powers. It was along the southern rim of Asia that the other powerful force emerging after the war, nationalism, had a pronounced impact on the geopolitical environment. As Western colonialism receded, a different import arrived from Europe: the Westphalian system of nation-states. Indeed, this region became ardently attached to that system, jealously guarding its national prerogatives and in some cases becoming conspicuously prickly in relations with the big powers.

One result of the interaction of bipolarity and nationalism was the emergence of neutralism, which became an organized group known as the nonaligned movement and attempted to go beyond resistance to superpower intrusions and to play a positive role in mitigating the effects of the Cold War. Several prominent neutralist leaders arose along Asia's southern rim, including India's Jawaharlal Nehru, Burma's U Nu, Cambodia's Norodom Sihanouk, and Indonesia's Sukarno. In other cases the interacting forces had different effects, as in Pakistan, which, to compensate for its weakness vis-à-vis India after the bitter partition, became part of the Western alliance system and also aligned itself with China as India and China became estranged. Vietnam offers still another narrative as an arena where bipolar pressures contested the force of nationalism, with a result that sharply contrasted with developments elsewhere in the region (and to which Chapter 9 is devoted).

## THE GENESIS OF NATIONALISM IN SOUTH AND SOUTHEAST ASIA

Nationalism in both South and Southeast Asia is an artifact of the Western colonization of both regions. When they emerged in the late nineteenth century, nationalist identities and sentiments in South and Southeast Asia reflected the indigenous people's response to the empire building of Western powers, which imposed their rule over colonial territories whose boundaries owed little to the ethnic, cultural, religious, and political frontiers that had traditionally defined both regions. In most cases, the leaders of nationalist movements were products of Western education, sometimes in the colonies, as was the case of Aung San in British Burma and Sukarno in the Dutch East Indies, and sometimes in the imperialist homeland itself, as was the case with Mohandas Gandhi in British India and Ho Chi Minh in Indochina. Schooled in the cultural assumptions and political tenets of the West but alienated by the disparity between Western ideals and practice in the colonies, these leaders became primary agents in recasting their own colonized societies into independent nation-states in the international order created by the West.

The resulting nation-states—for example, India, Indonesia, and the Philippines—are thus ironic creations. They reflected the adoption by indigenous elites of a thoroughly Western form of political organization, whose territorial claims were assumed in large part from colonies created by Western imperialism and whose assertions of national unity rested more directly on shared colonial experience than on continuity in historical tradition. The nation-state of the Philippines, for example, incorporates a sprawling archipelago that shares no history of precolonial unity or homogeneous cultural traditions, takes its name from the late-sixteenth-century monarch King Philip II of Spain, is predominantly Catholic in religion, has been governed by an elite reared under American colonial rule, and designates English, alongside "Filipino" (Tagalog), as its official language. The nationalisms that fueled the establishment of the contemporary nation-states of South and Southeast Asia are thus complex fabrications, combining elements of experience under homogenizing Western imperialist rule with precolonial cultural traditions recast to suit contemporary purposes. As such, nationalism has had a powerful impact on these new nation-states' interactions with one another and with the great powers of the postindependence era.

## British India

In the case of British India, the earliest discernible stirring of "Indian" nationalism appeared in the wake of the assumption of direct rule by the British Crown from the British East India Company after the Sepoy Mutiny in 1857. Agitation by Indians educated in British schools for greater participation in the British civil service that administered the colony led in 1885 to the creation of the Indian National Congress (INC). Over the next three decades, the INC debated its ultimate goals—expanded Indian representation within British colonial rule, autonomy under overarching British sovereignty, or outright independence. It also debated the tactics to achieve its goals, ranging from pressing for reform by working with the British administration, to noncooperation with it, to active and violent resistance to it. The INC also debated whether and how to collaborate in pursuit of its goals with other nationalist groups, the most important of which was the Muslim League, founded in 1906.

The British attempted both to accommodate rising nationalist pressures through reforms and to blunt and suppress them. The most important steps toward accommodation were the 1909 Morley-Minto reforms, which provided for greater Indian participation in the colonial administration and created the principle of "communal" representation for Muslims, and the 1919 Montague-Chelmsford bill, which established the principle of "dyarchy"—joint rule by the British and Indians. The latter reform was complemented, however, by extension into the postwar period of martial law provisions established during World War I for imprisonment for political agitation.

The end of World War I was a watershed in the rise of nationalism in British India, as in other colonized regions. The savagery of the war severely deflated the image of Western superiority in the eyes of Indian intellectuals, and it also weakened the European powers' capacity to impose their will outright in their colonies. As described in Chapter 1, the war also ushered a rhetoric of liberalism into international affairs that stressed the right of peoples to have a voice in their government, inspiring hope among nationalists that their goals might be achieved. By the end of the war years, the INC, which had split over tactics in 1907, had reunified and, thanks to the 1916 Lucknow Pact, was pledged to work together with the Muslim League. The 1919 Montague-Chelmsford reforms did not go far enough to satisfy the ambitions of the INC, which, outraged by the massacre of hundreds of assembled demonstrators in Amritsar in April 1919, adopted tactics of noncooperation and elected Gandhi as its new president.

Gandhi's tactics of *satyagraha*—noncooperation and nonviolent resistance—and his outreach to rural society expanded the INC movement and gave it a mass following, while also sustaining his leadership. In Lahore in 1929, the INC declared independence as its goal and elected Gandhi's collaborator Jawaharlal Nehru as its president. The British responded to the INC's subsequent campaign of civil disobedience first with suppression and then with new reforms, set down in the 1935 Government of India Act, which abolished dyarchy and provided for provincial autonomy through elections. After the ensuing provincial elections of 1937, the INC and Muslim League failed to agree on league representation of Muslims in provincial offices, and in 1940, after three years' failure to heal the breach, the Muslim League under Mohammed Ali Jinnah, a British-trained lawyer, declared an independent Pakistani state for Muslims as its goal.

The onset of World War II provided new opportunities both for the INC to press London for a promise of independence—a promise to "quit India"—in exchange for Indian support during the war, and for the Muslim League to consolidate its claim to represent Indian Muslims. New INC campaigns of civil disobedience in 1942 triggered new British attempts at suppression and the imprisonment of Gandhi and INC leaders. With Gandhi's release in 1944, negotiations began for outright self-rule that set the stage for the postwar INC–Muslim League struggle over what form that outcome would take.

### Southeast Asia

In Southeast Asia, the roots of nationalism similarly began in the late nineteenth century, when the final stages of administrative authority were consolidated in the British, French, Dutch, and (after 1898) American colonies.[3] In an era of accelerating strategic competition among the imperialist powers in Southeast Asia, centralized bureaucratic administrations through a secular civil service replaced former patterns of indirect, quasi-feudal rule in the colonial regions that had relied on the cooptation of indigenous traditional authorities and military force, both to consolidate the powers' hold over their colonies and to facilitate more systematic economic exploitation. Concurrent with these efforts at consolidation, new indigenous elites educated in modern schools in the colonies or in schools and universities in the colonial powers themselves sought careers in the new centralized administrations. These efforts at colonial consolidation also laid the institutional foundations and conceptual frameworks—the idea of a unified "Burma" or "Malaya" or "Philippines" nation under centralized bureaucratic administration—for the independent nation-states that emerged in Southeast Asia under the force of aroused nationalism after World War II.

Many of these educated Southeast Asians became the first nationalists, who, especially after World War I, as in British India, pushed for reform by working within the colonial system and for independence by working to overturn it. Their efforts drew inspiration not only from the experience of these indigenous elites with the framework of Western colonialism within their own societies. They also were inspired by Western liberal rhetoric after the war and the progress of nationalist movements in British India and in late Qing and early Republican China, the emergence of Japan as a regional power, and the success of a Marxist revolution in Russia in 1917.

In the Spanish Philippines, the first nationalistic stirrings emerged among educated *ilustrado* Filipinos (intellectuals), typified by the writer José Rizal, whose Propaganda Movement in the 1870s and 1880s sought equal standing for Filipinos as Spanish citizens.

In the mid-1890s, the beginnings of a revolutionary movement led in 1899 to the declaration of an independent Philippine Republic, which was brutally suppressed by the United States in the course of making the Philippines its colony in the Spanish-American War. The subsequent American reformist approach coopted many of the nationalist elites in governing the colony and held out the promise of independence, set down on paper in the Tydings-McDuffie Act of 1934.

In the Dutch East Indies, among the earliest nationalist organizations was Sarekat Islam, established in 1912 to advance reform on behalf of Muslims in the colony and which the Dutch colonial authority tolerated. In 1920, what became the Communist Party of Indonesia (PKI) was formed and established membership in the Comintern, but it was ruthlessly suppressed after its members led a local revolt in 1926. Finally, in 1927, Sukarno, a civil engineer, and friends in Bandung established the Indonesian National Party (PNI), which sought independence for the entire Dutch East Indies under the banner "One nation—Indonesia, one people--Indonesian, and one language—Indonesian."[4] Pursuing tactics of noncooperation with the Dutch authorities, Sukarno and other leaders were arrested and imprisoned in 1929 and the party was dissolved. The invasion of the Dutch East Indies by Japan in 1942 gave nationalistic Indonesians a new opportunity to advance their cause, as Sukarno and other nationalists, such as the Dutch-trained economist Mohammad Hatta, collaborated with the Japanese in hopes of pursuing an independent Indonesia.

In French Indochina, nationalism emerged out of a longer tradition of xenophobia and anticolonialism—first against the Chinese and then against the French. The transformation of anticolonialism to Vietnamese nationalism was furthered by the writings of Confucian scholars Phan Boi Chau and Phan Chu Trinh, who were inspired by revolutionary leaders including Sun Yat-sen in late-Qing China, leading to the Republican revolution of 1911, and by Japan's triumph in the 1904–5 Russo-Japanese War. Moderate French administration in the 1910s encouraged the collaboration of nationalistic reformers. But disillusionment with the West and its liberal ideals as a consequence of World War I and of the failure, from an Asian perspective, of the Paris treaties to live up to those ideals, as well as the Bolshevik Revolution in Russia, encouraged more radical trends. In 1927, the Vietnam Nationalist Party, modeled after the Chinese Kuomintang (KMT), was founded but suppressed by the French after resorting to radical violence. In 1930, Ho Chi Minh, who had worked and studied in France after 1911, founded the Indochinese Communist Party, which through the 1930s attempted to find an effective revolutionary strategy to pursue under conditions of concerted French suppression. The onset of World War II, however, presented Ho with new opportunities to advance his and his collaborators' cause of independence. In contrast to his Indonesian counterparts, who opted to work through the Japanese, and consistent with the long Vietnamese anticolonial tradition, Ho founded a Communist front organization, the League for the Independence of Vietnam (the Vietminh), in 1941 under a banner of rallying Vietnamese nationalism against the new Japanese colonial power. The success of this strategy made Ho's Vietnamese Communists the principal force to contest the French attempt to reassert colonial control after the war.

Similar patterns characterized the emergence of nationalism elsewhere in Southeast Asia. As Japan's defeat loomed, nationalist movements throughout South and Southeast Asia grew in strength and were poised to assert power in their own societies. As a result, the colonial states' desire to reinstate their power along Asia's southern rim was swamped by the tide of nationalism bursting forth after the war.

## PARTITION IN SOUTH ASIA

As the war ended, Britain's legendary strategy of divide and rule was quickly replaced by a policy of divide and run in the case of the empire's crown jewel, the Indian subcontinent. Churchill's aversion to presiding over the dissolution of the British Empire became moot when the Conservatives lost power in mid-1945. Two years later, the contending INC and Muslim League parties having been unable to agree on a unified India, the Attlee government imposed a plan for partition and scurried away. The partition of the subcontinent produced the new independent states of India and Pakistan (and of Burma, which until the 1930s had been ruled as part of British India). It also entailed splitting the provinces of Punjab and Bengal, which endured mass population transfers that accounted for much of the tragic carnage—upward of five hundred thousand killed in communal violence—that attended the British departure. The Bengal division led a quarter of a century later to still another partition when what had been East Pakistan broke away to become the independent state of Bangladesh.

### Divergent Strategies

Impelled by fundamentally different national identities and geopolitical interests, the resulting states of India and Pakistan pursued divergent grand strategies and opposing foreign policy orientations. India emerged as the giant of South Asia, with a population more than four times that of Pakistan, and dwarfing the smaller states of the region. Its economy, though poor and developing, was by far the largest in the region. Given these geopolitical advantages, India sought to secure its position as hegemon over South Asia, dominating its smaller neighbors and seeking to blunt the intrusion of external powers into the region. India's size and relative power also served New Delhi's ambition of establishing India as a major player in global politics, deserving of a seat on the UN Security Council.

As prime minister, Nehru advanced a foreign policy rhetoric of neutralism that served India's core national interests. In its renunciation of membership in either Cold War bloc, neutralism drew inspiration in part from the Indian path to independence and Gandhi's tactics in achieving it. Having struggled to free itself of British colonial domination, India was not about to subordinate its hard-won sovereignty to either of the superpowers. Neutralism also allowed New Delhi to attempt to play each superpower off against the other. It facilitated New Delhi's efforts to fend off efforts by either superpower to extend its reach into South Asia and so to sustain its position of hegemony in the region. Moreover, the rhetoric of neutralism also enhanced India's claim to moral leadership in world affairs.

In addition, the moralism of Indian foreign policy rhetoric helped to mask its readiness to use military force. As a new nation-state built on what had been a colonial empire, India faced a significant agenda of territorial unification. As have other new nation-states that were established out of similar circumstances—China and Indonesia come to mind—India has not hesitated to use military force to assert control over territories where it claims sovereignty or to sustain its hegemonic position in South Asia. With its forced accession to the Indian Union of the princely states of Junagadh and Hyderabad, its eviction of the Portuguese from Goa in 1961, its "forward policy" in contesting sovereignty over Aksai Chin in 1960–62, its intimidation of Sikkim, Bhutan, and Nepal, its intervention in the Sri Lankan civil war in the late 1980s, and its intervention in the Maldives in 1988, not to mention its successive conflicts with Pakistan over Jammu and Kashmir, New Delhi has resorted to military force as frequently as has the PRC, although its moralistic rhetoric of neutralism has obscured that reality in ways that China's Marxist-Leninist rhetoric did not.

As the weaker of the two major South Asian states, in contrast, Pakistan's national interests evoked a different foreign policy and security orientation. While India's interests called for efforts to keep the external powers out of South Asia, Pakistan's weakness with respect to India commended an approach of inviting external great powers into the region to balance and dilute Indian regional hegemony. In addition, Pakistan's even poorer economic status meant that it required the scale of developmental assistance that a superpower patron might provide. Finally, its Muslim population oriented Pakistan westward, toward the Middle East; given its long-standing historical ties with Southeast Asia, New Delhi tended to look east.

As both superpowers discovered in their Cold War search for assets in South Asia, the rivalry between India and Pakistan proved to be frustrating. Patronage of one tended to alienate the other, prompting its tilt toward the opposite side in the Cold War. As Washington soon discovered, moreover, aid that was intended to strengthen either India or Pakistan against the Soviet bloc was readily used more immediately against the other.

## Kashmir

A final point of contrast between the new nation-states of India and Pakistan was their diverging sense of national identity. Nowhere was this divergence more apparent than in the most enduring—and explosive—issue, the Kashmir question, which has remained on the agenda into the new century, now a confrontation between nuclear powers. Whether viewed as an acute symptom or the main cause of the Indian-Pakistani conflict, the Kashmir issue goes to the heart of the matter in that it represents in concentrated form the conflict between the antithetical ideological foundations of the two states. Pakistan—the name was coined to reflect major regions with Muslim populations (Punjab, the Afghans of the North-West Frontier, Kashmir, Sind, and Baluchistan)—was based on the two-nation theory advanced by Muslim leader Mohammed Ali Jinnah, who contended that the subcontinent was already divided into two nations, Muslim and Hindu, and thus these should be incorporated into two nation-states as successors to the British Empire.

(There is a historiographical school that says Jinnah actually did not desire partition but used it as a bluff to secure better terms for Muslims in a unified India.[5]) India, in sharp contrast, was founded on "the premise of civic nationalism"; that is, it was to be a secular state.[6] Kashmir, which would have been a prize in its own right due to its beauty and its strategic importance as a borderland, became a focus of the underlying conflict between the opposed conceptions of a state. For Pakistan it was a crucial irredenta whose Muslim majority should be gathered into the homeland of their communal kindred. Conversely, for India to surrender its claim to Kashmir—based on the accession to the new state of India by its maharajah, a Hindu—would derogate from its status as a pluralist state accommodating all communities. More concretely, it could spur separatists in other parts of the country—perhaps the Sikhs or Tamils—and trigger a fissiparous chain reaction. In addition, Srinagar, Kashmir's capital city, was also the hometown of the Nehru family.

The Kashmir issue was brought into the broader international arena when India referred it to the UN Security Council, citing Pakistani complicity in the Muslim unrest that prompted the maharajah's accession decision. Pakistan questioned the validity of that decision while denying Indian charges of aggression. Security Council resolutions in 1948 led to the creation of a commission to investigate and mediate the controversy, and mandated a plebiscite to determine the population's preference. A deadlock ensued that has persisted into the new century.[7] (The chair of the UN commission was a Czechoslovak diplomat, Joseph Korbel, father of one future U.S. secretary of state, Madeleine Albright, and mentor of another, Condoleezza Rice.[8])

## IMPACT OF THE COLD WAR IN SOUTH ASIA

India definitively turned away from the plebiscite route when Pakistan was drawn into the U.S. security orbit in 1954, first by an agreement in which Pakistan was provided American arms and training, and then when Pakistan became a member of the new Southeast Asia Treaty Organization, which was thrown together to deal with regional security following the Geneva accords on Indochina. The next year Pakistan joined still another part of the Western alliance chain, the Baghdad Pact, comprising Britain (still a major player in the Middle East), Turkey, Iraq, Iran, and Pakistan, with the United States officially having observer status. (This organization became known as CENTO, the Central Treaty Organization, after the overthrow of Iraq's British-installed monarchy in 1958.) Thus Pakistan became a link in a Cold War chain that extended from North America to Europe and along a huge arc from the eastern Mediterranean to the Pacific.[9]

India meanwhile played a leading role in the nonalignment movement, or "positive neutralism"—*neutralism* with its passive connotations being replaced as the favored term by *nonalignment*—whose leaders sought to take an active part in international affairs as a force independent of the superpowers locked in their Cold War. New Delhi sought to cultivate good Sino-Indian relations as a bulwark against the intrusion of outside forces in Asia and to serve the interests of "Asian solidarity." Thus, it supported Beijing's demand to be seated in the United Nations and was sympathetic to Chinese concerns generally. After the Geneva accords on Indochina in 1954, which chose India as chair of the three-member international control commission (reflecting its neutralist stance, the other two members—Poland and Canada—representing the opposing blocs), New Delhi's profile was given still greater prominence in Asian affairs. This also coincided with China's moderate approach in foreign policy in the mid-1950s, the period in which the "five principles of peaceful coexistence" were promulgated and Beijing renounced the export of revolution. Zhou Enlai signed agreements enshrining the five principles during visits to nonaligned India and Burma in 1954. (The five principles are mutual respect for each other's territorial integrity and sovereignty; nonaggression; noninterference in each other's internal affairs; equality and mutual benefit; and peaceful coexistence.)

These trends, sharply contrasting with the formation of the U.S. alliance system in Asia in the same years (see Chapter 7), were in dramatic display at the first Asian-African conference, held in Bandung, Indonesia, in 1955. Twenty-nine countries were represented, an impressive turnout considering that the vast wave of decolonization in Africa had not yet occurred. In addition to Nehru and other neutralist leaders from the region, the suave Zhou was in attendance as the face of a smiling foreign policy. While burnishing the PRC's image of conciliation and accommodation with its Asian neighbors, Zhou also used his stay in Indonesia to sign an agreement on the status of Overseas Chinese—a sensitive subject in the region—by requiring those with dual citizenship to choose which one to retain, and he joined Indonesian leader Sukarno in still another celebration of the five principles of peaceful coexistence.[10]

Thus, during this period Nehru's efforts to promote Asian solidarity and peaceful coexistence seemed to be paying off handsomely. Over time, however, geopolitical realities deflected India from its chosen path, bringing it into conflict with China and into alignment with the Soviet Union, culminating in a security treaty at still another period of hostilities with Pakistan in the early 1970s. With the advent of the new century, marked in particular by the terrorist attacks on the United States in 2001, India's relations with Washington underwent a marked improvement, to the point that there was talk of its joining the U.S. missile defense system proposed for Asia, and Washington offered a nuclear agreement with India (see Chapter 14).

## SINO-INDIAN CONFLICT

After the Communists' triumph in China, Nehru nourished hopes that his country and the "New China" would lead the continent in expunging the effects of colonialism and bolstering the forces of independence against the impact of the Cold War. These hopes were destined to be buffeted by geopolitical and nationalist imperatives, however, and eventually they dissolved into recrimination and border warfare. India and China formed diplomatic relations in early 1950, but danger signals were flashed later that year as the PRC set about establishing control by force over Tibet. India protested the Chinese moves; Beijing indicated its priorities by defining its action as liberating Tibet from the "Anglo-American imperialists and their running dog Nehru." Tibet, its buffer status during the British rule in India now having been overridden by the PRC's determination to fill out what it regarded as its natural borders, was destined to become a source of mutual distrust and conflict in the following years.

Having "stood up" to reclaim its historical status after a century of humiliation and domination from outside, China was intent on reestablishing its authority in the sensitive borderlands of Xinjiang and Tibet with their restive minority populations. As they revealed later when the Sino-Indian border dispute flared, the Chinese used an old caravan route from Xinjiang to move their troops into western Tibet in 1950. This route crossed the barren plateau of Aksai Chin (a Uighur word, Zhou Enlai was careful to point out); a major military road was constructed there in 1956–57 as China's main access route into Tibet from the west and became the area of contention in the western sector of the Sino-Indian border. Because Tibet as well as Xinjiang were defined as essential areas in Beijing's determination to extend its control over what it deemed its sovereign territory, there was little room for accommodating India's counterclaim. It was all the more irritating to India in that the area lies in the northeastern corner of Kashmir, thus overlaying another dispute on the bitter issue dividing India and Pakistan. Salt was poured into India's wounds in 1962 when Pakistan concluded a border agreement with China that involved areas in Kashmir. India was not mollified by the fact that the agreement was explicitly provisional pending a resolution of the Kashmir dispute.

India's claims, like China's, reflected the nationalist impulses of a newly independent state, in this case an intent to inherit the full territorial patrimony of the British Raj. The problem, however, was that British jurisdiction itself was based on weak grounds or begged the question of ownership. Aksai Chin was a no-man's-land, with conflicting claims resting on murky historical and cartographic grounds (each side even citing the tenth-century Ladakhi Chronicles[11]). In the eastern sector, the main disputed area had been delimited by the McMahon Line, running along the Himalayan ridgeline, and India's claim as successor to the Raj invoked the results of the 1913–14 Simla conference (after the fall of the Manchu dynasty in China), which was attended by representatives from Britain, Tibet, and China. The boundary agreement, however, had been a secret one between the British and Tibetan representatives; the Chinese, whether Nationalist or Communist, have insisted that they were never bound by its terms.[12]

After the rocky start of Sino-Indian relations when the Chinese Communists occupied Tibet, a halcyon period ensued in the mid-1950s. It was during this time of moderation in Chinese foreign policy that the celebrated five principles of peaceful coexistence were introduced, in the preamble to a 1954 Sino-Indian agreement regulating Indian trade and travel in Tibet. India acknowledged Beijing's authority over the "Tibet region of China." Events were soon to conspire, however, to disrupt this peaceful environment. For one thing, the building of the road across Aksai Chin, or more precisely, the disclosure of the road in a Chinese magazine in 1958, brought the border issue to the surface. The next year the Tibetan uprising against Chinese control erupted, with the Dalai Lama fleeing to India and gaining asylum. Mutual mistrust flared, exacerbated by Beijing's concern over Chinese Nationalist and American CIA support for Tibetan insurgents.[13] The collision course thus created led to border clashes in 1959 and a punishing Chinese military thrust that humiliated India three years later.

If geopolitical concerns could be insulated from nationalist sentiments, a deal involving trade-offs that would address these concerns to mutual advantage seemed plausible all along, and indeed the Chinese suggested it. In outline, this would require Indian acquiescence in China's possession of the Aksai Chin, thereby ensuring Chinese use of the strategic artery between Xinjiang and Tibet, in exchange for acceptance of India's claim to the territory lying below the McMahon Line. New Delhi has important strategic interests in having defensible borders along the eastern sector, which would be served by a boundary roughly along the ridgeline. Otherwise, its northeastern regions, beset by tribal unrest and friction stemming from immigration from elsewhere in India, are especially vulnerable to a Chinese invasion. For example, the Indian heartland is connected to the northeast by an extremely narrow corridor between Nepal and what was East Pakistan and is now Bangladesh; this corridor—the site of a Maoist insurgency arising in the 1960s to further complicate the situation—is accessible from a pass and valley leading down from Tibet.

Beijing was, of course, in a better position to barter than New Delhi, which was answerable in a democratic system to parliamentary and public opinion. Nehru seemed at first to adopt a conciliatory tone in discussing the border issue, doubtless hoping to preserve his hopes for Sino-Indian amity as a beneficent force in Asia, but he was soon engulfed by the enflamed nationalism sweeping the country. From the Indian perspective, China's offer to barter amounted to a demand for New Delhi to accept what was stolen in the western sector in exchange for Beijing's recognition of what already belonged to India in the east. Thus, the attempt at negotiations in the wake of the 1959 clashes foundered and the 1962 war followed ineluctably.

## OTHER SOUTH ASIAN DEVELOPMENTS

The Cold War intruded into the decolonized South Asian scene in various ways. As has been noted, Pakistan became a link in the Western alliance system, a development making India receptive to overtures from the other Cold War bloc. The post-Stalin Soviet leadership began courting the Indians in the 1950s, exchanging visits with Nehru and offering economic and diplomatic support to India (such as on the Kashmir question). Moscow's growing ties with "bourgeois nationalist" governments became a source of tension in Sino-Soviet relations when Beijing lurched to the left in the late 1950s; as will be seen, the Chinese were infuriated by Moscow's decision to take a neutral stance on the Sino-Indian border conflict (see Chapter 8). Meanwhile the Eisenhower administration, at least until the demise of Secretary of State Dulles and his antipathy toward neutralism, was cool toward India, but the two sides saw an opportunity to develop better relations as they found themselves with a common adversary, China. The Kennedy administration in the early 1960s pursued this opening by providing military aid to India in the interest of deterring China. The warming of U.S.-Indian relations, in turn, was counterbalanced by the close relationship developing between Pakistan and China.

The Sino-Indian conflict thus lent new complexity to the Cold War while adding complications to the subcontinent. New Delhi and Beijing scrambled to contest the buffer areas along the Himalayas. India regarded itself as the heir to the British Raj's spheres of influence in the small states to its north, Nepal, Sikkim, and Bhutan; it was intent on maintaining its protectorates over Sikkim and Bhutan, eventually simply annexing the former in 1975. The Chinese, for their part, cultivated relations with states in this region, dramatically contrasting what they portrayed as Indian obduracy on the boundary issue by concluding border treaties in the early 1960s with Afghanistan, Pakistan, Nepal, and Burma. In the case of Burma, in fact, the Chinese accepted the McMahon Line, offering further evidence of a willingness to concede that boundary line in exchange for Indian acceptance of China's control of Aksai Chin. The rivalry between India and China exhibited signs of a classic "security dilemma." Each side's moves to enhance its security in the buffer zones only stoked the suspicions of the other side, which in turn took measures to improve its security situation, thereby impelling a spiral of moves and countermoves heightening tension.[14]

## THE COLD WAR AND NATIONALISM IN SOUTHEAST ASIA

Truman's statement of 27 June 1950 after the outbreak of the Korean War had fateful implications for Asia by bringing the Cold War deeply into the region. In addition to committing the United States to involvement on the Asian mainland and reasserting an American role in the Chinese civil war, Truman called for increased military assistance to the forces of France and its allies in the Indochina conflict and for the dispatch of a military mission to "*provide close working relations*" with those forces (emphasis added). This in itself was not a reversal of policy, which had already occurred when the administration abandoned Roosevelt's vague hopes for trusteeship arrangements as a means to end European colonialism in the area. But the earlier shift reflected Washington's priority interest in buttressing France and the rest of West Europe against Soviet pressure; now the purpose was to buck up French resistance to Communist pressure in Asia itself. The impact of bipolarity thus began to be felt in Southeast Asia, an arena of revolutionary insurgencies that Washington perceived as instruments of the Soviet bloc's drive to global hegemony. Vietnam in particular was sucked into this bipolarity, with Ho Chi Minh—who once collaborated with the United States in the anti-Japanese struggle—now regarded as a tool of the Kremlin in its expansionist designs. This perception led ineluctably to the morass of the American war in Indochina.

Apart from the impact of bipolarity, there were other powerful geopolitical forces arising out of World War II, notably anticolonialism and nationalism, which fed the flames of revolution and radical change. But where French Indochina, like China, fell to Communism, other colonial areas in Southeast Asia rejected their imperialist overlords and produced a prickly nationalism that proved resistant to both Communist and Western pressure. How these divergent outcomes developed needs examination.

Southeast Asia is the product of diverse historical, cultural, and religious influences. It was the meeting point of the great Chinese and Hindu cultural influences, which interacted with a complex assortment of indigenous elements to produce a wide range of cultural formations. Major religions penetrated the area—Hinduism, Buddhism, Confucianism,

Islam, Christianity—and the linguistic variety is immense. The colonial era superimposed yet another layer of difference, with the British in Burma and the Malay Peninsula, the French in Indochina, the Dutch in the East Indian archipelago, and the Spanish and later the Americans in the Philippines. Yet notwithstanding these heterogeneous influences, Southeast Asia at the end of the war had several key shared characteristics. As has been noted, the war's sapping of the colonial powers' strength, the impact of Japan's military successes on the myth of Western superiority, the appeal of Western notions of self-determination, all created the grounds for ferment and change. Another shared feature was the outbreak of Communist-led insurgencies across the region, and the specter of Communist revolution seemed all the more menacing because of the presence of sizable and economically powerful ethnic Chinese minorities. These Overseas Chinese were feared as constituting a fifth column for the CPC, as a source of subversion and insurrection from within that was promoted by the new Communist regime in Beijing.

As it happened, the forces of nationalism, whose elites, as discussed previously, were firmly dedicated to transplanting the Westphalian system of nation-states to the region, proved a strong competitor to the forces of Communist insurgency and Cold War pressures. In some cases, notably Vietnam, it was the Communists who succeeded in capturing the mandate of nationalism; as a result, the Hanoi regime managed both to enter the socialist camp (as "the southeastern outpost") and to maintain its nationalist credentials. This enabled Hanoi to secure massive aid from its Communist allies while mobilizing its people to sustain decades of warfare against the "imperialists" and their "lackeys." In other cases the new nation-states became standard-bearers for neutralism, resolutely refusing to align with either camp. Burma even rejected membership in the British Commonwealth (unlike India and many other former British possessions). Rangoon's position seemed particularly precarious in view of the fact that it faced rebellion not only from the Communists but also from the minority nationalities, amounting to almost half of the country's population. The Malay Peninsula, beset by a Communist insurgency, did not acquire independence until almost a decade later than Burma (awaiting victory in the counterinsurgency campaign called "the Emergency"), and then became another ardent proponent of the Westphalian system.

Thailand presented a special case, having been only a semicolony while practicing an agile bandwagon diplomacy of accommodating the main external power (Britain before the war, Japan during its occupation of most of the region, and the United States after the war). The United States allowed the Thai elite who had collaborated with Japan to retain their status, and in return was given military bases and major influence in Thailand. In Burma and Indonesia, similarly, the nationalists who had collaborated with the Japanese became the postwar anticolonial and postcolonial leaders. The Philippines was different in still another way, having been a colony but promised independence by Washington in 1934 (the Tydings-McDuffie Act). That independence was heavily qualified during the Cold War, however, with the United States having major air and naval bases as well as enjoying important commercial privileges.

## THE INDONESIAN STRUGGLE FOR INDEPENDENCE

Indonesia's hard-won independence from stubborn Dutch efforts to stay on deserves particular attention because of the role that international pressure, including from the United States, played in that struggle in contrast to the case of Vietnam.[15] While London acquiesced in the dissolution of its South and Southeast Asian empire principally through negotiations that preserved economic ties with its former colonies, Paris and The Hague believed reassertion of control over their prewar colonies to be essential to sustaining their stature in postwar international relations, and so each contested nationalist efforts on behalf of independence with force.

As the war ended, the Netherlands was in no position immediately to assert control over its colony, and so, for reasons of their own, the British did so on the Netherlands' behalf, landing forces and occupying Jakarta on 29 September 1945. By that time, however, Sukarno and Hatta had already declared an independent Republic of Indonesia on 17 August, building on wartime promises by the Japanese of eventual independence and taking advantage of the power vacuum that emerged in the former colony with the Japanese surrender. They had already promulgated a constitution for the new republic, were elected president and vice president, respectively, and had begun to try to consolidate the republic's administration in areas where their strength was greatest—mostly Sumatra, Java, and Mataram—and to negotiate incorporation of the diverse principalities in the easternmost parts of the island chain. In contrast to Dutch opinion, which discredited Sukarno and Hatta and dismissed the new republic as the product of wartime collaborationists, popular opinion on the islands surged in favor of independence and behind the republic. Some of this support—the *pemuda* youth movement—promoted violent defense of the republic in Java and Sumatra, and managing this radical support, alongside the ambitions of other groups in the broader nationalist movement, complicated the republican effort.

Bloody clashes between republican forces and the British and, later, the Dutch led to negotiations sponsored by the British (who had no wish to become entangled in the struggle) and to the Linggajati (or Cheribon) Agreement in November 1946. By that accord, The Hague would recognize republican autonomy in governing Java, Sumatra, and Mataram, but Dutch sovereignty would prevail over a broader United States of Indonesia that incorporated those regions as well as the remaining islands to the east. In the wake of the agreement, Washington and London joined six other countries in extending de facto recognition to the republic. By June 1947, however, the agreement broke down and conflict erupted again; in response, the Dutch mounted their first "police action" to suppress the republic. The brutality of this campaign strengthened the Dutch position in the colony, but it also earned broader condemnation from the international community, including Britain, the United States, the Soviet Union, and the newly independent India, which viewed the republican struggle with increasing sympathy. A new round of negotiations, encouraged by the UN Security Council, produced in January 1948 the Renville Agreement (after the U.S. Navy ship on which the agreement was negotiated). The agreement reinstated the outlines of the Linggajati accord but modified it to reflect the reduced republican position on Java resulting from the Dutch action.

The agreement satisfied neither party, and over the next several months, negotiations called for by the Renville accord broke down. In December 1948 the Dutch opted to press their advantage by launching a second "police action" that exceeded the ferocity of the first. On the ground, the Dutch succeeded in occupying most of the republic's remaining territory and captured Sukarno, Hatta, and others among the republican leadership. The action, however, was a disaster for the The Hague internationally. Condemnation of the Dutch action was nearly universal, and included criticism from Washington, which up to that point had been sensitive to Dutch concerns even while sympathizing with the nationalists. American favor toward the republic had been strengthened in part by its suppression of two revolts—the Darul Islam Muslim uprising in May 1948 and the Communist attempt to establish an Indonesian Soviet Republic at Madiun in September 1948—which demonstrated to Washington the non-Communist and moderate orientation of the mainstream republican leadership. Under condemnation by a UN Security Council resolution of 29 January 1949, the Dutch finally agreed to open negotiations leading to outright independence for Indonesia. These culminated in The Hague Agreement of 2 November, by which an independent Indonesia became sovereign over all of the former Dutch Indies except western New Guinea, which remained under temporary Dutch control. On 27 December 1949, the United States of Indonesia was established.

As was the case of India and Burma, the brutal four-year struggle for Indonesian independence inclined the new nation-state toward a declared foreign policy of neutralism. The relative weakness of these new states internationally and the fragility of their hold on sovereignty over ethnically, religiously, and culturally diverse populations made such an approach to the escalating Cold War appealing. In addition, their difficult struggles to achieve independence made them sensitive to potential encumbrance of their hard-won independence by attachment to either superpower bloc. So it is not at all surprising that they were among the leaders of the nonaligned movement that got its start at the 1955 Bandung Conference.

## THE FIRST INDOCHINA WAR

We must take a closer look at developments in Vietnam to identify the factors that produced the outcome in Indochina, notably triumph by the Communist revolutionaries, which distinguished it from the rest of Southeast Asia. As mentioned previously, the founding of the Indochinese Communist Party came only in 1930, nearly a decade after that of its Chinese counterpart, which became its mentor and backer during the decades of struggle against the French and Americans. That it was a party claiming to represent all of Indochina foreshadowed the close relationship between the Vietnamese struggle and that of the Lao comrades in particular as well as the Cambodian Khmer Rouge. (Ho originally named it the Vietnam Communist Party, but the Comintern instructed him to change it to the more inclusive title.[16]) Not coincidentally, all three of the former dependencies of French Indochina fell to the Communists virtually simultaneously in 1975.

As in some other countries, Ho Chi Minh sought to capitalize on anti-Japanese nationalist sentiment by establishing a specifically Vietnamese nationalist united front, the

Vietminh, or League for the Independence of Vietnam. (Similarly, the Philippine Communists called themselves the Anti-Japanese Resistance League.) Ho, who had learned Marxism-Leninism in France and had close ties to the CPC, declared an independent Democratic Republic of Vietnam in 1945 after the surrender of the Japanese and dissolved the Indochinese Communist Party. With the French in control of the south and of major cities, the Communists established guerrilla bases to pursue the anticolonial struggle. The situation deteriorated, leading France in January 1950 to try a new formula by making Vietnam, Laos, and Cambodia independent "associated" states of the French Union. Bipolarity asserted itself, with the Soviet Union and the PRC recognizing the Democratic Republic of Vietnam (DRV; the North), and the United States and Britain recognizing the pro-Western government in Saigon headed by the former emperor Bao Dai. In the region, only Thailand recognized Bao Dai. Secretary of State Acheson portrayed the situation in strongly Cold War terms: The Soviet and PRC recognition of the DRV "should remove any illusions as to the 'nationalist' character of Ho Chi Minh's aims and reveal Ho in his true colors as the mortal enemy of native independence in Indochina."[17] Ho, like Mao, was thus ruled out as a potential Tito. It was in this context that the United States supplied arms to the French and China arms to the DRV. Vietnam had thus been drawn into the Cold War bipolar conflict.

The French, even with increased U.S. aid, proved incapable of suppressing Ho's forces. Paris declared that its burdens in Indochina were too heavy to sustain and sought political and military ways out. While offering measures for "perfecting the independence of the Associated States," France's military plans called for an offensive against the Vietminh main force in an effort to create a military situation that would enhance French bargaining power in the political negotiations.[18] It was as part of this effort that the French prepared for a decisive battle in the spring of 1954 at Dienbienphu, an isolated post along the Laos border in northern Vietnam that left the French at a perilous logistical disadvantage. They

### UNITED STATES PLANS TO PREVENT COMMUNIST EXPANSION IN INDOCHINA: NSC-64

It is recognized that the threat of communist aggression against Indochina is only one phase of anticipated communist plans to seize all of Southeast Asia. . . .

A large segment of the Indochinese nationalist movement was seized in 1945 by Ho Chi Minh, a Vietnamese who under various aliases has served as a communist agent for thirty years. He has attracted non-communist as well as communist elements to his support. . . .

It is important to United States security interests that all practicable measures be taken to prevent further communist expansion in Southeast Asia. Indochina is a key area of Southeast Asia and is under immediate threat. . . .

The neighboring countries of Thailand and Burma could be expected to fall under Communist domination if Indochina were controlled by a Communist-dominated government. The balance of Southeast Asia would then be in grave hazard.

National Security Council, document NSC-64, 27 February 1950, in U.S. Department of State, *Foreign Relations of the United States, 1950*, vol. 6 (Washington, DC: U.S. Government Printing Office, 1976 ), 744–47.

got the decisive battle they were seeking, but it was in favor of the Vietminh and marked the end of France's effort to retain its increasingly tenuous control over Vietnam.

Like 1945 and 1950, this was another crossroads where Western disengagement from Indochina may have been feasible at relatively low cost. As it happened, there was a meeting at this time of the Council of Foreign Ministers on European issues; it agreed to convene a conference on Korea and also to discuss Indochina. In addition to the four powers composing this group—the United States, Britain, France, and the Soviet Union—China "and other interested states" were invited. The conference took up the Indochina question a day after Dienbienphu's fall on 7 May 1954.

The Western powers had divergent approaches to resolving the Indochina conflict. France hoped for an armistice, leaving political negotiations for later, and to that end sought a leopard-spot regroupment of military forces so as to defer drawing political boundaries. Washington was keenly sensitive to anything that accorded legitimacy to the PRC or conceded loss of territory to Communist control. Indeed, during the siege of Dienbienphu, President Eisenhower had popularized the metaphor of the "domino theory" in the lexicon of international relations, meaning that the loss of one country would inexorably lead to a serial toppling of others in an onrush of Communist expansion. As for the British, partition was the favored option, thereby keeping the Communists as far north as possible while the campaign to defeat the insurgency in Malaya proceeded.[19] Foreshadowing Washington's troubles with its Saigon clients when negotiating a peace settlement in the 1970s, the Vietnamese anti-Communists resented their secondary role during the Geneva Conference.

The DRV retreated from its demands for early elections and for participation at the conference by its brother Lao and Cambodian parties, though the Communist Pathet Lao was allowed to regroup in two northern provinces pending elections. Moscow and Beijing, wishing to avoid confrontation with Washington, pressured the Vietminh to accept a compromise solution, a result that Hanoi resented and that would become a bitter topic in Sino-Vietnamese polemics in the late 1970s.[20] (The Vietnamese charged that the PRC had betrayed them three times, including in 1954. During these polemics Hanoi remained discreetly silent about the historical role of Moscow, with which it had now formed a friendship treaty to counterbalance the Chinese threat.) Thus, the setting was favorable for partition and an armistice, leaving an uneasy equilibrium that would take a second Indochinese war to resolve finally in favor of the Communists.

Hanoi's grudging acceptance of the Geneva Conference results was matched by Washington's less than wholehearted endorsement. The Final Declaration[21] listed the participants—the United States, Britain, France, the Soviet Union, the PRC, the two opposing Vietnamese governments, Cambodia, and Laos—but the document was left unsigned. (A detailed agreement on the cease-fire and military regroupment was signed by the French and DRV commanders.) Washington went no further in embracing the Geneva results than to issue a unilateral statement that "took note" of the accords and said the United States would not "disturb" them by the threat or use of force. This arm's-length posture, dictated by Washington's extreme aversion to conceding any further ground to Communism and especially to conferring legitimacy on the Chinese Communists, left the Geneva accords dangling in ambiguity. Moreover, in its unilateral statement the United States warned that it would view with grave concern "any renewal of the aggression" in violation of the Geneva agreements.[22] As events were to demonstrate, Washington resolved the ambiguity in a way that erased the declaration's emphatically explicit statement that the "military demarcation line" was "provisional and should not in any way be interpreted as constituting a political or territorial boundary." Moreover, the United States and the State of (South) Vietnam under Ngo Dinh Diem—the Catholic mandarin who proceeded to consolidate his control of the Saigon regime—refused to take part in the elections that according to the Geneva agreement were to take place in two years in order to unify the country. Instead, Washington began to take steps—military aid for Saigon, "nation building" in South Vietnam through economic and technical assistance, and inclusion of the non-Communist areas of Indochina within the structure of security pacts designed to contain Communist expansion in Asia—that were aimed at drawing a line beyond which the Communists were not to be allowed to penetrate. That line was the "provisional" military demarcation line at the seventeenth parallel of Vietnam that the Geneva Final Declaration said was not to be construed as a territorial boundary.

In a profusion of architectural metaphors, Senator John F. Kennedy reflected the thinking in Washington by declaring that South Vietnam represented "the cornerstone of the Free World in Southeast Asia, the keystone in the arch, the finger in the dike."[23] On the heels of the Geneva Conference, Secretary of State John Foster Dulles had proceeded to build this architecture in the form of a multilateral Southeast Asia Treaty Organization (SEATO) comprising the United States, Britain, France, Australia, New Zealand, the Philippines, Thailand, and Pakistan. In a bow to the constraints in the Geneva accords against any military alliance involving either half of Vietnam, SEATO did not include South

### GENEVA ACCORDS: MILITARY DEMARCATION LINE NOT A TERRITORIAL BOUNDARY

The Conference takes note of the clauses in the agreement on the cessation of hostilities in Viet-Nam to the effect that no military base under the control of a foreign State may be established in the [military] regrouping zones of the two parties, the latter having the obligation to see that the zones allotted to them shall not constitute part of any military alliance and shall not be utilized for the resumption of hostilities or in the service of an aggressive policy. . . .

The Conference recognizes that the essential purpose of the agreement relating to Viet-Nam is to settle military questions with a view to ending hostilities and that the military demarcation line is provisional and should not in any way be interpreted as constituting a political or territorial boundary. . . .

The Conference declares that . . . the settlement of political problems, effected on the basis of respect for the principles of independence, unity and territorial integrity, shall permit the Viet-Namese people to enjoy the fundamental freedoms, guaranteed by democratic institutions established as a result of free general elections by secret ballot . . . general elections shall be held in July 1956 under the supervision of an international commission. . . .

Final Geneva Declaration, 21 July 1954, in U.S. Department of State, *Foreign Relations of the United States, 1952–54*, vol. 16 (Washington, DC: U.S. Government Printing Office, 1981), 1540–42.

Vietnam as a member but brought it under the alliance's collective security umbrella by means of a separate protocol. (In mid-1954 the National Security Council had called for a "new initiative" to bolster the U.S. position in Southeast Asia, recommending "every possible effort, *not openly inconsistent*" with the armistice agreements, "to maintain a friendly non-Communist South Vietnam and to prevent a Communist victory through all-Vietnamese elections."[24]) This designated South Vietnam along with Laos and Cambodia as areas to be treated the same as the SEATO member countries in the event of an armed attack.

The pressure exerted on Hanoi by its Communist patrons to accept an accommodation that fell short of control over all of Vietnam reflected their broader interests—as would occur still again during negotiations on a settlement in the early 1970s. In the mid-1950s both Moscow and Beijing had moved toward more accommodating and less confrontational postures in foreign affairs. After the death of Stalin in March 1953, Moscow took steps in a variety of areas to seek a relaxation of tensions: a summit meeting with the United States and the other Western members of the Big Four, negotiation of an Austrian peace treaty and withdrawal of foreign troops, diplomatic relations with West Germany and Japan, and reconciliation with Yugoslavia. To these should be added the effects of the Korean and Vietnamese armistices in promoting a more relaxed international environment. Beijing, its stature enhanced by the military standoff with the United States in the Korean War and its diplomatic performance at the Geneva Conference, entered the "Bandung phase" of its foreign policy, professing a commitment to peaceful coexistence and reassuring governments in the region that it was not seeking their overthrow by promoting insurgencies. Further reassurance came from Zhou's offer at Bandung to negotiate with the United States on the Taiwan question, leading to the opening of Sino-American talks in August 1955. Later, in a period of a few weeks in late 1956 and early 1957, Zhou flaunted this benign phase of Chinese policy by visiting eight countries south of China's border as an evangel of Beijing's irenic message.[25]

Washington might have seen in these developments an opportunity to pull back from involvement in Indochina, but this proved to be one of the decision points in the 1950s and 1960s where the United States opted to dig in deeper. The Cold War mind-set, universalized in NSC-68 (see Chapter 7) so that a loss to Communist forces anywhere represented a threat to the global balance, perceived the dangers as outweighing the opportunities for peaceful disengagement. The containment strategy, the domino theory, and the hopes for nation building as a means of thwarting Communist penetration militated against a relaxation of the effort to draw the line against what were viewed as probes and tests coordinated by the Kremlin. The notion of credibility was central to this mind-set; not only were the resources and territory of a contested area at stake, but the resolve and determination of Washington were being tested. In this view, failure to pass the test would embolden Moscow and its clients to press their offensive even further, and demoralize U.S. allies that might question Washington's commitment, thereby tipping the balance of power away from what it called the "Free World."

## THE VIETNAM DIFFERENCE

Why were the Communists of Vietnam so conspicuously successful in their revolutionary effort while other Communist parties in Southeast Asia were stymied? What was the combination of factors that, taken together, distinguished the victorious Vietnamese Communists from their red brethren in the region in the first decade after World War II? Some of these factors the Vietminh shared with the Chinese Communists but were notably absent from other countries in the region.

- The Vietnamese Communists, like the Chinese, managed to capture the mandate of nationalism; they were widely perceived as having provided staunch resistance to the Japanese invaders and French colonizers. By successfully merging nationalism and revolution, the Vietnamese and Chinese Communists earned great credit for enabling their nations to "stand up" (in Mao's phrase) after years of being abased by foreign domination and humiliation.
- Their rivals as nationalists were faction ridden and often corrupt, and failed to develop united-front appeals that could isolate the Communists. The Kuomintang in China was crippled by the same afflictions. By contrast, the non-Communist nationalist elites that took power in Burma, Thailand, the Malay Peninsula, and Indonesia developed effective, broadly based organizations and armed forces that were able to marginalize and eventually overcome the Communists (even though Communist insurgents remained active for years afterward). Unlike Vietnam, where the Japanese allowed the Vichy French to administer the country, indigenous elites in the neighboring states acquired organizational and administrative experience under the Japanese occupiers. The Philippines' elite also had the advantage of the country's being granted independence shortly after the war in accord with the promise by Washington a decade earlier.
- There was a strong Communist insurgency in Malaya, but it was fatally crippled by being dominated by ethnic Chinese. The Vietnamese Communists, conversely, had an advantage because their rivals enjoyed the support of native Catholics, the religion imported by the colonizing French. This was reflected in the departure of hundreds of thousands of Catholics from north of the dividing line created by the Geneva accords. Diem himself was a devout Catholic whose brother was a bishop.
- The Vietminh profited from having a common border with China, an advantage that became particularly important after the establishment of the PRC in 1949, which provided a sanctuary for training Vietminh troops and a conduit for arms and other support for the Vietnamese comrades.

Although the Geneva accords temporarily halted the Vietminh's progress toward unification of the country, the factors promoting its success and the absence of comparable achievements by other Southeast Asian Communists had manifested themselves by the middle of the 1950s. The subsequent American involvement, becoming massive in the next decade, was not able to reverse the momentum that those factors had already generated. This would seem to undercut the argument that the U.S. intervention created conditions for the rest of Southeast Asia to overcome the challenge of their Communist insurgencies. The pattern of events in the region had already been established before the onset of the Second Indochina War, but the bedrock U.S. concepts of containment and credibility remained in place and dictated the inexorable slide into the next phase of the conflict.

# 7 THE U.S. ALLIANCE SYSTEM

There were fundamental differences in the geopolitical settings in which the two superpowers' alliance systems developed. The Soviet Union's system was determined by its situation astride the Eurasian landmass and its memories of enduring invasion from both flanks. Combined with the Kremlin's obsessive fear and mistrust of the outside world, this geopolitical setting led Stalin to seek buffer zones to provide strategic depth against its enemies. The symbol of Soviet military might, at least before the advent of intercontinental ballistic missiles in the late 1950s, was the tank. Strategic depth would buy time for Moscow to hurl its massive tank formations against invaders. Its Cold War adversaries saw those tank masses as a threat looming over the continent—the nightmare of Soviet armored might rampaging across the north European plain to subdue non-Communist Western Europe and tilt the global balance of power in favor of Moscow.

The United States, in contrast, was protected by oceans from its Cold War adversaries. Still, its concern about unfavorable shifts in the balance of power and its interest in maintaining an international trading system led Washington to develop an alliance system that eventually girded the globe. This began in 1947 with the Rio Pact, in which the United States joined all other states in the Western Hemisphere to form an alliance in which an attack on one was to be regarded as an attack on all other members—an updating of the Monroe Doctrine for the Cold War. Two years later came the founding of the North Atlantic Treaty Organization (NATO), again with all members obligated to aid any of the others under attack. The outbreak of the Korean War the next year served as a catalyst for erecting a network of alliances in Asia, mainly bilateral; a broader multilateral organization, SEATO, was created after the 1954 Geneva accords on Indochina in an effort to draw the line on Communist expansion in Southeast Asia. In 1955 NATO and the alliances in Asia were linked by the Baghdad Pact (later CENTO), which included two NATO members, Britain and Turkey (the United States had observer status), along with Iraq, Iran, and Pakistan (a member of SEATO, as was Britain). The Western alliance structure thus virtually encircled the globe. In the Asia-Pacific region, the chain of security relationships, augmented by control of Okinawa (returned to Japan in 1972) and islands in the western Pacific formerly held by Japan, afforded the United States both strategic depth and a forward presence for applying the containment policy, platforms for military action in the region, and domination of vital sea-lanes to ensure America and its allies access to trade and resources.

This vast geopolitical reach required the United States and its close ally, the traditional naval power Britain, to be able to project power across great distances. As a symbol of power-projecting capability, the aircraft carrier comes readily to mind. (It bears noting in this connection that the United States based an aircraft carrier in Japan, the keystone of its Asian security structure, and in 2005 even secured the nuclear-sensitive host country's consent to substitute a nuclear-powered carrier for a conventional one.[1]) More broadly, the various U.S. fleets—such as the Sixth Fleet in the Mediterranean and the Seventh Fleet in the Pacific—became widely known, and in hostile circles resented, as the means by which the American flag could be shown, and force inserted when required, in regions thousands of miles removed from the homeland.

## IMPETUS FOR THE U.S. ALLIANCE SYSTEM

Several factors conspired to prompt Washington to develop a system of security relationships in Asia. In the summer of 1949, as the Chinese Communists were sweeping to victory, the Soviets ended the American nuclear monopoly by conducting an atomic test. At the end of the year Mao Zedong made his first trip abroad, going to Moscow for protracted negotiations that eventuated in the signing in February of a Sino-Soviet treaty of alliance (see Chapter 8). These events produced a jolt of alarm in Washington and led to a programmatic document that greatly expanded and transformed the containment policy enunciated by George Kennan in the early postwar years. A draft of the document, known as NSC-68, was completed in April 1950 under the supervision of Paul Nitze, who became well-known for decades as a hard-line Cold Warrior. (At the time, Nitze was Kennan's successor as director of the State Department's Policy Planning Staff; his name now adorns Johns Hopkins University's School of Advanced International Studies, an institution of which he was a founder.) This document, however, languished on Truman's shelves for months; what gave the president pause was that its call for an accelerated, massive mobilization of military, economic, and ideological resources had grave budgetary implications (on the order of tripling defense spending), and this during a time when the Republican opposition was demanding spending restraints and the president himself was averse to big budgets.

The top secret NSC-68, which was given final approval at the end of 1950, significantly globalized, militarized, and ideologized the containment doctrine (so much so that Kennan came to disavow his own strategic offspring).[2] Where the original doctrine concentrated on protecting the industrial capacity and resources (including human capital) of Western Europe and Japan from Soviet encroachment, NSC-68 advanced a postulate that invested containment with a global writ: "The assault on free institutions is world-wide now, and in the context of the present polarization of power *a defeat of free institutions anywhere is a defeat everywhere*."[3] One consequence of this mind-set was a tendency to perceive all conflicts between Communists and their opponents as having more or less comparable implications for American security interests. This obscured differences between priority concerns and peripheral matters, and it lent a somewhat mechanistic rigidity to security policy. A Communist advance anywhere held implications for the credibility of containment and thus demanded a response. The Vietnam War would come to represent these implications.

The study had its origins in a request by the president to assess the implications of the Soviet Union's possession of atomic bombs and its possible development of thermonuclear devices (hydrogen bombs). In losing its monopoly on atomic weapons, the United States lost a deterrent to Soviet expansion; it was now up to the drafters of NSC-68 to map out the requirements for redressing what it determined to be a serious mismatch between commitments and capabilities. Accordingly, it called for an urgent remobilization and rearmament to produce the full spectrum of military means for inhibiting Moscow's drive for world power, if possible, or winning a war, if necessary. Otherwise, it warned, the United States would face an intolerable choice between capitulation and a global war of annihilation. (Note, as discussed in Chapter 9, that the doctrine of "flexible response" was fashioned in the 1960s to avoid that dilemma.)

### THE UNITED STATES GLOBALIZES THE CONTAINMENT DOCTRINE: NSC-68

The Soviet Union, unlike previous aspirants to hegemony, is animated by a new fanatic faith, antithetical to our own, and seeks to impose its absolute authority over the rest of the world. . . .

What is new, what makes the continuing crisis, is the polarization of power which now inescapably confronts the slave society with the free.

The assault on free institutions is world-wide now, and in the context of the present polarization of power a defeat of free institutions anywhere is a defeat everywhere.

National Security Council, document NSC-68, 7 April 1950, in U.S. Department of State, *Foreign Relations of the United States, 1950*, vol. 1 (Washington, DC: U.S. Government Printing Office, 1977), 234–92.

NSC-68 was also notable for its apocalyptic tone, the manner in which it saw the Cold War in ideological terms as a war between freedom and slavery: The Soviet Union, "animated by a new fanatical faith, antithetical to our own . . . seeks to impose its absolute authority over the rest of the world."[4] The document obsessively referred to "the Kremlin design" for world domination. Kennan's containment project had also found the wellsprings of Soviet expansionism in the Kremlin's ideological compulsion to extend its control within and beyond the Soviet boundaries; his approach, however, was rooted in classical realist considerations of counterbalancing Soviet power until the seeds of decay in that system led to its collapse internally. Interestingly, NSC-68 barely addressed this possibility, parenthetically dismissing the prospect of awaiting the Soviet Union's internal collapse because of overextension and other causes.[5] As is discussed in Chapter 11, this ultimately happened (though the argument could be made that those overextensions were induced by the high levels of mobilization of the West prescribed by NSC-68 and subsequent hard-line policy initiatives).

It was the outbreak of the Korean War, interpreted in the context of the other ominous developments in the Cold War as demonstrating an implacably hostile and monolithic Soviet bloc's intent to impose its will and system on the world, that tipped the scales in favor of adoption of NSC-68. As Secretary of State Acheson remarked in his memoirs, the dispatch of U.S. troops to Korea "removed the recommendations of NSC-68 from the realm of theory and made them immediate budget issues."[6] Truman's statement of 27 June 1950 had identified the war's outbreak as a watershed in the Cold War. His conclusion that the Communists had now gone beyond subversion to the use of "armed invasion and war" led to several fateful decisions (see Chapter 5): One was to engage in war on the Asian mainland, something for which Washington had a historical aversion; another was to interpose the Seventh Fleet in the Taiwan Strait to prevent military action from either side, thereby reasserting America in the Chinese Civil War; and still another was to sow the seeds of direct American involvement in the Vietnam War by dispatching a military aid mission there.

The Korean War was also a watershed in extending the containment doctrine to Asia, to be embodied in a structure of alliance relationships. The administration's Europe-first strategy, and its withdrawal from the Asian mainland to the "defensive perimeter" outlined in Acheson's famous National Press Club speech (Chapter 5), had already been under considerable stress from Republicans in Congress and even figures within the administration and military, notably General MacArthur.[7] As discussed later in this chapter, MacArthur had been advocating the defense of Taiwan as an urgent requirement of the U.S. strategic position in East Asia. This line was also propounded by vocal critics of the administration in Congress such as California senator William Knowland (mockingly known by opponents as the "senator from Formosa"). Once hostilities erupted in Korea, it was all but inevitable that Washington would extend containment to Asia. Fresh memories of appeasement at Munich and acquiescence in Japanese expansion into Manchuria provided the backdrop for American decision making as the Cold War turned hot in Korea. The Truman administration was under severe pressure for having "lost" China. It could not but shudder over the psychological impact that failure to step up to the challenge posed by Korea would have on the rest of Asia, not to mention the domestic repercussions in America. Moreover, Truman saw the Korea challenge as an opportunity to apply the principle of collective security in Asia.[8]

Thus, Washington set about assembling a posse of countries to intervene in Korea under the flag of the United Nations. It also began to construct a network of alliances to contain Communist expansion in Asia.

## U.S. SECURITY STRUCTURE IN ASIA

The network of mostly bilateral security relationships that Washington formed in Asia stood in sharp contrast to NATO, a multilateral collective security treaty committing each member to come to the defense of any other under attack. Rather than a single collective organization, Washington's treaties with its Asian allies formed a hub-and-spokes pattern, with Washington as the hub and the bilateral relationships as the spokes. The set of treaties possessed something of a systemic character by virtue of their almost cookie-cutter uniformity: Common procedures were prescribed, and each side was obligated to treat an attack on the other as dangerous to its own security and "to meet the common danger in accordance with its constitutional processes." The trilateral arrangement binding the

United States, Australia, and New Zealand (the Australia, New Zealand, United States Security Treaty, or ANZUS) fit the pattern of the bilateral treaties.[9] The ANZUS and Philippine treaties, coinciding with the peace treaty and the original bilateral security treaty with Japan, were designed to offer reassurance against a revival of Japanese militarism now that the occupation was about to terminate. The ones with the Republic of (South) Korea and the Republic of China (Taiwan) came in the wake of the Korean War and served to demonstrate that the U.S. writ of containment now extended to those areas (after having been excluded before the war). SEATO had still another context, the French withdrawal from Vietnam and its neutralization by the 1954 Geneva accords.

### UNITED STATES BEGINS BUILDING A SECURITY STRUCTURE IN ASIA: THE PHILIPPINES TREATY

The Parties . . . will consult together from time to time regarding the implementation of this Treaty and whenever in the opinion of either of them the territorial integrity, political independence or security of either of the Parties is threatened by external armed attack in the Pacific.

Each Party recognizes that an armed attack in the Pacific Area on either of the Parties would be dangerous to its own peace and safety and declares that it would act to meet the common dangers in accordance with its constitutional processes.

U.S.-Philippines Security Treaty, 30 August 1951, *U.S. Treaties and Other International Agreements, 1952*, vol. 3, part 3 (Washington, DC: U.S. Government Printing Office, 1955), 3947–51.

There were some variations in the cookie-cutter pattern. U.S. basing rights were contained in the treaties with Japan, South Korea, and the Republic of China; the Philippines and Thailand provided those rights in separate agreements. The treaty with the ROK defined the territory covered as being that under the respective parties' "administrative control," a formulation designed to limit U.S. obligations in the face of claims by the ROK to sovereignty over the entire peninsula. The Senate, in ratifying the treaty, was more explicit, attaching an "understanding" that the United States was not required to come to its ally's assistance except when there was an attack on territory recognized by Washington as "lawfully brought under the administrative control" of the ROK. (The concern over defining the territorial reach of U.S. obligations to an ally was especially evident at the time of the ratification of the pact with the ROC, as discussed later in this chapter.) The Japan treaty, concluded at the same time as the peace treaty (see Chapter 4), represented the biggest departure from the pattern, reflecting the special circumstances of that country's reentry into the international system. In this case there was no mutual defense obligation; instead, with Japan disarmed and unable to defend itself, the United States was given basing rights for forces that "may be utilized" to defend Japan as well as to maintain security in the Far East region. The treaty did, however, include the "expectation" that Japan would "increasingly assume responsibility for its own defense," a provision in conflict with the postwar constitution's renunciation "forever" of the nation's sovereign right of recourse to war and maintenance of a war potential. In a qualification designed to resolve that contradiction, the treaty stipulated that Japan would "always" avoid possessing "offensive" arms. This was the source of the recurrent Japanese exercise of wrestling with the demands for a defense capability within the tight bounds of constitutional limits.

A revised version of the treaty, concluded in 1960, imported into the U.S.-Japanese alliance the mutual defense provision found in the other treaties. The new treaty was crafted to conform more closely to Washington's other bilateral alliances and to appear less unequal in Japanese eyes. Thus it removed the provision for use of American forces to quell internal disturbances, and it added a provision for termination by either side after ten years (the other pacts provided for termination after a year's notice). Nonetheless, the revised version encountered extraordinarily widespread protests, reflecting considerable neutralist sentiment in Japan, and the threat of violence prompted cancellation of President Eisenhower's planned visit. In its revised form, again reflecting Japan's constitutional and political constraints, the treaty still departed from pattern by obligating the two sides to repel attacks only on areas under Japan's jurisdiction, not—as in the other mutual defense agreements—on U.S. territory in the Pacific region as well. In the case of the treaties with the Philippines and with Australia and New Zealand, the mutual defense obligation extended to the treaty partners' metropolitan areas, that is, to the American mainland as well as to territories in the Pacific. (It was this provision that Australia invoked after the terrorist attacks on the United States in September 2001, as did America's NATO partners.)

Why did Washington not simply follow the NATO model and create a multilateral collective security organization in Asia? Such an arrangement had in fact been contemplated, and a draft of a "Pacific Pact" was produced by Washington in the period after the jolt of the Korean War's outbreak mobilized American policymakers to press forward on a peace settlement with Japan. This organization would have comprised only island nations along with the United States, namely, Japan, the Philippines, Australia, New Zealand, and possibly Indonesia (the latter's willingness to participate being in question). The draft prefigured the formulation used in the bilateral and ANZUS treaties in calling on the parties to "act to meet the common danger" if any side was attacked. (An annex to the draft takes care to make the point that the proposed Pacific Pact differed as follows from the NATO treaty: In the NATO accord, each side "agrees" that it would take appropriate action in case of an attack on any participant, whereas in the Pacific Pact, the parties "declare" that they would do so.) Britain was conspicuously absent from the proposed membership, omitted because of U.S. Defense Department objections to a commitment to defend Hong Kong (and inclusion of the British would have raised the question of adding France with its commitment to retaining Indochina). Not surprisingly, the British objected to the project, and it was not seriously explored during the negotiations with the Japanese leading up to the peace treaty and bilateral pact concluded later that year. Thus the hub-and-spokes system emerged as the answer to U.S. security concerns in East Asia and the Pacific.[10]

One inhibition against a collective security system for the region may have been the strong animosity Japan's former victims felt toward that country, making it difficult to induce them to enter a security body alongside their recent oppressor. Moreover, the constitutional limitations on Japan's military role militated against its participation in a collective defense alliance. But why not have an Asian organization without Japan, just as West Germany was not originally a member of NATO? This may have reflected the Europe-first strategy that prevailed in American thinking; an Asian NATO might have been too ambitious and costly an undertaking given the resources being allocated to Europe. (This consideration was reflected in an early 1952 article by future secretary of state Dulles, who cautioned against overstraining American resources through a regional defense organization. He also noted that the treaties that had been concluded in Asia involved islands, where security was provided by air and sea power.[11]) Moreover, Europe possessed much more of a common cultural heritage, in contrast with the political and cultural diversity of Asia, and thus lent itself to formation of a collective security body to confront the nearby menace of the Soviet Union. A further obstacle was the strong nationalist and neutralist sentiment in Asia, reflected in the determination of such countries as India and Burma to guard their independence and steer clear of Cold War alignments. In contrast to Europe, where there was strong sentiment to overcome a history of destructive wars among nation-states, the new states in Asia were jealously protective of their new sovereignty and ill disposed to merging it in a multilateral body.

Finally, there may have been a sense of urgency about ending the occupation of Japan because of the outbreak of war in Korea, an event viewed as particularly foreboding against the backdrop of the Communist victory in China and the formation of the Sino-Soviet alliance; this left no time for working out a multilateral alliance embracing Japan. More than five years elapsed after the founding of NATO before the Western allies ended their occupation of Germany and the latter joined that multilateral organization. (A Japan specialist has argued that time pressures deriving from domestic Japanese complications caused the multilateral approach in Asia to be shelved.[12])

SEATO represented one attempt to fashion an overarching collective security body for Asia, but its representation in the region was paltry and its commitments weaker than those embodied in NATO. Washington's allies Thailand and the Philippines joined, as did Pakistan in the wake of its military aid agreement with the United States. The pro-Western Ceylon (now Sri Lanka) was initially receptive but stayed out after Burma, India, and Indonesia (which together with Ceylon and Pakistan composed the Colombo Powers, a precursor of the nonaligned movement) rejected the demarche as inconsistent with nonalignment. SEATO in fact amounted essentially to a cover for the United States and its anti-Communist partners to circumvent the neutrality provisions of the Geneva accords on Indochina in order to extend a security umbrella over the non-Communist areas of that peninsula. Washington also adapted SEATO's provisions for collective defense to reassure Thailand, which, unlike the other Southeast Asian member of SEATO, the Philippines, did not have a bilateral treaty of alliance with the United States. To relieve Bangkok's concern about a threat to its security from developments in neighboring Laos, Washington declared in March 1962 (in the Rusk-Thanat communiqué) that Thailand's security was vital to American interests and that in case of aggression the two countries would "act to meet the common danger" without prior consultation with the other SEATO members.[13] Washington thereby used a multilateral instrument to provide a bilateral security guarantee akin to those given in the treaties discussed earlier. A few weeks later, the Kennedy administration, facing a deteriorating situation in Laos, dispatched troops to northeastern Thailand, a move that cheered the Thais and checked a potential drift to a neutralist position by Bangkok.[14]

## THE TAIWAN ISSUE

The two Taiwan Strait crises in the 1950s had a strong impact on the superpowers' alliance relationships. The first, in 1954–55, further entrenched the American role in denying Taiwan to the Communists. The second, in 1958, provided a stern test to the Sino-Soviet alliance (discussed in Chapter 8). Though the eventual switch in American recognition from the ROC to the PRC went a long way toward normalization of Sino-American relations, a residual security tie between Washington and Taipei has persisted into the twenty-first century as a central factor in making the Taiwan Strait one of the potentially most explosive flashpoints in the world.

Through the mid-seventeenth century, Taiwan was not part of any China-based regime. In the 1660s, however, prefiguring developments of three centuries later, loyalists of the collapsing Ming dynasty fled to Taiwan and established a regime there as an alternative to the new Manchu Qing dynasty on the mainland. In 1683, they were eventually subdued by a Qing invasion, and the island was administered not as a Chinese province but rather as a subordinate territory of the Qing Empire, using the local aboriginal headman elite to govern a predominantly aboriginal population. Over the succeeding two centuries, Chinese immigration gradually tipped the balance in favor of ethnic Chinese. In the context of the 1884–85 Qing-French War over northern Vietnam, prompted by concerns over French designs on Taiwan, Beijing finally altered Taiwan's status, raising it to that of a province of China rather than a subordinate territory. Only ten years later, however, it was ceded to Japan after the Qing defeat in the Sino-Japanese War.

As we have seen (Chapter 2), World War II's Cairo and Potsdam declarations stated as the allies' "purpose" the return of Taiwan to Chinese sovereignty, and the Japanese surrendered the island to Nationalist troops. The victory of the Communists in the civil war prompted some rethinking of Taiwan's juridical status, though the Truman administration opted to disengage from the conflict while waiting for the dust to settle.[15] The shock of the outbreak of the Korean War, however, led not only to a renewed involvement in the civil war but also to a policy of treating Taiwan's status as "undetermined." In this view, there had been no legal instrumentality transferring sovereignty over Taiwan; the peace treaty with Japan, for instance, only removed sovereignty from the former colonial ruler without specifying where it now reposed.[16]

Taiwan's strategic significance had already been emphasized in General MacArthur's memorandum dated only days before the North Korean invasion of the South.[17] The commander of U.S. forces in the Far East depicted in stark terms what he called "a disaster of utmost importance" if Taiwan came under the control of a hostile power, and requested authorization to make a survey of the military measures required to prevent such an eventuality. (For years Soviet and Chinese propaganda distorted MacArthur's characterization of Taiwan as an "unsinkable aircraft carrier"—a metaphor he used to underline its value to the *enemy*—by claiming he wanted to control the island to use it for that purpose.) This memo, which was read to the meeting Truman held with his top advisers on the day the Korean War began, found expression in the president's statement two days later that occupation of Taiwan by the Communists would pose a direct threat to U.S.

forces. In this context, after ordering interdiction of the Taiwan Strait by the Seventh Fleet, Truman declared that Taiwan's future status "must await the restoration of security" in the Pacific, a peace settlement with Japan, or consideration by the UN.

The unresolved status of Taiwan seemed even more conspicuous after the Korean armistice in mid-1953 and the Geneva accords on Indochina a year later. As it would continue to be after normalization of U.S.-PRC diplomatic relations in the 1970s, American policy was calculatedly ambiguous regarding Taiwan and the offshore islands, which consisted of the Dachen group about two hundred miles south of Shanghai, and the Mazu and Jinmen (Quemoy) island groups alongside ports of Fujian Province across the strait from Taiwan. (The Penghus, or Pescadores, midway between Taiwan and the mainland, are not regarded as among the offshore islands.) Was the United States committed to defense of these vulnerably situated islands? What would be the implications of their abandonment to the Communists? How did Taiwan fit into Washington's network of security relationships in Asia? Beijing's effort to probe the extent of the U.S. commitment and the solidity of American relations with the ROC produced the first Taiwan Strait crisis, compelling Washington to face these issues.

The ROC saw the offshore islands' value both in strategic terms—such as for harassing and blockading mainland coastal areas—and politically as symbolizing its links to the mainland and its claim to representing all of China. (Beijing saw the latter point in similar terms, sharing the position that Taiwan was part of China, and thus did not regard a takeover of the offshore islands as a goal in itself.) In 1954 the Nationalists with U.S. support began reinforcing the islands. The Communists decried what they depicted as an effort by Washington to form a Northeast Asia Treaty Organization, a NEATO counterpart to SEATO, which would comprise the United States, Japan, the ROK, and the ROC. Against the background of calls for "liberation" of Taiwan, the Communists began shelling Jinmen in September and blockading the Dachens at the end of the year. Washington responded by deepening its involvement in the Taiwan issue by adding the ROC to the network of security alliances in Asia.

The new treaty, signed in December 1954, filled a gap in that network, the reach of SEATO's area of coverage having been carefully delimited to just below Taiwan. Though the U.S. commitment to defense of Taiwan was now formalized—and Taiwan now was included in the island chain marking the line of commitment in the western Pacific—Washington took care to leave enough ambiguity about the extent of that commitment so as to retain flexibility in its actions. The treaty defined the ROC's territories covered by the treaty as comprising Taiwan, the Penghus, and "such other territories as may be determined by mutual agreement" (Article 6). In an exchange of notes at this time, Washington constrained its ally's freedom of maneuver—given the danger of the United States being drawn into hostilities not of its choosing—by requiring joint agreement to use force except in the case of emergency. Meanwhile, President Eisenhower was given latitude for responding to the Communists' attacks on the offshore islands by a joint congressional resolution (the Formosa Resolution) authorizing the president to take military action to defend "certain territories" under the ROC's jurisdiction.[18] Such action, however, was to be undertaken only if attacks on the offshore islands were deemed by him to be part of an offensive against Taiwan. Consistent with this proviso, the ROC was induced to abandon the distant offshore islands, the Dachens, which were not stepping-stones for an invasion of Taiwan.

An easing of tensions in the Taiwan Strait coincided with Beijing's turn to a moderate approach to foreign relations. As noted in Chapter 6, this approach was especially on display at the first Asian-African conference, in April 1955, which provided the stage for Zhou Enlai's offer to enter negotiations with the United States on reducing tensions in the Taiwan area.[19] Talks began in Geneva that August (and lasted until early 1958, when they were discontinued by Beijing after Washington had downgraded them to below ambassadorial level). Beijing brightened the atmosphere a bit with gestures toward the Nationalists, including suggestions of a "peaceful liberation" of Taiwan and conciliatory offers to the Nationalists. This phase of Chinese policy was paralleled by similar moderation in Soviet behavior (reflected, for instance, by establishment of diplomatic relations with Japan). After the Chinese lurched back onto a militant path in 1957, they again probed the firmness of the U.S. commitment to Taiwan and the offshore islands in renewed artillery attacks in August and September 1958. On that occasion, however, the real test was the one posed to Beijing's alliance with Moscow. A watershed now loomed in that relationship.

## CONTAINMENT, COMMITMENT, AND CREDIBILITY

The structure of security relationships had given formal expression to the extension of the U.S. containment policy to Asia. Though there were elements of ambiguity, and the obligations undertaken by Washington to its Asian allies were somewhat weaker than those contained in the Rio and NATO treaties, the array of Asian alliances lent credibility to the American commitment to containment of Communism. As SEATO demonstrated, however, with its sparse representation from the area itself, the structure of U.S. alliances had large gaps due to the neutralist countries' aversion to bloc politics.

The greater clarity of commitment, with its intended deterrent effect, came at some cost to the treaty partners. The weaker side sacrificed some freedom of maneuver in exchange for enhanced security—a price the neutralists were not prepared to pay. Having renounced war as an instrument of policy, Japan in effect surrendered some of its sovereignty as the price of U.S. military protection. The Japanese parlayed this bargain into a concentration on economic development that produced the second-largest economy in the world. One result was to extract an added cost from the United States in the form of intense and at times bitter economic competition between these allies, and this was exacerbated by a perception among Americans that the Japanese were enjoying a free ride under the U.S. strategic shield. In other cases, the weaker partner was able to manipulate Washington's concern over the impact on its broader strategic interests of a defection by its ally, thereby complicating U.S. policymaking. These complications, for example, figured in the often-tortuous U.S. relations with Saigon during the Vietnam War. (Moscow had its own problems along this line, for example, restraining East Germany on sensitive German issues, or dealing with the independent policy proclivities of Warsaw Pact ally Romania.)

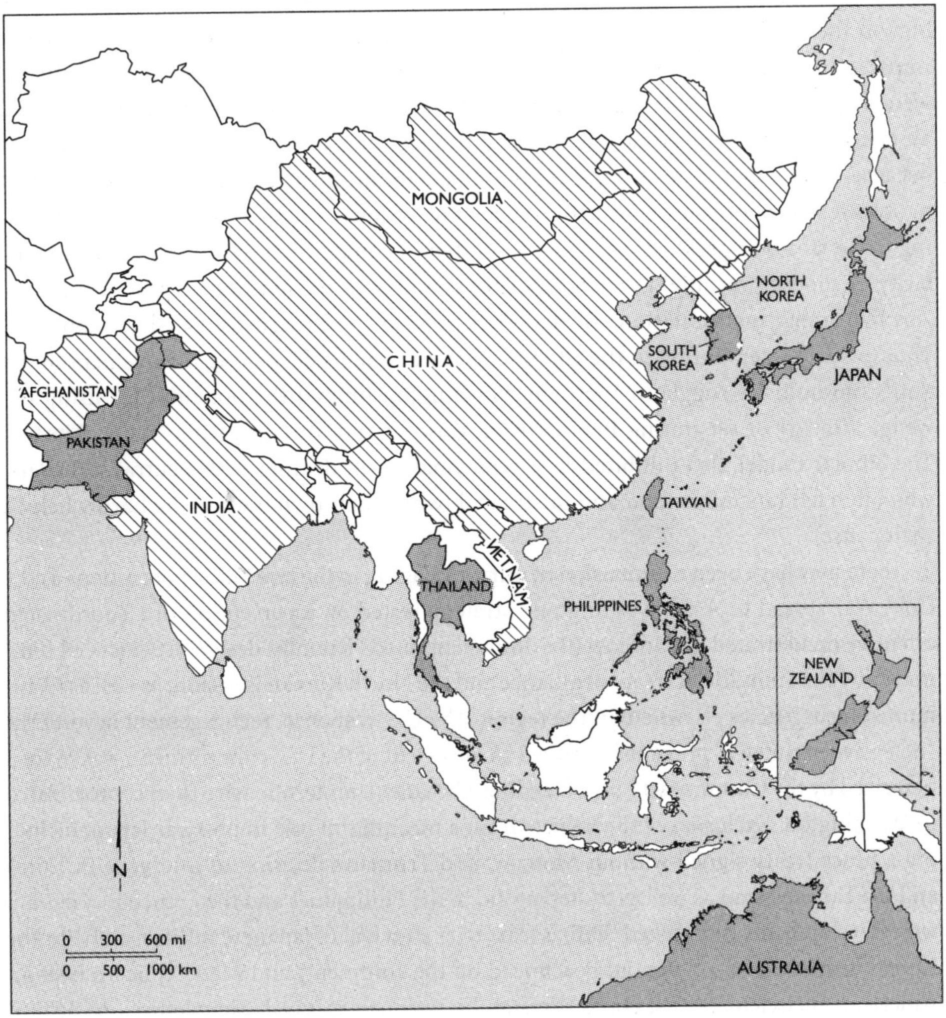


**Map 7.1** U.S. and Soviet Alliances in Asia

**Shaded areas indicate U.S. partners:** Philippines, 1951; ANZUS, 1951, Australia, New Zealand; Japan, 1951, rev. 1960; Republic of Korea (South), 1953; SEATO, 1954 (Philippines, Thailand, Pakistan, Australia, New Zealand, UK, France); Republic of China (Taiwan), 1954

**Diagonal lined areas indicate Soviet partners:** People's Republic of China, 1950; Democratic People's Republic of Korea (North), 1961; Mongolian People's Republic, 1966; India, 1971; Vietnam, 1978; Afghanistan, 1978

The sharper clarity of commitment was also gained at the price of rigidity and loss of flexibility in applying the doctrine of containment. In the zero-sum game of Cold War competition, a failure to meet a challenge anywhere represented a gain for the opposing bloc in the global balance sheet, and this was magnified by the perceived psychological impact of a defeat in demoralizing allies and emboldening enemies. Lines of containment were thus drawn without much regard for what were core and what were peripheral areas; an area might be ascribed far greater significance than its intrinsic geopolitical weight because of its implications for the credibility of commitments. One result was to distort or at least shape both superpowers' treatment of nationalism, that powerful force emerging in the postwar period alongside—and often in competition with—the force of bipolarity. A superpower might sacrifice flexibility and even pursue counterproductive policies by forcing manifestations of nationalism onto the Procrustean bed of bipolarity. Thus, by its reintervention in the Chinese civil war and its deepening involvement in the anti-Communist struggle in Vietnam, Washington limited the potential for using the wedge strategy of separating Beijing from Moscow and for cultivating "Asian Titos."[20] The bipolar model also inhibited U.S. policymakers in dealing with neutralist leaders, who often felt misunderstood and mistreated (while their own moralizing hardly helped their cause).

There may have been a dimension of mirror imaging in the two blocs' perceptions as the Cold War spread to Asia. Washington's strategy rested on a perception of a coordinated offensive orchestrated by Moscow (the aforementioned "Kremlin design"), evidenced ominously by the Sino-Soviet treaty of alliance and the North Korean invasion, as well as Communist insurgencies elsewhere in the region. The U.S. response, reengagement beyond the "defensive perimeter" previously defined as the extent of the U.S. commitment, was in turn perceived by the Communists as portending a broader counteroffensive than contemplated in Washington. Exclusion of the Soviets from a meaningful role in postwar Japan, including a peace treaty signed without Moscow, and Truman's decision to intervene in Korea and the Taiwan Strait as well as to step up aid to the Philippines and the French in Vietnam were developments that stoked Stalin's fears over a revival of Japanese militarism (with the Korean peninsula as a potential beachhead on the continent) and Mao's concern over an American encirclement that could threaten his regime's survival. The picture one gets, at least in retrospect, is one of mutually reinforcing perceptions that went well beyond the intentions of the respective sides, leading to a pattern of unintended consequences that propelled the process to still higher levels of mistrust.[21]

With one notable exception, the U.S. alliance system in Asia held up remarkably well. Higher geopolitical imperatives, including the radical transformation of Sino-Soviet relations that soon developed, led to the end of the treaty with the Nationalist Chinese regime on Taiwan. After the winding down of the Cold War, the Philippines terminated the American basing rights, but, as has been noted, these were not a part of the treaty in any case. The big exception was SEATO, which withered away after its primary purpose, providing a cover for extending the U.S. containment policy to Indochina, became moot with the triumph of the Communists. The anchor of the American alliance system in Asia, the security treaty with Japan, was buffeted over the years by economic competition and charges of free riding, but its central role in U.S. policy in the Asia-Pacific region persisted intact. In sharp contrast to this record of continuity, the axis of the socialist camp, Moscow's alliance with Beijing, began fraying in the late 1950s and had fallen apart by the middle of the next decade. It is to the origins of that astonishing story that we now turn.

# 8 THE SINO-SOVIET ALLIANCE

After Mao Zedong's famous declaration in mid-1949 that his new Communist regime would "lean to one side" in favor of the socialist camp,[1] it might have appeared that a smooth, almost ineluctable progression to a formal alliance with Moscow was in prospect. In the event, it was not an easy path to a goal cherished by Mao, who by now saw that a Tito-style neutralism was not an option and that both ideological affinities and strategic imperatives propelled the Chinese Communists into the Soviet big brother's embrace. But as had happened in the past and would recur in fateful ways in the future, Moscow's interests and those of its junior partner in the Communist movement did not mesh all that comfortably.

Stalin's approach comported with the manner in which he had negotiated the postwar settlements. His bedrock objective was Soviet security, whether in establishing a glacis in Eastern Europe to provide a bulwark and strategic depth against another invasion from the west, or in securing buffer zones to buttress the Asian flank. If at the end of World War II this meant negotiating with the Chinese Communists' enemies to secure these interests, then his ideological allies must bide their time and not expect full support from Moscow for their revolutionary aspirations. And while promptly extending diplomatic recognition to the People's Republic in October 1949, Stalin was characteristically cautious about underwriting the new regime's goals if he felt that this could provoke an American reaction inimical to Soviet security. Khrushchev later suggested to Mao that Stalin was reticent about negotiating an alliance with the PRC "be-

**MAO DECLARES NO THIRD ROAD BETWEEN SOCIALISM AND IMPERIALISM**

"You are leaning to one side." Exactly.... Sitting on the fence will not do, nor is there a third road. We oppose the Chiang Kai-shek reactionaries who lean to the side of imperialism, and we also oppose the illusions about a third road....

"Victory is possible even without international help." This is a mistaken idea. In the epoch in which imperialism exists, it is impossible for a genuine people's revolution to win victory in any country without various forms of help from the international revolutionary forces, and even if victory were won, it could not be consolidated.

Mao Tse-tung [Mao Zedong], "On the People's Democratic Dictatorship," 30 June 1949, *Selected Works of Mao Tse-tung*, vol. 4 (Peking: Foreign Languages Press, 1961), 411–23.

cause he thought an attack on China was possible and did not want to get involved in this."[2]

Mao's top lieutenant, Liu Shaoqi, who had been dispatched secretly to Moscow in the summer of 1949, around the time of Mao's "lean to one side" declaration, got a foretaste of the complexities that negotiations with Stalin would present. Though the Communists' conquest of the mainland was no longer in doubt, the arduous task of completing the revolution by seizing control of the islands occupied by Nationalist garrisons, principally Hainan and Taiwan, loomed. Stalin, consistent with his behavior in withholding or at least hedging support for the CPC in earlier phases of the revolution, refused to provide aid. He did, however, acknowledge the Chinese Communists' experience as a model for Asia and advised creation of an alliance of Asian Communists. But even this suggestion had an ulterior motive arising from Stalin's obsession with Soviet security. He was excluding the CPC and their Asian brethren from the European union of Communists, the Cominform (Communist Information Bureau), at whose founding meeting in Warsaw in September 1947 Soviet delegate Andrey Zhdanov barely discussed Asia and failed to mention China in his famous speech.[3] (Notably, Zhdanov propounded Moscow's two-camp thesis, confirming the bipolarity of the Cold War, which was now in full development.) By excluding the Asian Communists, the Kremlin simplified its management of the Cominform's affairs and insulated developments on the all-important western front from the vagaries of revolutionary activity in the East.

Stalin's obsessive concern with maintaining control of Communist affairs in Europe, expressed most dramatically in the expulsion of Yugoslavia from the Cominform, was also reflected in the unusual arrangement by which the PRC supervised its relations with Eastern Europe. The first PRC ambassador to Moscow was concurrently the vice foreign minister in charge of Eastern European relations, thus ensuring that Beijing's diplomatic roads to Eastern Europe all passed through Moscow.

## STALIN-MAO TALKS

Mao could have had no illusions about the task facing him in negotiating with Stalin. With the prospects uncertain, Mao took advantage of a gathering of Communist leaders in Moscow in December 1949 to celebrate Stalin's seventieth birthday; joining the festivities provided a cover for his visit should he come back empty-handed. The visit did not begin auspiciously: Mao was left to cool his heels in Moscow for most of the first two weeks after his arrival on the sixteenth, and as he later acknowledged to Stalin's successor Khrushchev, Stalin said he did not want to conclude a treaty with the PRC. The reason, as he pointed out to his visitor, was that a new treaty would jeopardize the Yalta settlement and thereby raise questions about the Soviet gains secured at the Crimean negotiations.[4] Mao, while far from being obsequious, was solicitous of Stalin's concern. Seeking to allay Stalin's suspicions over a Chinese interest in removing the taint on Beijing's sovereignty represented by the Manchurian concessions, Mao obligingly observed that the railroads and Port Arthur served both sides' interests. Mao's more overriding purpose came out in his suggestion that the Soviets provide aid for the prospective invasion of Taiwan, but

### 16 DECEMBER 1949: STALIN TELLS MAO NO NEW TREATY

Stalin: [The 1945 treaty between the USSR and the ROC] was concluded as a result of the Yalta agreement, which provided for the main points of the treaty (the question of the Kurile Islands, South Sakhalin, Port Arthur, etc.). . . . Keeping in mind this circumstance, we . . . have decided not to modify any of the points of this treaty for now, since a change in even one point could give America and England the legal grounds to raise questions about modifying also the treaty's provisions concerning the Kurile Islands, South Sakhalin, etc. . . .

Mao: In discussing this treaty in China we had not taken into account the American and English positions regarding the Yalta agreement. We must act in a way that is best for the common cause. . . . It is already becoming clear that the treaty should not be modified at the present time, nor should one rush to withdraw troops from Port Arthur.

### 22 JANUARY 1950: THE KREMLIN BOSS CHANGES HIS MIND

Stalin: We believe that the agreement concerning Port Arthur is not equitable.

Mao: But changing this agreement goes against the decision of the Yalta Conference?!

Stalin: True, it does—and to hell with it! Once we have taken the position that the treaties must be changed, we must go all the way.

*Cold War International History Project Bulletin*, nos. 6–7 (Winter 1995–1996), Woodrow Wilson International Center for Scholars, Washington, DC, 5, 8.

Stalin asserted his own priorities by emphasizing that what was "most important here is not to give the Americans a pretext to intervene."[5]

Stalin was to change his mind, however, and the way was opened for agreements that would provide a security guarantee for the PRC while also retaining Soviet rights in Manchuria. That Mao was in Moscow for more than Stalin's birthday festivities was disclosed in a TASS interview—agreed upon on 1 January 1950 and issued the following day—in which the Chinese leader said the *existing* Sino-Soviet treaty, a Soviet loan, and trade were topics of negotiation.[6] On the same day, he cabled Beijing that Stalin had agreed to have Zhou Enlai come to Moscow to negotiate and sign a *new* treaty.[7] The available documentary record is spotty for these events, but we have evidence that Stalin remarked to Mao nearly three weeks later, on the twenty-second, that Moscow had changed its mind regarding the old treaty, which "has become an anachronism" with the defeat of Japan. Moreover, when Mao, echoing Stalin's previous concerns, wondered whether replacing the existing treaty would contravene Yalta, Stalin replied with abandon, "True, it does—but to hell with it."[8] By this time the uncertain, tentative prospects facing Mao at the onset of his journey had turned into a clear path to a new treaty.

What motivations may have caused the shift in Stalin's wary approach? One may have been his concern that the newly victorious Chinese Communists, flush with a sense of rising national pride, would want to withdraw the Manchurian concessions embedded in the existing treaty. Mao seemed to have alleviated that wariness by expressing a shared concern about the possible negative impact of a new treaty on Yalta, thus implying that the Chinese were not demanding the elimination of the concessions. There was also Stalin's concern that a mutual security alliance with the PRC could draw the Soviet Union into a conflict with the United States as a result of Chinese actions—such as an invasion of Taiwan. That concern would have been assuaged by Washington's decision, announced by President Truman on 5 January, that the United States would "not provide military aid or advice" to the Nationalist forces on Taiwan or become involved in the Chinese civil war (although Truman added that Taiwan had adequate resources to obtain arms and would continue to receive U.S. economic assistance). The president's statement was based on a policy paper prepared the previous month concluding that Taiwan was not strategically important. This hands-off policy was further underscored by Secretary of State Acheson's remarks at the National Press Club in Washington a week later, drawing the U.S. defense perimeter off the Asian coast in such a way as to exclude Taiwan (see Chapter 5).[9]

While these statements of American policy surely reduced Stalin's apprehensions over being dragged by the Chinese into a conflict with the United States, his approach to the Moscow negotiations may have been shaped by another concern, namely the possibility—not fully excluded by Mao's leaning-to-one-side posture—of U.S.-PRC diplomatic relations and an amelioration of the tensions accompanying the Chinese Communists' seizure of power. Such a concern would have been fed by Britain's announcement on the sixth, a day after Truman's remarks, that it would recognize the PRC. As an insurance policy against improvement of Sino-American relations, Moscow now played up the U.S. role in Taiwan and encouraged Beijing's plans to seize Chiang's island redoubt.

In addition, Moscow dramatized its support on the Taiwan issue by arranging to walk out of the UN in protest of the PRC's exclusion. In the immediate wake of Britain's announcement, the Soviet foreign minister approached Mao to ask that Beijing issue a statement denouncing the Nationalist Chinese representation on the Security Council as illegitimate, to be followed by the Soviet walkout. This afforded Moscow an inexpensive way to further cultivate Beijing's trust—or so it may have seemed to the Soviets at the time; an unwelcome consequence, however, was that they were absent from the Security Council when it took up North Korea's invasion the following June.[10] (It is not necessary to overreach, as some scholars have done, by interpreting Moscow's gambit as a cynical move to push the PRC into a collision with the United States in order to deepen Beijing's dependence on its big brother. It was part of a pattern of moves—agreeing to a new treaty, putting time limits on the Manchurian concessions, and so forth—designed to solidify a relationship that by now offered little scope for an assertion of Chinese independence. Perhaps this is a choice between using Occam's razor in interpreting developments or being too Machiavellian by half.)

## TERMS OF THE ALLIANCE

The stage was now set for Zhou to travel to Moscow to negotiate the terms of the new alliance. Zhou, at that time premier and concurrently foreign minister, arrived on 20 January, and the negotiations culminated in the signing on 14 February of a Treaty of Friendship, Alliance, and Mutual Assistance, an agreement on a loan to China, and an agreement on the status of the Manchurian railroads and ports that had been Stalin's primary objectives in the bargaining over Soviet entry into the anti-Japanese war. Stalin extracted Chinese acquiescence (reprising the experience of the 1945 agreements with the Nationalist government) in maintaining Soviet satellite Mongolia's nominal independence—that is to say, independence from China. Completing Stalin's insensitive handling of the borderlands, a later agreement, dated 27 March, established joint-stock companies to exploit resources in Xinjiang. (Saifuddin, a Uighur who would have a long career as a leader in Xinjiang, was a member of the delegation to the Moscow negotiations.) As if all of this was not enough to fuel Chinese resentment, Beijing also had to agree to exclude non-Soviet foreigners from residing, investing, or trading in Xinjiang and Manchuria.

This package had elements of give-and-take and responded to the partners' different but largely compatible needs.[11] The terms of the alliance were largely an update of the 1945 Soviet pact with the Nationalist Chinese: Each side was obligated to render immediate military assistance in case the other was attacked by Japan or—in the updated version—"states allied with it." This added provision, a recognition of the bipolar postwar environment, paralleled one contained in Moscow's treaties with its Eastern European satellites, in the latter cases Germany being the country named. (In early 1949 Mao himself had suggested the Soviet-Polish treaty as a model for a Sino-Soviet pact.[12]) The treaties were thus phrased so as to reflect Cold War realities while playing on still-fresh memories of Axis aggression—and serving the propaganda role of portraying American efforts to rebuild the power of the former enemies as abetting the revival of militarism. In any case, Moscow was still in a state of war with Japan and Germany.

Through this mutual defense pact, China was brought under the Soviet security umbrella at a time when the civil war and consolidation of the CPC's power remained incomplete, a precarious campaign to invade Hainan and Taiwan being still on the agenda (Hainan was captured in April), and when the opposition Republican Party in the United States was condemning the Truman administration for weakness in the struggle against Communism and demanding stronger action. For Moscow the buffer zones so dear to Stalin were vastly expanded, with North Korea in Communist hands and now the alliance with the PRC providing the Soviet Union great strategic depth. Also, the West's attention and resources would be diverted in significant measure from Europe to the East. In the eyes of much of the world, there had been a significant shift in geopolitical weight in favor of the socialist camp.

As for the economic dimension, the loan agreement was hardly munificent; it paled in comparison with American grants to the Nationalists: China was provided three hundred million dollars over five years at a concessionary rate (as Mao had requested in early 1949). Nonetheless, the new alliance soon had significant economic implications for a China needing the Soviet Union as a major trade partner in view of Western hostility and trade restrictions imposed in 1951. For ideological as well as strategic reasons, China drastically reoriented its trade and aid relationships from the West and Japan to the Soviet

### USSR, PRC PLEDGE MUTUAL SECURITY AGAINST JAPAN OR ITS ALLIES

Both Contracting Parties undertake jointly to adopt all necessary measures at their disposal for the purpose of preventing the resumption of aggression and violation of peace on the part of Japan or any other state that may collaborate with Japan directly or indirectly in acts of aggression. In the event of one of the Contracting Parties being attacked by Japan or any state allied with her and thus being involved in a state of war, the other Contracting Party shall immediately render military and other assistance by all means at its disposal.

Treaty of Friendship, Alliance, and Mutual Assistance Between the People's Republic of China and the Union of Soviet Socialist Republics, 14 February 1950, in Sergei N. Goncharov, John W. Lewis, and Xue Litai, *Uncertain Partners: Stalin, Mao, and the Korean War* (Stanford, CA: Stanford University Press, 1993), 260–61.

bloc. Soviet aid projects in China, including capital goods and technical experts, played an important role in China's economic development in the 1950s.

Moscow's retention of its Manchurian rights, a subject that would fester in Chinese resentment of Soviet high-handedness, was subject to a termination date at the end of 1952 in the case of the railroads and Port Arthur—the latter, however, to be used jointly (formally at Beijing's request) in the event the mutual security provisions of the treaty of alliance were triggered. As for the commercial port of Dairen, its status would be considered after conclusion of a peace treaty with Japan. Whatever wounded pride the Chinese endured in this bargaining, the provisions on the Manchurian concessions marked a major advance from those extracted by Moscow from the Nationalists in 1945. Those earlier concessions contained no time limits short of the thirty-year term of the treaty itself.

More broadly, the alliance provided a framework for cooperation in China's transformation into a socialist state along the Soviet model. Their ideological affinities, based on a shared commitment to Marxism-Leninism, were translated into the full panoply of institutional forms: a highly centralized Leninist party claiming a monopoly on political authority; collectivization of agriculture; nationalization of industry, commerce, and finance; a command economy, with five-year plans determined by the party and administered by a state planning commission; and a widely encompassing penetration of the party's authority into all sectors—political, economic, social, and cultural.

At least as important as the ideological affinities was Stalin's awesome personal authority and mystique, enabling him to extract humiliating concessions from other Communist leaders and to exercise the willfulness demonstrated toward the Chinese. Mao and his colleagues nursed their resentments, but after the death of the *Vozhd* (leader) in March 1953 his successors found it prudent to assuage those grievances. Negotiations begun in late 1952 finally resulted a year later in a big increase in projects supported by the Soviets, and this was increased still more in 1954 during the visit by Stalin's successors, notably Khrushchev, who was outmaneuvering Georgy Malenkov in the Kremlin leadership sweepstakes.[13] Khrushchev hailed the "immense" significance for Asia of the Chinese revolution and announced that Moscow would sell to China the Soviet shares in the joint-stock companies and relinquish its rights to Port Arthur by the end of the next year. (In 1952, at China's "request" during the Korean War, the Soviet role in Port Arthur had been extended, while the Soviet rights in the Manchurian railroads were allowed to terminate at the end of the year as scheduled.)

The post-Stalin leadership needed to sweeten the pot to offset the loss of the dictator's mystique in the Communist movement. The Chinese also had a claim on Moscow for the losses and costs they incurred in pulling North Korea's chestnuts out of the fire. Now, with the Korean truce and a broader trend in the world toward a relaxation of tension, the setting was propitious for China to turn its attention to economic development along the Soviet model, as reflected in the first five-year plan. The scope of Moscow's involvement was shown in its role as China's main trade partner, totaling as much as half of that trade before peaking in 1959,[14] and in the extent of Soviet aid. By Beijing's own count, "hundreds of agreements and contracts" were torn up by Moscow when it precipitately withdrew the Soviet experts from China in 1960.[15] Khrushchev said at the time that there had been around fifteen hundred Soviet experts working in China in the late 1950s.[16]

The dense web of interparty and intergovernmental bonds formed a relationship that was regarded as transcending normal Westphalian relationships between nations. It represented a higher-level relationship known as "socialist internationalism," which entailed mutual obligations among Communist Party–ruled states deriving from their shared commitment to Marxism-Leninism. One implication of this "new type" of relationship was that lines between external and internal affairs were less sharply drawn than between nation-states in the realist paradigm. What happened within one member of the socialist camp had great resonance for the others, involving sensitive matters of legitimacy and authority, and this ineluctably became a source of tension, resentment, and conflict. We will be seeing manifestations in various forms, such as the demonizing during the Cultural Revolution of Mao's top lieutenant Liu Shaoqi as "China's Khrushchev" for favoring Soviet-style "revisionism"[17] and the so-called Brezhnev Doctrine, according to which a Communist state's internal affairs were subject to sanction by others (such as by invasion, as in the case of Czechoslovakia in 1968). An explosive instance was the manner in which Stalin's successor Khrushchev reassessed the role of the *Vozhd*, an initiative that produced convulsions in the international Communist body politic.

## REPERCUSSIONS OF DE-STALINIZATION

In the retrospective polemics that erupted in the 1960s, Beijing traced the origins of the Sino-Soviet schism to the CPSU Twentieth Congress in February 1956, the first since Stalin's death. That judgment was valid in large measure but must be qualified. At the congress Khrushchev introduced two sets of initiatives, one in a secret speech—soon leaked to the world—denigrating Stalin, and the other in an open report propounding a global strategy that took into account the realities of the nuclear age. The former did indeed lead to a chain of events that severely strained the socialist camp and started a process in which the Chinese increasingly staked their claim as a source of authority in the Communist movement. In the case of Khrushchev's strategic initiatives, however, it was not until Chinese policy took a sharp turn to the left more than a year later that these became disputed issues. (These initiatives, centering on the concept of coexistence between the socialist and capitalist systems, echoed policies adopted by Stalin's heir apparent, Malenkov, following the dictator's death. After besting Malenkov in the ensuing leadership competition, Khrushchev coopted his defeated rival's policies.)

Khrushchev's forceful indictment of Stalin's "cult of personality" and gross abuses of power set off shock waves in the socialist camp and posed the question of how to compensate for the loss of the autocrat's mystique in order to maintain cohesion in the Communist movement. The convulsions produced by de-Stalinization were manifested most acutely in Poland and Hungary. In Poland, Władysław Gomułka, once Stalin's victim for his "nationalist" deviation, returned to power on a crest of sentiment in the Polish party in favor of greater autonomy from Moscow. Even more explosively, the unrest in Hungary reached the point where the leadership under Imre Nagy declared its withdrawal from the Warsaw

Pact. In Beijing's view, Khrushchev had bungled miserably in his handling of the Stalin question, and both the need and the opportunity arose for the Chinese to strike a proper balance in assessing Stalin's role and in determining the scope of Moscow's authority in relation to that of the other parties.

In Beijing's assessment, Stalin was 70 percent correct and 30 percent incorrect—a formula that would be applied to the Chinese chairman himself after his death. This gave a clear preponderance of approbation while reserving a significant degree of blame for the leader's excesses. The seriousness with which Beijing approached this issue was reflected in the authoritative form in which the assessment was delivered: an editorial in the party paper *People's Daily*, with the ponderous title "On the Historical Experience of the Dictatorship of the Proletariat," which was "based on discussions at an enlarged meeting of the Politburo."[18] In a characteristic Maoist touch, Beijing placed the issue in a theoretical framework of "contradictions," such as between the leader and the people, in order to explain the negative aspects of the Stalin phenomenon. No one at the time could have failed to sense the implications of this issue for Mao's own status, and indeed the party took care to redress the excessive adulation of the chairman that had accompanied his consolidation of power. The CPC Eighth Congress, held seven months after Khrushchev's secret speech and five months after the editorial on de-Stalinization, played up the role of collective leadership and removed from the party constitution the previous version's obeisance to the "Thought of Mao Zedong" as the party's theoretical basis.[19] (The Seventh Congress, held in 1945, had enshrined Mao Thought in the constitution.)

The repercussions of de-Stalinization afforded Beijing an opportunity to begin carving out a role as an alternative source of ideological guidance in the Communist movement. The Chinese played a mediatory role during those tumultuous events, counseling Moscow not to take coercive measures as the Poles groped for more autonomy, and pressuring the Kremlin to take a moderate position during the first phase of the Hungarian developments. When the latter got out of hand and threatened Hungary's membership in the socialist camp, Beijing urged the Soviets to crack down, as they did, to suppress the uprising. The severity of the Hungarian crisis, and the questions the Stalin issue raised about whether it revealed basic systemic faults (as argued by Tito in his assessment of the Hungarian events), prompted the Chinese leadership to return to the subject in another *People's Daily* editorial, "More on the Historical Experience of the Dictatorship of the Proletariat," which sought to delineate which elements of the Soviet experience were of "universal significance" and which were not. The thrust of Beijing's approach to the turmoil in the socialist camp was to define a balance that would both restrain Moscow's "great-nation chauvinism," or excessive centralization in bloc affairs, and contain the tendencies toward "nationalism," or the assertion of autonomist claims by the smaller Communist countries.[20] It was a balance that the Chinese were not able to sustain.

Beijing's mediatory role was dramatized in the immediate wake of this second policy statement when Zhou Enlai interrupted an Asian tour to dash off to Moscow, Warsaw, and Budapest to pursue efforts to repair the damage to the socialist camp.[21] Complementing this diplomatic demarche was another attempt on the theoretical front to deal with the strains exposed by the Eastern European crisis through an elaboration of the concept of contradictions that had figured in the two editorials on de-Stalinization. In his speech "On the Correct Handling of Contradictions Among the People," delivered in February 1957, Mao cited the Hungarian experience as illustrating the need to deal properly with the conflicts of interest that continue in a socialist state lest enemy elements exploit them and endanger the socialist cause. This was followed later in the spring by a "rectification campaign" aimed at exposing and correcting the abuses of power that the Stalin issue had highlighted. Thus, Mao permitted "a hundred flowers to bloom and a hundred schools of thought to contend," an invitation to the Chinese people to vent their grievances and criticize the regime for its shortcomings and faults. A deluge of criticism was unleashed, producing such a challenge to the regime that the campaign was cut short after less than six weeks.[22] What followed was a fundamental shift in the Chinese leadership's approach across the board, a shift that set the stage for a severe testing of the Sino-Soviet alliance.

## BEIJING'S LURCH TO THE LEFT

In the year or so following the debacle of the hundred flowers campaign, the Chinese leadership took a decidedly leftist turn that created strains in the relationship with Moscow on several fronts. One thrust took a harder line toward the West, insisting that the Communist movement go on the offensive and thus downplaying the theme of peaceful coexistence that had been prominent in the mid-1950s. Beijing seized upon the Soviets' dramatic technological breakthroughs in the second half of 1957, the launching of the world's first intercontinental ballistic missile and artificial satellites (Sputniks), to proclaim that a "turning point" had been reached in which the East Wind (the socialist camp and its allies) now prevailed over the West Wind. Moreover, with this strategic edge now constraining the West's ability to threaten intervention, Beijing contended that the radical forces of the world, particularly in the third world, should seize the opportunity to pursue revolution.

At the same time, Beijing moved from its middle-of-the-road position between autonomist and centralist tendencies in bloc relations, coming down decidedly in favor of centralism. At a Communist summit held in Moscow in late 1957 to deal with the strains in bloc relations, Mao pressed the Soviets to take the lead in conducting the offensive against the West now that they held the strategic upper hand. In this second and last visit to Moscow, Mao declared that "the socialist camp must have a head, and that head is the Soviet Union," a polemical insistence that implied tougher discipline within the camp at the expense of the autonomist aspirations evident during the Eastern European unrest the previous year. A strong assertion of Soviet leadership was incorporated in the "Declaration of Twelve Communist and Workers' Parties" issued at the conference. Not surprisingly, Yugoslavia did not join the other Communist states in this declaration, though it signed another statement issued in the name of all Communist parties.[23]

Mirroring this shift to a leftist line in foreign and bloc relations was the emergence of a radical agenda in Chinese domestic policy displaying the same mark of impatience with the sluggish pace of change. Mao ordered a crackdown on the "rightists" who had joined in the outpouring of criticism of the regime during the abortive "blooming and contending," and he set the stage for the momentous program of radical change known as the Great Leap Forward. This program, which included the establishment of "communes" to exploit China's biggest resource, mass labor power, jettisoned the more gradualist Soviet model of socialist development that had been embodied in the PRC's first five-year plan. The party convened an extraordinary second session of the Eighth Congress, in May 1958, at which ambitious goals for an accelerated march to Communism were established, and those who "wanted to go slower rather than faster" were criticized. Two months later a resolution on establishing communes, noting that these would be the "basic social units of Communist society," declared the purpose to be "to prepare actively for the transition to Communism."[24] Thus, the Chinese were proposing to leapfrog the Soviets in reaching the avowed goal of the entire Communist movement, a breathtakingly bold challenge to Moscow as the leader and trailblazer of that movement. Not coincidentally, the cult of Mao was revived at this time, reversing the moves that had been taken two years earlier, at the time of the first session of the congress, when Beijing was following a moderate course.

## STRAINS IN THE ALLIANCE

Though Mao had issued a challenge to the Soviets to take a tougher line toward the West while he was in Moscow for the November 1957 summit, there was an effort to contain the corrosive effects of Khrushchev's de-Stalinization initiative on Sino-Soviet relations. The Stalin issue was not pursued; instead the Chinese submitted a draft on the question of "peaceful transition," which led to an exchange of drafts and to a compromise formulation in the conference declaration in which the Chinese (as they later claimed) accommodated the Soviet position in the interest of unity.[25] Also during this period the Kremlin sought to mollify the Chinese, most notably in agreeing to aid them in developing nuclear arms. The nuclear issue, involving as it did the most sensitive matters of strategy and alliance, was fated to be a catalyst in precipitating the Sino-Soviet schism.

Developments in the volatile Middle East provided a setting for Mao's challenge to the Soviets to meet their responsibilities as leader of the anti-Western forces. On 14 July 1958 the pro-Western Iraqi king Faisal was ousted in a coup in Baghdad, an event that not only ruptured the Baghdad Pact, a link in the chain of containment stretching from NATO to the U.S. alliances in East Asia, but also raised the prospect of further developments undermining the Western position in this strategic region. American and British forces were dispatched to Lebanon and Jordan to shore up these vulnerable countries; this also raised the possibility of further intervention to roll back the reversal in Iraq. The Chinese seized upon these developments to press Moscow to stand up to the West, but Khrushchev scrambled for a diplomatic way out, clearly desperate to avoid a clash with the Western powers.[26]

The accommodations that had been reached the previous year were now beginning to give way under the strains of divergent priorities, producing fissures in the alliance. It was in this context that the Soviet leader, accompanied by his defense minister, arrived suddenly in Beijing, evidently to settle the dust that had been raised by Soviet proposals for joint military arrangements, to which the Chinese had reacted bitterly, considering them an affront to their sovereignty. Several days before Khrushchev's arrival, Mao had vented his ire over the proposals—for a joint submarine fleet and joint naval communications facilities on the Chinese coast—in a heated conversation with the Soviet ambassador in which the chairman likened them to the joint enterprises imposed by Stalin at the beginning of the decade. Mao asked that his reaction be relayed to Moscow unvarnished and suggested that Khrushchev should reciprocate his own visit the previous year by coming to Beijing to discuss these issues.[27] Khrushchev would find this task an arduous one, as he increasingly was confronted by a need to keep the restless Chinese from straying from the fold.

Before the Soviet delegation's arrival at the end of July, Zhou had requested Soviet aid in producing missile-armed nuclear submarines, which, along with Moscow's agreement the previous year to aid the Chinese in developing a nuclear bomb, would represent another step toward cementing the alliance. The grounds of the alliance were shifting, however, with Moscow becoming wary of Chinese intentions and Beijing acutely sensitive to Soviet moves perceived as limiting Chinese independence. Efforts to resolve the alliance partners' differences were running up against conflicting imperatives: Moscow's attempt to reach an accommodation with the West at the same time as the Chinese were impatiently demanding a more forceful challenge to the status quo. On 31 March 1958 Moscow had announced a unilateral renunciation of nuclear testing, following up with a letter from Khrushchev to various leaders—among them President Eisenhower and Zhou—noting that with only three nuclear powers in the world it would be "comparatively easy" to reach agreement on discontinuing tests. Eisenhower and Khrushchev agreed to a meeting of experts to discuss means of monitoring compliance with a ban on testing. The Chinese, undoubtedly all too aware of the negative implications of this for the nuclear-aid promise from the Soviets, decided to pursue development of their own nuclear weapons.[28]

As later revealed in archival documents, Mao and Khrushchev had a testy exchange over the proposals for military cooperation during the latter's visit, even debating what the proposals were. A defensive Khrushchev found himself denying that Moscow was proposing a joint fleet (he claimed that he had even opposed the joint-stock companies that Stalin had demanded); his envoys had misrepresented the leadership's position on this matter, he explained. (His explanation may have been well-taken: He had delivered oral instructions to the Soviet ambassador in Beijing by telephone.) As part of his interest in reducing the burden of defense expenditures, Khrushchev sought to rely on nuclear-armed submarines in place of aircraft carriers, and he needed port facilities and communications facilities in China for these submarines in the Pacific theater.[29] His proposals, however, collided with Mao's acute sensitivity to any infringement on China's sovereignty. Regarding the proposed naval communications facility, Mao agreed on joint use but insisted that China retain ownership.[30] A feisty Deng Xiaoping later told the Soviets that acceptance of their proposals would have meant ceding "our entire coast to you" and that they were trying to bring China under Soviet "military control."[31] A similar point was pressed in the polemics of five years later, when the Chinese complained that in 1958 the Soviets had put forward "unreasonable demands designed to bring China under Soviet military control." These had been "firmly rejected."[32] Beijing's adamant refusal of Soviet requests for basing rights—at this time and during the Vietnam War—threw into sharp contrast the American access to bases in Japan.

## The Second Taiwan Crisis

The Chinese now made a move that seriously tested the alliance, choosing an arena where they could take the initiative rather than simply urging the Soviets to take more forceful action in an area such as the Middle East, where Beijing had little influence. This choice was the Taiwan Strait, where, as we have seen, Beijing had previously probed the firmness of the U.S. commitment to the Nationalist regime (see Chapter 7). A major meeting of the party's Military Affairs Commission lasting two months had planned an operation against the offshore islands; the decision to begin shelling the islands was made on 17 July. Mao put the decision in an international context, explaining that it was "our turn to create international tension" after the U.S. and British landings in the Middle East and to "support the Arabs' antirightist struggle." He also said that the action was in reaction to the Nationalists' harassment of the Fujian coast opposite the islands.[33] In addition, Mao used the new strait crisis to mobilize support for the Great Leap Forward.[34] Characteristically, when Mao pursued a radical agenda—such as at this time and during the Cultural Revolution in the next decade—his foreign and domestic policies overlapped and reinforced each other, making it an almost futile exercise to try to identify the dominant motivation (though a fierce commitment to independence and a closely related anti-Soviet animus were an abiding presence in Mao's thinking). Bombardment of the islands began on 23 August.

Whereas in the previous Taiwan Strait crisis Beijing had probed Washington's intentions in view of the ambiguity of its commitment to defense of Taiwan and the offshore islands, the new crisis had a broader context and an equally if not more momentous implication: not only a probe of U.S. support for Taiwan but also a test of support from the Soviet alliance for China's fundamental interests during a period when those interests were being pursued assertively. Resentments on both sides of the alliance were rooted in this episode, which served as a lesson to the Soviets that Beijing posed a danger to their interests by bringing them into potential conflict with the United States. For the Chinese it raised acute suspicions as to whether Moscow placed management of the Soviet-U.S. relationship above its responsibilities to China. The fundamental lesson both sides were to draw from events during this watershed period of the late 1950s was that their divergent strategic interests could not be accommodated within their alliance relationship.

Moscow bitterly resented what it regarded as Beijing's failure to consult adequately on the Taiwan Strait and other Chinese initiatives during this period. The Chinese, according to Moscow, "did not inform us in a timely fashion" of their intention to shell the islands, even though the decision had been made by the time Khrushchev and his defense minister arrived on 31 July. (The Soviets also complained that they were insufficiently informed about the PRC-U.S. ambassadorial talks that had begun three years earlier.)[35] Khrushchev would later recall that he had been informed only in general terms of plans to "bring Taiwan back under China's jurisdiction."[36] There was no reference in the communiqué on Khrushchev's visit to the liberation of Taiwan, though that had become a pressing theme in Chinese propaganda in the week prior to his sudden arrival (and then ceased until mid-August).[37]

The Chinese resented what they regarded as belated and inadequate Soviet support for their Taiwan Strait venture. Was it not understandable, however, that the Soviets were alarmed about the implications of that venture and measured their moves carefully? After Washington declared on 4 September that the United States would use its armed forces to defend the offshore islands if necessary, Foreign Minister Andrey Gromyko was dispatched secretly to find out what the Chinese were up to. Khrushchev "did not have any idea about our intentions" in shelling Jinmen (Quemoy), according to a Chinese account, which claimed that it was after Gromyko was assured that Beijing did not intend to involve the Soviets in a war that Khrushchev warned Eisenhower of Soviet support for China if it was attacked.[38] According to a letter from the CPSU to the CPC on 27 September, Gromyko had been told on the seventh that the Soviet Union would be expected to retaliate with nuclear arms only in case major and not just tactical nuclear weapons were used by the United States, a highly unlikely contingency.[39] (The Eisenhower administration—like its predecessor during the Korean War—had something of a habit of hinting at the use of nuclear arms to pressure adversaries at tense times.) It was on the day Gromyko received this assurance, and a day after Zhou had taken a major step toward defusing the crisis by calling for resumption of the suspended PRC-U.S. ambassadorial talks (promptly accepted by Washington), that Khrushchev wrote to Eisenhower that an attack on China would be regarded as "an attack on the Soviet Union."[40]

The compressed timeframe makes it difficult to sort out the precise causal sequence between Washington's announcement of 4 September and the dispatch of Khrushchev's letter three days later. According to some archival sources, Gromyko arrived in Beijing bearing a draft of Khrushchev's letter, to which the Chinese gave their assent; in that case, the Soviet leader's warning to Eisenhower was prompted by the U.S. statement of the fourth and preceded Zhou's demarche to reduce tensions with Washington. The fundamental fact remains, however, that Beijing's Taiwan Strait initiative was highly disturbing to the Soviets, and what Gromyko heard during his visit was particularly harrowing. In his account of what Mao told him about the prospective Soviet role if the U.S. resorted to nuclear arms against the PRC, Gromyko said he was "flabbergasted" when Mao proposed that after the Americans were drawn deeply into the Chinese interior the Soviets should "give them everything you've got"—which Gromyko interpreted as referring to a nuclear exchange. This led him to realize "how wide the gap" was on strategic issues between the two allies. He said nothing about carrying a draft of Khrushchev's letter.[41]

During the second Taiwan Strait crisis, the Kremlin had to strike a fine balance in meeting competing concerns. It had an overriding interest in avoiding any development that would trigger its commitment to China under the terms of the mutual security treaty, hence its acute concern over Beijing's aggressive moves. But the situation required enough of a show of Soviet support so as not to devalue the alliance in Beijing's eyes and thus lose any restraining influence on the worrisomely unpredictable Chinese. At the same time, the Soviet leadership was concerned that the United States and its allies might also devalue the Sino-Soviet alliance and thereby perceive an opportunity to capitalize on cracks in the solidarity of the socialist camp. If the enemy believed that the Soviet Union would remain on the sidelines in the event of an attack on China, Moscow warned, a "very dangerous situation" would arise that could lead to "a great calamity for the entire socialist camp."[42] The Chinese may have seen some logic to this at the time, but they also had a telling point in later polemics in charging that it was clear that the Soviets expressed their support for China only after "there was no possibility that a nuclear war would break out and no need for the Soviet Union to support China with its nuclear weapons." Making reference to the Soviet leader's letters of 7 and 19 September (the latter was rejected by Eisenhower because of its harshly threatening language), Beijing acknowledged that the situation remained tense at this time, which was the period during which the U.S. Navy escorted supply convoys from Taiwan to the offshore islands.[43] The critical phase had ended in early September, however, after a period of conspicuously tepid Soviet expressions of support for its ally. The PRC ceased the bombardment on 6 October, though later resuming it on alternate days in a bizarre and largely symbolic continuation of the campaign.[44]

## Widening Fissures

The implications of these events, and of the cycle of charges and ripostes they later evoked, were that Moscow had grounds for anxiety over its ally's readiness not only to push the Soviets toward a more aggressive approach to international issues but also to take initiatives without adequate consultation despite their potential for drawing Moscow into conflicts not of its choosing. That Khrushchev had to dispatch his foreign minister to Beijing to inquire as to its intentions so soon after his own visit underscored Moscow's tenuous influence over its ally. For their part, the Chinese may have in fact welcomed Khrushchev's statements of support during the crisis—Moscow cited a letter from Mao expressing gratitude for the "powerful support from the Soviet Union"[45]—but they had begun to chafe under the constraints they felt the Kremlin sought to place on their freedom of maneuver. As their later polemics indicated, the Chinese were particularly sensitive to any perceived effort by Moscow to exercise control by virtue of its possession of the socialist camp's strategic nuclear shield. The nuclear issue was becoming central to the divergence of interests that was to lead to open schism in the next decade.

Beijing had reason for wariness over Moscow's moves on the nuclear issue. The Soviet demarche on discontinuing nuclear testing would eventually lead to a test ban treaty that Beijing saw as an effort to exclude it from the nuclear club. Meanwhile Moscow began reneging on offers to aid the Chinese nuclear programs: Following Khrushchev's testy talks during his mid-1958 visit, Moscow stopped delivering technology for developing a nuclear submarine fleet, and in June 1959 notified Beijing of the termination of the agreement on producing nuclear arms. Moscow explained that efforts toward détente would be jeopardized if the West discovered that the Soviets were aiding China in producing a nuclear bomb.[46] More particularly, Moscow hoped to achieve a trade-off in which both China and West Germany would be kept out of the nuclear club.[47] The Soviet approach could only inflame Beijing's concerns over the Kremlin's priorities at the expense of Chinese interests.

The socialist camp, whose central leadership by Moscow the Chinese had so insisted upon in late 1957, was now showing serious cracks. Moscow would later offer a penetrating comment on the crux of the tension: "From our point of view, the very idea of a need to acquire their own nuclear weapons can be conceived by the leaders of a country whose security is guaranteed by the whole might of the socialist camp only when they have developed special aims and interests of some kind which cannot be supported by the military strength of the socialist camp."[48] From the Chinese point of view, of course, this begged the question. Beijing saw a need to acquire nuclear weapons because Moscow would not use its leadership, especially its strategic capability, to advance the purposes of its allies and instead subordinated their interests to its own overriding concern over managing the relationship with the other superpower. In short, the Soviet nuclear shield was being used to constrain the socialist camp rather than the common enemy.

Another grievance arose from the Sino-Indian border fighting in late summer 1959. During the 1950s, Moscow had cultivated relations with India, which did not pose serious problems for its relationship with Beijing given the warm Sino-Indian ties that had emerged during that time. Now, however, with the deterioration of Sino-Indian relations (see Chapter 6), Moscow had to choose between supporting its ally and maintaining its carefully nurtured relationship with that ally's big rival on the continent. The Kremlin treaded cautiously, offering a neutral comment on the border dispute delivered at a low level: a statement by the official TASS news agency. The statement sought to strike a balance between maintaining friendly relations with China based on "socialist internationalism" and maintaining the ties with India consonant with the principles of "peaceful coexistence." For Beijing this was a serious breach of Moscow's obligations (though, strictly speaking, Moscow was not obligated to come to China's assistance against a state not allied, directly or indirectly, with Japan, as stipulated in the Sino-Soviet treaty of alliance).

The TASS statement, as well as later polemics by both sides, put the border dispute in the broader context of East-West relations. The statement warned that the dispute was being used in the United States in an attempt to "obstruct a relaxation of tension and to complicate the situation" on the eve of Khrushchev's visit there.[49] In Beijing's interpretation, offered four years later, Moscow had "rushed out" the statement despite Chinese objections, thereby "siding with the Indian reactionaries" and seeking to "curry favor with the U.S. imperialists" ahead of Khrushchev's trip.[50] The conflicting interests increasingly dividing Moscow and Beijing were now being thrown into sharp relief. Khrushchev's successive visits, first to the socialist camp's main adversary and then to Moscow's principal ally, demonstrated this dramatically.

## Khrushchev's Summits

The very sequence of Khrushchev's visits in 1959 reflected the competing priorities that were straining the alliance. Instead of going first to his ally to discuss and coordinate policy toward the adversary, he proceeded first to tour the United States—the first visit by a Soviet leader—and engage in talks with Eisenhower in an atmosphere that the Soviet media celebrated as "the spirit of Camp David" (after the presidential retreat outside

Washington where Eisenhower hosted his Communist guest). The talks were intended to be a prelude to what became the abortive Paris summit conference of 1960; Khrushchev's hopes at the time for substantial progress in relations with the United States were reflected in his judgment that the president was one who "sincerely wants, like us, to end the Cold War."[51]

The Soviet leader next visited Beijing, attending the tenth anniversary of the founding of the PRC and engaging in acrimonious exchanges with the Chinese. Khrushchev chose this occasion to deliver a stinging public lecture to his hosts, crediting Eisenhower with a desire to relax East-West tension and warning against attempts to "test by force the stability of the capitalist system."[52] In private talks later during the visit, the smoldering Chinese resentment flared, particularly in the case of Foreign Minister Chen I, whose blistering attack on Khrushchev as a "time server" sparked a bitter exchange. (The Russian document transcribing the talks used the term *prisposoblenchestvo*, which Khrushchev may have taken to mean a charge of "opportunism," a serious accusation in the Communist lexicon. Another participant, the Chinese leadership's Soviet expert Wang Jiaxiang, sought to lower the temperature by noting that there was a "wrong translation" and no doctrinal accusation was intended.)[53] Both sides vented their grievances, addressing at length the Taiwan Strait crisis and the Sino-Indian border dispute.[54] Khrushchev observed that he did not understand Chinese policy on these issues, remarking plaintively that it was not normal for the Soviet Union as China's ally not to "know what the Chinese comrades may undertake tomorrow" in foreign affairs.[55]

## THE ROAD TO SCHISM

The alliance was now in deep trouble. The ideological, security, and economic bonds of "socialist internationalism" that had cemented the close relationship earlier in the decade were under severe strain from the two sides' conflicting priorities. What kind of an alliance was it anyway, if one side, Moscow, believed that its partner was taking risky actions without proper consultation, particularly if such actions could involve the Soviets in a conflict? From the Chinese perspective, Moscow was using the alliance as a straitjacket to constrain Beijing's area of maneuver and subordinating China's goals to Soviet interests. As for consultation, Khrushchev was hardly taking Chinese views into account while he pursued better relations with the United States. Moreover, the Chinese were hardly pleased to have Khrushchev sermonize in their own capital on the importance of stability in superpower relations. As they interpreted his counsel during the 1959 visit, his emphasis on the dangers of the Taiwan issue in view of the superpowers' respective alliances with the PRC and ROC amounted to a two-Chinas proposal, utterly anathema to Beijing. (The Chinese invidiously quoted Khrushchev as citing the Far Eastern Republic, an entity recognized by Lenin during the early years after the Bolshevik Revolution before eventually being reunited with Russia, as an example of a temporary expedient that could serve as a precedent for Beijing's handling of the Taiwan issue.)[56] The Sino-Indian border dispute was interpreted by both Moscow and Beijing as symptomatic of basic shortcomings in their alliance in the broader international context: Moscow saw Chinese involvement in the dispute as an effort to undermine the pursuit of peaceful coexistence, while Beijing viewed Moscow's neutrality on a conflict involving its own ally as an effort to "curry favor" with the imperialist enemy in order to foster the spirit of Camp David.[57]

A chasm had begun to loom in the Sino-Soviet alliance. Was it on the verge of fracture, or were the underlying mutual security interests too important to allow the alliance to be jettisoned in a dangerous world? Answers were to come in stages in the coming decade. In his classic study of the emergence of the Sino-Soviet conflict, published in 1962, Donald Zagoria took a middle position between one that saw the fundamental interests of the alliance as being too great to allow significant conflict and the opposite view that a fracture of the alliance was inevitable. Zagoria foresaw further conflict and competition but without a breakup of the alliance in view of the partners' overriding common aims. As it turned out, the Vietnam War, coupled with Mao's obsession with continuing revolution at home and abroad, rendered Zagoria's forecast too conservative.[58]

## ERUPTION OF IDEOLOGICAL WARFARE

In the first half of the 1960s, the Sino-Soviet alliance survived as a security structure but was severely buffeted by the ideological competition initiated by Beijing at the beginning of the decade. The watershed years of 1958–59 having demonstrated that Moscow would not use the socialist camp as an instrument advancing the interests of the Chinese and others dissatisfied with the status quo, Beijing decided to outflank bipolarity by undertaking an ideological and political offensive in which the third world was the arena for both challenging the West's influence and competing with the Soviets for leadership of radical anti-Western forces. This ideological campaign was accompanied by schismatic political maneuvers, resulting in factional splits within various Communist parties mirroring the conflict between Moscow and Beijing.

In characteristic Communist practice, the Chinese used a significant anniversary to launch their campaign, the ninetieth anniversary of Lenin's birth, in April 1960. The opening fusillade, a set of polemical commentaries, was known collectively as *Long Live Leninism*,[59] reflecting the thrust of the campaign against Moscow's alleged departure from fundamental Leninist principles. The Chinese offensive, registering Beijing's repulsion by the "Spirit of Camp David" animating Soviet policy, came on the eve of the East-West summit scheduled for the next month (aborted by an American U-2 spy plane's downing over Soviet territory).

In the first phase of this ideological war, the two sides observed fraternal protocol by avoiding attacks on each other by name. Instead it was fought through the use of code words and proxies: Beijing criticized "revisionism" and the Yugoslavs as archrepresentatives of that heresy, while Moscow condemned "dogmatism" and its Albanian avatars. Beijing's indictment of Moscow's revisionism can be encapsulated as aimed at the "three peacefuls"—peaceful transition, peaceful coexistence, and peaceful competition. Though the Chinese were to trace these deviations to the twentieth CPSU Congress in 1956, they themselves had promoted peaceful coexistence during the moderate phase of their foreign policy in the mid-1950s; they had also cultivated relations with neutralist governments such as Nehru's. But as Beijing's line swerved sharply to the left in 1957, it began taking vigorous exception to efforts to seek a relaxation of East-West relations. These were not mere matters of arcane doctrinal dispute; rather, the Chinese viewed Moscow's doctrinal initiatives in the post-Stalin period as serving to freeze the international order, putting off revolutionary change in the interests of stability and at the expense of the forces in the world whose aspirations for radical change were thereby thwarted.

Moscow defended the doctrine of peaceful coexistence as an adaptation to the realities of the nuclear age, in which a new world war would be catastrophic. This may have been a revision of Lenin's thesis on the inevitability of war as long as imperialism existed, as the Chinese argued, but in the Kremlin's view Beijing was being dogmatic in resisting recognition of those realities. Moreover, in conditions of strategic stalemate between the two superpowers, the Communists would advance their cause by means of peaceful competition, in which the superiority of the socialist system would both lead to overtaking the West in economic development and serve as a powerful attraction to Marxism-Leninism. As for peaceful transition, Moscow sought to foster good relations with nationalist governments such as Nasser's Egypt and Nehru's India. These were not to be targets of revolutionary civil war lest Soviet influence be undercut and, in a worst case prospect, the entangling alliances in a bipolar world lead to an escalation of local conflicts into nuclear confrontation between the superpowers.

Beijing's position was not a total negation of these doctrines. Rather, the Chinese objected to Moscow's elevation of peaceful coexistence to that of a "general line"—strategic doctrine—of the Communist movement, whereas they regarded it (during this period) as a tactical expedient appropriate only in certain limited circumstances. The Chinese argued, moreover, that peaceful coexistence applied only to relations between the socialist and imperialist camps, not to the conflict between imperialism and the oppressed peoples in the third world, and that it was the latter "contradiction" that now provided the motive force for world revolution. Similarly, Beijing acknowledged, grudgingly to be sure, the possibility of a peaceful road to power by Communists but argued that this would be rare and its prospects not to be overstated lest the revolutionary will be emasculated.[60] In Beijing's view, Soviet cultivation of "bourgeois nationalist" governments stood in the way of revolutionary advance by Communist and other radical forces. Particularly galling to the Chinese was the way it led Moscow to its neutral posture on the Sino-Indian border dispute despite the Sino-Soviet alliance.

The situation deteriorated rapidly in 1960 under the impact of the Chinese polemical campaign and as both sides lobbied for support at Communist Party congresses and meetings of Communist front organizations. A measure of Moscow's exasperation came in the middle of the year when it withdrew its large contingent of experts from China, wreaking further havoc on an economy in utter disarray from the Great Leap Forward debacle and suffering massive famine. In an attempt to halt the slide toward schism, another international party conference was convened at the end of the year. This time, though, the Soviets were impelled to submit the dispute to the jurisdiction of the broader international Communist movement, the eighty-one Communist parties whose representatives gathered in Moscow to discuss the issues dividing the two giant parties (in contrast, the key deliberations at the 1957 conference were conducted by the ruling parties). Moreover, the 1960 conference statement contained a formulation significantly diluting Moscow's authority in the movement. Whereas the 1957 statement proclaimed the Soviet Union to be the head of the socialist camp and world Communist movement (at Chinese insistence, as has been noted), the new one simply recognized Moscow as the "universally recognized vanguard" of the movement. This was hardly more than acknowledging that Communist revolution had begun in Russia.

The 1960 statement was largely an ambiguous document with nods to both sides' positions without definitively resolving their differences—more a collation than a compromise of views, in the words of one acute scholar.[61] The conference failed to contain the polarizing forces that had been unleashed; instead the atmosphere became increasingly charged by damaging polemical forays by both sides. The Chinese seized on the Cuban missile crisis of 1962 to heap scorn on Moscow's "adventurism" in installing the missiles and then its "capitulationism" by removing them under U.S. pressure. Khrushchev taunted his tormentors by contrasting India's forcible takeover of the Portuguese colony of Goa with China's toleration of Hong Kong's status as a British possession and Macao as Portuguese. The increasingly nasty exchanges finally erupted into open and direct polemical warfare in 1963. Beijing issued a comprehensive competing agenda for the Communist movement, presenting a frontal challenge to Moscow's primacy and positioning the Chinese to assume the leadership of "revolutionary Marxism-Leninism."[62] The Kremlin responded with its own wide-ranging rebuttal and indictment of Chinese positions.[63] There was now little room for accommodation between two Communist rivals on the road to schism.

The atmosphere was thus poisoned for interparty talks that took place in Moscow in mid-1963. (The CPC delegation was headed by its general secretary, Deng Xiaoping.) These talks, officially to prepare for a new international party conference to pursue the unity that both the Soviets and the Chinese piously professed to seek, failed miserably, in sharp—and revealing—contrast to the successful conclusion of the overlapping Anglo-American-Soviet negotiations on a limited nuclear test ban treaty. The interparty talks lasted from 5 to 20 July, when they were "suspended." The test ban negotiations opened on 15 July and concluded on the twenty-fifth. (In a revealing coupling of events, Mao received the leader of the pro-Chinese faction of the Australian Communists on the day that the test ban negotiators initialed the treaty.)

Beijing reacted furiously to the signing of a treaty that it viewed as an effort to exclude it from the nuclear club and as representing "a US-Soviet alliance against China pure and simple."[64] Moscow's riposte, while emphasizing that the Soviet nuclear shield had served China and the rest of the socialist camp, included hints that this shield would be withdrawn if Beijing insisted on pursuing its "special aims," a warning in effect that the Sino-Soviet alliance itself was in grave jeopardy. (See the passage quoted earlier.)

The success of the test ban negotiations and the failure of the Sino-Soviet talks having sharply clarified the situation, Khrushchev now proceeded to accept the reality of a schism and to rally support within the Communist movement for a new international party conference, this time to excommunicate or at least isolate the Chinese and end the compromises and accommodations that had marked efforts to maintain unity in the movement.

He was not, however, fated to preside over such an undertaking. For reasons having mainly to do with domestic issues but also intertwined with international policy, including the China question, a coalition of Khrushchev's colleagues ousted him in October 1964—an event that coincided with China's first nuclear test.[65] A high-powered Chinese delegation headed by Zhou Enlai went to Moscow for the next month's Bolshevik Revolution anniversary celebrations to probe the new Soviet leadership's readiness to meet Beijing's demands. That the Sino-Soviet conflict ran much deeper than the personal rivalry between Khrushchev and Mao was demonstrated by Beijing's assessment of the new Kremlin leaders' policy predilections: "Khrushchevism without Khrushchev." As discussed in Chapter 10, Khrushchev's successors made a significant gesture toward reducing the ideological conflict with Beijing, but supervening events, notably the escalation of American involvement in Vietnam, converted Moscow's seemingly conciliatory initiative into a source of bitter tension that finally led to the collapse of the alliance.

## IMPACT IN ASIA

Beijing's ideological offensive in the early 1960s fractured individual parties in various regions of the world, but it was in Asia that there was a significant impact on *ruling* Communist parties. Moscow's Mongolian satellite, while buffeted by the polemical storms, remained within the Soviet orbit; elsewhere, however, Beijing gained important inroads that eroded Soviet authority in Asia. The polarizing force of the Sino-Soviet rivalry caused China's other two neighboring Communist states, North Korea and North Vietnam, to gravitate toward Beijing at Moscow's expense. Though both Pyongyang and Hanoi, recognizing the importance of the Soviet strategic umbrella for their security, took care to avoid alienating the Kremlin, they found themselves leaning toward the Chinese positions on key issues. This was reflected in their antipathy toward the test ban treaty, for instance, and more generally toward Moscow's pursuit of détente with the West. Also, a Stalinist of Kim Il Sung's ilk could hardly have looked kindly on Moscow's de-Stalinization program.

There were structural reasons for the ideological affinities that enabled Beijing to register considerable success in attracting its Korean and Vietnamese comrades. The three Communist regimes saw themselves as each being confronted by a hostile U.S.-backed rival government in a divided country. They thus perceived America and its projection of power abroad as the chief obstacles to the completion of their revolutions. For Moscow to reach an enduring accommodation with Washington would mean an indefinite postponement of that goal, or even worse, a threat to the security of these regimes.

The Sino-Soviet ideological rivalry, meanwhile, viewed in the context of a relaxation of Soviet-U.S. relations and Beijing's appeal to radical anti-American forces, caused a rethinking in Washington's hopes for driving a wedge in the Moscow-Beijing axis. Whereas earlier American hopes centered on the potential for Chinese nationalism to draw the PRC away from Moscow, now they were placed on prying the Soviets away from a China increasingly viewed as the most dangerous source of instability in the world. Washington persistently sought to enlist Soviet help in coping with the Vietnam quagmire and to appeal to common interests in containing what was perceived as Chinese adventurism and expansionism. As it turned out, Washington eventually relied on Beijing to help ease its exit from Vietnam and formed a quasi-alliance with the Chinese to contain Soviet power. The Vietnam conflict, to which we now turn, was crucial to this remarkable turn of events.

# 9 THE VIETNAM WAR

The Vietnam War ("the American War" to the Vietnamese), also known as the Second Indochina War, presents a paradoxical picture in retrospect. At the time, from the late Eisenhower administration until the Paris settlement in 1973, the stakes of the conflict were perceived as being momentous. For Washington, while varying over time in its identification of the source of danger, what was at stake was no less than the credibility of U.S. commitments worldwide, on which the stability of the international system depended. For their part, the Vietnamese Communists saw the conflict as a life-or-death struggle to complete the revolution to which they had devoted their careers and to reunify all of Vietnam and dominate Indochina. Given these perceptions, the enormous destruction and expenditure of blood and treasure were in some sense proportionate to the stakes involved.

In retrospect, however, one can ask whether the conflict was really much ado about not very much. The Communists did indeed reach their revolutionary goals, but so did the other formerly colonial countries in the region without anything approaching the level of death and devastation suffered by the parties to the Indochina conflict. U.S. credibility did not suffer the kind of blow that would undermine global stability. Did Washington and its allies misperceive the implications of a Communist victory in Indochina? Were there points after 1954 when the United States could have reversed the logic of intervention and produced an outcome substantially like what developed with the eventual Communist success? In short, was it all a meaningless if monumentally destructive contest of wills that made little difference after all?

The picture may be more complicated. Did the American intervention buy time for Indochina's neighboring countries, which thereby were able to obtain their independence without incurring the terrible costs suffered by the peoples of that peninsula? A positive answer to that question would make a net assessment of the U.S. action more difficult. In an even broader geopolitical context, what was the relationship between the Vietnam War and the strategic realignment of the superpowers and China that transformed the geopolitical landscape in the 1970s? Might it be said that the peoples of Indochina paid an enormous price, including the murderous reign of the Khmer Rouge in Cambodia and hundreds of thousands of boat people fleeing Vietnam after the U.S. withdrawal, but that the global benefits, including an end to the Cold War and its potential for producing World War III, justified their sacrifices? We return to these issues after examining the logic and imperatives behind Washington's commitment of its resources and credibility to a subregion that had little intrinsic significance but was invested with stakes of astonishing proportions.

## AFTER THE GENEVA ACCORDS

The 1954 Geneva accords ending the First Indochina War (the one involving the French) were inherently ambiguous and unstable (see Chapter 6). Washington, having only "taken note" of the agreements and promising not to "disturb" them, chose not to take this opportunity to disengage along with the French, at a time when both Moscow and Beijing were following a moderate course. Instead, it construed the "provisional" military demarcation line along the seventeenth parallel as a segment of the global line of confrontation with its Cold War adversary. From this premise followed the logic of intervention: nation building in the southern half of Vietnam, the commitment of U.S. prestige and credibility, and the gathering momentum of involvement that proved so difficult to arrest.

Meanwhile Hanoi, having acceded to its Communist patrons' pressure to negotiate the Geneva accords, engaged in its own nation building by pursuing postwar reconstruction and land reform as the two-year period that Geneva had stipulated for elections to reunify the country elapsed. As an article in the party's ideological journal, which was reprinted in the party daily, put it a few months after the election deadline, the North Vietnamese Communists "must not allow the winning over of the South to detract from the requirements of consolidating the North."[1] This priority must have been welcomed by Moscow and Beijing, given their conciliatory tendencies in that period.

By the end of the decade, however, the priority accorded to building socialism in the North gave ground to a renewed pursuit of armed struggle in the South. The Third Congress of the (Communist) Vietnam Workers Party in September 1960 formally endorsed this shift, and a united front organization under Communist control, the National Liberation Front of South Vietnam, was established to seek broad support for the campaign. The Saigon regime referred to the front as Vietcong, or Vietnamese Communists. Two years later a southern branch of the Vietnam Workers Party, the People's Revolutionary Party, was founded under the guise of independence from the North.[2] These ideological and organizational developments were accompanied by a "drastic intensification of revolutionary activity" in the South.[3] The Second Indochina War was looming on a darkening horizon.

## THE LAOS "MESS"

An overture to the larger Vietnam drama was played in Laos, which had gained independence at the 1954 Geneva Conference but was destined to be buffeted and enveloped by the gathering turbulence in its bigger neighbor. Indeed, President Eisenhower's briefing of his successor regarding Indochina was dominated by what he called the "Laos mess."[4] The outgoing administration regarded Laos as the key to stability in the region—the cork in the bottle, in Eisenhower's imagery—and believed American intervention would be required if a political settlement could not be achieved.

Throughout the 1950s, various efforts, some with more success than others but none with lasting effect, had been made to integrate the contending forces in Laos into a coalition government. The Communist Pathet Lao, founded in 1950 to fight the French and to oppose "international imperialist intervention," along with its united front organization, the Neo Lao Hak Sat (Lao Patriotic Front), entered a coalition in 1957 that brought together two princes who were half brothers, Souvanna Phouma and Souphanouvong, and permitted the Neo Lao Hak Sat to operate as a legal party while integrating the Pathet Lao forces in the Royal Lao army.[5] Centrifugal forces could not be contained, however, and the superpowers were active in supporting the contending sides. The Eisenhower administration and the CIA, using its Air America operation and supporting tribesmen in combating the Communists, backed the rightists; the Soviets lent their support to the leftists; and the situation became still more complicated when a paratroop commander, Kong Le, staged a coup in 1960 to oppose the pro-U.S. rightist government. Souvanna Phouma returned as prime minister, pledging to pursue a policy of "true and wise neutrality," but Washington viewed neutralism with suspicion, and in any case Laos's strategic position in sharing a long border with Vietnam was less than propitious for pursuit of a neutral course. This was the messy backdrop as the new Kennedy administration prepared to confront the Communist challenge in Indochina.

## Flexible Response and Counterinsurgency

The Laos situation seemed to illustrate a gap in Washington's arsenal for contending with what were perceived as challenging trends in global affairs: the "winds of change" sweeping the formerly colonized areas of the world, particularly the "national liberation movement" with its anti-Western thrust. The Dulles policy of "massive retaliation" was designed to prevent repetitions of the Korean experience, with its protracted, frustrating, and inconclusive fighting by American ground troops. Washington had flexed its nuclear muscles at times of incipient crisis (such as over the Taiwan Strait), and there had been talk of using nuclear weapons to stave off Communist conquest in Indochina. But if the political and diplomatic costs were disproportionately high, and the risks of sparking a major war too dangerous, Washington was left emptyhanded for dealing with a situation such as that in Laos, where the Communist forces were gaining ground despite aid for the anti-Communists. The alternative outcomes looked unwelcome: use of massive force, including nuclear arms; a reprise of the Korean experience; or default to the Communists and another experience like "the loss of China."

Though Eisenhower had warned Kennedy that the "mess" in Laos might require American military intervention, the new administration elected instead to pursue negotiations for the neutralization of that strategically sited country. With veteran negotiator (and former New York governor) Averell Harriman leading the American delegation at a reconvened Geneva Conference in 1961–62, an agreement was arduously reached on a Declaration on the Neutrality of Laos.[6] Attended by the participants of the 1954 conference as well as by the members of the International Control Commission for monitoring the accords reached then—India, Poland, and Canada—and neighboring countries Burma and Thailand, the new conference decreed that Laos would not enter into any military alliance or allow foreign military bases, and specifically disavowed the protection of SEATO. Another Lao coalition government, comprising Prime Minister Souvanna Phouma as head of the centrists and leaders of the rightist and leftist forces, was formed to try to steer the neutralist course ordained at Geneva.

Even if this coalition could have survived in an isolated geopolitical setting, itself a dubious prospect given the country's inherent political instability, the location of Laos alongside Vietnam doomed it to being sucked into the rising level of conflict prompted by the recrudescent insurgency in the South. The so-called Ho Chi Minh Trail, a network of roads and paths along Laos's border with Vietnam, provided the conduit for the Communists to send cadres, troops, and supplies in support of the campaign against the Saigon regime. First as the site of a "secret war" conducted by the United States, and later as an open battleground as the Americans and their allies tried to stanch the flow down the trail, Laos became ineluctably drawn into the Vietnam conflict.

In these circumstances, the Kennedy administration faced another of the decision points posed by the Vietnam conflict: whether to seek a broader neutralization to include Vietnam, thereby dislodging the Saigon regime in favor of a coalition government that would negotiate a settlement with Hanoi, or to dig in deeper to preserve South Vietnam's independence. Choosing the latter led Washington to fashion the doctrine of flexible response, one that deployed a range of military, political, and economic tools to respond to different levels and types of challenge. The challenge posed by Vietnam—the insurgency rising in the South in the 1960s—was the most pressing case of the "national liberation movement" that was transforming the third world into a principal battleground of the Cold War.

## THE NATIONAL LIBERATION MOVEMENT

Early in January 1961, as the Kennedy administration was preparing to assume office, Soviet leader Khrushchev delivered a major address that deeply impressed the incoming president. Khrushchev was commenting on the international Communist conference held in Moscow a couple of months earlier at which the role of national liberation wars was one of the contentious issues. According to Khrushchev, the Soviets had "assured" the conference participants that Moscow would "spare no efforts to fulfill its internationalist obligations" (the Chinese were questioning this readiness with increasing polemical force) but had "proposed that this wording not be included" in the documents of the Communist movement. In a passage discussing national liberation wars, in which he cited the Vietnam conflict, Khrushchev intoned that such wars were "not only admissible but *inevitable*, since the colonialists do not grant independence voluntarily."[7] In effect, the Soviet leader seemed to be conceding unilaterally a point that he had resisted at the international party conference.

Khrushchev's speech "made a conspicuous impression" on Kennedy, who was alarmed by the Kremlin leader's "bellicose confidence" in achieving victory through "rebellion, subversion and guerrilla warfare."[8] In this instance, however, as was recurrently the case in American perceptions of Soviet intentions, Khrushchev's seemingly aggressive declaration needed a close examination, one that placed it in a Sino-Soviet as well as an East-West context. Khrushchev felt a need to fend off criticism from the hard-line Chinese (as well as hard-liners in the Kremlin), but he also needed to balance this against the imperatives of superpower relations, especially the need to avert world war in the nuclear age. A failure to appreciate this balancing act tended to lead Washington to exaggerate the threat suggested by Soviet pronouncements, prompting a cycle of heightened threat perceptions by the superpowers.

A close reading of Khrushchev's speech shows that he took care to qualify Moscow's commitment to its "internationalist obligations." Thus, while conceding to hard-liners that national liberation wars were inevitable, Khrushchev introduced a new distinction that enabled him to maintain a balance between Chinese pressure and a strategy of peaceful coexistence with the West. He distinguished local wars between states from wars of liberation that began as "an uprising by the colonial peoples against their oppressors and changed into guerrilla warfare," and he coupled local wars with world wars as containing the potential to develop into global nuclear war—the prospect the strategy of coexistence, a primary target of Chinese criticism, was designed to avoid. He went a bit further in suggesting the implication of this dialectical reasoning by citing the events in Cuba as an uprising against the U.S.-supported Batista regime and pointedly noting that the United States "did not interfere in that war directly with its armed forces."[9] In other words, national liberation wars could run their course without broader consequences so long as the big powers avoided direct military involvement.

Khrushchev may have raised the issue of support for national liberation movements at this point, having excluded it from the statement issued by the Moscow conference a few weeks earlier, in order to take into account developments in Laos during the intervening period. At the end of 1960 the Soviets had begun airlifting military supplies to buttress the neutralist and leftist forces facing a severe challenge from rightists backed by the United States. Moscow now coupled this demonstration of concrete aid to a national liberation struggle with acceptance of the proposal initiated by Cambodia's Prince Sihanouk to reconvene a new Geneva conference to guarantee the beleaguered little kingdom's neutrality, hoping thereby to arrest a slide toward a broader conflagration in Indochina that would complicate Khrushchev's efforts to manage relations with the West. When Washington rejected the Laos settlement as a model for a broader deal and made the decisive move to intervene in Vietnam, Moscow would find its balancing act increasingly difficult to maintain as the fighting escalated.

## ROOTS OF ESCALATION

With the Laos model of neutralization off the table as an approach to a Vietnam settlement, the Kennedy administration with its can-do spirit rolled up its sleeves to take on what was perceived as a challenge to the containment policy. In effect Washington did not accept Khrushchev's distinction between the national liberation movement and other wars; the former had the potential to undermine U.S. credibility and the whole edifice of containment that Washington had built over the years of the Cold War, and thus could lead to a situation in which global nuclear war was the ultimate outcome. As the Pentagon study of the American intervention put it, Vietnam was "the only place in the world where the Administration faced a well-developed Communist effort to topple a pro-Western government with an externally aided pro-Communist insurgency." It was "a challenge that could hardly be ignored."[10]

Washington responded quickly. The number of American advisers in Vietnam was increased and Special Forces dispatched to train the South Vietnamese in counterinsurgency; Hmong tribesmen in Laos were trained and armed by the CIA to act against the Ho Chi Minh Trail; Vice President Lyndon Johnson was assigned the mission of delivering assurances of American support directly to Saigon; the president's military adviser, General Maxwell Taylor, architect of the counterinsurgency doctrine, recommended significant expansion of aid to arrest the deterioration of the situation in the South.[11] The Military Assistance and Advisory Group, which was established to support the French after the outbreak of the Korean War, was raised to a Military Assistance Command, Vietnam, to direct the rapidly rising level of American involvement, with the amount of military aid doubling and the number of advisers tripling in the first couple of years of the Kennedy administration.[12] The strategic hamlet program developed by the legendary British counterinsurgency guru Sir Robert Thompson was adopted to isolate the people in fortified settlements so that the Vietcong would not have access to food, recruits, and intelligence—removing the guerrilla fish from the water nourishing a people's war.[13] The program was better suited, however, to the Emergency in the Malay Peninsula, where it got its fame. There the predominantly ethnic Chinese guerrillas were trying to survive in the alien waters of the Malay people. American observers ruefully noted how the Vietcong seemed to have access to intelligence enabling them to penetrate U.S. military bases, not to mention Vietnamese hamlets.

Meanwhile efforts at "nation building," seeking to transform South Vietnam into a nation-state by developing its economy and political institutions along modern lines, were severely complicated not only by a deteriorating security situation but also by political infighting in the South. The Buddhist majority, alienated from the Catholic-dominated regime, caused repeated crises with its demonstrations and protests, seared into the world's consciousness by dramatic instances of fiery self-immolation by monks. This elicited further repressive measures by the regime, notably raids by special forces under President Ngo Dinh Diem's brother, Ngo Dinh Nhu, on Buddhist pagodas in various cities.[14] In the summer of 1963 the cauldron of instability was further stirred by coup plotting among the South Vietnamese military, who were in contact with, and enjoyed the acquiescence of, U.S. officials. The new American ambassador, Henry Cabot Lodge, the Kennedy-Johnson ticket's vice presidential opponent in 1960 and therefore a source of bilateral cover for the administration's actions, was instructed to support efforts to remove the troublesome Nhu (who was also suspected of pursuing contacts with Hanoi for a possible plan to neutralize the South); failing that, the United States must "face the possibility that Diem himself [could] not be preserved."[15] The plotting in the summer of 1963 fizzled out, but it was revived a couple of months later, again with American complicity. Washington told Lodge that while it did not "wish to stimulate [a] coup," it would not "thwart a change of government or deny economic and military assistance to a new regime."[16] Given the eagerness of Lodge and his Saigon mission to see Diem and family removed from power, this in effect gave the green light to the conspirators. Three weeks before Kennedy's assassination they effected their coup, going so far as to execute Diem and Nhu after their capture in a church following their escape from the presidential palace.

Kennedy's assassination, on 22 November 1963, marked the end of another phase in American involvement in Vietnam. That year had seen a pattern of events that opened prospects for disengagement in a more favorable global geopolitical environment: Kennedy's conciliatory speech at American University in June had cleared the atmosphere of U.S.-Soviet relations; the successful conclusion of the nuclear test ban treaty coupled with the collapse of Sino-Soviet talks that summer indicated Moscow's readiness to give priority to better relations with the West over the needs of the Communist movement; more specifically in the Indochina context, the removal of Diem opened the door to a search for neutralization of South Vietnam, an approach promoted by French President Charles de Gaulle. It is a matter of speculation whether Kennedy would have made a turn away from his administration's deepening commitment to an anti-Communist Saigon regime, though it is not easy to imagine how the momentum toward American involvement would have been reversed or even limited. After all, the removal of the Ngo brothers was not viewed as a way to clear the road toward a Laos-type settlement. What in fact developed was a cycle of deeper involvement in which Hanoi and Washington matched each other's steps in what amounted to a process of "escalating stalemate."

## THE COMMUNISTS' COMMITMENT

Meanwhile, Hanoi was intensifying its commitment to the insurgency in South Vietnam. A North Vietnamese party plenum held in December 1963 identified as "the key point" at that stage the need to "*rapidly strengthen our military forces in order to create a basic change in the balance of forces between the enemy and us in South Vietnam.*" Stressing the necessity of defeating the enemy's military forces in order to achieve victory in the revolution, the plenum underscored that "*armed struggle plays a direct and decisive role.*"[17]

This emphasis on armed struggle was also reflected in Hanoi's drift toward Beijing in the Sino-Soviet competition. In mid-1963 an article in Hanoi's ideological journal *Hoc tap* by General Nguyen Chi Thanh, a southerner and member of the North Vietnamese party's Politburo, stressed the North's crucial and integral role in the insurgency: "The powerful North Vietnam and the revolutionary movement of the South Vietnamese people are mutually complementary and must be closely coordinated." The issue of the role of revolutionary violence, a key topic in the Sino-Soviet dispute, was addressed in the article's assertion that if fear that "firm opposition to US imperialism would touch off a nuclear war, then the only course left would be to compromise with and surrender to US imperialism."[18] Signaling its approval, Beijing republished the article.

No less a figure than Le Duan, the Vietnam Workers Party secretary-general, weighed in on the Chinese side, scorning "some people" who placed détente over other goals. Speaking at the December plenum, he indicated that there were elements in the Hanoi leadership who had "come under the influence of modern revisionism"—the code word for the Soviet leadership.[19] The next month Le Duan led a delegation—which included fellow Politburo member Le Duc Tho, later to be Henry Kissinger's interlocutor at the secret Paris negotiations—on a visit to Moscow. Tellingly, the announcement on the results of the visit said that the two sides had a "frank and useful exchange of views"—a frigid formulation signaling significant differences.[20]

While Hanoi was tilting toward Beijing at a time of intensifying Sino-Soviet conflict, Khrushchev was abandoning his balancing act aimed at containing the dispute with Mao and maintaining influence in the radical Asian wing of the Communist movement at the same time as he pursued détente with the West. Now the Soviet leader was moving to disengage from Indochina, press the dispute with China to the breaking point, and give clear priority to management of superpower relations. This trend was one of the policies that his successors tried to reverse after ousting him in October 1964.

## INTRODUCTION OF U.S. TROOPS

The potential opening to a search for a settlement in the last year of the cruelly shortened Kennedy administration not having been taken, the new Johnson administration, composed largely of holdovers, moved ahead resolutely on the road of escalation. Four days after the assassination, a National Security Council memorandum accepted the premises of U.S. involvement in defining the purpose as being "to assist the people and Government [of South Vietnam] to win their contest against the externally directed and supported Communist conspiracy."[21] One of the premises underlying the logic of escalation was that the "provisional" line established by the 1954 accords for a regrouping of military forces was now a border between sovereign states. Another was that failure to maintain the independence of South Vietnam would severely damage American credibility, thereby undermining the global containment policy and eroding the U.S. security structure. Accordingly, the Johnson administration stepped up the counterinsurgency campaign—covert operations against North Vietnam including intelligence overflights, bombing of Laos to impede the supply pipeline along the Ho Chi Minh Trail, commando raids along the coast—all in the hope that "progressively escalating pressure" combined with warnings of potential devastation of the North would compel Hanoi to end the insurgencies in South Vietnam and Laos.[22]

The administration seized on highly questionable events in the Gulf of Tonkin—the waters washing North Vietnam's coastline—in August 1964 to take further steps on the path of escalation. Washington claimed that in two murky incidents in international waters, North Vietnamese torpedo boats had fired at American destroyers, neither of which was damaged. (The Democratic Republic of Vietnam [DRV] defense minister during the war, General Vo Nguyen Giap, reportedly told his counterpart, Robert McNamara, in 1995 that the first attack was ordered by a local commander, not Hanoi, and that the second one "never occurred." A top secret internal history by the U.S. National Security Agency, released to the public in November 2005, said that 90 percent of the intercepts of North Vietnamese communications relevant to the second incident were omitted from the documents sent to policymakers, resulting in "deliberately skewed" evidence.[23]) Seeing what it wanted to see, the Johnson administration ordered retaliatory air strikes against the North and secured carte blanche from Congress—the Gulf of Tonkin Resolution—to undertake "all necessary measures to repel any armed attacks against the forces of the United States and to prevent further aggression."[24] Whatever signal of military resolve this action conveyed, the resolution, adopted unanimously in the House of Representatives and with only two dissents in the Senate, provided domestic cover for Johnson, who was under fire from his presidential campaign opponent, Barry Goldwater, for failing to take strong enough action in Vietnam. LBJ simply pocketed the resolution and did not expand the war further at this time, disavowing interest in a "wider war" and portraying Goldwater as a warmonger. His landslide victory that November, however, set the stage for the decisive moves up the ladder of escalation in the next year.

With the political and military situation deteriorating in South Vietnam, Washington envisaged a program consisting of two phases of gradually intensifying air strikes: The first phase would consist of action against infiltration routes in Laos and reprisal attacks after provocative acts by the Vietcong; the second, after the Saigon government had become more effective or could "only be kept going by stronger action," would proceed to a progressively expanded air campaign against the North, including possibly mining of its ports and a naval blockade.[25] It was only a matter of time before events offered the opportunity for deeper American involvement.

This opportunity appeared with a Vietcong attack on an American military base at Pleiku, which, as it happened, coincided with a visit to South Vietnam by the holdover national security adviser, McGeorge Bundy. In a memorandum for the president prepared

### CONGRESS APPROVES ACTION TO REPEL ATTACKS: THE GULF OF TONKIN RESOLUTION

Whereas naval units of the Communist regime in Vietnam . . . have deliberately and repeatedly attacked United States naval vessels lawfully present in international waters, and have thereby created a serious threat to international peace; and

Whereas these attacks are part of a deliberate and systematic campaign of aggression that the Communist regime in North Vietnam has been waging against its neighbors and the nations joined with them in the collective defense of their freedom; and

Whereas the United States is assisting the peoples of Southeast Asia to protect their freedom and has no territorial, military or political ambitions in that area, . . . be it Resolved . . . That the Congress approves and supports the determination of the President, as Commander in Chief, to take all necessary measures to repel any armed attack against the forces of the United States and to prevent further aggression.

The United States regards as vital to its national interest and to world peace the maintenance of international peace and security in Southeast Asia.

U.S. Congress, Gulf of Tonkin Resolution, August 1964.

en route home, Bundy laid out the rationale for a policy of "sustained reprisal" against the DRV, reemphasizing the key reason for American involvement: that U.S. international prestige and influence were "directly at risk" in Vietnam.[26] Bundy frankly acknowledged the Vietcong's "astonishing" tenacity, a trait that amazed the Americans. (General Taylor, for example, called their ability to rebuild their units and maintain morale one of the "mysteries of this guerrilla war."[27]) The former Harvard dean explained the "overriding" importance of combating "a widespread belief that we do not have the will and force and patience and determination to take the necessary action and stay the course."[28] In an annex to his report, Bundy made clear that this belief resided "in the minds of the South Vietnamese and in the minds of the Viet Cong cadres," which were the "immediate and critical targets" of the American campaign.[29] Bundy minced no words—in this secret document—in asserting that the policy being enunciated had been developed "in the days just before" the attack on Pleiku, which had created "an ideal opportunity" for initiating the policy.[30] Such were the origins of the air campaign against the North, code name Rolling Thunder.

The steps to escalating involvement soon began. Two detachments of Marines landed in South Vietnam in March 1965, at first to provide security for U.S. installations but soon assigned to counterinsurgency operations in surrounding areas—the enclave strategy. This in turn led to a strategy of "search and destroy," associated with General William Westmoreland, the U.S. commander in Vietnam, and aimed at "attriting" the enemy to the point where the South could be pacified and Hanoi would be compelled to negotiate on terms acceptable to Washington. Meanwhile, the impact of the growing American presence was complemented by the stabilization of Saigon's political situation when Young Turks in the military seized power and ended the chaotic period of revolving-door coups and countercoups. General Nguyen Van Thieu became commander of the armed forces, Air Marshal Nguyen Cao Ky the prime minister, the two later becoming president and vice president, respectively, after controversial elections in 1967. Thieu's position became progressively stronger, to the point that he was later able to impede the Nixon administra-

## SECRET BUNDY MEMO PLANS "SUSTAINED REPRISAL" AGAINST NORTH VIETNAM

The situation in Vietnam is deteriorating, and without new U.S. action defeat appears inevitable. . . . There is still time to turn it around, but not much. . . .

We believe that the best available way of increasing our chance of success in Vietnam is the development and execution of a policy of *sustained reprisal* against North Vietnam—a policy in which air and naval action against the North is justified by and related to the whole Viet Cong campaign of violence and terror in the South. . . .

We emphasize that our primary target in advocating a reprisal policy is the improvement of the situation in *South* Vietnam. Action against the North is usually urged as a means of affecting the will of Hanoi to direct and support the VC. We consider this an important but longer-range purpose. The immediate and critical targets are in the South—in the minds of the South Vietnamese and in the minds of the Viet Cong cadres. (emphasis in original)

McGeorge Bundy memorandum for President Johnson, 7 February 1965, in U.S. Department of State, *Foreign Relations of the United States, 1964–1968*, vol. 2, *Vietnam* (Washington, DC: U.S. Government Printing Office, 1996), 175.

tion's efforts to negotiate an extrication of the United States from the Vietnam quagmire. An even more significant measure of the importance of the stabilized leadership in Saigon can be found in the pertinacity with which Hanoi insisted on Thieu's removal as a fundamental negotiating demand. In at least this important respect, the American intervention had a meaningful effect in reversing a seriously deteriorating situation produced by political instability in the South.

## INTERNATIONAL COMMUNIST POLITICS

The new stage of American involvement took place at a time of significant changes in the international Communist movement. In fact, the two developments intersected dramatically in February 1965, four months after Khrushchev's ouster, when Premier Aleksey Kosygin (who with the party chief, Leonid Brezhnev, and the head of state, Nikolay Podgornyy, composed the new leadership troika) visited Hanoi as the bombs from Rolling Thunder were beginning to fall on the North. In the joint communiqué on the visit, Moscow pledged to "strengthen the defense capacity" of the DRV,[31] and later that summer the two sides signed an agreement providing for substantial military and economic assistance, including advanced weaponry now needed to combat the U.S. air assault. Also during this period, the new Soviet leadership signaled its deepening political involvement by permitting the Vietcong to open a mission in Moscow and endorsing Hanoi's four-point proposal in April for a Vietnam settlement.[32] These moves gave substance to the post-Khrushchev Kremlin's line of united action, which was intended to reverse the erosion of Soviet influence in Asia, reduce the intensity of the rivalry with China, and use aid to the Vietnamese comrades as a fulcrum for strengthening Moscow's hand in determining the outcome of the Vietnam conflict.

Chinese reaction to the new Soviet approach was somewhat ambiguous for a while. An authoritative PRC Government Statement on 9 February condemning the onset of Rolling Thunder warned that the DRV "is a member of the socialist camp and all other socialist countries have the unshirkable international obligation to support and assist it with actual deeds." Five days later, on the fifteenth anniversary of the Sino-Soviet treaty of alliance, the party organ *People's Daily* trumpeted that the two countries "will inevitably fight shoulder to shoulder" against "all aggressors who venture to invade the socialist camp." The Chinese leaders, in an anniversary message to their Kremlin counterparts, declared that the bombing of North Vietnam was "not only an aggression against the DRV, but also an aggression against the entire socialist camp."[33] Thus, Beijing seemed to be taking a line consonant with Moscow's call for united action.

In another move to lay aside the ideological competition with the Chinese in the interest of united action, the post-Khrushchev leadership postponed indefinitely the preparations that the deposed Kremlin leader had put in motion to convene a new international Communist conference that would isolate Beijing. What had been touted as a "preparatory" meeting was postponed for three months and diluted to a "consultative" session that effectively shelved the project until it could be revived at a "suitable" time. There had thus been a detour from what under Khrushchev was going to be a road to full schism.

The Chinese, however, were not quite receptive to Moscow's irenic gestures. A high-powered delegation under Zhou Enlai had attended the Bolshevik anniversary celebrations in the Kremlin a few weeks after Khrushchev's ouster, but Beijing concluded dismissively that the new Soviet leadership was committed to practicing "Khrushchevism without Khrushchev." The Chinese were not appeased by the shelving of the schismatic international party conference: The new Soviet leaders had simply "taken over Khrushchev's revisionism and splitting lock, stock, and barrel, and they have carried out his behest for a divisive meeting very faithfully."[34] As for Moscow's call to eschew polemics, Beijing insisted that it would continue its campaign without abatement. Indeed, Moscow's united-action offer became a central target of Chinese vituperation, with a polemical assault coming on the heels of Kosygin's Asian tour. Chinese suspicions over Moscow's intentions were fanned rather than assuaged by the post-Khrushchev leadership's approach, thus greatly complicating the Soviet aid program for North Vietnam. The Chinese claimed later that year, after a debate over how to respond to the growing crisis to their south (see Chapter 10), that Kosygin stressed to them en route to Hanoi in February the need to help the United States "find a way out of Vietnam." This would become a motif in Beijing's criticism of the Soviet line for the next few years.

## ESCALATING STALEMATE

The impact of the American intervention and a stabilized leadership structure in Saigon having staved off the collapse that had seemed imminent, Washington may have believed it had found a strategy for repelling the Communists' campaign to unify the country under their control. With more U.S. troops pouring into the country, General Westmoreland was authorized in mid-1965 to "commit U.S. troops to combat independent of or in conjunction with" Saigon's forces.[35] Another fateful step had been taken, an escalating American involvement that gradually assumed the burden of the fighting in an open-ended commitment.

There were two inherent problems facing this strategy. One was that the enemy could also move up the ladder of escalation. An estimated two hundred thousand North Vietnamese reached draft age each year, enabling Hanoi to replace its losses and match Washington's commitment of rising troop levels.[36] Infiltration from the North exceeded five thousand men a month by 1966.[37] The DRV's war-making capacity was greatly augmented by aid from its patrons to the north. The Soviets supplied modern weapons, such as antiaircraft batteries and missiles, and several thousand Soviet technicians participated in operating this vital equipment. The Chinese were a major presence, with several hundred thousand troops providing logistical and engineering support and helping to maintain supply lines.[38] According to Kosygin, in 1965 the Chinese even offered to dispatch troops to Vietnam to engage in the fighting but were rebuffed by Hanoi.[39]

The other problem was that by assuming the burden of fighting, the United States created a dependence that eventually ill served its South Vietnamese allies. When the Americans finally did depart, they left behind an extensively equipped South Vietnamese army and a stabilized leadership, circumstances in which Saigon would seem to have a good chance of staying out of the Communists' grasp. When the crunch came, however, and American support was constrained by domestic factors, the South Vietnamese armed forces crumbled rapidly and ignominiously.

The reality of the stalemate was impressed brutally on the American consciousness with the Communists' Tet Offensive, which began at the end of January 1968. What has been depicted as a "massive, coordinated assault against the major urban areas" of the South was punctuated by penetration of the U.S. Embassy compound in Saigon and seizure of the ancient Citadel in Hue, seat of the Vietnamese emperors. Hue, the scene of particularly vicious fighting, was not retaken until after almost three weeks. The offensive failed in its maximum goal of sparking a general uprising, but it had a huge psychological impact in demonstrating how strong and resilient the Communists had remained three years after the introduction of American combat units and the ever-rising troop levels. According to the chairman of the U.S. Armed Forces Chiefs of Staff, General Earle Wheeler, Tet had been "a very near thing" and had inflicted "a severe setback" on the pacification program, with the Vietcong now "to a large extent" controlling the countryside.[40] The effect was to call into question the achievements of American intervention and the prospects for overcoming the stalemate by further injection of troops. Would the United States envisage a massive presence in Vietnam in perpetuity in the face of rising discontent on the home front? Or would it expand the war geographically, at the risk of a repetition of the Korean experience and Chinese intervention?

Tet proved to be a fundamental turning point for the Johnson administration. Wheeler's assessment came after consultations with Westmoreland, who called for an increase of more than two hundred thousand troops and an offensive strategy that would involve amphibious attacks north of the demilitarized zone (DMZ) and actions against the sanctuaries in Laos and Cambodia. The latter actions in fact would be undertaken by the next administration, but Johnson had now lost his appetite for the battle. Secretary of Defense McNamara having been eased out, with his doubts about the war remaining under public wraps (until he issued his mea culpa years later[41]), his successor, Clark Clifford, ordered a searching reevaluation of policy on Vietnam. The realization was now setting in that further escalation would not succeed in eroding Hanoi's determination or its capacity for sustaining its campaign to unify Vietnam. The time had come for a serious attempt to pursue negotiations.

## PURSUIT OF NEGOTIATIONS

Hanoi had made it clear that unification was a goal no less sacred to its cause than the quest for independence that had animated its struggle against the French. Washington, however, regarded the division of Vietnam as a line to be defended in the Cold War. Each side thus had huge stakes in the outcome of the struggle to determine the political future of South Vietnam. Their goals seemed irreconcilable, but the escalating stalemate, punctuated by the psychological impact of Tet, pushed them to the negotiating table as the only way out of the impasse.

Another factor was becoming an important part of the calculus: the rising salience of the Vietnam War in American politics. The escalation of American involvement had been accompanied by growing protests, first mainly within the academic world, but in the wake of Tet the effects began to be felt in an area dear to President Johnson's heart, elections. Dovish Senator Eugene McCarthy gained a surprisingly high vote in the first of the 1968 presidential primaries, New Hampshire, and this was followed by Senator Robert Kennedy's entry into the contest for the Democratic nomination. Johnson threw in the towel, dramatically, by announcing in a television address on 31 March that he would not seek another term. Seeking to entice Hanoi into negotiations, he declared that the bombing of North Vietnam would be confined to the area just above the DMZ and offered to end all the bombing "if our restraint is matched by restraint in Hanoi." He said the United States was ready to talk about peace at anytime and any place. Within days Hanoi agreed to hold talks, which began in May but deadlocked over North Vietnamese insistence on an unconditional bombing halt and American demands for reciprocity by a reduction of the insurgency in the South. Indeed, the two sides haggled at length over the shape of the negotiating table and other procedural issues, raising the prospect of a stalemate on the negotiating front, at least until a new president could make decisive moves toward a settlement.

In order to break the deadlock, Johnson announced on 31 October, only days before the presidential election, that the bombing would be halted unilaterally. Saigon objected to proposed four-party talks including the Vietcong, but after Richard Nixon's electoral victory, President Thieu agreed to send representatives to the Paris talks. (There has been controversy over whether Nixon's representatives connived with Thieu to delay assent to the talks until after the election in order to prevent the Democratic candidate, Hubert Humphrey, from reaping any benefit from the breakthrough.) The scene was now set for the new administration to pursue what it had touted as a "secret plan" for ending the war.

The architect of the plan, the Harvard foreign affairs specialist Henry Kissinger, had written an article for *Foreign Affairs* before Nixon's inauguration (in fact, Kissinger had been Nelson Rockefeller's adviser during the latter's unsuccessful try at the nomination) outlining an approach to Vietnam negotiations. Kissinger in effect rejected the premise of American involvement as being required by the containment policy, acknowledging that Washington may have overstated the stakes in Vietnam, but he pressed another line to justify hanging tough: that "the commitment of five hundred thousand Americans has settled the issue of the importance of Vietnam." According to this line of reasoning, the task now facing the United States was to extricate itself from the quagmire with a minimum impact on its global position. Any solution other than ending American involvement "honorably" could "unloose forces that would complicate the prospects of international order."[42] "Whatever our original war aims," Kissinger later wrote, "by 1969 our credibility abroad, the reliability of our commitments, and our domestic cohesion were alike jeopardized by a struggle in a country as far away from the North American continent as our globe permits."[43]

The new administration's approach led to abandonment of the vain hope for mutual withdrawal, by North Vietnamese as well as Americans, from the South. It also lent an aspect of ambiguity to Washington's claim that the line of division drawn by the 1954 Geneva accords was a territorial boundary between independent nation-states; allowing a foreign army to remain in South Vietnam would vitiate that premise. The Nixon administration sought to reverse the process of American escalation while strengthening the Saigon regime so that it could contest with the Communists the political future of the South. This meant that instead of the Americanization of the war, as pursued by the previous administration, Washington would now adopt a policy of "Vietnamization" that would permit American withdrawal without serious damage to U.S. credibility.

The new policy was an application of a strategy that became known as the Nixon Doctrine. First introduced in a rambling press conference on Guam in mid-1969, then elaborated in a television address in November, the strategy rested on three principles: The United States would honor its treaty commitments, thus maintaining the alliance structure of containment; it would provide a strategic shield against a threat by a nuclear power against a country allied to Washington or one whose survival was vital to U.S. security; and "in cases involving other types of aggression" it would furnish military and economic assistance, but the country directly threatened would be expected "to assume the primary responsibility of providing the manpower for its defense." It was the third element that defined Vietnamization. Nixon declared that his administration had a plan for a complete withdrawal of ground troops from Vietnam and their replacement by South Vietnamese forces "on an orderly scheduled timetable." He warned, prophetically as it turned out, that if "increased enemy action jeopardizes our remaining forces in Vietnam, I shall not hesitate to take strong and effective measures to deal with that situation"—what became the intensified bombing and the mining of DRV ports.[44]

The administration complemented the withdrawal plan with a second, more authoritative negotiating track in Paris. In addition to the ongoing publicized talks, Kissinger met secretly with Xuan Thuy, the functionary who represented the DRV at the talks, and, more significantly, with Politburo member Le Duc Tho, the "special adviser" who could actually negotiate and would rendezvous in Paris with Nixon's adviser to explore each side's real positions. Kissinger also conferred in Washington with the Soviet ambassador, Anatoly Dobrynin, in the hope of enlisting Soviet pressure on Hanoi.

Removal of the demand for mutual withdrawal from South Vietnam may have been a necessary condition for a settlement, but it did not prove sufficient until a rocky four years of the Nixon administration had been traversed. As Kissinger learned from a secret meeting with Xuan Thuy in the first year (stopping over in Paris after accompanying Nixon on the trip that included the Guam press conference adumbrating the Nixon Doctrine), Hanoi demanded fulfillment of two conditions, one military and the other political, which it insisted were integrally linked. The military issue required a complete American withdrawal; the political demand was for removal of the top Saigon leadership and its replacement by a coalition of the Provisional Revolutionary Government, or PRG (as the National Liberation Front was now called), and elements of the Saigon regime favoring "peace, independence and neutrality"—a formula hardly reassuring to anyone familiar with Communist behavior in Cold War coalition arrangements. The Communists held a particularly strong card in these negotiations: the American prisoners of war, now hostages to Hanoi's demands. Even unilateral American withdrawal would not secure release of the POWs or produce a settlement.[45]

In Kissinger's view, to overthrow the Thieu government would be to do for the Communists what they could not do for themselves and "an act of dishonor that would mortgage America's position for a long time to come." Hanoi's demand on this point remained "the single and crucial issue that deadlocked all negotiations" until Hanoi withdrew it in October 1972.[46] The problem now facing Washington was how to break the linkage of the two issues and thus permit an American withdrawal along with the POWs without dismantling the Thieu government.

## NEW ESCALATION AMID DE-ESCALATION

Vietnamization and the progressive withdrawal of American ground troops was de-escalation in one sense, but there was another sense in which the Nixon administration intensified the military pressure. Indeed, the two were related: Washington perceived an urgent need to inhibit Hanoi's opportunities for exploiting the receding American presence. This new form of U.S. escalation took two forms: expanded operations into areas neighboring Vietnam and heavier bombing of the North. A political risk attended these moves, however, by provoking sharpened domestic criticism and doubts about the administration's bona fides in pursuing an exit from the conflict, not to mention the continuing casualties the Americans incurred even as troop withdrawals were taking place.

One form of the new escalation consisted in a widening of the war into the adjacent countries of Cambodia and Laos in an effort to cut the supply lines, the Ho Chi Minh Trail, from North Vietnam and remove Communist sanctuaries along the South Vietnamese border. In the spring of 1970, after Prince Sihanouk had been overthrown by an anti-Communist junta headed by General Lon Nol, Nixon ordered an "incursion" into Cambodia by South Vietnamese and U.S. forces to attack the sanctuaries, in particular to remove Hanoi's "nerve center," the Central Office for South Vietnam, which was said to be the headquarters directing the Communists' military activities in the South. In one of Nixon's most quoted—and derided—statements justifying his decisions in the war, the president offered a stark portrayal of what was at stake: "If when the chips are down, the world's most powerful nation acts like a pitiful giant, the forces of totalitarianism and anarchy will threaten free nations and free institutions throughout the world."[47] That was an odd echo of the Truman Doctrine of 1947!

Sihanouk's ouster ended the policy of neutralism he had adopted in the mid-1950s and had pursued precariously as the Vietnam War flared again in the 1960s. He had tolerated North Vietnamese sanctuaries inside his country and acquiesced in the secret American bombing begun early in the Nixon administration, but these activities had been limited to the less-populated areas along the South Vietnamese border. Now, however, the Vietnamese Communists were driven deep into Cambodian territory, and that country became embroiled in a conflict that ended with the triumph of the murderous Khmer Rouge—which at this time were supported by Hanoi—and the ensuing killing fields, which claimed between two and three million people. Sihanouk himself took refuge in Beijing, which sponsored a united front of forces opposed to the U.S. presence and the pro-U.S. regimes of Indochina. Also formed was the National Front of Kampuchea, which joined Sihanouk and some nationalist Cambodian elements with the Khmer Rouge.[48]

The incursion aroused an enraged reaction in America, and demonstrations became even more massive after a confrontation with Ohio National Guard troops resulted in the killing of four students at Kent State University. Congress joined the fray by overwhelmingly voting to rescind the Gulf of Tonkin Resolution of 1964, and there were attempts to legislate restrictions on the administration's conduct of the war. Nixon's decision to broaden the war into Cambodia may have bought valuable time for the disengagement process, as intended. In Kissinger's account, the Saigon regime "needed time to consolidate and improve its forces," while Hanoi's "offensive potential had to be weakened by slowing down its infiltration and destroying its supplies. It was a race between Vietnamization, American withdrawal, and Hanoi's offensive."[49] It also served, however, to constrict the administration's freedom of action in the face of rising domestic discontent and the American people's loss of patience.

The need to buy time for Vietnamization was also adduced for another operation across South Vietnam's border, this time into Laos in early 1971. After the ouster of Sihanouk and the closing by his successors of the port of Sihanoukville—a conduit for supplies from the DRV to its forces in South Vietnam—the Ho Chi Minh Trail along Laos's border with Vietnam became even more essential to Hanoi's logistical effort. Anticipating an increased effort to prepare for a major offensive during the election year of 1972, Washington sought to preempt this move by a cross-border drive by Saigon's troops with U.S. air support—the United States being prevented from using its ground troops by a congressional ban imposed after the Cambodia incursion. The South Vietnamese troops incurred severe losses before withdrawing after six weeks of heavy fighting.[50] The operation may not have been a reassuring test of Vietnamization but was deemed by Kissinger to have disrupted the supply system enough to enable the allies "just barely" to blunt the major Communist offensive launched the next spring.[51]

## CHINESE REACTION

In addition to the domestic fallout, Washington had to ride out harsh reaction from Beijing at a time when the two sides were engaged in their delicate dance toward a new relationship (see Chapter 10). Citing the incursion into Cambodia, Beijing canceled the Sino-American ambassadorial talks scheduled for 20 May 1970 in Warsaw, in the process expressing solidarity with the anti-U.S. forces in Indochina and implicitly presenting a contrast with Moscow's uninterrupted talks with the United States on strategic arms control. (In another contrast, Moscow recognized the Lon Nol government in Phnom Penh.) The Chinese used that date instead to issue a rare statement by Mao (the first in more than two years) with a resounding title, "People of the World, Unite and Defeat the U.S. Aggressors and All Their Running Dogs." Five days later Beijing signed a special aid agreement with the DRV, the first one supplementing the annual aid accords and the first one specifying military as well as economic aid.[52] Yet, notwithstanding these moves to exploit the storm of protests engulfing the Nixon administration at home and abroad, Beijing pulled its punches and even took conciliatory measures designed to keep open the door to better relations with Washington.

Beijing's reaction to the operation in Laos in 1971, though on this occasion lacking the flourish of another statement by Mao, was notably pointed about the danger posed to Chinese interests. For the first time in years directly linking China's security to military developments in Indochina, Beijing warned against "spreading the flames of war" to China's doorstep. Zhou led a delegation with a strong military representation on a visit to Hanoi, where he pledged that China would "take all necessary measures, not flinching even from the greatest national sacrifices" to deter the United States—a warning of intervention that had not been voiced in recent years. Still another supplementary aid agreement was signed with Hanoi.[53] Yet again, however, Beijing tempered its warning to Washington against going too far in Indochina by pronouncing the situation there as being "unprecedentedly" fine, as if to say that there was no reason why Sino-American rapprochement could not proceed so long as Washington gave priority to this higher strategic interest.

## CONTINUED NEGOTIATIONS

Hanoi was pressing for U.S. withdrawal on a certain date combined with decapitation of the Saigon leadership structure, to be replaced by a three-part coalition consisting of the PRG, neutralists, and elements from the Saigon government other than the top leaders. Nixon countered with a proposal, disclosed in a speech on 7 October 1970, calling for a standstill cease-fire along with a halt to all U.S. bombing, a total U.S. withdrawal, and a political settlement, though not one meeting the "patently unreasonable" demand for dismantling the Saigon leadership.[54] In the secret talks, the administration made crucial concessions that largely satisfied two of the essential conditions set by Hanoi for a settlement: offering to set a date for total withdrawal and dropping the demand for *mutual* withdrawal, provided there was no further North Vietnamese infiltration. A political settlement would be left to the peoples of Indochina. This proposal, given to the DRV on 31 May 1971, "marked a turning point" in Vietnam negotiations, according to Kissinger, and was "in its essence" what Hanoi accepted sixteen months later.[55] Early the following year, Nixon went public about the secret contacts, revealing that there had been twelve such meetings. He cited his willingness to set a deadline for withdrawal and President Thieu's willingness to step down a month before internationally supervised elections for a new Saigon government.[56]

Next, Nixon found a dramatic stage on which to raise the pressure on Hanoi to meet his negotiating terms: the trip to China in February. In the Shanghai communiqué, the United States cited its latest proposals (formally joined by Saigon); the Chinese routinely expressed support for the PRG's position, including the "two key problems"—meaning the political and military issues that Hanoi had insisted were inseparable and interdependent. Beijing's support, however, was less than would have been seen by the casual eye (and Hanoi would hardly have been watching casually), for the Chinese had been interpreting Nixon's withdrawal moves from Vietnam as an opportunity for improved Sino-American relations. Thus, the Chinese had resisted explicit endorsement of Hanoi's insistence on the inseparability of the military and political issues; rather, they treated U.S. military withdrawal as the basis for a settlement.[57] In the Shanghai communiqué, the United States offered to reduce its military presence on Taiwan "as the tension in the area diminishes." In other words, a Vietnam settlement would serve Beijing's fundamental interests, and Hanoi's own interests would not be allowed to interfere.[58]

Hanoi could read the geopolitical writing on the wall and decided to use the U.S. election year to attempt a military breakthrough to shore up its negotiating position—what Kissinger has called the Communists' "last throw of the dice" before serious negotiations could proceed. The DRV launched a major offensive in the spring of 1972, with three divisions pouring across the DMZ and others entering South Vietnam from Laos and Cambodia.[59] As for the implications for the United States, Kissinger perceived huge geopolitical stakes: A collapse in Vietnam would put American foreign policy "in jeopardy," would render the U.S. negotiating position at the upcoming Moscow summit "pathetically weak," and might lead China to "reconsider the value of American ties."[60] In short, a failure in Vietnam would undermine the triangular structure of global politics that the Nixon administration had labored to construct.

Kissinger went to Moscow in April for secret talks (revealed only after his return) to prepare for the summit and to negotiate an agreement on limiting strategic arms (the negotiations known as the Strategic Arms Limitation Talks, or SALT), which he said was largely completed during this visit. He also sought Soviet pressure on the DRV to restrain its military offensive or at least to obtain Moscow's acquiescence in forceful U.S. counteractions. These measures, announced by Nixon on 8 May, crossed a threshold that Washington had theretofore avoided: mining of Haiphong harbor and a naval blockade of the DRV combined with massive bombing of the North. The intended effect was to increase pressure on Hanoi to turn to serious negotiations by constraining its military offensive: The Soviet supply pipeline would be cut, and bombing of rail and road lines from China would hinder efforts to circumvent the blockade.[61] Washington accompanied these military actions with moves in the triangular arena that appealed to Moscow and Beijing to place higher strategic interests over their obligations to Hanoi. In both the speech and a private communication to Brezhnev, Nixon observed that Washington and Moscow were "on the threshold of a new relationship" as they neared "major agreements" on nuclear arms limitation and other issues. He complemented this move with a letter to the Chinese saying that "the short-term perspectives of a smaller nation" should not "be allowed to threaten all the progress we have made."[62] With Nixon being welcomed to Moscow despite the punishment its guest was inflicting on North Vietnam, the geopolitical geometry was putting Hanoi into a tight box. This was brought further home to Hanoi by a visit from Soviet President Podgornyy to brief the North Vietnamese on the Moscow summit; meanwhile, Kissinger went to Beijing to brief the Chinese, emphasizing to Zhou that Washington's relationship with Beijing "is infinitely more important for the future of Asia than what happens in Phnom Penh, in Hanoi, or in Saigon."[63] Hanoi now had to face the sobering implications that the big powers' triangular politics held for its position in the struggle for control of South Vietnam.

Within days of Nixon's departure from the Moscow summit in May, where agreements were reached capping offensive missile launchers—the first time the superpowers had agreed to limit strategic arms—and freezing antimissile deployment, Hanoi began to take stock of these realities. Taking note of Nixon's statements in Moscow along with his military measures against North Vietnam, Hanoi plaintively wondered aloud whether its patrons could "distinguish right from wrong" and between "who is one's friend and who is one's foe." Hanoi's anguish was expressed even more pointedly a few months later when the party's daily organ, *Nhan dan*, lamented that Nixon's policies were abetted by those who entered the road of "unprincipled compromise. . . . The imperialists pursue a policy of détente with some big countries" in order to "bully the small countries and stamp out the national liberation movement."[64] Authoritative editorials in August leveled one of the gravest charges in the Marxist lexicon—"opportunism"—at unnamed but unmistakable targets, concluding that the Vietnamese Communists were being subjected to "terrible pressure" not only from the American military actions but also from "tendencies of compromise from outside."[65]

In these circumstances the pressure to come to a negotiated settlement was too powerful for either side to resist, and they moved swiftly toward agreement. Hanoi progressively diluted its demand for a tripartite coalition government in Saigon, and by October had abandoned the project. In September the PRG, which was to have been a member of such a coalition, issued a statement accepting the realities: A political settlement should "proceed from the actual situation that there exist in South Vietnam two administrations, two armies, and other political forces."[66] The Communists acquiesced in what they called "the oft-expressed desire of the American side": a two-stage process consisting of a cease-fire and U.S. withdrawal along with the POWs, to be followed by negotiations on South Vietnam's political future while "the two present administrations in South Vietnam will remain in existence."[67] This was a crucial concession, severing what Hanoi had insisted were the integral "two points," the military issue—U.S. withdrawal—and the political issue—removal of the Saigon leadership in favor of a coalition government. Now a settlement was devised to leave the political evolution to take place after U.S. withdrawal but with the DRV troops remaining in South Vietnam. (This had been the line pressed by Beijing, a major source of Sino-Vietnamese tension as the Chinese moved toward a new relationship with the United States.[68])

Kissinger famously declared in October that "peace is at hand," but Thieu objected to a settlement that left North Vietnamese forces in the South. Nixon sought to appease Thieu by offering his "absolute assurance that if Hanoi fails to abide by the terms of this agreement it is my intention to take swift and severe retaliatory action."[69] Then, when Hanoi reacted angrily to U.S. efforts to change the provisions to meet Thieu's objections, Washington undertook twelve days of intensive B-52 attacks during the latter half of December, the first time those aircraft had been used on a sustained basis over the northern part of the DRV. This was Nixon's last roll of the dice, according to Kissinger, as North Vietnam's spring offensive had been theirs.

## THE PEACE SETTLEMENT AND THE "POSTWAR WAR"

When negotiations resumed in early January 1973, it took only a few days and minor changes for the settlement to reach its final form. Hanoi could see that an easily reelected Nixon had no need to make concessions beyond those already offered when the election was still ahead. As for Saigon, Nixon made it brutally clear to Thieu that he had "irrevocably decided" to proceed with the agreement and gave the hapless South Vietnamese leader a deadline by which to sign on. Thieu met the deadline, Nixon's Inauguration Day.[70] The U.S. presidential election no longer provided leverage for deflecting the administration from its course of withdrawal.

The "Agreement on Ending the War and Restoring Peace in Viet-Nam"[71] reflected the underlying conflict between Hanoi's insistence on a united Vietnam and Washington's demand that the South Vietnamese be free to determine their political future. Thus, the agreement registered U.S. acknowledgment of Vietnam's independence and unity while also containing provisions for the South Vietnamese people to exercise self-determination. The modalities for reconciling these competing demands were as follows:

- After a standstill cease-fire to begin that month, the United States would withdraw all its military personnel along with its POWs.
- The "armed forces of the two South Vietnamese parties" would be permitted to replace unusable arms on a piece-for-piece basis. The "question of Vietnamese armed forces in South Viet-Nam"—a euphemism for the DRV troops in the South—was to be settled by the two South Vietnamese parties.
- The South Vietnamese people would determine their future through "genuinely free and democratic general elections under international supervision." The elections would be organized by a National Council of National Reconciliation and Concord, which was to operate on the basis of unanimity. Reunification of North and South Vietnam was to be carried out on the basis of "discussions and agreements" between the two parts without coercion.

The settlement thus reflected the crucial concessions made by the warring parties in the preceding two years (not the same terms, despite the claim of many critics, as were available earlier, before those concessions). Of special significance for Hanoi, the absence of a requirement for mutual withdrawal served to rectify what must have been seen as a historical mistake: its acquiescence in the regrouping of its forces to the north of the seventeenth parallel in 1954. Hanoi was now determined to retain its capabilities in the South. On the other hand, its demand for the decapitation of the Saigon leadership structure had been successfully resisted; the National Council, by virtue of the requirement of unanimity, was a pale resemblance of the coalition government doggedly pursued by the Communists until the geopolitical pressures deriving from the Nixon summits in 1972 broke their will.

The settlement was a fragile structure, and the land grabbing that took place before its signing continued afterward. It did, however, provide cover for what Washington could call an honorable withdrawal and afforded "a decent interval" before the core issue of the conflict—South Vietnam's political future—was resolved by force of arms. A cohesive

### VIETNAM PEACE ACCORDS LEAVE NORTH'S FORCES IN SOUTH

The question of Vietnamese armed forces in South Viet-Nam shall be settled by the two South Vietnamese parties in a spirit of national reconciliation and concord, equality and mutual respect, without foreign interference, in accordance with the postwar situation. . . .

The reunification of Viet-Nam shall be carried out step by step through peaceful means on the basis of discussions and agreements between North and South Viet-Nam, without coercion or annexation by either party, and without foreign interference. The time for reunification will be agreed upon by North and South Viet-Nam.

Paris Peace accord, 17 January 1973, accessed at www.aiipowmia.com/sea/ppa1973.html.

Saigon leadership possessing large and well-equipped armed forces—the fourth-largest air force on the planet, for instance—seemed to be in a strong position to contest the future of South Vietnam. The U.S. intervention had substantially reversed the conditions that portended an early collapse in the 1960s: a volatile leadership situation, deep-rooted internal discontent, disintegrating authority in the countryside. Hanoi had counted on an unraveling of the Saigon political structure by its demands for a coalition government, but now it faced an adversary with considerable assets to deploy against the Communists.

There was a fatal weakness afflicting the Saigon regime, however. If American intervention had saved it by taking on the burden of the fighting and inflicting massive punishment on the Communists, this also created a dependence that undermined Nixon's program of Vietnamization. Moreover, Nixon's assurance of continuing support to Saigon was undercut by severe domestic constraints, particularly as embodied in the War Powers Act, passed by Congress over Nixon's veto ten months after the signing of the Paris agreement. This legislation required the president to inform Congress within forty-eight hours of deployment of military forces and to withdraw them in sixty days unless given explicit congressional authorization. When the Communists went on the offensive in March 1975, the Saigon regime collapsed precipitately. After vainly trying to retain what had been Cochin China, the southernmost section of Vietnam, Thieu resigned on 21 April. By May Day the Communists were able to fly their flag over Saigon, now renamed Ho Chi Minh City. Meanwhile the Khmer Rouge had entered Phnom Penh, and in August the Pathet Lao seized control of Laos. Indochina was now Communist.

In July 1976 North and South were formally united under the new name of the Socialist Republic of Vietnam. The feared bloodbath after the Communists' triumph did not materialize, but large-scale reeducation camps were established to further subdue the southerners. Another serious strain resulted from the nationalization of private enterprise, hitting hard at the ethnic Chinese community in particular. Massive emigration (the boat people) reflected the depth of discontent with the new rulers. Tensions already present in Sino-Vietnamese relations became further enflamed over various issues, such as treatment of ethnic Chinese, border demarcation, and ownership of islands in the South China Sea. Paralleling these tensions were those between the Vietnamese and the Khmer Rouge. As discussed in Chapter 10, all of this erupted into an invasion of Cambodia by the Vietnamese, followed closely by China's incursion into Vietnam. The Third Indochina War had arrived.

## LESSONS OF VIETNAM

Politicians, like generals (and perhaps scholars), fight the previous war, and the Vietnam War yielded a rich crop of lessons for future conflicts. Among the lessons drawn was that the incrementalism characteristic of the U.S. escalation needed to be replaced by a strategy with clear objectives and the resources and tactics required to meet those objectives (as in the so-called Powell Doctrine, named after the U.S. Armed Forces chief of staff during the first Gulf War, Colin Powell, who had been a junior officer in Vietnam and became secretary of state in 2001). In contrast, the incremental approach was improvisational, taking whatever measures were required to avert immediate defeat. Another lesson was the crucial role of domestic opinion; public support was required to provide staying power and the resources in manpower and materials needed to meet long-term objectives. Prevarication, concealment, and secrecy beyond what is operationally necessary, while serving to sweep problems under the rug and away from public scrutiny in the short term, have a tendency to come back to bite policymakers and undermine the very credibility they were seeking to preserve.

There is also the question of whether the containment policy, applied to Vietnam after the shock of the Communist invasion of South Korea, was too rigid in conception. Was Saigon, as was said in support of intervention, the Berlin of Asia? More broadly, could SEATO be compared to NATO in its implications for U.S. credibility and commitment? The questions suggest their answers, at least in retrospect.

Then there is the matter of the domino theory. Did the intervention buy time for Indochina's neighbors to develop themselves as nation-states and to withstand the Communist insurgencies that threatened to engulf them? Or, as discussed earlier (see Chapter 6), were the circumstances in Vietnam sufficiently different from those in other Southeast Asian countries that there is no reason to assume that developments in those countries would be affected substantially by the success of the Communists in Indochina in gaining power?

Still another way to approach the lessons of Vietnam is to examine the dilemmas that faced policymakers trying to avert the Communist takeover. The lessons mentioned previously need to be examined in the context of these dilemmas.

- Each step of escalation raised the stakes for the United States, thus becoming a self-fulfilling prophesy. As each step raised the stakes, the more important it was to take the next step in order to protect the higher stakes. As Kissinger observed, whatever doubts one might have had in the late 1960s about the wisdom of the intervention, the commitment of more than half a million troops and the loss of thirty-one thousand lives had settled the issue of whether the outcome in Vietnam was important.[72] A similar logic had informed each stage of escalation.
- U.S. administrations were haunted by the specter of the "loss of China," but they felt constrained in the actions they could take in Vietnam by fear of a reprise of the Chinese intervention in the Korean War. Johnson remarked privately that "what they said about us leaving China would just be warming up, compared to what they'd say now."[73] At the same time, policymakers took care to limit the bombing

of North Vietnam and to avoid movements of ground troops that might provoke a Chinese response. As mentioned previously, Beijing reacted sharply when Saigon's troops aided by the United States conducted an operation into Laos in 1971. The Chinese delivered a message that moving the ground war beyond South Vietnam and into a state bordering the PRC could be expanding the war to a point at which their security was endangered.

- The U.S. air war against the North and ground actions in the South were needed to compensate for the Saigon regime's weakness, but each step up the ladder of escalation by Washington could be matched by a corresponding rise in Soviet and Chinese support for the North. With Hanoi able to replenish its supplies and to maintain a steady and even increased flow of infiltration into the South, Washington would need to take still more forceful measures, creating a vicious circle that it sought to escape for years—and then did so only as a result of developments on a global strategic level.
- To achieve military gains, or at least avert defeat, Washington increasingly Americanized the war, but this had the effect of creating South Vietnamese dependency. Then, with gradual U.S. withdrawal and Vietnamization of the ground war, a large and well-equipped South Vietnamese army proved to be psychologically crippled and quickly crumbled under the onslaught of the Communist forces.

The most important lesson, but the most difficult to apply, is the need to subject to critical cross-examination the assumptions underlying intervention; in this case, that loss of Indochina would lead to the fall of other states in Asia and beyond like a row of dominoes, and that it would undermine U.S. credibility. Those assumptions were invalidated after the fact of intervention. As for Johnson's fear of the domestic repercussions of a loss of Indochina in the absence of intervention (as in the "loss of China"), what happened was that intervention was what produced the domestic backlash that drove him out of Washington.

So did the Vietnam War have results that, from a broad geopolitical perspective, redeemed the enormous costs in blood and treasure exacted from its participants and the people in its midst? Even putting aside the dubious proposition that the U.S. intervention bought the time required by the neighboring countries' non-Communist elites to consolidate their new nation-states, did the war have a transforming impact on the international environment by producing a strategic realignment involving the superpowers and China? And did this development play a role in the ending of the Cold War and the demise of the Soviet Union? It is to these issues that we turn in the next two chapters.

# 10 STRATEGIC REALIGNMENT

The Kremlin's post-Khrushchev leadership registered significant gains in its effort to reassert Soviet influence in East Asia by reversing the ousted leader's moves to disengage from Indochina and lead the Chinese out of the international Communist movement. The line of "united action" in support of the Vietnamese comrades appealed not only to Hanoi, a recipient of crucial Soviet assistance, but also to Pyongyang, which like Hanoi had drifted toward the Chinese side in opposition to Khrushchev's "revisionist" policies. Premier Kosygin showed the Soviet flag in a trip in early 1965 to the East Asian Communist capitals; his message was invested with added urgency by the initiation of American bombing of North Vietnam during the visit. Moscow also took care to support its call for an end to ideological conflict by shelving what was to have been a schismatic new international conference of Communist parties (see Chapter 9).

The escalation of the American intervention in Vietnam provided a propitious setting for the new Soviet line and its appeal for a closing of ranks behind the comrades under attack. Here was a new Kremlin leadership, purged of a leader who had become a symbol of irresoluteness toward the imperialist enemies, that was prepared to stand up for the socialist camp's interests and to provide concrete aid to an ally in a time of dire need. Was it not time for the Chinese to reciprocate in kind, to put aside their ideological challenge to Moscow, to repair the damage to bloc unity in the face of pressing geopolitical imperatives? The Chinese leaders would spend much of the year sorting out their answers to these questions.

## THE CHINESE DILEMMA

The Chinese were confronted with a dilemma in this decision making: whether to accept an accommodation with Moscow, and thus risk a reassertion of Soviet influence in an area where it had been seriously eroded by Beijing's ideological challenge; or to reject the Soviet offer, raising the prospect of isolation in the international Communist movement and undercutting the deterrent effect of the Sino-Soviet alliance at a time of rising hostilities on China's southern border. As we have seen, the Chinese had played up themes of mutual security in the socialist camp in February 1965, at the time of the American air attacks on North Vietnam and on the anniversary of the Sino-Soviet treaty. What followed was a pattern of sharp shifts and clashes of line bespeaking leadership debate and reflecting the high stakes involved, not only geopolitically but also in Chinese domestic politics.[1]

Moscow's appeal for an end to polemics had little effect: The ideologues in Beijing returned to the offensive in the wake of Kosygin's Asian tour. They seized upon the innocuous "consultative" conference in Moscow in March—the one that had originally been intended as a "preparatory" meeting for the schismatic international conference envisaged by Khrushchev—to fan the ideological flames by castigating the new Soviet leadership and rejecting its overtures. The anniversary in June of the programmatic "general line" introduced by Beijing in 1963 as an alternative platform for the Communist movement afforded a tailor-made opportunity to sharpen the lines of conflict, both with the Kremlin and within the decision-making elite in Zhongnanhai (the Chinese leadership compound). This came through forcefully in a highly authoritative joint editorial on the anniversary by the CPC's daily organ and its ideological journal:

- The article referred defensively to the "more covert, more cunning, and more dangerous" tactics being followed by the post-Khrushchev leadership. Taking note of the "honeyed" words about unity coming from Moscow, it acknowledged the pressure on Chinese decision making from the escalating Vietnam War by warning that the Kremlin was seeking to capitalize on aspirations for "closer unity of the revolutionary forces in face of the US imperialists' rabid aggression."
- Rebuffing Moscow's appeal to set aside the ideological competition, the editorial posed the question "confronting the Chinese Communists today" as one of whether to carry the fight "against Khrushchev revisionism to the end or whether to stop halfway." The Soviets were "pretending to be quite accommodating," but "we should not be misled by the various guises and tricks of Khrushchev's successors and give up our principled struggle."

Anyone advocating an accommodation with the Soviets was delivered a stern rebuke: "It would be wrong to exercise unprincipled flexibility, to create ambiguity and confusion on questions of principle on the pretext of flexibility." The editorial defined the choice in stark terms: "If we were to abandon our principled stand and accommodate ourselves or yield to the Khrushchev revisionists . . . it would be a grave historical mistake. . . . It is imperative to carry the struggle against Khrushchev revisionism through to the end."[2]

The polemical thrusts of the editorial had several target audiences: the Kremlin and its "cunning" line of united action; the international Communist movement, especially those elements that might be responsive to that line; and also those in the Chinese leadership who might see the advantages of an accommodation with the Soviet Union at a time of expanding warfare south of the border. Though its overtures were being rebuffed by Beijing, Moscow had dealt itself a strong hand in the Communist movement, enabling it to recover ground lost in recent years to the Chinese ideological onslaught. The other East Asian Communist capitals, Hanoi and Pyongyang, now veered back toward the center in the Sino-Soviet dispute; indeed, their resentment of Chinese intransigence at a time when the socialist camp was under siege in Indochina was hardly concealed by the prudent neutrality they felt obliged to project.

The defensiveness that showed through in the editorial's strident language pointed to divided councils in Beijing over the wisdom of the radical, uncompromising stance being propounded. Who among the Chinese leadership might have counseled the flexibility the editorial was so vigorous in rejecting? A likely source would have been the professional military, the group whose institutional interests dictated concern over issues of preparedness for the contingencies posed by developments in Indochina and the implications of the deteriorating alliance with Moscow—an alliance that had been played up in February at the time the United States initiated its sustained air campaign against North Vietnam. (The *People's Daily* editorial on the anniversary of the alliance was titled "Struggle to Safeguard Sino-Soviet Unity." See Chapter 9.) In fact, these concerns were expressed during this period by a key figure in the military establishment, the chief of staff of the People's Liberation Army (PLA), Luo Ruiqing, a Politburo member, whose speeches and statements emphasized the importance of preparedness ("it makes a world of difference whether or not one is prepared once war breaks out") and the deterrent value of the socialist camp (the United States could be deterred "*provided* that we are good at uniting the socialist camp") while warning in urgent terms of a Korea-type war breaking out in Vietnam and spreading to China.[3] Luo in effect was calling for just that flexibility and accommodation the anti-Soviet radicals were denouncing.

The conflicting approaches were thrown into sharp relief by a *People's Daily* commentary on V-E Day, which scorned the "sham unity" offered by "Khrushchev's successors" as designed to abet Soviet-U.S. collaboration at the expense of the Vietnamese comrades. In his major statement on the same occasion Luo had avoided a direct attack on the new Kremlin leadership and its call for unity, referring ambiguously to "revisionists like Khrushchev"; instead he emphasized the central role of the socialist camp comprising a billion people (which, given the population totals of that time, necessarily included both China and the Soviet Union). The *People's Daily* article merely referred offhandedly to "a socialist camp consisting of a number of socialist countries."[4]

It devolved to the defense minister, Lin Biao, who played a highly politicized role in that position, to propound a strategy that would serve several interrelated purposes: maintain and even deepen China's independence of Moscow, avert the danger of war spreading north from Indochina, and thus leave the way clear for Mao to institute his latest campaign to ensure and invigorate his revolutionary mission and legacy. (Lin had been a military hero during the war against Japan and the civil war but had been largely inactive until being tapped to be defense minister in 1959 to restore ideological and political control over the military.) As presented in his celebrated tract on people's war pegged to the anniversary of the defeat of Japan (V-J Day),[5] Lin's strategy was to decouple the Vietnam conflict and China's security, thereby minimizing the danger of becoming embroiled in that war and undercutting the need for better relations with the Soviets. This approach counseled the Vietnamese Communists, facing a rising infusion of American power, to dig in for protracted guerrilla warfare rather than to confront U.S. forces frontally and risk a reprise of the Korean War. It also prescribed a policy of self-reliance for the Vietnamese comrades, who must be ready to carry on the fight independently "even when all material aid from outside is cut off." All but spelling out the message, Lin warned against relying on foreign aid even from socialist countries "which persist in revolution," meaning countries like the PRC and not the Soviet Union.

Western reaction to Lin's strategy statement largely missed the implications of his call for the Vietnamese Communists—and the Chinese—to engage in a low-risk response to the American intervention. Rather than seeing it as an effort to contain the flames of war lest China become involved in another Korean-style conflict, Western perceptions were bewitched by the specter of a Maoist-inspired world revolution sparked by a Communist success in Indochina (the domino theory again). Lin fed this fear by universalizing Mao's doctrine of people's war, with the third world being the "countryside" that would encircle and eventually bring down the "cities," that is, the developed industrial world. In this worldview, unsurprisingly, there was no place for the socialist camp, which was simply left unmentioned by Lin (as a clue to his message, this was like the dog that did not bark in the Sherlock Holmes story).

Luo Ruiqing disappeared from view in late 1965 and was purged, at Lin's instigation, for resisting the injunction to give priority to politics, that is, to place ideology over professionalism.[6] A major policy statement issued in that period undertook to explain the "astonishingly abrupt changes" that were taking place.[7] In a forceful and venomous rejection of Moscow's united-action line, it demanded that "a clear line of demarcation both politically and organizationally" be drawn and any accommodation with the Soviets be foreclosed categorically. Sino-Soviet schism was now complete; the alliance had become an empty shell. The Chinese now entered a period of "great upheaval, great division, and great reorganization," causing "drastic divisions and realignments" in the world.

It can be seen from this discussion that the Vietnam War was a crucial factor in the collapse of the Sino-Soviet alliance. An observer contemplating the development of events in early 1965 might very well have predicted that the escalation of American intervention in Vietnam would cause Hanoi's two big Communist patrons to close ranks at a time of emergency. This seemed all the more likely in that the post-Khrushchev leadership offered to put aside the ideological competition that had pushed the two allies apart earlier in the decade. Moreover, as indicated by the Chinese strategic debate evoked by the new Soviet line in the context of rising hostilities in Indochina, there was a strong current of opinion favoring maintenance of the alliance as a deterrent factor in Washington's decision making. Indeed, there was much concern in the West at the time that American escalation in Vietnam would drive the Communist giants back together, if for no other reason than to maintain a deterrent against a reprise of the Korean War.

Instead, Mao and the radical wing of the Chinese leadership took steps that flouted what seemed like conventional wisdom. It was precisely because of the broad appeal of the new Soviet line that Mao pushed the alliance to the breaking point. Given the considerations discussed earlier, it is ironic that American escalation in Vietnam, far from causing a reconstitution of the Sino-Soviet alliance, caused its final fracture. By the end of 1965 it was an empty shell (though, as will be discussed, it was not formally terminated until the end of its thirty-year term). Beijing embarked on a new mass campaign to erase all traces of Soviet influence; this included politicizing the professional military, an interest group the Soviets had hoped to cultivate. Moscow, dismayed at the rejection of its call for united action and alarmed by Chinese animosity, proceeded to take major steps to fortify its security; a treaty of alliance, clearly aimed at China, was signed with the Mongolian People's Republic at the beginning of 1966, and the Soviets began to amass troops along the Chinese border. What's more, the logic of events led to a transformation of the Sino-American relationship and emergence of a quasi alliance to counterbalance Soviet power. This represented an inversion of the situation at the time U.S. intervention in Vietnam was being designed, a time when President Johnson saw developments there as part of a wider pattern of Chinese expansion. Now China was to be enlisted as a strategic partner to resist an increasingly assertive Soviet Union.

## THE CHINESE CULTURAL REVOLUTION

In 1965, as the debate over China's defense posture was taking place, Beijing announced the abolition of military ranks, signaling a reversal of the PLA's "modernization and regularization" that had been instituted a decade earlier under Soviet guidance, and undercutting Luo's call for preparedness across the spectrum of conventional and nuclear capabilities.[8] Subsequent commentary, pegged to the PLA anniversary on 1 August, underscored the significance of the military's political and ideological role while minimizing the importance of professionalism.[9] The policy conflict at this time was recounted a year later on the PLA anniversary in a *Liberation Army Daily* editorial identifying it as the third of three major struggles between the professional military and Maoist ideological lines since the founding of the PRC. Deriding emphasis on military preparedness as "bourgeois regularization" of military affairs, the editorial stressed Lin Biao's role in strengthening political and ideological work in the PLA.[10]

The politicized and ideologically indoctrinated PLA served as the model institution in the vast upheaval that erupted in the middle of 1966 known as the Great Proletarian Cultural Revolution. This latest mass campaign by Mao, who had retreated to the "second line" of leadership as his colleagues sought to put the country back together again after the ravages of the Great Leap Forward, represented still another attempt to sustain the revolutionary élan that he feared would be dissipated if the country were allowed to lapse into the "revisionist" and "bourgeois" practices of the Soviet Union or the "feudal" habits of old China. The youthful Red Guards, supported by the PLA, were unleashed to humiliate and bring down the party and government apparatus. No less a figure than Mao's top lieutenant, Liu Shaoqi, damned with the sobriquet of "China's Khrushchev," or "the No. 1 person in authority taking the capitalist road," became a victim of an ever-widening purge. (Deng Xiaoping was the "No. 2" revisionist.) Eventually, with the nation spiraling into anarchy and the administrative structure shattered, the PLA was ordered to restore order and take control. Defense Minister Lin himself soared to the top, second only to Mao, and was constitutionally enshrined as Mao's designated successor at the CPC's Ninth Congress in 1969 (the first in more than a decade).

The Cultural Revolution by its very nature was virulently anti-Soviet. In Mao's eyes, relations with Moscow and Chinese domestic politics were virtually indistinguishable; hence his determination to reject Soviet overtures, whatever the cost in international isolation and a degraded deterrent against American power, as he sought to eradicate all traces of Soviet influence in Chinese affairs. In the early years of the Cultural Revolution (which officially lasted from 1966 to 1976, when Mao died and his radical acolytes, the Gang of Four, were arrested), massive demonstrations punctuated the rabid anti-Soviet campaign, and the Soviet embassy came under a virtual siege in February 1967. (At that time the embassy's swimming pool was filled up to serve as a reservoir in case the water supply was cut off.) The Red Guards even changed the name of the street on which the Soviet embassy was located to "Anti-Revisionism Road" (though failing to have the meanings of red and green in traffic lights reversed, on the ground that the Communist color red should denote advancement rather than stopping).

Moscow was not slow to perceive the perils Mao's anti-Soviet campaign portended. It mounted a vigorous propaganda counteroffensive against "Mao Zedong and his group," an anathematizing formula that licensed efforts to unseat the Maoist leadership as usurpers of power. (This formula had been used earlier in the decade against the Albanian leader Enver Hoxha.) It also prepared for more than a war of words: A Treaty of Friendship, Co-operation and Mutual Aid with Moscow's Mongolian satellite in January 1966 permitted the stationing of Soviet troops there, and in the next few years combat troops were transferred to the east in a massive buildup along China's borders that exceeded forty divisions by the end of the decade.

## SYSTEMIC CHANGE IN GEOPOLITICAL RELATIONS

Two developments, far apart geographically, interacted in ways that transformed the geopolitical landscape. One was the Soviet-led invasion of Czechoslovakia in August 1968 to squelch the liberalization movement there that posed grave ideological challenges to the Soviet bloc. The other development was the Nixon administration's moves to disengage from Vietnam and prepare for a post-Vietnam environment in Asia. Beijing's response to these developments, combined with Washington's readiness to explore a new relationship with China, produced powerful systemic effects, setting in motion a sequence of events that led to a major realignment of geopolitical relations.

Beijing bitterly denounced the invasion of Czechoslovakia as a naked display of "social imperialism," meaning imperialist behavior under the banner of socialism. The Chinese had no sympathy for the reform movement known as the Prague Spring, having sharply criticized the far less extensive liberalization pursued by Khrushchev. The significance of the new charge of social imperialism was that the Soviets were now being placed in the enemy camp; they were not just ideological backsliders along the revisionist path. Zhou Enlai underscored this by resurrecting the concept of a socialist camp, which had faded from the Chinese lexicon after the onset of the Cultural Revolution, for the purpose of publicly burying it. Delivering a withering indictment of the Kremlin in a speech at the North Vietnamese embassy on the DRV National Day (2 September), Zhou declared that the Soviet leadership had "long since destroyed the socialist camp which once existed." His reference to the socialist camp in this context was revealingly gratuitous. In the same breath he directly quoted Moscow's own reference not to the socialist camp but to the "socialist community," a more positive term (meaning the panoply of political, economic, and cultural as well as military relations binding the Soviet bloc) favored by the Soviets over one redolent of the Stalinist two-camp era.[11] Why had Zhou injected a reference to a concept that neither Moscow nor Beijing was currently invoking?

The timing and venue of Zhou's statement provide the answer. In the twelve days since the invasion of Czechoslovakia, the North Vietnamese had endorsed the Soviet decision; what is more, they had called it a necessary action to preserve *the socialist camp*. For Hanoi, Moscow's move demonstrated a willingness to sacrifice other interests to defend the socialist camp. Moscow in fact incurred two costs from its decision, though both proved to be temporary: Plans to open strategic arms limitation talks with the United States (to have been announced on what turned out to be the day after the invasion of Czechoslovakia) were derailed and not put back on track for more than a year; and the revived project for another international Communist Party conference to isolate the Chinese had to be shelved (to be mounted finally the following spring after extensive lobbying by the Soviets). Both of those projects being deemed undesirable by Hanoi (which did not send a delegation to the party conclave in Moscow), the Soviet decision to intervene in Czechoslovakia proved Moscow's bona fides in Hanoi's eyes as a defender of the interests of the socialist camp.

It was small wonder, then, that Beijing was infuriated by the North Vietnamese, and that Zhou would use their embassy and national day as the forum to express exasperation at their drift into Moscow's embrace. "It is high time," Zhou thundered, that "all those who cherish illusions about Soviet revisionism and US imperialism woke up." Zhou thus signaled the emergence of two significant trends in international Communist relations: the perception of the Soviet Union as China's primary enemy—his statement marked the first time in years of polemics that the United States was not listed first in the order of enemies—and Beijing's growing estrangement from Hanoi, which would culminate in the Chinese invasion of Vietnam eleven years later.

Also in the wake of Czechoslovakia, Beijing introduced an ominous new dimension to the Sino-Soviet polemics, the border dispute, which had been kept under wraps even as just about every other possible topic was aired in acrimonious exchanges. This served both to warn Moscow against further adventures in Eastern Europe (such as against the maverick Romanians, who denounced the invasion of Czechoslovakia and were on good terms with Beijing) by suggesting possible Chinese mischief making on the eastern front, and to sharpen Beijing's portrayal of the Soviets as imperialists (the "new tsars") who had seized territories from weaker nations. During that winter the Chinese began to change the rules of the game along their riverine borders with the Soviet Union, challenging Soviet patrols (which according to Moscow were following "established border procedures") and eventually engaging in lethal firefights that kept the border in a high state of tension for much of 1969.[12] A broad consensus has emerged that it was Chinese behavior that caused the border crisis, but views vary widely on the motivation. One perspective, applied also to other crises such as the 1958 Taiwan Strait crisis, has Mao provoking heightened tensions in order to mobilize support for his radical domestic initiatives. Another interpretation is that Beijing feared a Soviet attack on the basis of the so-called Brezhnev Doctrine of limited sovereignty—that Moscow was obligated to intervene if the socialist order was threatened in another Communist country. It would be anachronistic, however, to explain Chinese behavior immediately after the invasion of Czechoslovakia in terms of a doctrine that was only adumbrated in low-level commentary the month after the invasion of Czechoslovakia and was not articulated authoritatively until Brezhnev's address to the Polish party congress that November, long after Beijing had raised the border issue publicly and taken other steps that transformed its foreign policy. Moreover, Moscow over the previous two years had already put in place its strategy to combat the deviant turn taken by the Maoist leadership, both politically—applying the anathematizing formula "Mao Zedong and his group" (discussed earlier)—and militarily, by the buildup of troops along the Chinese border. The origins and context of the Brezhnev Doctrine indicate that it applied to Warsaw Pact countries, not at all to China.

It was concern over Moscow's growing influence in East Asia and Hanoi's embrace of Soviet policy—reversing the trends of the first half of the decade—that primarily motivated the transformative Chinese policy changes in the wake of the invasion of Czechoslovakia. These changes need to be understood in the context of Beijing's overriding interest in challenging the reassertion of Soviet influence in the region after the ouster of Khrushchev. Beijing's vehement rejection of the post-Khrushchev Kremlin's offer of unity behind the Vietnamese, and the virulent anti-Soviet dimension of the Cultural Revolution, were salient features of this context. It also bears noting that when the Chinese posited "three obstacles" to Sino-Soviet normalization in the 1980s (see Chapter 11) it was Soviet support for Vietnam's occupation of Cambodia that topped the list—not the Soviet military presence in Afghanistan or even the more direct threat posed by the Soviet troops massed along China's border.

Fear of a Soviet attack did arise after months of severe tension and skirmishes along the border. The border crisis erupted first in March 1969 in fighting over an uninhabited island—Zhenbao in Chinese, Damanskiy in Russian—used only for fishing and other minor economic purposes, and spread that summer to other islands and to areas in Central Asia. Beijing charged that the Soviets were trying to occupy areas that belonged to China even according to the "unequal treaties" imposed by tsarist Russia in the nineteenth century (which annexed the vast territory north of the Amur River and east of the Ussuri). These included six hundred islands on the Chinese side of the main channel of the border rivers, which Beijing claimed to be the boundary according to the *thalweg* principle of international law. The center of the main channel of navigable rivers, the *thalweg*, defines the boundary except in special cases where by treaty or long-established peaceable occupation the boundary runs along one bank, giving sovereignty over the whole river to the other riparian state. Also contested were twenty thousand square kilometers in the Pamir Mountain region of Central Asia. While demanding negotiation of a comprehensive "new equal treaty" to erase the humiliation visited on a weak China, Beijing offered to take the old treaties as the basis for determining the boundary, thus indicating that it did not intend to press wide-ranging irredentist claims. Nonetheless, this demand pitted China's acute sense of historical grievance against Moscow's extreme aversion to submitting territorial settlements to renegotiation (as reflected also in its rejection of Japan's claims to the southernmost islands in the Kuril chain, the obstacle blocking a peace treaty to formally end World War II).

Finally, at the end of a long hot summer of border tensions and skirmishes, the two sides moved toward negotiations. This took place in the context of severe Soviet warnings, in particular a *Pravda* editorial article (a highly authoritative party commentary) on 28 August warning of the growing Chinese nuclear arsenal and of the threat to the rest of the world that a nuclear war posed,[13] and fervent appeals by Hanoi for ending strife in the Communist movement. Ho Chi Minh, who died in early September, left a "testament" solemnly pleading for Communist unity. The Chinese, who for years had censored North Vietnamese statements on this subject, broke precedent and republished the text of Ho's appeal (a surprising action that led one of the current authors to conclude at the time that the probability of large-scale Sino-Soviet war erupting was extremely low). Premier Kosygin, who had attended Ho Chi Minh's funeral in early September, had reached Soviet Central Asia on his return home before backtracking to Beijing for discussions with Zhou Enlai. The Soviets had suggested a meeting, according to a Chinese account, but Beijing's response arrived after Kosygin had left Hanoi; Zhou's arrival there also came after the Soviet premier's departure. The Chinese found still other ways to demean Kosygin: They confined the meeting with Zhou to the Beijing airport, and their frigid account—the two premiers had "a frank conversation"—contrasted with Moscow's more constructive report of "a conversation useful to both sides" (Moscow omitted noting that the meeting was held at the airport).[14]

Moscow had sought throughout to defuse the crisis and made a series of conciliatory gestures in an effort to escape the burdensome challenge being posed by the Chinese. The border talks that opened in October largely comported with Beijing's terms: rather than a resumption, as Moscow proposed, of the 1964 Sino-Soviet "consultations" devoted to "clarifying" sections of the border, with a Soviet border guard officer heading a technical delegation, the two sides entered into "negotiations" at the level of deputy foreign ministers. These talks served to contain tensions rather than resolve territorial issues—the two sides even quarreled over what was agreed at the Kosygin-Zhou meeting—but a breakthrough eventually occurred when later a Soviet leader conceded Beijing's position on the *thalweg* issue as part of a major package of proposals on Asian security (see Chapter 11).

In addition to raising the border issue, the Chinese undertook other significant steps to position themselves for what they termed a "historic new stage" of development. On the domestic front, they completed the process of erecting new administrative structures, dominated by the military, to replace the shattered party apparatus. This was a transitional phase, and in October 1968 a lengthy CPC Central Committee plenum officially called for a new party congress, the first step in reconstituting the party and restoring Communist normalcy. Beijing also was fashioning a notably more flexible, less ideological approach to the external world, replacing the "Red Guard diplomacy" that had wreaked such havoc on its foreign relations (at one point the PRC had only two ambassadors stationed abroad).

Two telling examples illustrate this trend: Beijing made an abrupt turnabout in its relationship with Tito's Yugoslavia, now treated as a friend (for strategic reasons) after years of being vilified as the arch-heretic (for ideological reasons); and it put aside the Maoist evangelism that had so irritated foreign Communists. During the Cultural Revolution Beijing had elevated Mao to equal status with Marx and Lenin in the Communist pantheon, claiming that he had brought the international Communist movement to the new era of Marxism-Leninism-Mao Zedong Thought. A month after the invasion of Czechoslovakia, the Chinese retracted this provocative claim by signaling that Maoist ideology applied only to China and that other Communist parties were to apply the universal principles of Marxism-Leninism to the specific conditions of their own countries. (Later, however, in a reflection of shifting political developments, the party congress held in April 1969 adopted a constitution that incorporated the universalist claim for Maoist ideology and enshrined Lin Biao as Mao's successor designate.[15] In still another switch, the Tenth CPC Congress, in 1973, which put a new leadership structure in place after the Lin Biao affair—in which Lin died in an aircraft clash while fleeing after purportedly attempting a coup against Mao—removed the Cultural Revolution claim that Mao had raised Marxism-Leninism to a new and higher stage.[16])

The potentially most significant shift, however, occurred in Beijing's posture toward the United States, theretofore the principal enemy and the target of fire-breathing vituperation. This shift had a seismic impact on the geopolitical landscape, one effect being to raise the old "wedge" policy to the level of a "strategic triangle."

## SINO-AMERICAN RAPPROCHEMENT

Events surrounding the Vietnam War were central to this development. After having relentlessly denounced the Vietnam peace talks that began in the spring of 1968, the Chinese made an about-face later in the year, shifting from adamant opposition to openness to a negotiated settlement. This shift coincided with the election of Richard Nixon that November in the wake of Johnson's moves to curtail the bombing campaign against North Vietnam and the expansion of the Paris talks. Undoubtedly taking note of Nixon's professed interest in escaping from the Vietnam quagmire—including "a secret plan" to do so—and in drawing China into the international community, Beijing issued a public offer to conduct meaningful talks with the United States. Proposing to resume the stalled Sino-American ambassadorial talks in Warsaw after the newly elected administration had taken office (Beijing had postponed the session scheduled for May 1968 so as not to compromise its posture of total opposition to Hanoi's agreement to negotiate with Washington), the Chinese insisted that the talks should concern fundamental issues rather than "haggling over side issues"—an allusion to American proposals (especially from the Democratic Party) to improve the atmosphere through modest steps like exchange programs—and that the objective was an agreement based on the five principles of peaceful coexistence.[17] Considering the wrath that the Chinese had for years directed at the very idea of peaceful coexistence with the American imperialists, this was clearly intended to be a strong signal of a readiness for a new relationship. The signal was further amplified when Beijing took what at the time was the extraordinary step of publishing the text of Nixon's inaugural address in January, including his hope that no nation would remain in "angry isolation" (an echo of his 1967 *Foreign Affairs* article) from the international community.[18] Chinese commentary on the inauguration was mockingly derisive, portraying the United States as in a state of ineluctable decline into a sea of troubles at home and abroad. It may have seemed to be a cascade of propaganda sound and fury signifying nothing positive, but its significance (again, like that of the dog who didn't bark) lay in Beijing's failure to pass judgment on key substantive issues. The Chinese had thus kept the door open for serious dialogue, as proposed in November. This willingness to skirt contentious issues was brought into sharp relief by Beijing's contrasting treatment of remarks by the new president at his first press conference and similar remarks by Japanese Prime Minister Sato Eisaku on the same day. Both said there would be no change in their policies until Beijing changed its approach, but reports in the official Chinese media carefully avoided direct mention of Nixon's comments on China policy while castigating Sato for having made "the outrageous demand" that Beijing change its policies.[19]

Both sides were now preparing for a post-Vietnam era. From its earliest days, the Nixon administration began exploring ways of opening communications with Beijing. Steps were taken that ranged from symbolic gestures such as beginning to use the official name People's Republic of China—one of the gestures, like Beijing's publication of Nixon's inaugural address, that required no response from the other side but began to invest a measure of credibility in each side's signals of interest in a new relationship—to using intermediaries such as Pakistan and Romania to convey Washington's message. It was during a visit by Romanian President Nicolae Ceausescu that Nixon became the first American president to use China's official name. Significantly, he did so in a toast to Romania's good relations with the United States, the Soviet Union, and the People's Republic of China—a neat reference to the three nations about to become players in triangular diplomacy.[20] Both Romania and Pakistan had been on Nixon's itinerary when he first enunciated the Nixon Doctrine at Guam in mid-1969, a doctrine that explained the policy of retrenchment in Asia and in effect called for a return to the pre–Korean War policy of avoiding ground wars in Asia.

Beijing's antennas would have been tuned in to signals of American retrenchment. Of all the campaign oratory during the presidential election of 1968, Beijing's official media publicized only a fragment, in a news dispatch explaining that Nixon was elected "after he called for the necessity to 'reduce our commitments around the world in the areas where we are overextended' and to 'put more emphasis on the priority areas,' namely, Europe and other areas" (the interior quotations are Nixon's words). Similarly, after the inauguration Beijing quoted Kissinger, the newly appointed national security adviser, as acknowledging that U.S. global strategy had been a failure and that America was "no longer in a position to operate programs globally."[21] Although the Vietnamization process of disengaging from Indochina was clouded by outbreaks of intensified warfare, provoking Chinese warnings against going too far, the two sides were able to sustain the momentum toward a changing relationship.[22]

What was driving this momentum was a shared purpose in counterbalancing the perceived rise of Soviet power. Washington needed to arrest the decline in American power and prestige by escaping the Vietnam morass without suffering a humiliating blow to its credibility. Moscow's interest and success in gaining influence in Hanoi had made it disinclined to risk its gains by serving as a partner in U.S. efforts to temper the Vietnamese Communists' intransigence. The Soviet gains had also infuriated the Chinese, as we have seen. Washington therefore turned to Beijing for help in extricating the United States from Vietnam; by removing the American presence from China's south and negotiating an accommodation on the Taiwan obstacle, Nixon sought to prepare the ground for realizing the goal articulated in his 1967 *Foreign Affairs* article of drawing China back into the world community.[23] Moreover, by fashioning a new relationship with China, Washington would at the same time create a counterweight to growing Soviet power.

The Chinese were making parallel calculations in determining how to respond to rising Soviet and declining American power. Having placed the Soviets in the enemy camp as "social imperialists" after the invasion of Czechoslovakia, Beijing adopted a strategy that defined Moscow as the main enemy while pursuing an opening to the United States, viewed now as a secondary threat, as it was withdrawing from the south and signaling an interest in a new relationship. During the 1969 border crisis, four veteran marshals had been commissioned to assess the strategic situation and the menace posed by the Soviet military concentrations and warnings. The four marshals discounted the likelihood of war, and one of them, former foreign minister Chen I, urged the leadership to "pursue a breakthrough" in Sino-American relations by capitalizing on the strategic "contradiction" between the United States and the Soviet Union.[24] After Kissinger's dramatic visit two years later and the invitation to Nixon to visit China, Beijing used a canonical 1940 work by Mao, "On Policy," to explain the strategy of distinguishing between "the principal enemy" and adversaries of "secondary importance" in order to make use of the latter to isolate the former.[25]

Because much of this signaling process was arcane or kept in tightly held channels (though the Chinese invitation to an American Ping-Pong team to visit in April 1971 after the world championships in Japan was a highly publicized omen of progress), the world was astonished to learn in July 1971 that Nixon had dispatched Kissinger on a secret visit to Beijing (flying surreptitiously out of Pakistan) and that the American president, who had made his career out of hard-line anticommunism, had been invited to China. The results of Nixon's visit the following February ("the week that changed the world," in Nixon's hyperbole) reflected the shared geopolitical needs that had drawn the two-decades-long adversaries into a new relationship. Most of the famous Shanghai Communiqué followed an unusual if not unique format, insisted on by the Chinese against American resistance: Each side issued a separate statement of its positions on various international issues (these positions had been thoroughly aired in their discussions).[26] This format—more parallel communiqués than joint communiqué—afforded the Chinese as well as the Americans a way of reassuring their allies that the new relationship would not be at their expense. Thus, rather than a convergence of views across a range of issues, what brought the old antagonists together was essentially twofold: a shared perception of the Soviet Union as an aggressive and ascendant power, providing an incentive to develop a relationship to counterbalance Moscow's growing geopolitical weight; and signs of American disengagement from Indochina, which, along with the Nixon Doctrine, signified a reduced threat to China and a reduced likelihood of a collision between China and the United States in Asia. To enable this relationship to take hold, however, required a measure of accommodation (as distinct from—and more than—an agreement to disagree) on the Taiwan issue, identified by Beijing as "the crucial question obstructing the normalization of relations." It would take nearly seven years before formal normalization, in the form of full diplomatic relations, could be achieved, and the Taiwan issue would remain as a potential flashpoint in the next century, but a formula was crafted in the Shanghai Communiqué that enabled the two sides to enter into a new strategic relationship.

The Chinese reaffirmed their bedrock claim that the PRC government represented all of China, including the "province" of Taiwan; that the "liberation" of Taiwan was China's internal affair in which no other country had a right to interfere; and that the United States must withdraw its armed forces from Taiwan. (Beijing later modified its terms in the interest of greater flexibility and appeal, substituting "peaceful reunification" for "liberation" and referring to Taiwan more generally as "a part" of China—thus adopting the phrasing used by the United States in the Shanghai Communiqué. This was intended to leave broad room for negotiations with Taiwan on how to define its formal relationship with the PRC.) The United States used an artfully ambiguous formulation to accommodate Beijing's demand without abandoning its relationship with the Nationalist government on Taiwan. In the communiqué the U.S. side "acknowledges" (*renshi dao*) that "all Chinese on either side of the Taiwan Strait" considered Taiwan to be part of China and that it "does not challenge" that position. In a pathbreaking agreement in 1970 establishing diplomatic relations with the PRC, Canada had simply "take[n] note" (*zhuyi dao*) of Beijing's position on Taiwan, but because of its special relationship with Taipei, the United States was required to go beyond the noncommittal Canadian formula (though a draft offered to the Chinese had unsuccessfully tried to use it). Thus, the United States was able to use a point of agreement between the Communists and Nationalists (who agreed on the one-China principle) to

### A BREAKTHROUGH IN SINO-AMERICAN RELATIONS: THE SHANGHAI COMMUNIQUÉ

[N]either should seek hegemony in the Asia-Pacific region and each is opposed to efforts by any other country or group of countries to establish such hegemony. . . .

The Chinese side reaffirmed its position: The Taiwan question is the crucial question obstructing the normalization of relations between China and the United States; the Government of the People's Republic of China is the sole legal government of China; Taiwan is a province of China which has long been returned to the motherland; the liberation of Taiwan is China's internal affair in which no other country has the right to interfere. . . .

The U.S. side declared: The United States acknowledges that all China on either side of the Taiwan Strait maintain that there is but one China and that Taiwan is part of China. The US Government does not challenge that position. It reaffirms its interest in a peaceful settlement of the Taiwan question by the Chinese themselves.

US-PRC joint communiqué during President Nixon's China visit, 27 February 1972, in Robert S. Ross, *Negotiating Cooperation: The United States and China, 1969–1989* (Stanford, CA: Stanford University Press, 1995), 265–69.

navigate around the treacherous Taiwan obstacle. Further, in affirming its "interest" in a peaceful settlement of the Taiwan issue, the United States posited "the ultimate objective" of withdrawing its forces from Taiwan, meanwhile reducing those forces as "the tension in the area diminishes." This formulation, which had appeared in earlier U.S. communications, represented the link between the winding down of the American presence in Vietnam and an accommodation on the Taiwan question. It provided further incentive to the Chinese to aid in reducing tensions, that is, to assist American disengagement from Vietnam. Beijing's readiness to accept this linkage helps explain its turnabout on the Vietnam question in late 1968 and its divergence from Hanoi's insistence on the integral nature of the military and political issues (see Chapter 9). On both the Vietnam and Taiwan issues the Nixon administration sought to separate the military and political aspects, leaving the latter to a historical evolution. (During the negotiations, Nixon asked the Chinese to allow him "running room" to reach full normalization, but the Watergate scandal and his resignation upset the expectation that this would be achieved in his second term.)

The accommodation on the Taiwan issue was the enabling condition for a transformed Sino-American relationship. The shared strategic purpose underlying this development was addressed in a section of the Shanghai Communiqué that registered agreement between the two sides (a rarity), one in which the United States agreed to base relations on the five principles of peaceful coexistence as proposed by Beijing in its démarche following Nixon's election. The two sides committed themselves to opposing efforts by any country to establish "hegemony" in the Asia-Pacific region—a code word for the expansion of Soviet influence and power. (Later, Beijing applied the term to the United States, including in joint communiqués with Moscow, when the geopolitical balance had shifted in favor of Washington.) They also agreed, in a bow to Beijing's abiding suspicions over a Soviet-U.S. condominium at the expense of lesser powers, that major powers should not collude with one another to divide the world into spheres of influence. In the pursuit of triangular diplomacy, Washington would need to balance its interests in negotiating improved relations with Moscow and its concern not to stoke Beijing's suspicions. Mao later complained that Washington was using China in its dealings with Moscow, telling a visiting American leader that the United States wanted to stand on China's shoulders (here he tapped on his shoulders) while engaging the Soviets.

## NEW GEOMETRIES OF POWER

Now, however, it was Moscow's turn to be apprehensive about being left out in the cold. A telling indication of its concern was the decision to host Nixon as scheduled three months after his China visit despite the heavy bombing of North Vietnam and mining of its ports. There were much higher stakes now than Vietnam, and Moscow could not afford to be left out of the game. Cold War bipolarity had been transformed in a fundamental way, but it would be going too far to say that an era of tripolarity had arrived. Only the two superpowers possessed a comprehensive nuclear arsenal and global reach. China's geopolitical weight was regional; it was in the Asia-Pacific region that the new Sino-American relationship had a major impact, including on the roles and maneuvering of the superpowers.

Washington sought to use the new triangular configuration to play the "China card" against the Soviets; the Chinese now had the American connection as a counterweight to Soviet pressure. For its part, Moscow tried to contain and isolate China in Asia and in the international Communist movement. In June 1969, against the background of Beijing's more flexible initiatives since the invasion of Czechoslovakia and at a time of acute tension during the border crisis, it convened another world party conference for that purpose (this time attended by only seventy-five parties, compared with the eighty-one represented at the 1960 meeting, the ruling East Asian Communist parties notably being among the absentees). The conference featured a clamorous chorus of anti-Chinese polemics, but Brezhnev's proposal for an Asian collective security system—in essence a project for containment of China—proved to be a nonstarter despite Soviet efforts to give it traction in subsequent years.

The process of Sino-American rapprochement imparted a powerful impetus to change in international affairs in the 1970s. The PRC reentered the international system after the self-imposed isolation of the Cultural Revolution, beginning a process of integration that gathered extraordinary momentum in the following decades. It had taken the China seat in the United Nations in the fall of 1971, after Kissinger's blockbuster trip to Beijing knocked down the remaining barriers to its entry that Washington had managed to maintain up to then. A spate of diplomatic recognition agreements during this period included those with its Southeast Asian neighbors Malaysia in 1974 (in addition to resumption of normal ties with Burma that year) and Thailand and the Philippines a year later; each of these were beset by Communist-led revolutionary movements, but Beijing now downplayed "export of revolution" in favor of normal political and economic relations.

The tectonic shifts in the geopolitical landscape in the 1970s registered two "Nixon shocks" on Japan. U.S.-Japanese relations, though beginning to be troubled by trade frictions, had weathered two potentially destabilizing challenges in the 1970s: an agreement on the reversion of Okinawa to Japanese administration (prepared by the Nixon-Sato communiqué of November 1969, formalized in 1971, and effectuated in 1972) and the automatic renewal of the security treaty in 1970 in the absence of a decision by Tokyo to invoke the one-year notice of termination. It was the fate of Prime Minister Sato, who successfully managed those challenges and pursued policies favorable to the United States in the face of considerable opposition, to be rewarded with the two Nixon shocks.[27] One *shokku* was the abrupt transformation of the Sino-American relationship after two decades of animosity and confrontation. There had been tensions in U.S.-Japanese relations over Tokyo's desire to "separate politics and economics" in order to pursue trade with China, but the Japanese had been constrained to follow Washington's lead in isolating the PRC and maintaining ties with the ROC. Now they had to scramble to deal with the reconfigured geometry of relationships, and they did so by outpacing the Americans in establishing full diplomatic (though yet not fully normalized) ties with the PRC barely more than a half year after the Nixon visit. Six years later, as Sino-American negotiations on normalization were under way, Japan signed a peace and friendship treaty with the PRC that finally normalized relations by formally ending World War II between them and that included the anti-Soviet clause on opposing hegemony.[28] This produced the following result, which was illustrative of the realignments taking place: Beijing had concluded a peace treaty with the state that was explicitly named as the target of the still formally existent Sino-Soviet alliance (Beijing gave notice the next year of its termination of the Sino-Soviet treaty), while Moscow remained unable to conclude a formal peace with that state and was now the implicit target of the Sino-Japanese treaty.

The second *shokku* came in August 1971, on the heels of Kissinger's trip to Beijing in July and the announcement of Nixon's forthcoming visit. Not only America's geopolitical standing but also its financial condition—especially the strength of the dollar—had been sapped by the Vietnam involvement, leading Nixon to scuttle the Bretton Woods system by abandoning fixed exchange rates. This threatened to damage Japan's exports by the resulting appreciation of the yen, a threat made even more immediate by Nixon's decision at the same time to impose a surcharge on imports. Thus, in successive months Nixon had astonished the world with dramatic moves that had transformative effects on the international system.

Ten days before Nixon announced that he would be going to Beijing, thereby setting the stage for the "triangular diplomacy" of the two superpowers and China, he had introduced still another geometric image for the changing international landscape. In an acknowledgment of the remarkable economic advances of Japan and Europe as well as the trend in the latter toward a regional identity and institutions, he declared that a pentagonal structure of power had emerged: America, Europe, the Soviet Union, China, and Japan. The two Nixon shocks reflected an effort to adjust American strategy, geopolitical and economic, to this new reality.

The Japanese were not alone in their region in sensing the geopolitical ground shifting under them. The startling development in Sino-American relations produced a "Nixon shock" for the South Koreans and a "Mao shock" for their northern rivals. For the former, U.S. policy shifts—notably the Nixon Doctrine, portending disengagement from Asia, and the opening to China—raised doubts about the durability of Washington's commitment to old allies like Saigon, Taipei, and Seoul itself. For Pyongyang, which had pursued a fiercely independent line by maintaining a balance between its two big Communist allies while depending on them for security and economic support, Mao's invitation to Nixon posed the danger (shared, of course, by Hanoi) that its patrons would compete for a U.S. connection rather than for favor in the DPRK. ROK president Park Chung Hee reacted by acquiring increasingly authoritarian power and eventually staging an internal coup, justifying his actions by reference to the geopolitical changes taking place in the region. He and Kim Il Sung engaged in their own exchange of secret emissaries in the spring of 1972, culminating in another surprise to the world in the form of a North-South joint statement issued in July, a year after the announcement of Mao's invitation to Nixon. The statement pledged the two sides to seek unification, making the point that this was to be pursued by "independent" means without "external imposition or interference."[29]

While this process was set in motion by the shock waves from the Nixon visit, the two sides may have had differing intentions in taking this step: Seoul seeking a less menacing environment on the peninsula in the changing geopolitical environment, and Pyongyang trying to draw the South away from the U.S. military embrace. Underlying differences and mistrust as well as North Korean terrorist actions impeded the evolution of the process, though there was an exchange of Red Cross delegations in the wake of the joint statement, and extensive contacts and exchanges took place in the next decade. The U.S.-ROK military alliance, particularly the annual joint exercises that elicited Pyongyang's thunderous denunciations, proved to be an insurmountable obstacle. It was not until after the end of the Cold War transformed the geopolitical environment even more that a summit meeting was arranged. By that time Kim Il Sung had died and been replaced by his son, and a democratized South Korea had undergone a generational change in attitudes toward inter-Korean relations.

## DEVELOPMENTS IN SOUTH ASIA

The Indian-Pakistani relationship had a dynamic of its own, with the Kashmir issue producing a second war in 1965, but we need to take a look at the evolution of events in the subcontinent to see how this became an arena for the broader geopolitical contests. The emergence of the Sino-Indian border conflict in the late 1950s set in motion significant shifts in relationships between the subcontinent rivals and outside powers. Extensive diplomatic exchanges and a Nehru-Zhou summit in April 1960 in New Delhi (Zhou's trip also included Burma and Nepal, both countries having reached boundary agreements with Beijing) failed to close the yawning gap between the two sides. To avoid acquiescence in the status quo as proposed by Beijing, which New Delhi regarded as acceptance of Chinese occupation of its territory, the Indians began a "forward policy" of patrolling in disputed areas, interposing posts and patrols between Chinese positions. The Chinese, naturally suspecting that India was preparing to try to force them out, repeatedly warned of "grave consequences" if the Indians persisted in pressing forward. A heedless and woefully unprepared India was about to suffer those consequences.[30]

Aggressive Indian patrolling in the face of stern Chinese warnings produced a combustible situation awaiting only a spark to ignite a conflagration. The spark came from a Chinese move in 1962 to dislodge a forward Indian position recently established in a tiny parcel of land in the western extremity of the eastern sector, at the junction of China, India, and Bhutan. This area was located between the McMahon Line as cartographically delimited and the boundary according to New Delhi's version along a higher ridgeline a few miles farther north. As in their border dispute with Moscow, the Chinese complained that India had tried to occupy areas beyond even the boundary it claimed on the basis of existing treaties. Beijing disputed the legality of those treaties but offered to take them as the basis for a comprehensive negotiation of a border settlement.

This was one of the striking parallels between China's border disputes with India and with the Soviet Union. Another was the extreme reluctance of Moscow and New Delhi to acknowledge the existence of a territorial dispute, each insisting that only minor adjustments or clarifications of specific and limited slices of the border could be addressed rather than an overall negotiation—hence the Indian distinction between "talks" and "negotiations," and the Soviet one between "consultations" and "negotiations." Also, in each case Beijing called for observance of the status quo, which it termed "the line of actual control," pending a comprehensive settlement. (However, in the dispute with India, Beijing rejected the McMahon Line because China had not been a party to the Simla Convention that adopted it, whereas in the disagreement with the USSR, the nineteenth-century treaties Moscow invoked as determining the boundary were signed by the Chinese authorities of the time.)

The situation in the eastern sector had been quiet since the skirmishes in 1959, but three years later, the Chinese reacted to the Indian movement north of the McMahon Line by taking up threatening positions, as they had against the Indian forward posts in the west. India responded by trying to evict the Chinese, precipitating a Chinese assault in October to drive the Indians back below the McMahon Line. After a lull of a few weeks, Beijing concluded that New Delhi was not going to abandon the forward policy and launched an offensive in both east and west that threw the Indians out of the North-East Frontier Agency (NEFA, through which the McMahon Line ran) and overran their posts in the area claimed by Beijing in the west. NEFA later became an Indian state, Arunachal Pradesh, an action drawing a sharp Chinese denunciation because of its implication of foreclosing a negotiated settlement of the region's status.

The offensive had lasted only a few days when Beijing startled the world by announcing a cease-fire and withdrawal behind the lines of actual control as of November 1959. There was speculation at the time about outside forces determining the Chinese decision, including possible Soviet pressure—though in fact Moscow had moved from its neutral posture to endorse Beijing's proposals at this time, which coincided with the Cuban missile crisis and a need to show Communist unity for deterrence purposes. Beijing's own explanation for its operation should be given due weight: that its goals were to "shatter Indian plans to alter the border status quo" by force and to "create conditions for a negotiated settlement."[31] To be sure, there were scant early prospects for achieving the latter goal, given the psychological conditions of a humiliating blow to India's national pride and the military conditions of having to negotiate from a position of weakness—conditions hardly conducive to entering negotiations. But the Chinese action certainly fulfilled the other objective—that of smashing India's forward policy and thereby realizing Beijing's need for maintenance of the status quo for the foreseeable future. The Sino-Indian border dispute was thus placed on the shelf where reposed those issues that were "left over from history" and could be left pending for future resolution.

The Chinese action also inflicted a blow to India's nonaligned stance. At New Delhi's request, the United States dispatched an aircraft carrier from the Pacific, though the crisis was over before it reached the Bay of Bengal.[32] Military missions from the United States and Britain arrived, preparing the way for substantial military assistance in the next three years. Washington cut off this conduit when the Indian-Pakistani War of 1965 over Kashmir erupted (see later in this chapter), and Moscow—which had veered back away from supporting Beijing after the Cuban missile crisis ended—became India's main supplier. Meanwhile Pakistan, alarmed at the U.S. arms relationship with its enemy, was receiving military aid and diplomatic support from China, nurturing a close relationship that insulated Pakistan from the spillover effects of the Chinese Cultural Revolution soon to ignite.

The Anglo-American mission sought to use the arms-supply relationship as leverage to induce the South Asian foes to restart negotiations on the enduring Kashmir issue. Talks were held from the end of the year until May 1963 but ended in a stalemate. Meanwhile the two sides were making moves that intensified suspicion and mistrust. India was whittling away at Kashmir's special status and bringing it into closer control from New Delhi, with adverse implications for Pakistan's irredentist claims. Pakistan, consolidating its relationship with China, provoked an Indian rebuke by ceding territory in Kashmir to the PRC. During this period the Pakistanis had reason to see a window of opportunity for action on Kashmir, one that would begin to close as India pressed forward with the military modernization that it had undertaken after the 1962 debacle. With India in disarray—political infighting and Nehru's death in 1964 raised questions about that country's vulnerability—Pakistan may have seen this as an opportune time to make its move.[33]

In August 1965 Pakistan began infiltrating insurgents into Indian-held Kashmir in the hope—vain, as it turned out—that an insurrection would catch fire. Battles between the Pakistani and Indian armies developed, including an Indian horizontal thrust into Pakistani Punjab that expanded the battleground beyond Kashmir. The UN issued a call for a cease-fire, to which both sides acceded in mid-September. The Pakistanis had reason to be disappointed by their China connection; nothing much came of Chinese warnings to India, including a threat of mischief making in India's eastern sector.[34] India lost the arms-supply connection it had established with the United States and Britain, which cut off the supply after the outbreak of hostilities between India and Pakistan. Moreover, while the United States was preoccupied with its escalating involvement in Vietnam, the way was cleared for Moscow to take the leading role in South Asia, which it did by mediating the Tashkent Agreement in January 1966 to end the second war over Kashmir.

With the United States disengaged from South Asia while embroiled in Vietnam, and the Chinese in the throes of the Cultural Revolution, the subcontinent was at the periphery of broader regional and global developments. This was to change in the next decade, however, as the dynamics of Pakistan's internal affairs led to another war with India, one that intersected significantly with the emerging Sino-American rapprochement and the nascent strategic triangle. Long-festering tensions plagued relations between Pakistan's two wings, separated by a thousand miles of Indian territory and by fundamental ethnic and linguistic differences. There had been long-standing agitation in Bengali-speaking East Pakistan over the status of Urdu as the official national language as well as grievances over West Pakistani—especially Punjabi—domination of the military officer corps and the elite civil service. These tensions boiled over after elections in December 1970 revealed a highly polarized electorate, mirroring the differences between the country's east and west. In East Pakistan the Awami League, led by Sheikh Mujibur Rahman, advocated greater autonomy for the predominantly Bengali population there and won an overwhelming victory. At the same time the party of another charismatic figure, Zulfikar Ali Bhutto, gained a smashing success in West Pakistan. Significantly, neither party won a single seat in the other wing of the country. When the two sides could not agree on constitutional changes to meet the East's demands, President Yahya Khan ordered a military crackdown, Mujibur Rahman was arrested for treason, and civil war erupted.

India perceived both cause and opportunity for intervention during its adversary's travails. The turmoil in East Pakistan generated millions of refugees flowing into India's northeast and West Bengal, producing a humanitarian crisis while imposing heavy economic and demographic burdens on India. Not only would an influx of Muslims from East Bengal affect the communal balance, but the areas adjoining East Pakistan were subject to minority unrest as well as radical Marxist insurgencies, which stoked Indian fears of fissiparous tendencies wracking their country. But India also saw in the situation a strategic opportunity: A collapse of Pakistani authority in the country's eastern wing would remove the threat of a two-front confrontation with India's enemy. It also offered the possibility of reducing India's vulnerability to the Sino-Pakistani relationship that had developed in the past decade.

India's early stages of intervention consisted of training and equipping the East Pakistani insurgents and providing them sanctuary and political support. Eventually, in December, Indian artillery and troops were directly assisting the insurgents, provoking a Pakistani preemptive air strike in the west, which led to a short war between the armies of India and Pakistan that ended with a cease-fire in mid-December. (Pakistan's motives are unclear. It may have hoped that its action would prompt the international community to exact a cease-fire that would give time for the insurgency in East Pakistan to be broken.) A new state, Bangladesh, was born. The Indian and Pakistani leaders, Indira Gandhi (Nehru's daughter) and Bhutto (who had replaced the disgraced Yahya Khan as president), met at the old British colonial summer capital of Simla the following summer to negotiate an agreement by which India returned Pakistan's POWs and territory captured in the fighting. The two sides abjured the use of force on the Kashmir dispute and changed the name of the cease-fire line to the Line of Control. (There was speculation—hotly contested—that Bhutto agreed to convert the LOC to a permanent boundary line, thereby ending Pakistan's claim to all of Kashmir.[35])

India's crucial role in the amputation of Pakistan's eastern wing brought what had begun as an internal conflict in Pakistan into the broader geopolitical arena at a time of tectonic shifts in the international landscape. Washington—or at least the White House, given the divisions in the Nixon administration itself as well as in American political circles in general—perceived the developments in South Asia through the prism of the emerging triangular structure of global affairs. At the very time that the East Pakistan crisis was brewing, the United States and China were engaged in a delicate minuet of signaling in which Pakistan served as the main communication channel and then as the logistical base for Kissinger's secret trip to Beijing in July. Four weeks after that trip came what Kissinger termed a "bombshell," the signing of a Soviet-Indian Treaty of Peace, Friendship and Cooperation in which the two sides agreed to take "appropriate effective measures" in case of an attack or threat of attack.[36] There is a question about the gestation time for this treaty. Indian and Soviet officials have been cited (by Kissinger) as saying it was a year in the works.[37] That it was not simply an abrupt reaction to Sino-American developments would be consistent with Moscow's moves during this period to conclude treaties with various friendly third world countries; treaties were signed with Egypt and Iraq as well as India. A senior Indian foreign ministry official at the time said that the Soviet-Indian treaty had been under negotiation since the mid-1960s.[38] In any case, highlighting a phase of increasing Soviet support for India, the timing of the treaty's conclusion seemed chosen to offset the new Sino-American nexus.

### INDIA FORMS SECURITY LINK WITH THE USSR

Each High Contracting Party undertakes to abstain from providing any assistance to any third party that engages in armed conflict with the other Party. In the event of either Party being subjected to an attack or a threat thereof, the High Contracting Parties shall immediately enter into mutual consultations in order to remove such threat and to take appropriate effective measures to ensure peace and the security of their countries.

Treaty of Peace, Friendship and Cooperation between the Government of India and the Government of the Union of Soviet Socialist Republics, 9 August 1971, in Sumit Ganguly, *Conflict Unending: India-Pakistan Tensions Since 1947* (New York: Columbia University Press, 2001), 164–67.

The South Asian foes now had treaty commitments from their respective superpower supporters, while Moscow's former ally China was finding common cause with the United States in resisting the expansion of Soviet influence and power. The security relationship gave India an added increment of deterrence vis-à-vis China along with diplomatic support (especially Moscow's veto power in the UN Security Council) and economic and military assistance. Pakistan had its long-standing alliance with the United States, though the embargo on arms since the 1960s and divided councils in Washington over support for a military regime engaged in repressive action in East Pakistan cast a cloud over that relationship. As for Pakistan's China connection, that had been somewhat devalued by Beijing's failure to do much in 1965 or during the current crisis to bare its teeth of deterrence to the Indians.

In these circumstances, the Nixon-Kissinger team, fixated on the upcoming China summit and concerned about the effects on the global equilibrium of the humiliation of a longtime ally by a Soviet-armed India,[39] perceived high stakes in the South Asian conflict, warranting a show of American power. Washington ordered an aircraft carrier force to enter the Bay of Bengal, ostensibly for rescuing Americans threatened by the hostilities but actually for deterring Indian ambitions. In Kissinger's account, the independence of Bangladesh was inevitable, but the manner in which it was achieved was important. Hence, Washington pressured Islamabad to return East Pakistan to civilian rule and proceed to a political settlement of the crisis. According to Kissinger, however, India would not wait for this process to unfold, instead pressing its advantage to a military conclusion, its ultimate aim being to dismember Pakistan in the west—or at least seize Pakistani-occupied Kashmir—and establish Indian predominance in the subcontinent. Kissinger had "no doubt" in his mind that New Delhi's offer of an unconditional cease-fire in the western sector was a "reluctant decision" resulting from Soviet pressure, "which in turn grew out of American insistence, including the fleet movement and the willingness to risk the [Moscow] summit."[40]

Indian commentators, of course, dispute that interpretation, though they cannot credibly deny that New Delhi seized an opportunity to improve its geopolitical situation. In contrast to Kissinger's view that East Pakistan was bound to become independent but India would not wait for a political evolution, the Indians believed that they needed to act quickly lest the Pakistani military manage to suppress the insurgency.[41] According to

Kissinger's own interpretation, the Soviet-Indian treaty served to remove New Delhi's fears that Moscow would close its military pipeline and that China might intervene. Yet, even given this backing, India chose not to press the campaign in the west and limited its gains to Bangladesh independence, a substantial enough reward but hardly the dire prospect of Pakistan's disintegration portrayed by Kissinger. The costs of an Indian drive to further dismember Pakistan would have been high, both in military terms and in India's international standing. It was one thing to intervene in the east to relieve a humanitarian burden caused by a brutal military repression. To proceed to additional amputations and occupation of territory in West Pakistan or Kashmir would have elicited worldwide opprobrium and undermined New Delhi's foreign relations, and it might have sparked a chain reaction involving China and the superpowers. Notwithstanding Kissinger's overblown warnings of aggressive Soviet intentions, Moscow would have been loath to allow its new South Asian ally to engage in such provocative behavior. (Kissinger's fevered geopolitical imagination conjured up a nightmare of worst-case analyses, and these sometimes become self-fulfilling prophecies, as would have been the case if American overreaction had led to a Soviet-U.S. or Sino-Soviet collision. Kissinger cites an intelligence source for the belief that India was intent on dismembering West Pakistan and destroying its armed forces, but that seems to be an exaggerated interpretation of the report.)[42]

## THE SOVIET CHALLENGE

Though Kissinger's depiction of the gravity of the South Asian developments was overdrawn, there were regional as well as global trends in the 1970s that were alarming to both Washington and Beijing. India's success in dismembering Pakistan in 1971 and North Vietnam's triumph over the South four years later were achieved through the use of Soviet-supplied arms. Along with the rising concentration of Soviet forces along its borders, these developments confronted China with a new threat of encirclement. Where previously it felt menaced by a ring of hostile states aligned with the United States, prompting the newly established PRC to enter into a countervailing alliance with the Soviet Union, it now was being enveloped by rivals on three sides at a time when American power was receding in the region.

For its part, Washington observed with concern the rise of Soviet power and its implications for global equilibrium. The Cuban missile crisis in 1962 had demonstrated the USSR's strategic inferiority and discredited Khrushchev's attempt to redress the imbalance on the cheap by emplacing the missiles in Cuba while reducing the burden of maintaining a huge conventional force structure. After ousting him, Khrushchev's Kremlin colleagues undertook an across-the-board military buildup, transforming the USSR from a land-based Eurasian power to one with a global reach and strategic parity with its superpower rival. At the same time Moscow pursued the policy of peaceful coexistence, or détente, which encompassed efforts to regulate the arms race through negotiations with Washington. The Strategic Arms Limitation Talks led to the signing during Nixon's June 1972 Moscow summit of an interim agreement (SALT I) capping ICBMs for five years; an antiballistic missile (ABM) treaty was also signed in the interest of stabilizing the strategic balance.

Another Nixon summit a year later produced a pledge by the two sides to strive for a "permanent" agreement by the end of the following year, but the Watergate scandal during the election of 1972 and the ensuing attempted coverup led to Nixon's resignation in disgrace in August 1974. Gerald Ford, Nixon's successor, held a summit with Brezhnev in Vladivostok that November (Ford had already been scheduled to visit Japan and the ROK when the summit was thrown together), producing guidelines for SALT II, but détente was now flagging and arms control negotiations losing momentum. It was not until the third year of the administration of Ford's successor, Jimmy Carter, that SALT II was finally signed, but it stalled in the Senate and faded away after the Soviet invasion of Afghanistan.

There are several measures of the extent of the decline of détente. For one, plans for Soviet leader Brezhnev's summit visits to the United States were scuttled in three successive years (1974–76).[43] For another, the very term *détente* fell into disfavor and was banned from the Ford administration's lexicon as the 1976 election approached and hard-line critics—notably Ronald Reagan, a challenger for the Republican nomination—charged that the Soviets were using détente as a smokescreen while building up their military might. The critics of détente were also exercised over Soviet activities in the third world, where Moscow supplied arms to its clients and provided logistical support for Cuban intervention. The collapse of the dictatorship in Portugal led to the breakup of that country's empire in Africa and a struggle for control in which the superpowers supported rival groups (in Angola there were three rival forces, one supported by the Chinese). A Marxist-oriented regime took power in Angola and signed a friendship treaty with the USSR. Also in the 1970s the Soviets gained ground in the Horn of Africa after the fall of Ethiopian Emperor Haile Selassie and the end of his country's long relationship with the United States. These Soviet advances in areas possessing rich resources and strategic significance heightened concern over what was perceived as Moscow's relentless march to global dominance.

Moscow's intervention in Afghanistan at the end of the decade was regarded as a crucial threshold in its advance. There, a central arena of the Great Game between the British and tsarist empires in the nineteenth century, which had ended with a formal agreement to respect Afghanistan's status as a buffer between the rival empires, had now become an arena in the zero-sum game of superpower competition.[44] Until a Marxist-led group seized power in 1978, Afghanistan had maintained a largely neutral stance. To be sure, given its historical rivalry with U.S.-allied Pakistan, Afghanistan had leaned toward Moscow. In the late nineteenth century, the British, seeking control of the Khyber Pass, had seized an area in the far northwest of their possessions on the subcontinent that was inhabited by Afghan (Pashtun) tribes (which lent the second letter in the acronym later used for Pakistan—Punjabis, Afghanis, Kashmiris, and so on). The British drew a boundary, the Durand Line, so as to include that area within their empire. This was the root of the Pashtunistan question, posing a challenge to Pakistan's sovereignty over territory it inherited from the Raj and creating an irritant in Afghan-Pakistani relations. (Afghanistan expressed its grievance on this issue by being the sole country to vote against Pakistan's admission to the United Nations.) Now, as part of the South Asian dynamic in which Pakistan joined the U.S. alliance system, Moscow enjoyed some leverage with Kabul. Yet, notwithstanding competition between the superpowers to increase their respective levels of influence, the situation was tolerable for both sides until the Saur (April) Revolution of 1978, which came after a period when Kabul was moving toward a more strictly neutral position and was cultivating ties with the pro-Western Pakistan and Iran.

The regime produced by the revolution was led by a Marxist party, the People's Democratic Party of Afghanistan (PDPA), which had the trappings of a Communist Party (central committee, Politburo, and the like) but for tactical reasons claimed to lead a neutral country that was a member of the nonaligned movement. (The new regime's leader told the Soviet ambassador a few weeks after the revolution that "Afghanistan, following Marxism-Leninism, will set off on the path of building socialism and will belong to the socialist camp," but that this must be pursued "carefully" and revealed to the people only later.[45]) The PDPA purported to lead the country on the path of "national democracy," comprising policies of land reform, women's liberation, and secularization. Consistent with this posture, Moscow did not officially treat the new regime as a member of the socialist camp. It did, however, enter into a Treaty of Friendship, Good Neighborliness, and Cooperation (signed in December 1978), one of the series of friendship pacts in the 1970s—such as the ones with India, Egypt, and Iraq—by which the Soviets formalized their special relationship with third world countries.

Notwithstanding the gains accruing to Moscow from having a pro-Soviet regime in an area of competition with the West, the Soviets found themselves with a client state that posed serious problems, not unlike those faced by Washington in dealing with its Chinese and Vietnamese clients before their defeat by Communists. The PDPA was riven by factionalism and pursued repressive policies that left it with a dwindling base of support in the country. The party itself was divided into feuding factions: the more radical Khalq (Masses) dominated by the Pashtuns, the largest ethnic group, and the Parcham (Banner), comprising the second-largest group, the more urban Tajiks, and others. Even worse, two Khalq leaders atop the government engaged in murderous rivalry, leading to the ouster and death in September 1979 of President (and party leader) Nur Mohammad Taraki and his replacement by Hafizullah Amin, who pursued increasingly radical measures. Already there had been a rise of armed opposition by Islamic groups and mutinies within the armed forces, including one in Herat in which Soviet advisers and their families were massacred. Now, in the late months of 1979, Moscow's consternation over the effects of Amin's policies in alienating vast segments of the population was compounded by fears that he was seeking to rescue his situation by moving away from the Soviets and into the embrace of the United States, Pakistan, and China. The Kremlin feared that Amin would "pull a Sadat," that is, follow the Egyptian leader's precedent by abrogating the friendship treaty with Moscow and expelling the Soviets.

By the end of 1979 Moscow perceived a gravely deteriorating situation with adverse consequences for its position in the superpower competition that had become especially acute during the decade. After making the necessary military preparations and parallel political arrangements, the Soviets intervened in late December to liquidate Amin and install a Parcham leader, Babrak Karmal, who was brought from abroad to do Moscow's bidding. This action represented the first time since the formation of the socialist camp that the Soviets had intervened militarily across a border outside the Warsaw Pact. Thus, it was widely interpreted as crossing a threshold with momentous significance (as discussed in the following section). What were the Kremlin's motivations and calculations; what goals did it envision for this action?

One line of interpretation, probably not the consensus view at the time (and not shared by official Washington) but confirmed by archival accounts of the Kremlin's deliberations,[46] explains the intervention as reflecting Moscow's determination to preserve its political and economic investment in Afghanistan and to defend its strategic interests in the region. Moscow had taken the opportunity of the April 1978 coup (which arose out of Afghan internal dynamics rather than Soviet plotting) to enhance its position in the zero-sum game of Cold War geopolitics, but now it found itself on the defensive as the Kabul regime's situation deteriorated and an opportunity seemed to be arising for gains by the other superpower. Not unlike actions by the United States to resist geopolitical inroads in its neighborhood by leftist forces (such as the Johnson administration's intervention in the Dominican Republic and Reagan's in Grenada), the Kremlin perceived a dangerous development close to home that required military means to forestall. Moreover, the Soviet border with Afghanistan was a particularly vulnerable one, with similar ethnic groups professing Islam inhabiting both sides of the border (much like the vulnerability felt by the Chinese with respect to Xinjiang). And the Soviet military districts in Central Asia were significantly weaker and undermanned compared with those deployed near the western and eastern borders of the USSR.

Until the situation threatened to become irretrievable without drastic action, the Kremlin had been loath to go beyond aid and advisers to Kabul. Yuriy Andropov, the KGB chief who (along with the foreign and defense ministers) was entrusted with assessing the Afghan situation, expressed this reluctance in March 1979—at the time of mutinies in the Afghan army and anti-Soviet atrocities—when he ruled out as "entirely inadmissible" Soviet military action to suppress the insurgency.[47] Foreign Minister Gromyko mused on the negative repercussions intervention would have on détente, arms control negotiations, "and much more." One aspect of that "more" was Moscow's obsessive concern over anything having implications for the Sino-Soviet rivalry. "China, of course, would be given a nice present," Gromyko remarked ruefully.[48] (A scholar working in archival sources has stated that the Politburo troika assessing the Afghanistan situation was in favor of intervention in early 1979 but was overruled by Brezhnev, for whom détente was an overriding concern.[49])

Finally, however, Moscow's strategic calculus determined that intervention was unavoidable if Soviet security was not to be endangered in a vulnerable area. The Soviets viewed their decision in the context of perceived U.S. efforts "to achieve unilateral military advantages in regions that are strategically important to the USSR."[50]

An example of American unilateral moves that had rankled Moscow was Kissinger's maneuvering after the Israeli-Arab October War to exclude it from Middle East decision making. (The USSR was the cochair with the United States of a conference for negotiating the peace, but Kissinger circumvented that forum by conducting his famous "shuttle diplomacy" between Middle Eastern capitals.) The Soviets were also highly sensitive to the possibility that the Americans could use Afghan soil after a collapse of the Marxist regime to install the facilities for monitoring Soviet missile tests that were lost to the Iranian

Revolution in 1979. (Any Soviet hopes that the anti-American revolution in Iran would present opportunities such as those initially promised by the Afghan coup were dashed when the Islamic revolution took an anti-Communist turn.) This fear was not merely paranoia; the CIA in the spring of 1979 had surveyed Afghanistan as a possible site for the monitoring stations.[51] In the middle of that year, well before the Soviet decision to intervene, President Carter had approved covert support for the Islamic resistance, the mujahideen.[52]

By the end of the year the Kremlin faced three unpalatable alternatives: the collapse of the Kabul regime and its replacement by an anti-Soviet Islamist movement, a reorientation by a panicky Amin toward Pakistan and the United States, or direct Soviet military intervention to defend Moscow's strategic position. The superpowers perceived the situation in diametrically opposite terms; both could not be correct, and both could be wrong, and to a large degree were. Moscow saw a danger that Afghanistan could be "turned into an imperialist bridgehead on our southern border."[53] In Washington's eyes, this strategically located country offered the Soviets a gateway to warm-water ports and to the oil riches of the Persian Gulf.[54] Claiming that their security interests left them with no choice, the Soviets invaded, executing Amin and installing the compliant Karmal. This was the threshold event that so alarmed Washington: Carter said in a television interview that the Soviet action had "made a more dramatic change in my opinion of what the Soviets' ultimate goals are than anything they've done in the previous time I've been in office."[55] He asked the Senate to indefinitely postpone further consideration of SALT II, signed the previous June, and adopted a series of measures to demonstrate to Moscow that the United States could no longer do business as usual with the USSR. The impact of the intervention also imparted new impetus to Sino-American cooperation.

## THE SINO-AMERICAN RESPONSE

Having embarked on the process of normalizing their relations, Beijing and Washington watched with apprehension as Moscow's power and influence expanded in the 1970s far beyond the boundaries of the Soviet bloc. While relishing its position at the fulcrum of the triangular relationship, the Nixon administration had to reassure the Chinese that its dealings with Moscow would not be at their expense. Kissinger tended to pander to the Chinese, even cynically telling them that Washington sometimes took tough measures against the Soviets even if an issue was more contrived than real—an allusion to Washington's nuclear alert during the 1973 Arab-Israeli War when Moscow threatened to intervene unilaterally if Washington rejected a proposal for joint action to restrain the Israelis, restraint that Kissinger himself also desperately sought. He would also hint to the Chinese that the Nixon administration pursued détente with Moscow for domestic reasons. The administration reassured the Chinese that full diplomatic normalization was on its agenda, though pleading for "running room" to reach that objective while building a domestic consensus for the hard choices that meeting Beijing's requirements on the Taiwan issue would entail. As an interim step agreed upon during Kissinger's visit in February 1973 (after Nixon's reelection and the signing of the Vietnam peace agreement), the two sides established liaison offices in their respective capitals.[56]

Several factors conspired to complicate and retard the normalization process. The Watergate scandal, for one, weakened the presidency and caused Washington to repeatedly postpone consummation—to Beijing's bemusement and consternation. There were also complications on the Chinese domestic front. Opposition from radicals in the Chinese leadership was overcome during the early phases of Sino-American rapprochement, but after an uneasy compromise between moderate and radical elements at the CPC's Tenth Congress in 1973,[57] there was renewed criticism of the American connection and its implications. Thus, while Nixon was heading toward disgrace and resignation, Zhou Enlai, his and Kissinger's principal interlocutor in the negotiations, was weakened by both physical and political ailments (he died in January 1976).[58]

At the same time that the normalization process was stalling, the Chinese were also losing patience over Washington's handling of détente with Moscow. They persistently hectored American leaders over what was depicted as appeasement of Moscow (a recurring theme was an analogy with pre–World War II, when the West was said to have accommodated the Germans while trying to direct their aggression to the east). Another gambit was to express an interest in inviting to Beijing the U.S. secretary of defense, James Schlesinger, a notable opponent of détente. Senator Henry Jackson, another prominent hard-liner, visited Beijing at the same time that Nixon was holding his last summit in Moscow, in mid-1974. (Nixon's successor, Gerald Ford, eventually had enough of internal conflicts within his foreign affairs team, dismissing Schlesinger in November 1975. He also relieved Kissinger, who had been named secretary of state two years earlier, of his concurrent title of national security adviser, and recalled George H.W. Bush from his post as the U.S. liaison representative in Beijing to be director of the CIA.) Mao pressed these concerns over the adverse effects of Watergate and Washington's pursuit of détente with Moscow during Kissinger's visit in November 1973, which was the last occasion on which the two sides were able to issue a joint communiqué until the Carter administration in the late 1970s.

Though lack of progress on normalization precluded issuance of a joint communiqué, President Ford used his visit to China at the end of 1975 to reaffirm his intent to achieve that goal after the election the next year (yet another time the goal line was moved back). For their part the Chinese recited their litany of warnings about the dangers of détente and appeasement of Soviet expansionism, and their list of complaints about U.S. economic and technology assistance to the USSR. The seriously ill Zhou had been replaced by Deng Xiaoping as the principal negotiator. (Deng had been rehabilitated in 1973 several months before the Tenth Congress. He fell again in 1976 after Zhou's death, only to rise again in July 1977, following Mao's death in September 1976 and the purge of the radical Gang of Four a month later.) The assertive Deng pressed the Chinese demands for normalization, namely, severing of U.S. diplomatic relations with the ROC, abrogation of the security treaty, and withdrawal of U.S. troops. The two sides thus had begun talking about the modalities of achieving normalization, though they were now doing little more than marking time.

The advent of the Carter administration in 1977 did not immediately lend new momentum to the process. Sino-American normalization was a major item on the new administration's agenda, but it was subordinate to other foreign policy goals, notably, SALT II and a Panama Canal treaty, both of which required shoring up domestic support. Not only would the latter requirement dictate caution on the normalization process lest valuable political capital be expended, but the Carter administration at the outset took a sanguine view of Soviet actions and thus in effect diluted the importance of the anti-Soviet basis of Sino-American relations. As in the case of its predecessor, the administration contained divided councils on these issues—Secretary of State Cyrus Vance put priority on negotiations with Moscow, and National Security Adviser Zbigniew Brzezinski was more inclined to play the China card. During the first year the Vance line was in the ascendancy, and his visit to Beijing in August failed to push the normalization process forward. The United States, taking into consideration the effects on domestic opinion, said that to realize normalization it would require an official presence in Taipei, though without formal diplomatic representation, and would need to issue a public statement of its interest in a peaceful settlement of the Taiwan issue. Deng dismissed these conditions as amounting to a switch in liaison offices, and he challenged Washington to make up its mind and meet Beijing's three demands.[59]

It was during the Carter administration's second year that a breakthrough was achieved. Not surprisingly, this coincided with an emerging hard line toward Moscow and the ascendance of its avatar, Brzezinski, who was given a mandate to travel to Beijing in May 1978 to convey the administration's readiness to make up its mind as demanded by Deng. The discussion in Beijing, focused in large measure on a common need for coping with "the Polar Bear," included an extensive review of global affairs, with Brzezinski updating the Chinese on U.S.-Soviet relations, SALT, and Soviet weapons developments. Signaling the advent of a new stage in Sino-U.S. security ties, the American delegation included a Defense Department representative and a science and technology official. Two months later, a delegation led by Frank Press, the president's science adviser, negotiated agreements on science and technology cooperation with the Chinese.

To underscore its serious intent about proceeding with normalization after years of marking time, Washington set a date, the first day of 1979, for completing the process. The Panama treaties had been completed, the presidential election would not be coming until a year later, and Carter was now prepared to take a tougher approach toward the Soviets, in which enhanced ties with China would play the role it had assumed when the relationship first developed earlier in the decade. (In a decision indicative of this shift, Vance was overruled in his attempt to strike a balance by timing a planned visit by Soviet Foreign Minister Gromyko to coincide with Brzezinski's China trip. Gromyko's visit was postponed.) According to the instructions given to the U.S. liaison representative in Beijing, Leonard Woodcock, a former union official experienced in negotiations, the United States was prepared to meet Beijing's three conditions but required an understanding on the nature of the American relationship with Taiwan after normalization. To cite Brzezinski's circumlocutionary mantra on this crucial issue, that understanding concerned "the historically transitional period" of the U.S. relationship with the people of Taiwan.

The Carter administration made effective use of multiple channels in negotiating the normalization agreement. The formal talks were held in Beijing between Woodcock and

Foreign Minister Huang Hua (except when he was ill and replaced by his deputy), extending from July until Deng inserted himself for the climactic meetings in December to close the deal. Back in Washington, Brzezinski met with the PRC liaison representative to maintain the strategic dialogue that had stood him in good stead during his Beijing visit, as it had during the early days of Sino-American rapprochement. Chinese complaints about U.S. arms transfers to Taiwan were relegated to a lower level, the Chinese deputy representative delivering protests to Assistant Secretary of State Richard Holbrooke. In addition, Carter made a highly significant intervention in mid-September when he received the new Chinese representative, Chai Zemin, who was told that continuing U.S. trade with Taiwan after normalization would include "the restrained sale of some very carefully selected defensive arms." The president defended this decision as a way to deter Taiwan from turning to other sources or developing nuclear weapons to offset the PRC's overwhelming demographic advantage. At one of the Beijing sessions, in late August, Huang had complained that Woodcock's position was no better than the one taken by Vance in his failed visit the previous year. Huang insisted that Washington must cut all military ties with Taiwan. At the next session, a few days before Carter's intervention, the arms issue was not raised.

The Americans tried to tread with utmost care in addressing the highly sensitive arms issue. One way was to refer to the president's September statement to the Chinese representative without spelling it out, leaving it to the Chinese whether to pursue the subject. At a meeting in early December the Chinese expressed to Woodcock their "emphatic" objection to a continuation of arms sales to Taiwan, but they did not identify it as an insurmountable obstacle to a deal. Some ambiguity developed regarding the relationship of further arms sales and the U.S. offer of a moratorium on arms transfers while the one-year notification of the termination of the U.S.-ROC treaty ran its course. (Brzezinski had gotten the idea of invoking the notification procedure upon learning in 1978 that Beijing intended to follow the terms of the Sino-Soviet treaty by giving a one-year notice to Moscow of its intent to terminate the treaty at the end of its thirty-year term, in 1980.[60] There was a political logic to this idea, but of course the situations were not strictly analogous: Moscow and Beijing continued to recognize each other and maintain diplomatic ties, but Washington maintained a formal treaty relationship for a year with an entity that it no longer recognized as a state—a contradiction in terms.) Deng asked for clarification of this point when he took over the negotiations in mid-December, having just consolidated his position as China's paramount leader (see Chapter 12). He accepted Woodcock's distinction between invoking the terms of the treaty requiring a year's notice and the pledge not to sell arms to Taiwan for a year, which implied a resumption of sales thereafter. The American representative, however, remained uneasy over the arms issue and urged Carter not to make a direct public statement on the matter in view of Chinese sensitivities. But the administration had its own domestic concerns, which required an explicit offer to supply arms to Taiwan as a way of providing some assurance against Beijing's use of force against Taiwan, and thus instructed Woodcock to seek an immediate meeting with Deng to ensure that there was no misunderstanding on this issue. The stage was set for concluding the normalization settlement:

- Deng reacted sharply to Woodcock's statement, asking why the arms issue had been raised again and whether Carter would say publicly that the sale of weapons to Taiwan would continue after 1979—that is, after the moratorium and the lapsing of the treaty with the ROC. Told that Carter would do so, the Chinese leader vented his objections but avoided making the issue a deal breaker, appealing instead for the president to be vague and ambiguous on the subject. Thus the two sides in effect agreed to disagree on this most sensitive subject, kicking the can down the road while pursuing their overriding interest in counterbalancing Soviet power. The Chinese, according to Premier Hua Guofeng's statement when normalization was announced, had "made it clear that we absolutely would not agree" to continuing arms sales to Taiwan. "Nevertheless, we reached an agreement."[61] (Some observers do not accept the interpretation that the two sides agreed to disagree.[62])
- The anti-Soviet basis of the relationship stood out in the joint communiqué on normalization[63] (dated 1 January but issued on 15 December Washington time to avoid premature leaks), which was only a fraction of the length of the Shanghai Communiqué. At Deng's insistence, the communiqué retained the antihegemony clause, but it otherwise eschewed the third-country issues that had been extensively addressed in the 1972 document. In his statement, Hua stressed this aspect in claiming that the agreement contributed to the struggle against "both [Soviet] global hegemony and [Vietnamese] regional hegemony.[64] In the joint communiqué the United States again "acknowledge[d]" the Chinese position that Taiwan is a "part" of China. It bears noting, however, that the Chinese engaged in some linguistic legerdemain in their translation of "acknowledge" on this occasion. Previously, in the Chinese version of the Shanghai Communiqué it was translated as *renshi dao*, but it was now rendered in the normalization communiqué as *chengren*, a term not only with a more positive sense but also the very one used for diplomatic "recognition"; a Chinese reader comparing the Shanghai and normalization documents would see a stronger U.S. undertaking to meet Beijing's claim.
- The United States had asked the Chinese during the negotiations not to contradict its statement of interest in a peaceful settlement of the Taiwan issue. Beijing largely heeded this request, though taking care to note that resolution of the Taiwan question "is entirely China's internal affair."[65]
- The Taiwan Relations Act, passed in April 1979 after arduous negotiations between the administration and legislators concerned about the treatment of an old ally, provided the legal basis for maintaining what the United States said in the joint communiqué would be "cultural, commercial, and other unofficial relations with the people of Taiwan."[66] One aspect of this legislation sharply resented by Beijing was its definition of Washington's commitment to arms transfers to Taiwan. In addition, the act stated that Washington would view any effort to change the status quo in the Taiwan Strait by other than peaceful means "a matter of grave concern," creating a doctrine of "strategic ambiguity" by which Washington would neither say that it would intervene in the event of military hostilities nor say that it would not.

**THE UNITED STATES RETAINS SECURITY LINK WITH TAIWAN: THE TAIWAN RELATIONS ACT**

[T]he United States decision to establish diplomatic relations with the People's Republic of China rests upon the expectation that the future of Taiwan will be determined by peaceful means; . . .

[A]ny effort to determine the future of Taiwan by other than peaceful means, including by boycotts or embargoes, [will be considered] a threat to the peace and security of the Western Pacific area and of grave concern to the United States. . . .

[T]he United States will make available to Taiwan such defense articles and defense services in such quantity as may be necessary to enable Taiwan to maintain a sufficient self-defense capability. . . .

The President is directed to inform the Congress promptly of any threat to the security or the social or economic system of the people of Taiwan and any danger to the interests of the United States arising therefrom. The President and the Congress shall determine, in accordance with constitutional processes, appropriate action by the United States in response to any such danger.

Taiwan Relations Act, adopted by U.S. Congress 10 April 1979, in Ross, *Negotiating Cooperation*, 273–83.

In the immediate wake of the euphoria created by the normalization agreement, an ebullient Deng, named *Time* magazine's "Man of the Year," made a triumphant visit to America featuring lighthearted acts such as donning a Stetson hat in Texas. It would soon become evident, however, that the Chinese had some serious geopolitical uses in mind for their enhanced America connection.

## EXPLODING TENSIONS

The late 1970s saw polarizing forces become more pronounced in Asia as well as globally. As already noted, the Carter administration shifted in its second year to a hard line toward Moscow, giving renewed impetus to the faltering effort to normalize relations with Beijing. Parallel with the developments leading to Sino-American normalization, Moscow and Hanoi were moving ever closer as regional tensions heightened. In February 1978 a Soviet offer to improve relations with China was rebuffed. By contrast, a half year later Beijing concluded a peace treaty with Tokyo—a goal continuing to elude Moscow—that contained the anti-Soviet antihegemony clause. Meanwhile, the Soviets were drifting into their own version of the Vietnam quagmire in Afghanistan, a deepening involvement formalized by the friendship treaty signed in December.

During this period Hanoi began introducing collectivization measures in South Vietnam that adversely affected the ethnic Chinese there and embittered relations between the PRC and Vietnam, already strained by Beijing's readiness to subordinate Vietnamese interests to its higher geopolitical imperatives. The Vietnamese also had strained relations with their former Cambodian allies, the Khmer Rouge, with whom long-simmering tensions and border disputes produced skirmishes and recriminations. Hanoi moved deeper into Moscow's embrace by joining the Soviet economic bloc that summer, and in November the two sides' security ties were strengthened by the signing of a treaty of peace and cooperation. Meanwhile, Washington shelved negotiations on normalizing relations with Hanoi, a project that was pushed aside lest it impede the Sino-American talks.

The gathering tensions exploded in late 1978 when the Vietnamese invaded Cambodia, quickly ousting the Khmer Rouge from Phnom Penh and establishing Vietnam's historical goal of hegemony in the region. Hanoi may have been emboldened by its enhanced security links with Moscow, but the Chinese meanwhile had strengthened their hand by the normalization of relations with the United States. In February 1979, soon after Deng's victory lap in America, the Chinese surged across the Vietnam border to teach their erstwhile friends a lesson. The purported cause of the Chinese incursion was repeated Vietnamese border provocations, but the punitive strike served a broader purpose of restraining Hanoi in its regional ambitions. If the Chinese thought they could replicate their decisive attack on India in 1962, they were to learn some lessons of their own from the battle-hardened Vietnamese; plagued by combined arms deficiencies and command-and-control problems, the Chinese troops did not acquit themselves particularly well (and as the Indians had earlier, they began taking steps to remedy these shortcomings). But as in that previous conflict, the Chinese goals were limited and did not include a march to the Vietnamese capital. Though the Vietnamese were not dislodged from Cambodia at the time, Beijing nonetheless had delivered the message that Vietnam's huge neighbor to the north was prepared to use force to protect its interests in the neighborhood. Less than three weeks after invading, the Chinese announced their withdrawal, but they left behind a tense situation that compelled the Vietnamese to maintain troops on the border.

Thus the Third Indochina War had been launched. This time the Chinese and Americans found themselves supporting the same side (there were non-Communist elements in the resistance movement against Hanoi's puppet regime, but the awkward reality for the United States was that the notorious Khmer Rouge formed the backbone and musculature of the insurgency). Deng had informed Carter of China's impending action, but Carter had done nothing to dissuade him. In fact, during the Chinese operation Brzezinski met with the PRC's representative in Washington daily to pass on intelligence concerning Soviet activities.[67] Meanwhile, Moscow served as principal supporter for the Vietnamese military moves, garnering as a reward the use of the major Cam Ranh Bay naval base constructed during the American presence as well as a signals intelligence facility.[68]

These polarizing tendencies culminated at the end of 1979 with the Soviet invasion of Afghanistan. Moscow's action, contrasting with the U.S. humiliation in the Iranian Revolution and the seizure of American diplomats in Tehran, deepened the widespread perception, shared by Washington and Beijing, of a dangerously aggressive Soviet thrust toward global predominance. A SALT II agreement was signed in June 1979 at a summit meeting in Vienna, but prospects for ratification were clouded by the loss of the facilities in northern Iran that monitored Soviet missile tests, thus impairing U.S. capabilities of determining Soviet compliance with the treaty provisions. This became another subject of deepening Sino-American collaboration. During his U.S. visit Deng had offered to cooperate in intelligence collection against the Soviet Union, and the two sides thereafter agreed on establishment of facilities in Xinjiang to replace the monitoring sites in Iran.[69]

The monitoring sites were a closely held secret at the time, but expanding Sino-American security ties were on display for all the world—and of course for the Kremlin, brooding over the implications of this trend—when the U.S. secretary of defense, Harold Brown, visited China in January 1980. That the Soviets had just invaded Afghanistan prompted Carter to resolve differences within his administration over military ties with China by authorizing his defense secretary to offer the sale of "nonlethal" military equipment. The Soviet action was perceived as crossing a threshold; now another one was crossed with the initiation of an arms relationship between America and China. By the early 1980s the strategic realignment had produced an anti-Soviet coalition, what the Chinese called a united front against Soviet hegemony. As it would turn out, though it certainly did not seem so at the time, this marked both the high tide of the expansion of Soviet influence in the world and the concomitant climax of Sino-American collaboration to resist that tide.

# 11 THE END OF THE COLD WAR

The sorry spectacle of Kremlin gerontocrats dropping one after another like a row of dominoes closed with one of the most fateful leadership shifts in the century. The arrival of a new generation at the top of the Soviet hierarchy in the person of the fifty-four-year-old Mikhail Gorbachev set in motion the policy changes that would lead to the dismantling of the Soviet Union and the end of the Cold War. This denouement caught everyone, not least Gorbachev and his colleagues, by surprise. Perhaps those who had followed the liberalization process in Czechoslovakia in 1968 could have understood the dynamics and anticipated the runaway changes, the crucial difference being that "big brother" was available and willing to dam the flow of events before it was too late in that earlier drama but there was no one to play that role two decades later.

## SOVIET LEADERSHIP SUCCESSION

The agony of the Kremlin's succession crisis began with Leonid Brezhnev's increasing frailty and then his death in November 1982, followed by the demise in February 1984 of his successor, Yuriy Andropov, and in March 1985 of Konstantin Chernenko. Gorbachev's accession made him the fourth Soviet leader in the short span of two and a half years. Deriding the long Brezhnev era as one of stagnation in Soviet development, the new leader sought to reinvigorate a country that was falling embarrassingly behind its Western rivals. Systemic constraints and halfway measures proved to raise expectations much higher than achievements, however, not only dooming Gorbachev's career but also consigning the Soviet Union to the scrapheap of history.[1]

Long-term trends had left the Soviet Union in a rut: a highly inefficient command economy, ecological ravages, Brezhnev's "stability of cadres" (a reaction to Khrushchev's "harebrained" reorganization schemes), and a crushing burden of military expenditures (again a reaction to Khrushchev's fitful efforts to divert resources into economic sectors outside the military-industrial complex). As Gorbachev learned only upon reaching the top, military costs devoured 40 percent of the state budget instead of the announced 16 percent, and 20 percent of gross national product instead of 6 percent.[2] Strategic parity with the United States had been achieved at a staggering cost, and now the Kremlin was confronted with a Reagan administration intent on pressing an expensive arms race to new limits. This also came at a time when the props supporting a rotting economy had been removed, the precipitous fall in oil prices in the mid-1980s coinciding with a severe drop in oil production in the Soviet Union. The country had been living on borrowed time thanks to the mirror opposite circumstances in the previous decade: The huge spikes in oil prices (following the Arab-Israeli War in 1973 and the Iranian Revolution in 1979) had come just as the rich Siberian oilfields became available. From 1973 to 1985 energy exports accounted for 80 percent of hard-currency earnings, financing the military buildup and imports of Western technology and grain.[3] Gorbachev's timing was hardly propitious.

## CHALLENGE TO THE SOVIETS

In the wake of its invasion of Afghanistan, the Soviet Union faced a more vigorous challenge from the West. In his final year in office, President Carter had submitted a budget increasing defense spending by 5 percent in real terms, asked the Senate to defer consideration of the SALT II agreement reached in 1979, organized a boycott of the 1980 Olympic Games in Moscow, and applied various economic sanctions on the Soviet Union. This was but a foretaste of his successor's prescription for reversing what was perceived as relentless Soviet advances under the cover of détente. President Reagan presided over the largest peacetime military buildup in history, and he startled the world by proposing what he called the Strategic Defense Initiative (popularly referred to as "Star Wars"), a technologically ambitious and politically contentious project for launching satellites that would destroy missiles before they could reach the territory targeted (a project that would violate the ABM treaty, considered by arms control advocates as a cornerstone of strategic stability). He also advocated, in what was known as the Reagan Doctrine, that the United States move from the negative posture of containment and take "the offensive with a forward strategy" for rolling back Communism and combating the "Evil Empire."[4] In effect—and the administration acknowledged as much—this was a challenge to the Brezhnev Doctrine that once a country became Communist it must remain so even if this required Soviet intervention. From Afghanistan to Nicaragua, from Angola to Cambodia, Reagan had thrown down the gauntlet to the Communists.

Reagan's hard-line stance was fortified by Britain's Conservative Party leader Margaret Thatcher, who became prime minister the year before his election. His hand was also strengthened by NATO's success—in the face of widespread antinuclear protests in Western Europe and an intense Soviet propaganda and covert action campaign seeking to divide the West—in remaining firm behind plans to install a new generation of intermediate-range missiles in the European theater to counter the powerful and accurate Soviet SS-20s. He also found a kindred spirit in Asia, Japanese Prime Minister Nakasone Yasuhiro (forming the "Ron and Yasu" duo), who pledged to have Japan take a stronger geopolitical role more commensurate with its status as an economic superpower. Japan had reached that status by following a path of economic development along successive stages, from labor-intensive manufacturing (textiles, steel, shipbuilding) to capital-intensive sectors (electronics, automobiles), finally becoming the world's principal banker as the United States was transformed from the leading creditor to the leading debtor nation in the world. By the 1980s Japan's exports accounted for a tenth of the world's total, including more than a fifth of America's imports. Japan's economic "miracle," its stunning success in capturing export markets, and its vast capital accumulation (leading to purchases abroad of iconic properties such as Rockefeller Center in Manhattan and Hollywood film studios), led a bemused world to contemplate the sources of its remarkable achievements—as reflected in such titles as *Japan as Number One* and *Trading Places: How We Allowed Japan to Take the Lead*.[5]

Nakasone sought to translate that economic power into a more muscular role in security affairs. At a time of heightened Cold War tensions after the collapse of détente in the late 1970s, he aligned his country closely with the United States and China, including on such issues as Afghanistan and Cambodia, and committed his country to defending the sea-lanes up to one thousand miles from the homeland. He called Japan "an unsinkable aircraft carrier" as a bulwark against the Soviets, and he abandoned the ceiling of 1 percent of gross national product for military expenditures (though that ceiling was breached only once, barely, in 1987).[6]

It was in this context of deepening Cold War strains and a reinvigorated challenge from the United States and its allies that the new Kremlin leadership sought to fashion a policy of reform, called *perestroika* (reconstruction). In addition to attempting to spark an "acceleration" of economic production, the program sought to animate the support of the population by a policy of *glasnost* (openness), giving the media an exhilarating free rein and fostering political pluralism. The effect, however, was to unleash forces that caused the Communist Party to lose its hold on power. Long-repressed ethnic nationalism found explosive expression. The centrifugal forces straining the Soviet empire led to the astonishingly rapid collapse of Communism in Eastern Europe and then of the multiethnic Soviet Union itself.

## "NEW THINKING" IN FOREIGN AFFAIRS

Much of the impetus for the imperial retreat that occurred in the late 1980s came from Asia, where the heavy Soviet military presence imposed a significant burden on Moscow's treasury. According to Eduard Shevardnadze, the Georgian leader appointed by Gorbachev to replace Gromyko as foreign minister, the war in Afghanistan cost sixty billion rubles and the confrontation with China at least two hundred billion; a "colossal military infrastructure" had been built along the Chinese border.[7] Gorbachev also may have been intent on relieving himself of this burden in order to focus on his goal of integrating the Soviet Union into "the common European home." In what he called "new thinking" in foreign affairs, Gorbachev renounced the Marxist-Leninist doctrine of class struggle on the international stage and stressed shared "humanistic" values, thus in effect discarding the Iron Curtain into the junkyard of history.

Addressing his first CPSU Congress as party chief, a year after his accession, Gorbachev signaled the significant changes that were about to germinate. He took special note of the gradually improving relations with the Soviet Union's "great neighbor, socialist China," thereby reinforcing a process that was to culminate before the end of the decade in full Sino-Soviet reconciliation (as discussed later in this chapter). Most notably, he called Afghanistan "a bleeding wound," a remarkable and highly significant admission that the Soviets were mired in an intractable conflict and would need to find a way out.[8] Several months later, in July 1986, Gorbachev set out his Asian agenda in a watershed policy statement delivered in Vladivostok, a venue chosen to dramatize his message to the Soviet Union's neighbors.[9] Gorbachev again pointed to favorable progress in Sino-Soviet relations and took the occasion to announce steps toward relieving China's concerns over the massive deployment of Soviet forces along its borders: a reduction of forces in Afghanistan in the interest of spurring a negotiated settlement, consultation with Mongolia regarding a "considerable" withdrawal of Soviet troops from that ally's territory (thus reversing the buildup that followed the Soviet-Mongolian treaty of 1966), and an offer to discuss with China "a balanced reduction of forces" along their borders. In what seemed almost an offhand remark, he also offered to accept the Chinese position claiming the *thalweg* as the boundary in riverine borders, thereby conceding the crucial juridical issue in the border dispute and opening the way to a settlement.

These offers were to bear fruit and lead to a significant Soviet retrenchment in Asia. Within a few years the Soviets evacuated Afghanistan, the confrontation with China was ended, and the basic elements of a border settlement were put in place awaiting only final details. At this early stage, however, Moscow was reluctant to leave the field to its rivals in Indochina, where its ally Vietnam was supporting a client regime in Cambodia against a resistance backed by the United States, China, and ASEAN. Fending off international

---

**THE BEGINNING OF THE END OF THE COLD WAR: GORBACHEV IN VLADIVOSTOK**

At present . . . the question of withdrawing a large part of the Soviet troops in Mongolia is being considered. . . .

An appreciable improvement in our relations [with China] has taken place in the past few years. I want to reaffirm that the Soviet Union is prepared, at any time and at any level, to discuss with China in the most serious way questions of additional measures to create an atmosphere of good-neighborliness.

Let the basin of this mighty river [the Amur] unite the efforts of the Chinese and Soviet peoples in using to their common benefit the very rich resources existing there and in engaging in water-resources construction. . . . Officially, the border could run along the main navigation channel [*thalweg*]. . . .

It was stated from the rostrum of the 27th CPSU Congress that we are prepared to bring home the Soviet troops who are in [Afghanistan]. . . . [T]he Soviet leadership has adopted a decision that I am officially announcing today: Before the end of 1986, six regiments—one tank regiment, two motorized infantry regiments and three anti-aircraft regiments—will be returned from Afghanistan to the homeland, with their authorized equipment and arms.

Mikhail Gorbachev speech on Soviet Asia policy in Vladivostok, 28 July 1986, *Pravda*, 29 July 1986. "Condensed text" in *Current Digest of the Soviet Press* 38, no. 30 (27 August 1986): 1, 3–8, 32.

pressure to end support for Vietnam's role in Cambodia, Gorbachev claimed that a Cambodia settlement depended on the normalization of Sino-Vietnamese relations

## THREE OBSTACLES

The Chinese took a wait-and-see posture toward Gorbachev's initiatives. Deng Xiaoping provided an authoritative response in September, taking a wary but open approach ("a cautious welcome" to what was "new and positive") and reiterating Beijing's demand that Moscow remove the "three obstacles" to normalized relations: withdrawal from Afghanistan, reduction of forces along China's borders, and cessation of Soviet support for Vietnam in Cambodia.[10] Choosing the very issue on which Gorbachev had been least forthcoming, Deng emphasized the Cambodia issue as the "key" obstacle, though he left the door enticingly open by saying he would be happy to meet with Gorbachev if that obstacle were removed. The Soviets took the opening by making another in the series of concessions that had now begun to characterize Gorbachev's approach; departing from their previous refusal to include Cambodia in their semiannual talks with the Chinese, they allowed that topic to be put on the table at the next round in October. By August 1988 this had evolved to the point that a special meeting was dedicated specifically to the Cambodia issue.

Still another concession was calculated to reassure the Chinese that Gorbachev was serious in his intentions. In the contentious Soviet-American negotiations over the deployment of intermediate-range nuclear forces in Europe, Washington had acceded to Moscow's demand that it be permitted to have one hundred of these missiles in Asia while they were being barred from Europe. But now, in 1987, Gorbachev unilaterally offered to give up this right, paving the way for elimination for the first time of a whole category of nuclear weapons. Gorbachev's announcement was originally delivered in an interview with the Indonesian paper *Merdeka*, thus underlining its significance for Asia, and was given extensive publicity in the Soviet media.[11]

As it was constrained to do in 1954 and again in 1972, Hanoi read the geopolitical writing on the wall and began following Moscow's lead in withdrawing from its overstretched position. (Hanoi also adopted its own version of *perestroika*, called *doi moi*.) In the early 1980s the Vietnamese, seeking to reduce the pressure applied by the coalition aligned against their presence in Cambodia, had committed themselves to partial withdrawals, but the Chinese kept the pressure on by demanding unconditional withdrawal. Now, with its indispensable patron intent on removing this obstacle to Sino-Soviet reconciliation, Hanoi announced in May 1988 that it was withdrawing fifty thousand troops from Cambodia by the end of the year, with more to follow; the remainder were to be out by the following September. The "key" obstacle to normalization of Sino-Soviet relations had been removed.

This series of announcements was capped by Gorbachev's dramatic proclamation at the UN General Assembly in December 1988 of sweeping troop withdrawals and arms reductions.[12] He spoke of the "de-ideologization" of international relations and of the principle of "freedom of choice," in effect a renunciation of the Brezhnev Doctrine justifying intervention in Communist countries and a signal of the toleration that would be extended to the sweeping collapse of Communist regimes in Eastern Europe that occurred the following year. He announced a unilateral reduction of a half million troops, which would include most of those in Mongolia and a total of two hundred thousand withdrawn from Asia. The Sino-Soviet confrontation was drawing to a close.

## CROSSING THE TERMIZ BRIDGE

Moscow had realized early in its adventure in Afghanistan that a military solution was unlikely given the weak political base of its clients in Kabul and the tenacity of the Islamist resistance (with obvious parallels to Washington's experience in Vietnam). As reflected in his startling reference to Afghanistan as a bleeding wound (at the party congress in 1986), Gorbachev recognized the need to escape the quagmire; already in late 1985 the Politburo decided to withdraw forces as soon as feasible, and Moscow was signaling its concern over Kabul's political weakness.[13] This concern led to the removal of Babrak Karmal, the leader who had been installed when the Soviets intervened in late 1979 but who proved incapable of broadening the regime's base. Mohammad Najibullah, his replacement (first as party chief in May 1986 and then as president a half year later), was told by Gorbachev in late 1986 that the Soviets would be out in no later than two years and that he should shore up the regime's position through promoting a more inclusive political process known as "national reconciliation."[14]

At first Gorbachev sanctioned an offensive in Afghanistan, perhaps to demonstrate the futility of the military option but more likely to secure better conditions for a negotiated settlement.[15] There was no move, however, to expand the Soviet troop presence in an attempt to overwhelm the resistance, which at this time received massive assistance from the United States, China, Saudi Arabia, and Iran, with Pakistan as the main conduit, and which by late 1986 was further enhanced by the provision of handheld Stinger antiaircraft missiles to combat the intensified use of air power and new tactics by the Soviets. On the other end of the technological spectrum, thousands of mules were imported from China to transport arms to the resistance. UN-mediated talks between the Kabul government and Pakistan provided a diplomatic platform for a settlement, which took the form of a package of accords signed in Geneva in April 1988. In addition to agreements between Kabul and Islamabad, one of which took note of Moscow's commitment to a phased withdrawal of its troops to be completed by early 1989, a "Declaration on International Guarantees" underwritten by the two superpowers was issued.[16] An effective agreement to end external supplies was unattainable at the time, however, with Washington insisting on maintaining "positive symmetry"—meaning it would continue to supply the resistance so long as Moscow provided aid to the Kabul regime.

The Soviet commander led his last contingent of troops across the Termiz bridge into Soviet Uzbekistan on schedule in February 1989. To the surprise of many, Najibullah was able to remain in power until the superpowers finally agreed, in late 1991, to stop supplying their Afghan clients. Najibullah finally fell in April 1992, outlasting Gorbachev and even the Soviet Union itself.

## SINO-SOVIET NORMALIZATION

Moscow and Beijing had been preparing the ground for a better relationship since the early 1980s, following the period of sharply polarized Soviet-U.S. and Sino-Soviet relations in the previous decade (as discussed in Chapter 10). Reagan's campaign oratory during the 1980 presidential election had disturbed the Chinese by his calls for upgrading U.S. ties with Taiwan. The new Reagan administration at first tried to buy off Beijing by offering arms, but this undervalued the PRC's commitment to a one-China policy. Moscow meanwhile seized the opportunity to fish in troubled waters: Brezhnev used a speech in Tashkent in March 1982 to remind the Chinese that Moscow had unwaveringly supported their position on the Taiwan issue. He also made the point that Moscow did not deny that China's system was socialist, removing an ideological issue dating back to the 1960s. Eventually, after extremely arduous negotiations, Washington and Beijing concluded an agreement in August of that year according to which the United States committed itself to capping the level of arms supplies to Taiwan and to "gradually" reduce them. (Reagan, however, unilaterally wrote a secret codicil conditioning the level of arms provided to Taiwan "entirely on the threat posed by the PRC."[17])

Beijing by now had concluded that a more balanced position between the two superpowers would better serve its interests, one that was ratified at the CPC's Twelfth Congress that September as an "independent" foreign policy. Beijing may have been stung by a realization that Washington was using the China card against the Soviets without taking due consideration of the PRC's vital interests. It may also have concluded that with the intensifying American challenge to the Soviets there was less need for the U.S. connection to counterbalance pressure from Moscow, affording the Chinese space in which to pursue a more equidistant line between the superpowers. In any case, Beijing and Moscow now proceeded to take steps to foster improved ties. Bilateral talks—which had been proposed by Beijing in February 1979 when it formally declared its decision to terminate the treaty of alliance with Moscow, but had been derailed by the Soviet invasion of Afghanistan—were now put on track. The Chinese and Soviet parliaments exchanged visits in 1983–84, and enough trust had accrued for a five-year trade pact to be signed in 1984. There were also signs pointing to a resumption of long-ruptured party ties, as in fraternal salutes to "Comrade" Gorbachev at the time of Chernenko's funeral in March 1985. Vice Premier Li Peng, in Moscow for the funeral, reciprocated Brezhnev's gesture three years earlier by calling the Soviet Union a socialist country.

While the two sides were registering progress in removing the three main obstacles on the path to normalization of relations, they were also clearing away the underbrush that had accumulated over the decades. Thus, in the 1980s they ceased jamming the radio broadcasts that each beamed in the other's languages and closed clandestine stations—as well as Moscow's purportedly unofficial Radio Peace and Progress—responsible for the most vitriolic, even subversive polemical attacks. (The quirkiest practice in the broadcasting wars involved Radio Beijing's Russian service, whose multiple programs beamed daily to the USSR were all jammed—except for one program each day that was broadcast backwards!) In the late 1980s the disrupted border talks resumed, with Gorbachev's acceptance of the *thalweg* principle having opened the way to fruitful negotiations. An exchange of visits by the foreign ministers prepared the ground for a visit to Beijing by Gorbachev in May 1989, the first Sino-Soviet summit meeting in three decades.

Officially at the invitation of China's president, Yang Shangkun, Gorbachev's visit symbolized the normalization of relations between the two countries, including ties between the two Communist parties. In addition to his host, Gorbachev met with the paramount leader Deng, party chief Zhao Ziyang, and Premier Li Peng. Since coming to power, the Soviet leader had pointed to affinities between the two countries in their pursuit of economic reform, but the normalization of relations had proceeded from geopolitical rather than ideological premises, as the removal of the three obstacles demonstrated. Progress on this front was registered in the joint communiqué, in which the two sides abjured the pursuit of hegemony—in the earlier period a code word for the expansion of Soviet power—and stressed their interest in resisting attempts by others to impose their will. All of this reflected the strategic shifts that had taken place during the decade, with the reassertion of American strength and the concomitant Soviet disengagement.

The two sides agreed to press ahead toward a boundary settlement and to reduce their forces along the border to a level commensurate with normal relations between good neighbors. Border negotiations thereupon made good progress, though the finishing touches were not applied until the new century and crucial compromises were achieved (see Chapter 13).

The charismatic Gorbachev's visit coincided with other developments, such as the death of former CPC General Secretary Hu Yaobang, a symbol of liberalizing tendencies; the seventieth anniversary of the May Fourth student protests; and the eruption of demonstrations in Tiananmen Square demanding reform, that provided a dramatic backdrop to the normalization of Sino-Soviet relations. Though the Soviet leader had cited a shared interest in economic modernization in pushing forward the normalization process, the events of that spring underscored the fundamental divergence in the reform paths the two countries were pursuing. In particular, *glasnost* and the introduction of elements of political pluralism by Gorbachev were anathema to China's Leninist leadership. Thus, the demonstrations produced awkward moments during the visit, notably Gorbachev's meeting with Zhao, the reform-minded party chief who faded from the public scene a few days later and was disgraced the next month as the leadership mounted a bloody crackdown on the demonstrators. In a remarkable revelation—remarkable in having been made to a visiting leader at a delicate time in Chinese domestic affairs—Zhao disclosed that notwithstanding Deng's formal retirement from the Politburo it had been agreed that major decisions would be referred to him. In effect Zhao was indicating that he was being overridden by Deng on how to respond to demands for more extensive change, and inviting the inference that Zhao was a man of his times like Gorbachev but was being held in check by the older generation.[18]

Criticism that rained on Zhao after his disgrace resembled that directed at Gorbachev by Soviet conservatives—internal Chinese documents reportedly criticized "revisionist" developments in the Soviet Union—but ideological strains did not impede further development of relations.[19] Moreover, the Tiananmen Square crackdown in June produced even sharper tensions in Sino-American relations, seriously darkening the atmosphere and prompting an arms embargo against China. (Washington's effort to contain the fallout with two visits in the wake of the Tiananmen incidents by President Bush's national security adviser, Brent Scowcroft, created a backlash in American domestic opinion that imposed added constraints on Sino-U.S. relations.) In any case, ideological interests did not determine relations between Moscow and Beijing at this time. Premier Li's visit to Moscow the following April produced agreements on economic cooperation and principles governing troop reductions along the border as well as optimistic assessments of the ongoing border negotiations. In a *Pravda* interview at the time, Li somewhat tentatively observed that the Soviets had not "renounced the ideals of socialism," but he added that normal relations should be maintained "even if" they were to do so.[20]

The Leninist Chinese regime certainly did not join the cheering from much of the rest of the world as the astonishing changes of late 1989 swept across Eastern Europe. The fall of the Berlin Wall in November symbolized the end of the Iron Curtain, and the countries once embraced in the Soviet empire shed their Marxist-Leninist systems one after another (the domino theory finally vindicated) and looked to "Europe" as their natural home. It had to be particularly unnerving to Beijing to see the tide of change reach China's borders when Mongolia discarded Communism in 1990, and then the Soviet Union itself imploded at the end of the next year. Still, notwithstanding the profound distaste the Beijing leadership had for these developments and their implications for China, there was no interruption in the process that had gathered steam through the 1980s and now proceeded apace. Indeed, the way was now clear for Beijing and Moscow to form what they hailed as a "strategic partnership," in which they found mutual interests in coping with the challenging environment of a single superpower in a unipolar world.

## IMPACT ON THE KOREAN PENINSULA

A significant dimension of the Gorbachev leadership's effort to revitalize the economy by *perestroika* at home and retrenchment abroad was a fundamental reorientation of the country's foreign economic relations. This was to produce a particularly dramatic effect on the Korean peninsula, causing profound geopolitical shifts along with basic changes in trade relations. The result was that in a few years, as the Cold War was winding down, the ROK was recognized by Moscow and its Eastern European allies (as well as Yugoslavia), and both South and North Korea (grudgingly in the latter's case) entered the United Nations. Meanwhile, the Chinese, following the post-Mao pattern of giving priority to economic over political change, had been increasing their trade relations with South Korea to a level many times greater than that with their North Korean ally. In 1992, two years after Moscow's recognition of Seoul, Beijing followed suit, gaining the additional benefit of ending the ROK'S diplomatic ties with Taiwan. Washington, however, concerned about North Korea's nuclear ambitions, did not follow the pattern of cross-recognition by recognizing Pyongyang.[21]

The Olympic Games held in Seoul in September 1988 set the stage for these dramatic developments.[22] A few weeks earlier the new ROK president, Roh Tae Woo, had expressed interest in improved relations with the Communist countries, helping pave the way to their participation despite Pyongyang's objections. Gorbachev seized the occasion to deliver another major Asian policy statement. Speaking in the Siberian city of Krasnoyarsk on the day before the Olympics opened, he noted a "highly promising process" under way in the Asia-Pacific region since his watershed Vladivostok speech two years earlier. In addition to holding out the prospect for developing economic ties with South Korea, he proposed multinational talks to reduce military forces in the area where his country, China, Japan, and the two Koreas converge.[23] This was followed by invitations to two leading opposition leaders (and future ROK presidents), Kim Dae Jung and Kim Young Sam, to pay visits in the first half of 1989 hosted by Moscow think tanks, and the dispatch a year later of a special envoy (Anatoliy Dobrynin, the former ambassador to the United States) to Seoul to relay Gorbachev's readiness to meet with ROK President Roh Tae Woo. Such a meeting took place a couple of weeks later, in San Francisco, where the Kremlin leader had traveled after summit talks with President George H.W. Bush.

Pyongyang watched this rapidly developing situation with alarm and fury, which erupted in a public outcry after Foreign Minister Shevardnadze arrived in the North Korean capital in September 1990 to deliver the brutal message that Moscow was going to recognize Seoul. An authoritative Commentator article in the party organ *Nodong sinmun* vented Pyongyang's ire under a bitter headline, "'Diplomatic Relations' Sold and Bought with Dollars."[24] The North Koreans deplored Moscow's move as a violation of the Treaty of Peace, Friendship, and Mutual Assistance and as recognizing the South's international legitimacy and hence freezing the division of the peninsula. Particularly galling was that the Gorbachev-Roh meeting had taken place on American soil.

The Commentator article's reference to the economic motives behind Moscow's move was certainly apt. By the year of Gorbachev's Krasnoyarsk speech, the Soviets were shipping 1.9 billion dollars in goods to North Korea while receiving less than half that in return, a heavily subsidized trade relationship that accounted for three-fourths of the DPRK's total trade.[25] With the relationship now placed on a commercial rather than a concessionary basis, the crucial Soviet support for North Korea's economy was removed, causing a sharp drop in imports from the Soviet Union and severe economic privation. At the same time, while removing still another burden from Moscow's overextended commitments to its allies, the Kremlin managed to extract from South Korea loans totaling three billion dollars, including cash to relieve the bleak economic situation in the Soviet Union. In short, Moscow had undergone a remarkable role reversal in its dealings with the peninsula; instead of acting out of ideological and strategic motives as the DPRK's patron, the Soviet Union had become a supplicant of the capitalist ROK.

Beijing's road to recognition of Seoul was a longer one, with origins in the Dengist program of opening China to global trade relations.[26] Pyongyang's leverage in dealing with its big Communist patrons—its ability to profit from their competition for influence—had been undercut by the Sino-Soviet normalization, leaving the way open for them to pursue relations with the South. In late 1990, a few months after Moscow established diplomatic ties with Seoul, the Chinese opened trade offices in South Korea. Like the Soviets, the Chinese put trade relations with the DPRK on a commercial rather than concessionary basis. After visits by the Chinese premier and foreign minister in 1991 carrying the message that Beijing did not oppose dual admission of the two Koreas to the UN, Pyongyang saw no choice but to join the world body along with the ROK.

In addition to the economic gains in developing ties with Seoul, Beijing also successfully demanded that the ROK terminate its diplomatic relations with Taiwan, eliminating the latter's last toehold on the continent. Beijing and Seoul exchanged recognition in September 1992, followed a couple of months later by a visit to China by Roh Tae Woo.

## THE CAMBODIAN SETTLEMENT

The transformed geopolitical environment produced by Soviet retrenchment decoupled local and regional issues from the broader strategic context that had been superimposed by the Cold War. Previously Washington—along with Beijing after the emergence of the strategic triangle—deplored Moscow's readiness to seize opportunities in regional conflicts to extend its geopolitical reach while seeking to insulate these moves from the East-West or Sino-Soviet context. Thus the Nixon administration sought to exact costs from the Soviets in these circumstances by the policy of linkage, making progress in such matters as trade and arms control conditional on Soviet restraint in the third world. But with Moscow in retreat and Soviet power removed from the equation, those regional issues no longer were burdened with Cold War implications, opening the way for negotiated settlements.

In the case of the Cambodian conflict, the age-old Vietnamese-Khmer rivalry, flaring into firefights and recriminations after (and even before) the Communist victories in the two countries, had been encrusted with layers of conflict from outside the region. The collision between Hanoi's quest for hegemony in the region and the Khmer Rouge's fierce nationalism set the stage for the Third Indochina War, and like its predecessors it sucked in a variety of external forces. As has been seen, China invaded Vietnam to teach the lesson that the latter could not ignore the former's interests in the region, the latest chapter in a long story of Sino-Vietnamese rivalry. Meanwhile, the ASEAN countries shared with China and the United States a determination to reverse Hanoi's intervention in Cambodia to impose its client regime. On the broadest strategic plane, Cambodia had salience in the strategic triangle as a case of Moscow's use of surrogates to extend its geopolitical power.

After the Vietnamese invasion, the United States, Japan, and the European Community imposed economic sanctions, ASEAN exerted diplomatic pressure, and arms supplies from the Chinese to the Khmer Rouge and from Washington to other resistance groups based along the Thai-Cambodian border intensified the strains and costs of the occupation. A coalition government with Sihanouk as head of state, comprising the Khmer Rouge and two non-Communist groups (a royalist faction loyal to Sihanouk and a nationalist faction headed by a former prime minister, Son Sann), was formed in 1982 to provide cover for international support for the widely reviled Khmer Rouge, which was thus able to retain its UN seat as Democratic Kampuchea while its rival, the Vietnamese-installed People's Republic of Kampuchea, remained an international pariah. A stalemate persisted through the decade, until Gorbachev's disengagement initiatives removed the Cambodia obstacle from Sino-Soviet and Sino-Vietnamese relations.[27]

Hanoi's decision to withdraw its troops cleared the way for negotiations, but a sticking point concerned transitional arrangements for the period before a final settlement. In a situation of acute mistrust and animosity, the contending Cambodian sides were loath to share power and surrender their weapons during the transition. Moreover, their main external patrons had not been able to reach agreement on this point; during Gorbachev's visit to China, the two sides expressed their shared concern over civil war in Cambodia, but the Soviet leader would not go along with Beijing's proposal for a quadripartitite coalition government under Sihanouk's titular leadership during the transition. Against the background of Hanoi's announcement the previous month that its troops would be withdrawn by September regardless of whether ASEAN-sponsored negotiations by the Cambodian parties had been successfully completed, extraregional forces began to exert their influence by calling an international conference that opened in Paris in July. The conference, cochaired by the former colonial overlord, France, and the strongest ASEAN country, Indonesia, brought to the table the four Cambodian parties, the Security Council permanent members, and regional powers, but it still foundered on the issue of dismantling the Phnom Penh administration before elections.

Eventually, in a process plagued by false starts and impasses, but facilitated by warming Sino-Vietnamese relations and pressure from China and the United States, agreement was reached on a UN-approved plan creating a Supreme National Council comprising the Cambodian factions, which in turn would delegate executive powers to a UN Transitional Authority in Cambodia (UNTAC). In mid-1991 agreement was reached regarding demobilization of troops and elections, and a few months later control over security affairs and finance was turned over to UNTAC. Pursuant to "A Comprehensive Political Settlement of the Cambodian Conflict" signed in Paris in October 1991, a twenty-two-thousand-strong UN peacekeeping force (headed by a Japanese, Akashi Yasushi), the largest ever assembled by the world body, arrived to supervise the cease-fire and prepare for elections. Though obstructed by the Khmer Rouge, elections drawing a massive turnout and certified as fair by the UN were held in 1993, resulting in formation of a coalition government within a constitutional monarchy headed by Sihanouk. His son, Prince Norodom Ranariddh, and the Phnom Penh government leader Hun Sen became co–prime ministers. Meanwhile, no longer serving as an instrument in broader geopolitical contests, the Khmer Rouge was deprived of external supplies and withered away as an insurgent force. Cambodia's strategic significance had faded along with the Cold War.

## ASEAN AND REGIONALISM

In view of ASEAN's role in the Third Indochina War and the winding down of the Cold War in Asia, a review of the organization's evolution from its minimalist origins is in order here. The Association of Southeast Asian Nations, which had been founded in 1967 as the U.S. intervention in Vietnam was reaching its height,[28] had become by the time of the Cambodian negotiations the most developed of Asian regional organizations. In the first years after decolonization the region was hardly more than a geographic expression, plagued by territorial disputes, rebellions, and an armed confrontation (*konfrontasi*) arising in the

**NO EXTERNAL INTERFERENCE IN SOUTHEAST ASIA: THE ASEAN CHARTER**

[T]he countries of South-East Asia share a primary responsibility for strengthening the economic and social stability of the region and ensuring their peaceful and progressive national development, and . . . are determined to ensure their stability and security from external interference in any form or manifestation. . . .

[A]ll foreign bases are temporary and remain only with the expressed concurrence of the countries concerned and are not intended to be used directly or indirectly to subvert the national independence and freedom of States in the area. . . .

ASEAN, Bangkok Declaration, 8 August 1967, accessed at www.aseansec.org/1212.htm.

1960s from Indonesia's opposition to formation of what it regarded as the neocolonialist Federation of Malaysia (comprising the Malay Peninsula and parts of Borneo). The ouster of the militant Indonesian leader Sukarno in 1966 following an abortive coup the previous year—which had led to an anti-Chinese bloodbath and severing of the Beijing-Jakarta axis that Sukarno had promoted—opened the way for establishment of ASEAN. The original five members—Indonesia, Malaysia, the Philippines, Singapore, and Thailand—were joined by Brunei in 1984 when it gained its independence from Britain. It was after the ending of another confrontation in the region, the one arising from Vietnam's invasion of Cambodia, that the three Indochinese countries were added to ASEAN, along with the military-ruled Burma (renamed Myanmar).[29]

ASEAN's status as Asia's most developed regional organization has been more a matter of default than a reflection of a substantial level of integration, particularly compared with the development of multilateral institutions in Europe. It was not conceived as a robust body that would be much more than the sum of its parts. Its guiding principles, known as the "ASEAN way,"[30] were minimalism in institutional development, informality and consultation to achieve unanimity in decision making, and thus an inherent reticence about going beyond a consensus based on the least common denominator. Still, this helped to create an atmosphere in which the members began to develop a sense of regional identity; the leaders were now associating with one another rather than mainly with their former colonial masters. A predecessor organization, the Association of Southeast Asia, had foundered on territorial conflicts (in particular, conflicting claims in Northern Borneo between the Philippines and Malaysia), but now a conciliatory spirit served to defuse old issues.

As the timing of its creation in the midst of the escalating Second Indochina War suggests, ASEAN represented an effort to strengthen its members' resistance to the perils of Communist insurgency and ethnic rebellion. (Indeed, the Communists viewed it as hardly different from SEATO in its purposes.) It was not an alliance by any means, being created by the Bangkok Declaration, not a treaty. Four of the five founding members had security relationships with extraregional powers, and two of them, the Philippines and Thailand, were participating in the Vietnam War; this led Indonesia, cherishing its neutralist credentials, to require a passage in the declaration's preamble affirming that all foreign bases were temporary. As a regional organization, ASEAN afforded the Philippines a way of asserting its regional identity, rather than being perceived as an outpost of Latin America or a U.S. dependent; similarly, it offered Thailand, the other SEATO member in the region, a counterbalance to its close military ties to the United States, and Malaysia a complement to its links to Britain and the Commonwealth; Singapore gained a regional home after its divorce from the Federation of Malaysia; and post-Sukarno Indonesia now had the prospect of playing a positive, nonthreatening regional role.[31]

The Communist triumphs in Indochina in 1975 prompted a search for a higher level of cohesion, producing a Treaty of Amity and Cooperation in February 1976.[32] In addition to urging heightened cooperation in pursuing economic development, the treaty established a mechanism for conflict resolution, a council comprising ministerial-level representatives that would offer its good offices and mediation to disputing members. It also explicitly opened the door to accession by other Southeast Asian states (and later by extra-regional states). Given the new geopolitical realities, this was a way of promoting regional security by an inclusive approach to membership combined with a noninterventionist ethos, accommodating ideologically diverse members.

It took the jolt of Vietnam's invasion of Cambodia at the end of 1978 to impart real momentum to ASEAN's cohesion and sense of purpose. The organization's response to the new geopolitical challenge was complicated by differences in strategic perspective. Malaysia and Indonesia saw Indochina as a buffer against Chinese influence; now, given acute Sino-Vietnamese antagonism, they no longer were concerned about Hanoi as an instrument of Chinese expansion. By contrast, the Thais, historical rivals with the Vietnamese over the Mekong basin, could now view China as a counterweight to Vietnam's expanded power in the immediate region. Notwithstanding these divergent perspectives, ASEAN saw the Vietnamese action as an affront to its most-prized principle, the sanctity of national sovereignty, and rallied around Thailand as the frontline state. Bangkok had accepted the reality of Vietnamese hegemony over Laos (though it involved removal of a monarchy, a sensitive subject, and brought Vietnamese influence up to the Thai border), but it could not tolerate the geopolitical implications of the invasion of Cambodia. With Thailand providing a conduit for arms from China and the United States to Cambodian resistance groups as well as providing sanctuary along the Thai-Cambodian border, ASEAN projected a united diplomatic front that helped isolate the Vietnamese until the

### ASEAN OFFERS CONFLICT RESOLUTION: TREATY OF AMITY AND COOPERATION

To settle disputes through regional processes, the High Contracting Parties shall constitute, as a continuing body, a High Council comprising a Representative at ministerial level from each of the High Contracting Parties to take cognizance of the existence of disputes or situations likely to disturb regional peace and harmony.

In the event no solution is reached through direct negotiations, the High Council shall take cognizance of the dispute or the situation and shall recommend to the parties in dispute appropriate means of settlement such as good offices, mediation, inquiry or conciliation. . . . When deemed necessary, the High Council shall recommend appropriate measures for the prevention of a deterioration of the dispute or the situation.

The foregoing . . . shall not apply to a dispute unless all the parties to the dispute agree to their application to that dispute. However, this shall not preclude the other High Contracting Parties not party to the dispute from offering all possible assistance to settle the said dispute.

ASEAN Treaty of Amity and Cooperation in Southeast Asia, 24 February 1976, accessed at www.aseansec.org/1654.htm.

time came when they could no longer bear the costs in Cambodia (particularly, of course, after Moscow was no longer willing to underwrite them).

ASEAN's cohesion had become a significant factor, but its own modest expectations as a regional body stood in sharp contrast to the strong multilateral regional organizations developed in Europe. NATO from its beginning was a mutual security body committing all members to the defense of the others. The evolution of the European Union, conceived as a way of overcoming traditional rivalries (beginning by pooling the coal and steel industries of France and Germany, opponents in three wars in the previous three quarters of a century), has moved in the direction of supranational institutions—a parliament, judiciary, even a common currency among some members. ASEAN, and Asia generally, have fallen far short in evolving regional institutions. Where Europe sought to overcome the excesses of nationalism after long experience with nation-states, Asia had seen the emergence of newly independent states jealous of their hard-won sovereignty. There have been, however, two functional counterparts of the European multilateral bodies that did serve some of the same security and economic purposes. The extensive network of U.S. alliance relationships, mainly bilateral, constituted a formidable security structure (the hub-and-spokes structure described in Chapter 7) along the rim of Asia. (Actually, until NATO's post-Cold War expansion, all of its members also were littoral states.) And as part of its Cold War strategy, Washington opened the vast American market to friendly Asian countries. This was all the more important in that the latter, in particular the ASEAN members, pursuing a labor-intensive and export-oriented development strategy, had economies that were more competitive than complementary.

The end of the Cold War, along with China's rapid integration into the global economy, raised the possibility of Asia's achieving higher levels of multilateral organization. Broader security and economic bodies did evolve; at the same time, transnational issues such as terrorism and health acquired higher salience, posing new challenges to a regional order deeply committed to the Westphalian system of nation-states.

# 12 THE RISE OF CHINA

Since the end of World War II, Asia has seen the rise of several centers of power that now configure the international politics of the region. Japan's high-speed economic growth in the 1960s made it the world's second-ranking economy by 1970. Japan's national wealth, together with its close collaboration with the United States, also made its military the most technologically sophisticated force in East Asia, and Tokyo a significant player in regional and global politics. India emerged at the end of the Cold War as a rising power in Asian politics. Its tough practice of power politics made it the hegemon of the South Asian subcontinent, and its market-oriented reforms since the early 1990s propelled its economy to become one of the ten largest in the world. Building on a zealous defense of hard-won national sovereignty based on principles of noninterference and nonalignment, the ASEAN bloc steadily enhanced its capacity to sustain its solidarity and engage the region's major powers in a security dialogue through the ASEAN Regional Forum after 1994. And despite a decade of political and economic turmoil and catastrophic atrophy of the Red Army, post-Soviet Russia emerged in the first decade of the new century as a significant center of power in the region.

## CHINA'S ASCENDANCE

The rise of China, however, has in many respects followed the most dramatic trajectory among these ascending powers. When the People's Republic was established in 1949, China was weak and poor. It had endured seven years of war with Japan and another four of civil war. Its economy was in shambles because of the destruction of war and ravaged by hyperinflation stemming from the ROC's mismanagement of monetary policy. The civil war was not over. The new regime faced resistance in the south and southwest, and the ROC, while vanquished on the mainland, held out on Taiwan, hoping to rebuild and renew the civil war. Britain retained its colony in Hong Kong, and Portugal continued to hold Macao.

Internationally, the regime's legitimacy was in question. In the first year of its existence, Beijing was recognized by a total of eighteen countries, eleven of which were fraternal

Communist states of the Soviet bloc. No European great power recognized the PRC. Once the Korean War began in June 1950, Washington's debate over whether to recognize Beijing was resolved decisively in favor of continued recognition of the ROC as the legitimate government of China, and Washington launched a diplomatic effort to encourage other capitals to do the same. China—the ROC—had been a signatory of the 1945 San Francisco treaty founding the United Nations, and after 1949 the Chinese seat in the UN General Assembly and on the Security Council continued to be held by the ROC.

Today, China is an established power in the international order. Its economy in the early years of the new century had reached fourth place in size (or even higher by some measures), after the United States, Japan, and Germany, and it was among the top five trading nations. Its military modernization program, begun in 1985, was making China a rising power in Asia's security affairs. Although the ROC on Taiwan continued to resist reunification with the mainland, Beijing recovered sovereignty over Hong Kong in 1997 and Macao in 1999. After replacing the ROC in the UN in 1971, the PRC came to be recognized as the legitimate government of China by all but about two dozen of the world's 192 countries.

The course of China's spectacular rise in the global order from its uncertain beginnings was decisively shaped by its international environment. For the PRC's first two decades, it was an outcast in the international system. It could not advance its national interests through conventional diplomacy, nor could it participate in the American-dominated international economy to address China's development. After its accession to the UN and the subsequent wave of diplomatic recognition by other nations in the international system, Beijing became an insider, able to address the international order through normal state-to-state diplomacy. With Washington's concurrent dropping of the economic embargo against the PRC, Beijing could increasingly engage in international trade and attract foreign investment to pursue its developmental agenda.

China's rise over the following decades reflects a combination of two factors. One factor—and the one most widely credited—was the rise to power in the late 1970s of leaders whose priorities differed fundamentally from those of Mao Zedong, the man who had led the Communists to victory in 1949 and who dominated the PRC's politics until his death in 1976. In particular, the rise to power of Deng Xiaoping and the policies of reform that he began launched China onto its spectacular ascent in international affairs. The other factor was the emergence of an international context that made Deng's policies possible and effective.

As China's economy has grown, its weight in international affairs has grown accordingly, prompting debate among its neighbors and beyond about how Beijing would use its new strength. In a significant measure, the central problem of Asia's international relations over the past century and a half has been the weakness of China, creating an enormous power vacuum in the strategic center of the continent. Up to a point, the resurgence of Chinese power helps to fill this power vacuum and to stabilize a region that in modern times has suffered from a complex imbalance of power. Whether the growth of its power beyond that point threatens to make China a new element of instability in Asia will depend on several factors that make projection both difficult and a critical issue facing this era.

## CHINA AS REVOLUTIONARY OUTSIDER

Upon establishment of the PRC on 1 October 1949, the national agenda of the "New China" incorporated three major priorities. One was national unification—the termination of the civil war with the ROC and the recovery of territories lost to foreign powers over the preceding century or, in the cases of Tibet and Xinjiang, lost because of a weak regime. A second priority was national development. The central lesson of the preceding century of defeat and encroachment by the Western great powers and Japan was that development of the elements of modern national strength was critical to survival in the contemporary international order. No Chinese regime, no matter what its ideological commitment, could ignore this fundamental reality, and Mao and his fellow Communist revolutionaries, as Marxist-Leninists, were thoroughly committed to modernizing China. Marxism-Leninism, however, is a modernization theory with a particular emphasis—the simultaneous creation of a social and economic order liberated from the exploitation and inequities that, according to the theory, capitalism promoted. Thus, while seeking to modernize the country, the Chinese Communists, as their third priority, were also committed to the transformation of Chinese society.

The CPC brought several assets to this agenda. One was apparent popular support for the regime. China's people were weary of war and eager for peace and stability. The Communists benefited from popular alienation from the Kuomintang, whose mismanagement of the economy had lost it the support of the population of China's large cities and whose ruthless suppression of dissent had lost it support among China's professional and intellectual elites. The CPC benefited from an image of discipline and incorruptibility, and the party's nationalistic appeals engendered patriotic support for the new regime.

Another asset was the CPC leadership's unity around Mao Zedong. Mao had used the late years of the war against Japan to consolidate his leadership by purging opposition within the party. The 1942–43 Yan'an "rectification" campaign eliminated the International faction—leaders around Wang Ming (Chen Shaoyu) whose connections with the Comintern and whose training in Marxism-Leninism in the Soviet Union had made them the dominant CPC faction in previous years. In 1943 the new supreme leadership post of party chairman was created for Mao, and in April 1945 the Seventh CPC Congress confirmed a top party leadership dominated by Mao's cronies, including Liu Shaoqi, Zhu De, Zhou Enlai, and Chen Yun. These men became the PRC's top leaders in 1949.

Perhaps the most critical asset, however, was the new regime's close relationship with the USSR. The Sino-Soviet alliance concluded between Stalin and Mao in Moscow in February 1950 (see Chapter 8) was much more than a marriage of strategic convenience. It brought with it major commitments of Soviet advice, assistance, and aid that helped transform China's economy, society, army, and political order along Stalinist lines. With Soviet assistance the PRC launched its First Five-Year Plan (FYP) in 1953, modeled after the first Soviet FYP initiated under Stalin's leadership in 1928. This effort included the erection of an economic planning bureaucracy—the State Planning Commission, modeled after the USSR's Gosplan—which performed the basic tasks of directing the economy through production quotas in place of the operation of market-based pricing according to supply and demand signals. This command system allowed the new regime to mobilize resources and production toward sectors that it considered national priorities—especially heavy industry—and to slight other sectors—such as consumer goods—that it did not.

After an initial three years' effort to restore economic stability by curbing inflation and to redistribute agricultural land through land reform, the regime launched its program of incremental collectivization of agriculture. This began with the formation in 1952 of mutual aid teams among farmer households (whereby groups of neighboring farmers assisted one another during the planting and harvest seasons), followed in 1953 by the creation of lower agricultural producer cooperative (APC) farms (in which farmers pooled their still privately owned land and tools, farmed it together, and then divided the harvest proportionately). Finally, during the "high tide" of collectivization in 1955–56, higher APCs were established, in which private ownership of land and tools pooled in the lower APCs was abolished and the harvest was divided under a system of points allotted according to work performed across the growing season. By 1956 roughly one hundred million farming households that had received plots of private land thanks to land reform five years earlier worked in a system of nearly half a million collective farms. A comparable program of nationalizing industry and commerce began in 1955, producing the system of state-owned and collective industrial enterprises and state stores that characterized China's economic order until the 1980s. Moscow aided this effort in the First FYP by contributing 156 industrial plants, built largely in the Manchurian northeast, and it dispatched several thousand advisers to assist in the transformation of China's economic order along Stalinist lines.

The transformation of China's economy also enabled the transformation of society. As agriculture was collectivized and industry and commerce nationalized, China's people were regimented into "work units," which henceforth became the primary locus of identity, not only in their working lives, but also with respect to virtually everything else. Similarly, schools and universities, medical institutions, and other professional institutions were taken over, and all media were transformed into state-owned and party-controlled entities. The transformation of society along these lines enabled the new regime both to mobilize China's society behind its agenda—as it did in the great campaigns of the PRC's early years—and to monitor it for dissidence and opposition.

The PRC's political institutions were erected on the premise of the CPC's primacy as a Leninist party holding a monopoly of power, which penetrated deep into the country's political, economic, and social life. This power was also exercised through a parallel—but subordinate—structure of Soviet-style government bodies. In 1954 Beijing convened the First National People's Congress (NPC), which adopted the PRC's first socialist constitution, modeled after the 1936 USSR constitution, drafted under Stalin's supervision. The NPC itself was adapted from the USSR's parliament, the Supreme Soviet, and the new executive branch of the Chinese state, the State Council, was modeled after the USSR's Council of Ministers. The mechanism of coalition politics used in the first years, the Chinese People's Political Consultative Conference, became a united-front body that served, using Lenin's term, as a "transmission belt" to convey regime policies into society and to mobilize popular support for them.

Finally, Moscow aided Beijing in transforming the People's Liberation Army (PLA) into a modern, more professionalized military force.[1] The PLA that defeated Chiang Kai-shek and fought American and other UN forces in Korea was largely an infantry force that had been built up during the Sino-Japanese War, armed with captured Japanese and ROC weapons, and commanded without formal officer ranks. In Korea, it faced American forces that were vastly better equipped technologically and so took staggering losses—estimated at 980,000—even while fighting the war to a stalemate. In that context, Moscow gave Beijing massive military assistance. Soviet advisers helped to train a modern Soviet-style officer corps, establishing military academies and inaugurating ranks in 1955. Moscow helped Beijing create the PLA Navy and Air Force, provided the production designs for MiG fighters and short-range and medium-range bombers, and enabled the PRC to build its first submarine. In 1955 Moscow gave Chinese physicists access to the Soviet research facility at Dubna, inaugurating the PRC's nuclear program.

The first decade of the PRC was thus strongly shaped by the new regime's close association with Moscow and the Soviet bloc. The 1950 Sino-Soviet treaty linked the PRC into the Soviet bloc system of bilateral security treaties engineered by Stalin in the late 1940s. China's new economic system was linked into the Soviet bloc economic order through barter trade agreements, and China's broader international trade was severely limited by the Chinese currency's nonconvertibility. China's new military forces, while not directly under the command of the USSR, as the forces of the East European states were, complemented and collaborated with Soviet Red Army forces in Asia.

The impact of the Korean War reinforced these linkages. Even before Chinese forces intervened in Korea, the Truman administration responded to the North Korean attack on the South in June 1950 by deciding not to recognize Beijing and to continue diplomatic relations with the ROC on Taiwan while freezing the Chinese civil war by ordering the U.S. Navy's Seventh Fleet to interdict the Taiwan Strait (see Chapter 5). Once Chinese forces entered the war in October, Chinese dependency on Moscow for military aid expanded. After the United States imposed a trade embargo in 1951, the PRC was all the more reliant on economic relations with the Soviet bloc. Moreover, as the United States built its system of security alliances in the western Pacific in 1951–55 (see Chapter 7), China's security was heavily dependent on the alliance with the USSR.

Though Beijing enjoyed some relations beyond those with the Soviet bloc, particularly in South and Southeast Asia, these stood out in a context in which Beijing still had very few others. On its fifth anniversary in 1954, the PRC was still recognized by only twenty-four countries.

In a setting in which Chinese and Soviet ideological affinities and national interests seemed to converge while the U.S. containment policy became further consolidated in the region, Beijing's relationship with Moscow was a critical determinant of both its foreign relations and the direction of much of its domestic policies. "The growing strength, unity, and solidarity of socialist countries form the cornerstone that safeguards world peace," Vice Premier Chen Yi declared in his foreign policy report to the Eighth CPC Congress in 1956. "The Chinese people regard the consolidation and development of the unity and cooperation of their own country with the Soviet Union and the people's democracies as a task of first-rate importance," he went on, concluding that "the alliance between China and the Soviet Union has become a powerful guarantee of peace in the Far East and the world."[2]

The deterioration of the Sino-Soviet relationship in the late 1950s and its outright demise in the 1960s (as discussed in earlier chapters) therefore had catastrophic consequences for both China's foreign policy and its national agenda. With respect to security, at a time when American hostility continued unabated, the Sino-Soviet alliance was by the mid-1960s a dead letter. Worse, as the American combat engagement in Vietnam escalated in 1965, the Soviets themselves began a massive buildup of forces on their borders with China and in Mongolia. Thus, in the late 1960s Beijing faced the dire prospect of a growing military menace from both superpowers, adding a Soviet threat in the north to an increasingly assertive American involvement to the south.

In addition, China lost the patron of the PLA's modernization. In 1959, as a means of pressuring Beijing to bend on issues in the emerging Sino-Soviet split, Moscow cut off military assistance. Beijing had benefited from nearly a decade of major Soviet investment in modernizing the PLA and had built its defense doctrines on the premise of security collaboration with Soviet forces. With Soviet aid cut off, Beijing now had to rely on its own defense industries to equip the PLA, without Soviet guidance and material support. Therefore, improvements in PLA hardware had to come through tinkering with Soviet designs acquired in the 1950s, at a time when both Soviet and American designers were already moving ahead with new generations of weapon systems.

As the credibility of the Soviet commitment to the Sino-Soviet alliance waned in Chinese eyes in the late 1950s, therefore, Beijing began to revise its defense doctrines. In 1959 it began to revive the doctrine of "people's war" that the CPC had deployed in the struggle against Japan, replacing the doctrine based on collaboration with the USSR that had prevailed across the 1950s. Facing the looming potential for war with either or both superpowers, the PLA now prepared to deploy the most significant assets it still had—China's huge territory and population. In the event of an attack by either the USSR or the United States, the PLA would trade space for time, "luring the enemy in deep" and waging a long war of attrition against a vastly more sophisticated and technologically equipped adversary. This strategy meant that Beijing could not expect to hold its existing industrial base in the northeast or in the coastal provinces. In 1964, therefore, Beijing initiated its "third front" deployment of industrial development deep into the interior, in the southwest and northwest provinces, an irrational step on purely economic grounds but one that made sense from the logic of "people's war."[3]

To suit this strategy, the ranks of the PLA's ground forces swelled, reaching four million by the 1970s. Thanks to Soviet assistance in the 1950s, China could still produce and modify Soviet weapons systems, but now production was geared toward producing hardware adapted to the revived doctrine of people's war. Chinese defense plants in the 1960s produced thousands of battle tanks to supplement its burgeoning ground forces and thousands of fighter aircraft to interdict an invading superpower force. Other aspects of military modernization that did not suit the people's war strategy were ignored, in particular, development of the PLA Navy. In keeping with the decentralized command system mandated by people's war, in 1965 the PLA abolished ranks, which had been established only a decade earlier.

There was one area of defense modernization—the development of strategic weapons—that was allocated enormous resources. With the withdrawal of Soviet military assistance in 1959, and with Moscow reneging on Khrushchev's promise to supply China with a working nuclear reactor the year before, Beijing had to go it alone in this effort. The PRC nevertheless succeeded in testing its first fission bomb on 16 October 1964—two days after the fall of Khrushchev. In 1966 it tested its first hydrogen bomb, and in 1970 it succeeded in launching its first satellite, which beamed the revolutionary song "The East Is Red" back to audiences on Earth.

The emergence of the Sino-Soviet split also had a profound impact on the PRC's economic development strategy. In 1956, as Beijing was shaping its Second FYP, to run from 1958 to 1962, Moscow informed Beijing that it could not afford the scale of assistance that it had provided during the First FYP; moreover, the Chinese would have to begin to repay the loans that Moscow had extended up to that point. By 1960, when Moscow cut off all economic and technical assistance to China and pulled out Soviet advisers, Beijing had lost its primary economic patron at a time when the United States still denied Chinese access to the broader world economy.

Partly in response to these events but also in response to some of the social side effects of economic development during the First FYP, the CPC leadership began to debate alternative development approaches. Up to 1956 the party leadership around Mao had maintained broad agreement that the direction of economic development through the First FYP was correct. The Stalinist approach seemed to address the imperatives of rapid economic development and the ideals of revolutionary social transformation in tandem. The economy grew at an average annual rate of roughly 11 percent, and as a result of agricultural collectivization and the nationalization of industry and business, the party had worked a true social revolution, disenfranchising the old exploiting landlord and capitalist classes and creating new privileged sectors among urban workers.

At the same time, new dilemmas emerged with these successes. The Stalinist economic strategy rested on extraction of gains from agriculture to invest in heavy industry. This approach worked successfully through the 1955 "high tide of collectivization," but the gains from agriculture thereafter began to plateau. In addition, the hierarchical planning system had emergent inefficiencies and produced an imbalance among sectors. Finally, the approach produced new social elites—enterprise managers, technicians, and, most of all, party and state bureaucrats—whose emergence seemed to violate the egalitarian ideals for which the revolution had been fought.

As these new problems emerged, the presumption that economic modernization and egalitarian social ideals could be accomplished simultaneously proved illusory. The party leadership would have to choose between alternatives that emphasized one goal at the expense of the other. The leadership could choose to pursue economic modernization over satisfaction of the party's revolutionary egalitarian ideals, or it could choose the opposite. Different leaders naturally made different choices between the two goals and their associated policies, and over time, to put it in simplified terms, two broad camps emerged within the leadership that were committed to two alternative approaches to reconciling these dilemmas. One approach, gradually coalescing around Liu Shaoqi and Deng Xiaoping, favored emphasis on economic modernization. These and similarly inclined leaders argued that achievement of the revolution's social ideals could be accomplished only as the overall prosperity of the economy rose sufficiently to make egalitarian distribution possible. The other approach, strongly associated with Mao, stressed fulfillment of egalitarian goals first. Mao argued that pursuit of these goals—through higher levels of collectivization, obliteration of class and other distinctions in society, and mobilizing ever larger numbers of people through mass campaigns—would enable satisfaction of the economic modernization goals because people would be more productive working for the common good than they would in pursuit of self-interest.

In a setting of declining Soviet aid commitments, debates over development strategy were resolved in 1957 in favor of Mao's perspective. The resulting Great Leap Forward initiated a drive for accelerated economic development with the goals of overtaking Britain in fifteen years and America in twenty-five. Agriculture was pushed to an even higher level of collectivization than in 1955–56, as 485,000 APCs were merged in the summer of 1958 into some twenty-five thousand "people's communes." More than huge farming collectives, the communes were to become concurrently centers of industrial production—manifested most famously in the "backyard" steel furnaces. The communes also combined the rural labor force with professionals and intellectuals sent down from the city in the name of obliterating the gap between "mental" and manual labor. Paramilitary methods of organization mobilized the commune labor force to push for accelerated production.

The resulting pattern of economic development produced an effectively cellular economy, by which each commune was intended over time to become self-sufficient in both agricultural and industrial production. This arrangement complemented the shift in defense strategy in 1959 to "people's war"; if some region of China were carved off by an invading superpower force, then the loss of that region to China's overall economy could be minimized because the rest of China's economic cells could sustain the war effort to defeat the invading enemy.

The failure of the Great Leap was as dramatic as its initiation was bold. Across the 1959–61 period—later termed the "three bitter years" in China—grain production actually declined by nearly 15 percent and industrial production retreated by more than 20 percent, while the economy overall declined by roughly 12 percent. By China's own statistics, between twenty and thirty million people died of starvation over these years.[4] Moscow's withdrawal of aid and advisers came in the midst of these years, and Beijing blamed the failure of the Great Leap on Moscow and on disastrous floods and droughts. But the brunt of these disasters can be attributed to Mao's grotesque policies.

This calamitous failure produced a wholesale retreat in development policy after 1960. Mao went into political eclipse, while leaders favoring a moderate development approach associated with Liu Shaoqi and Deng Xiaoping dominated the agenda. At the Eighth Central Committee's Ninth Plenum in 1961, they put forward a program of economic recovery that reflected their own alternative development approach, emphasizing economic production over achievement of egalitarian revolutionary goals. It was in this context that

Deng uttered his remark, made famous in the reform era of the 1980s, "Black cat, white cat—what's the difference as long as the cat catches mice!" Under this new approach, China's economy recovered. The communes were not dissolved, but their operation was internally decentralized, allowing more pragmatic management of agriculture to take hold. In industry, wage differentials and other approaches to stimulate production were restored. Economic growth resumed at double-digit rates in 1962–65.

The post–Great Leap economic policies prevailed through the remainder of the Mao era, but now China's development had to proceed without major inputs from its former patron, the USSR. Chinese trade with the Soviet bloc continued, but in the early 1960s in particular, Beijing took care to run up consistent surpluses in its trade balances in order to repay Soviet loans taken out in the preceding years. In 1965 Beijing triumphantly announced the last of its loan payments ahead of schedule. By the mid-1960s, however, growth was slowing, averaging annual rates of 4 to 5 percent over the decade after 1965. China's economic development proceeded across the entire period from the Great Leap to the 1970s on an autarkic basis, the heyday of Beijing's policies of "self-reliance." In heralding self-reliance, however, Beijing was effectively making a virtue out of a necessity in the context of the continuing Western economic embargo and loss of Soviet economic patronage.

Finally, the Sino-Soviet split fed into the emergent divisions in Chinese leadership politics. Mao's hard-line dogmatism in the dispute with Moscow complemented his views on how to address China's economic development dilemmas, embodied in the Great Leap Forward. From his perspective, the erroneous policies of the Khrushchev leadership were mirrored among his own colleagues in their advocacy of moderate economic development policies. As he moved to reassert his power in leadership politics in the mid-1960s, therefore, he saw his antagonists in the Soviet Union and in the leadership of his own party as advancing the same ideologically "revisionist" principles. His drive to unseat "China's Khrushchev"—Liu Shaoqi—and his henchmen in the CPC leadership was thus intertwined with the broader struggle against Khrushchev and his successors in the USSR.

The resulting Great Proletarian Cultural Revolution, launched in the summer of 1966, turned China upside down over the ensuing two years.[5] By the time Mao moved to consolidate the new political order resulting from the Cultural Revolution, at the CPC's Ninth Congress in April 1969, he had succeeded in removing many of his former opponents in the leadership. In this struggle he drew on the support of the PLA, whose reorientation in the early 1960s to fight people's war also served Mao's purposes of reindoctrination by means of the famous "little red book"—the *Quotations of Chairman Mao*, edited by Mao's "closest comrade in arms," Defense Minister Lin Biao. He also drew on the support of radical leftist intellectuals as the Cultural Revolution's propaganda force, and he mobilized millions of China's youth into Red Guards and workers as "revolutionary rebels," serving as the shock troops of its political assaults.

The Cultural Revolution's real victors, however, were the PLA, whose leaders constituted roughly 45 percent of the new Central Committee appointed at the Ninth Congress in 1969. The party leadership had been shattered in the assaults of the Cultural Revolution, and in its place a highly factionalized party elite competed to advance contending agendas by appealing to one strain of "Mao thought" against the others. As Mao's health declined visibly in the early 1970s, the power struggle intensified, now embittered by the politics of Mao's succession.

Internationally, the split with Moscow isolated China and contributed to the radicalization of Chinese foreign policy. In 1963, as the split broke into public view, Beijing attempted to rally a new international Communist movement of "genuine Marxist-Leninist parties" that rejected Moscow's "revisionist" line of "peaceful coexistence" with the West. It competed for leadership of a new "international united front" against both Moscow and Washington in the third world, and pressed efforts to establish diplomatic relations among the new nation-states of Africa and elsewhere in the third world. By the mid-1960s, Beijing began to advertise Mao's model of people's war as having universal application and to promote the utility of the *Quotations of Chairman Mao* to revolutionary struggles everywhere. Beijing renewed direct support to Communist insurgencies in South and Southeast Asia, training guerrillas in south China and hosting clandestine radio stations beaming revolutionary propaganda on their behalf. By 1969, Beijing had established diplomatic relations with nearly forty countries, but in the first years of the Cultural Revolution, "Red Guard diplomacy," with its insufferable Maoist evangelism, had a devastating impact on the PRC's foreign affairs. In 1967, Red Guards even took over the Foreign Ministry for a week, and Maoist zealots laid siege to the Soviet embassy (located on the renamed "Anti-Revisionism Road") and burned the British consulate in Beijing. The fire-breathing polemics in the foreign affairs section of Lin Biao's political report to the Ninth CCP Congress in April 1969 vividly demonstrated the radical extremes to which Chinese foreign policy had been pushed.

Across the first two decades of its existence, the PRC was an outsider to the Western-dominated international order. The rise of China's alliance with the USSR locked it into Moscow's alternative world order in a period of unrelenting American hostility toward Beijing. The demise of the Sino-Soviet alliance intensified Beijing's isolation, leaving it in a position of weakness facing dual adversaries in the USSR and the United States and with no recourse but to rely on itself for China's development.

## CHINA AS POSTREVOLUTIONARY INSIDER

Ironically, it was at this point, when Beijing seemed at its most isolated and most radical, that its position in the international order changed fundamentally. The strategic realignment that resulted from Washington's rapprochement with Beijing in the 1968–72 period was a watershed in international affairs and in China's place in the world (see Chapter 10). With the PRC's accession to the UN in 1971, countries began immediately to switch diplomatic recognition from Taipei to Beijing. When the United States dropped its economic embargo in 1971, China could begin to trade in the broader world economy. In addition, on the basis of a convergent interest in opposing Soviet power, the United States and the West were now willing to collaborate in strengthening China's military capabilities. Where China up to this point had been a revolutionary outsider in the Western-dominated international system, it was now a legitimate insider in world affairs, able to rely on conventional diplomacy to pursue its national interests and on interaction with the international economy to develop its national strength. It could also address the Taiwan question as the increasingly recognized legitimate government of China, making Taipei the outsider.

Although China's rising strength in international affairs is conventionally associated with the reform policies launched in the late 1970s, the trajectory actually began in the early 1970s, stemming from the watershed change in China's place in the international order. In the period between 1970 and 1975, the PRC gained the recognition of fifty-five foreign capitals. Over the years between 1972 and 1978, China's trade volume quadrupled, reaching roughly twenty billion dollars. In January 1975, at the Fourth National People's Congress, Premier Zhou Enlai reintroduced the four modernizations—the call to build "a modern agriculture, industry, science and technology, and national defense" by the year 2000. The four modernizations had been first enunciated in December 1964 but had been dropped with the onset of the Cultural Revolution. Their reappearance in 1975 marked a return to giving priority to economic modernization over the egalitarian revolutionary ideals long associated with Mao. Meanwhile, with the possibility of upgrading PLA weapons with Western technological assistance, Beijing began to shift its defense doctrines in favor of what it called "people's war under modern conditions." With improved military hardware, Beijing could more actively attempt to stop a Soviet invasion at the frontier and to defend the large industrial cities of the northeast.

Across the 1970s, Beijing's foreign policy discourse changed in step with its increasingly insider status in world politics. The class-based revolutionary rhetoric gave way gradually to a more flexible foreign policy couched in terms of nation-state relations. Appeals to "proletarian internationalism" gave way to policies defined on the basis of national interest. Calls to rally "international united fronts" against "imperialism" and Soviet "social-imperialism" were replaced by condemnation of "hegemony" by "superpowers"—terms that appeared nowhere in Lin Biao's formulations at the 1969 party congress.

The emergence of these changes was constrained by two realities. One was the persisting polarization of leadership politics in Beijing, exacerbated by the struggle to succeed Mao. The other was the persisting limitation on relations with the two powers most important to Beijing, the United States and Japan. Richard Nixon's visit to China in 1972 had opened the way to normalized U.S.-China relations but only with the establishment of quasi-official "liaison offices" in each other's capital. The two sides anticipated an early establishment of full diplomatic relations, but this was delayed by circumstances in each capital—the power struggle in Beijing attending Mao's declining health, and Nixon's resignation in disgrace in 1974. Although Tokyo had established diplomatic ties with Beijing during the visit of Prime Minister Tanaka Kakuei in September 1972, full normalization of relations awaited conclusion of a peace treaty formally ending World War II between China and Japan, an issue that for a number of reasons could not be resolved quickly.

The power struggle to succeed Mao was prolonged and intricately complex—illustrated by Deng's rehabilitation from Cultural Revolution disgrace in 1973 and his purge again in April 1976. When Mao died that September, the succession struggle ended suddenly within a month with the arrest of Mao's Cultural Revolution radical faction—the Gang of Four—and the emergence of the dark horse leader Hua Guofeng. Over the next several months, Hua worked to consolidate his power on the basis of sustaining Mao's legacy and of continuity with Mao's Cultural Revolution doctrines. Over the early months of 1977, Hua called on China to uphold the "two whatevers": "Whatever decisions Chairman Mao made, we will uphold; whatever instructions Chairman Mao gave, we will unswervingly uphold." He had contravened Mao's wishes (following long-standing CPC practice) to be cremated and had the chairman embalmed in the manner of Lenin in the USSR. Following the precedent of Lenin's tomb in Red Square, Hua had a mausoleum built at the south end of Tiananmen Square in the heart of Beijing, where Mao's taxidermied remains could forever be venerated by China's public. He personally supervised the editing of a fifth volume of Mao's works, emphasizing themes that comported with Mao's views leading to the Cultural Revolution.

Despite these efforts, Hua was a weak candidate to succeed Mao and was unable to resist a broad coalition of leaders committed to moving China away from the ideology and policies of the later Mao era. Hua was forced in the summer of 1977 to accede to Deng's return to the leadership. At the CPC's Eleventh Congress that August, Hua hailed Mao as "the greatest Marxist-Leninist of the contemporary era" and, while declaring the official end of the Cultural Revolution begun in 1966, he insisted that future cultural revolutions would be necessary. At the same party congress, nevertheless, a rehabilitated Deng was appointed the CPC's third-ranking leader.

Over the next year, Deng waged a masterly campaign to overturn the legitimacy of Mao's Cultural Revolution ideas as the basis for party policy and, correspondingly, Hua's claim to leadership. To do this, Deng effectively used Mao against Mao, reviving the same Yan'an-era slogans that Mao himself had used to unseat the International faction. Mao had argued in Yan'an that the Soviet-trained Wang Ming faction's understanding of Marxism-Leninism was divorced from the current realities of China's social revolution and that the correct path lay in applying Marxism-Leninism's "truths" to the "facts" of China's concrete circumstances. Arguing that the CPC must again "seek truth from facts" as Mao did in Yan'an, Deng asserted that the party must seek to apply the principles and methods of Marxism-Leninism to China's contemporary realities. Mao's ideas had been valid in their time, Deng argued, but where they departed from contemporary circumstances, they should be abandoned in favor of new approaches. By applying the methods of Marxism-Leninism anew to China's contemporary realities, the CPC could advance China's progress under a banner of what Deng later—in 1982—called "socialism with Chinese characteristics."

Deng's adroit moves to establish a new leadership consensus behind his views while marginalizing Hua were ratified at the Eleventh Central Committee's Third Plenum in December 1978. At the plenum, Deng revised the CPC's "general task"—its foremost mission—from waging "class struggle," Mao's obsession, to advancing China's economic modernization. With these victories at the watershed Third Plenum, Deng transformed the party's guiding ideology, making possible the legitimate pursuit of policies that would have been condemned as "counterrevolutionary" and as "taking the capitalist road" in Mao's heyday. On the basis of that party platform emerged the array of economic, social, and political reforms that propelled China on its ascent in world affairs. (Deng's official titles did not reflect his real status in the leadership, which is why outside observers typically referred to him as China's paramount leader.)

The policies of what was explicitly called "reform"—previously a dirty word in the political vocabulary—launched in the Deng era after 1978 drew fundamentally from the views on China's development alternatives that he had shared with others in the Chinese leadership in opposition to Mao in the post–Great Leap period. Deng's policies also proceeded from two new points of departure. One was that Deng and his allies believed firmly that Mao's views in his later years were profoundly wrong and that the Cultural Revolution in particular had been a national catastrophe. Deng's views on China's direction ahead therefore rested on the conviction that the "revolutionary" politics that Mao had espoused and movements like the Cultural Revolution must not be allowed to recur.

Second, Deng saw that China's international setting had changed profoundly. Thanks to its decade of high-speed growth, Japan had emerged as the world's second-ranking power and, in the perspective of some, was on its way toward displacing the United States as the world's leading economy. In addition, by the late 1970s, East Asia's "four little dragons"—South Korea, Taiwan, Hong Kong, and Singapore—were undergoing a comparable economic takeoff by deploying export-led growth strategies in the world economy. If these smaller, Confucian-based societies could manage dramatic economic growth, Deng asked, then why could not the greater dragon of socialist China do the same? More broadly, in a famous speech to a conference of Chinese scientists in 1978, Deng pointed to an emerging revolution in science and technology. The advent of computers, lasers, biotechnology, satellites and telecommunications, miniaturization of electronics, and nuclear energy, he noted, was rapidly changing the criteria by which national strength would be defined in the future.[6] Not only was China not catching up with the world's advanced societies, Deng argued, but it was rapidly falling farther behind.

As Deng campaigned in 1978 to end the Mao era in China's politics, he also moved to relieve the other major constraint on the type of policies he sought to implement. In August 1978, Beijing finally concluded a peace treaty with Tokyo, officially ending World War II between the two countries and normalizing Sino-Japanese relations. Four months later, the watershed Third Plenum having confirmed Deng's status as China's paramount leader, Beijing and Washington finally arrived at agreement on full diplomatic relations. With these steps, the limitations placed on Chinese collaboration with the world's two largest economies were removed. Over the next year, Washington granted most-favored-nation trading status (now known as "normal trading relations") to the PRC, providing the lowest tariff rates on imports that the United States granted to almost all trading partners, and agreed to its accession to the World Bank and the International Monetary Fund, enabling the PRC to draw on loans to accelerate its development.

The economic policies that Deng and his reform coalition launched in the wake of the Third Plenum, broadly speaking, sought to restore markets to China's economy, to revise the role of the state with respect to the economy, and—under the banner of "opening up"—to engage the international economy in China's development.[7] In an important first step in agricultural policy, a household contract system was adopted whereby the state continued to own the land but now individual farmers made their own planting decisions and could sell their crops in open markets. (In October 2008 another step was officially adopted: granting farmers the right to lease out or transfer land allotted to them, thereby creating a land market and providing enhanced protection against arbitrary expropriation.) As agriculture moved toward full-scale market pricing, the people's communes were dissolved in 1980 and distribution through state stores was abolished. Over the first five years of the new system, overall grain production increased by a third.

In industry, beginning in 1984, Beijing authorized new approaches to transforming the often inefficient state-owned enterprises through leasing arrangements, corporatization through the sale of public shares, and other methods. The object of these arrangements was to discard the social welfare, political, and other roles of these enterprises so that they could begin to operate solely according to rational economic criteria in an increasingly market-driven economy. These goals entailed not only a radical restructuring of the enterprises themselves but also new reforms to create institutions to manage unemployment, retirement, labor benefits, and other functions that the old state-owned enterprises had fulfilled. The complexity of these industrial reforms meant that progress was slow and implementation continued into the new century. Meanwhile, Beijing tolerated the rebirth of a legitimate private sector in China's economy, a sector that quickly grew at faster rates than the traditional state sector. In step with these changes, Beijing began incrementally to transition to full-scale market pricing, gradually releasing prices on categories of commodities and abolishing fixed prices in state stores. As these reforms advanced, Beijing shifted from the former mandatory state economic plans to "guidance plans," and the role of the formerly powerful State Planning Commission receded until, in the 1990s, it was reorganized into an economic forecasting bureaucracy.

Deng's first steps to engage the international economy were the creation of four "special economic zones"—three in Guangdong Province, facing Hong Kong and Macao, and one in Fujian, facing Taiwan. In an emulation of the export-driven growth policies of other East Asian economies, these zones were granted tax breaks and special privileges to facilitate their production for international markets. Similar privileges were granted to fifteen coastal cities in 1985, and with the launching of the "coastal policy" in 1987, similar rights were extended throughout the coastal areas and beyond. To facilitate the growth of China's trade relations, Beijing became an observer in GATT in 1985 and applied to resume China's membership (suspended in 1950) in 1986. Meanwhile, Beijing encouraged foreign investment in China's economy. By the end of the 1980s, Western corporations flocked to do business with joint-venture partners in China, joined after 1987 by Taiwanese investors, who, with Taipei's lifting of a long-standing ban, could now transfer their operations to China to take advantage of lower labor costs. By the early 1990s, foreign business was everywhere in China; the world's largest McDonald's, for example, was on Wangfujing Street in central Beijing.

The impact of these reforms on China's economy was dramatic. In the decade after the 1978 Third Plenum, GDP grew at an average annual rate of 9.8 percent. The impact on the livelihood of China's people was comparably significant, although early advances in rural incomes did not keep pace with rising prosperity in China's cities. The advance in prosperity may be measured by the mildly sexist sociological observation that in the early

1980s, young women seeking a prospective husband sought someone who could provide the "three revolving things"—a wristwatch, a sewing machine, and a bicycle; by the end of the decade, young women sought prospective husbands whose income could provide a stove, a washing machine, and a VCR.

As China's economy surged, Beijing also moved to address its security situation. In the early 1980s, Beijing began a careful, incremental effort to improve relations with Moscow, which itself saw an opportunity to capitalize on strains in Sino-American relations by signaling an interest in ameliorating the noxious atmosphere poisoning Sino-Soviet affairs. These steps advanced even though the Soviet military threat on China's frontiers continued and despite Moscow's succession difficulties that began with the death of Leonid Brezhnev in 1982 (see Chapter 11). The steps toward normalizing Sino-Soviet relations proceeded along with continuing expansion of ties with the United States and Japan, even while Beijing was taking care to distance itself from Washington on the plane of strategic relations under its new "independent foreign policy line," launched in 1982.

In this context, Deng put forward a new, highly authoritative assessment of China's security environment at a Central Military Commission meeting in June 1985.[8] For the first time in its history, Deng concluded, the PRC no longer faced the imminent threat of attack by either of the two superpowers. Therefore, the massive preparations that had been made over the previous three decades to fight a prolonged, potentially nuclear war with the USSR or the United States were no longer necessary. Instead, China needed to be prepared to fight the next tier down of potential security conflicts, primarily on China's immediate periphery. In that light, Deng revised China's defense doctrines, dropping the former call to be prepared to fight "people's war under modern conditions" in favor of a new doctrine of being prepared to fight "local, limited wars."

The new doctrine designated five major missions for the PLA:

- Winning wars on China's continental periphery quickly and decisively, before they could escalate into prolonged, debilitating conflicts;
- Presenting a sufficient stick to complement the carrot of Beijing's "peaceful reunification" pitch to Taiwan, launched on New Year's Day 1979, to win resolution of the Taiwan question on terms acceptable to Beijing;
- Establishing power-projection capabilities to make credible Beijing's territorial claims in the East China Sea with respect to Japan and in the Spratly Islands in the South China Sea;
- Defending China's vulnerable coastline, again the backbone of China's industrial base thanks to Deng's economic reforms, against foreign naval attack; and
- Ensuring the survivability of China's hard-won nuclear deterrent against an adversary's first strike.

As of 1985, the PLA was poorly equipped to take on these tasks. Thanks to the people's-war orientation of PRC defense doctrines, the PLA was a huge infantry-based force of more than four million prepared to try to meet a massive Soviet ground assault. But this force had "short arms and slow legs"—it lacked rapid-deployment capabilities to

### DENG XIAOPING REVISES CHINA'S SECURITY POLICY

[Since 1978] we have made two important changes in our assessment of the international situation and in our foreign policy. The first change is in our understanding of the question of war and peace. We used to believe that war was inevitable and imminent. Many of our policy decisions were based on this belief, including the decision to disperse production projects in three lines, locating some of them in the mountains and concealing others in caves. In recent years, we have come to the belief that only the two superpowers, the Soviet Union and the United States, are in a position to launch world war. . . . In fact, the American and Soviet peoples themselves do not support war. The world is vast and complex, but if you analyze the situation you will find there are only a few people who support war; most people want peace.

We should also recognize that the new revolution in science and technology all over the world is developing vigorously and that economic strength, science, and technology play an outstanding role in worldwide competition. Neither the United States nor the Soviet Union, nor the other developed countries, nor the developing countries can afford to ignore this. Thus we can conclude that it is possible that there will be no large-scale war for a fairly long period of time to come and that there is the hope of maintaining world peace. . . .

The second change is in our foreign policy. In view of the threat of Soviet hegemonism, over the years we formed a strategic line of defense—a line stretching from Japan to Europe to the United States. Now we have altered our strategy, and this represents a major change. People around the world are talking about the big triangle composed of the Soviet Union, the United States, and China. We don't put it that way because we have a sober estimate of our own strength, but we do believe that China has considerable influence in world affairs. . . . In accordance with our independent foreign policy of peace, we have improved relations with the United States and with the Soviet Union. China will not play the card of another country and will not allow another country to play the China card, and we mean what we say. This will enhance China's international status and enable us to have more influence in international affairs.

Deng Xiaoping, speech to the 4 June 1985 Central Military Commission meeting, in *Selected Works of Deng Xiaoping*, vol. 3, *1982–1992* (Beijing: Foreign Languages Press, 1994), 131–33.

---

China's diverse border regions. China had the world's largest air force, composed largely of nearly five thousand fighter aircraft that had been built on modified Soviet designs of the 1950s to complement the people's-war strategy of the 1960s and 1970s. China had a brown-water navy of nearly one hundred submarines serving as a coastal defense force but no means to repel a modern naval power farther out at sea, as required to defend the now vulnerable industrial coastal provinces.

China had a tiny nuclear deterrent of five intercontinental ballistic missiles with ranges sufficient to strike the western United States and western USSR, and a force of roughly seventy intermediate-range ballistic missiles capable of reaching targets in much of Asia but not beyond. These missiles were based haphazardly in mountain caves and in forests to avoid detection by Soviet or American satellites; moreover, they were liquid fueled, which meant that they could not be kept in launch-ready status. To launch a second strike, China's missiles would have to survive an adversary's first strike, and then be fueled and armed with their warheads. Survival of this tiny force was in serious doubt because of the increasing accuracy of both Soviet and American missiles, because of the development by

Moscow and Washington of missiles carrying multiple warheads, and because China had no early-warning radars that made "launch on warning" possible. The PLA had attempted to establish a strategic dyad by building a pair of ballistic missile submarines, and it had successfully test-launched a missile from a submarine in the early 1980s. But one of these two Xia class submarines was never commissioned and the other proved not to be seaworthy.

Finally, the PLA remained heavily politicized and, without a professional officer corps, lacked the discipline of modern militaries. The technical capabilities of PLA soldiers were low, and many could not read or drive a truck, much less operate the increasingly sophisticated technology of modern warfare.

In view of these shortcomings, Deng launched a series of reforms designed to enable the PLA to address the new missions he assigned it. Military academies that had been suspended in the 1960s were restored and new ones established to train an increasingly specialized military; ranks were formally restored in 1988. Where Mao had stressed that "men, not weapons" win wars, Deng declared that under contemporary conditions "men *and* weapons" would be decisive. The PLA was reduced in size from four million in 1985 by a million and a half. Its remaining ground forces were regrouped into military regions, reduced in number from eleven to seven, whose forces were configured to address the terrain and missions specific to them. The PLA also developed rapid-response units—"fist units"—that could be deployed rapidly to win conflicts quickly and decisively on China's periphery. With missions beyond those assigned under the people's-war doctrine, the navy and air force received new emphasis, working to develop new capabilities to fight in more diverse contests and to complement ground forces in joint warfare. The PLA also worked to develop a new generation of solid-fueled long-range missiles that could be deployed on mobile launchers, as well as shorter-range missiles for tactical purposes.

Deng launched this military modernization effort on the premise that increased spending on defense could not exceed the economic growth rate overall. Funding for PLA modernization therefore had to come from a variety of off-budget sources, including foreign arms sales (roughly 4 percent of world volume in the 1980s), reductions in PLA forces, and, most significantly, production of goods for sale in China's civilian markets by China's defense industries. As China's overall economy grew, state allocations could grow in step. While such increments in the defense budget grew slowly in the early phase of the modernization effort, after 1989 they grew at consistently double-digit rates. Even so, as the absolute value of Chinese defense spending grew, the relative proportion of such allocations in the overall state budget remained stable at roughly 9 percent into the new century.

With the advance of the economic reforms and the launching of the military modernization effort in 1985, the foundations for China's rise in world affairs were laid. Over the 1980s, thanks to the reforms and to the normalization of relations with the Soviet Union (see Chapter 11), China enjoyed its most prosperous and secure decade since the 1839–42 Opium War. From an international perspective, China seemed to be the most successful and progressive Communist state, and across the decade from 1979 to 1988, Deng Xiaoping was *Time* magazine's "Man of the Year" twice.

## THE POST–COLD WAR ERA

The PRC's striking successes in domestic and foreign affairs during the first decade of reform under Deng's leadership were troubled by new dilemmas at the end of the 1980s, as the Cold War drew to a close. For a Chinese Daoist, this reflected the eternal alternation of yin and yang; for a Marxist-Leninist, it demonstrated the operation of the dialectic; for a pragmatist like Deng, it was just one damned thing after another.

For instance, the successes of economic reform promoted prosperity unevenly in Chinese society and so social jealousies and tensions grew. These reforms also engendered consequences that divided the coalition of leaders around Deng who had supported the reforms. In addition, as China's economy moved more and more to a market basis, it naturally saw the emergence of a business cycle of overheated expansion and inflation. The largest wave yet of inflation struck in the summer of 1988, splitting the party leadership over how to deal with it. In the fall of that year, the regime announced a three-year program of economic retrenchment that put new reforms on the back burner, a signal victory for conservative leaders over liberalizing reformers backed by Deng and CCP General Secretary Zhao Ziyang. When student demonstrations erupted in April 1989, a split party leadership responded haltingly, provoking even larger demonstrations joined by people from all walks of life. In May, the regime declared martial law after resolving the leadership split in favor of party conservatives, and on the night of 3–4 June, the regime authorized lethal force to clear the demonstrations.

The international consequences of the suppression of the demonstrations were catastrophic for the regime. Where China had been seen as the leading reforming Communist country throughout the 1980s, it now looked like a political fossil in the hands of an aging party leadership out of touch with the concerns of its own people. This sentiment was intensified the following fall, when one by one the Communist regimes in the Eastern European bloc dissolved once Soviet leader Mikhail Gorbachev made clear that Moscow would not intervene militarily as it had in Hungary in 1956 or in Czechoslovakia in 1968. The G7 group of developed states imposed a series of sanctions on Beijing for its suppression of the Tiananmen demonstrations, and although some of the sanctions were rolled back after a year, the damage to the PRC's international image and prestige was lasting.

Two years later, in December 1991, the Soviet Union itself dissolved. For Beijing, the dissolution of the motherland of socialism, with which it had painstakingly normalized relations after twenty-five years of deep hostility only two years earlier, was a deep psychological blow. Perhaps the most significant consequence of the Soviet demise, however, was the sudden emergence of an American-dominated unipolar system. Washington emerged from the Cold War overwhelmingly dominant along all major dimensions of international power—economic strength, military power, political influence, and soft power. How to deal strategically with an international order under an American hegemon and at the same time deal bilaterally with an American economy with which the PRC's own economy had become increasingly interdependent became a key dilemma for Beijing with the end of the Cold War.

Exactly how Washington would use its new dominance to reshape the international order became a question of fundamental concern to Beijing. During the Cold War, Beijing had proven itself to be a balance-of-power player, tilting toward the weaker of the two superpowers against the stronger. In the 1950s, Beijing sided with Moscow in an era of predominant American strength; in the 1960s, as both superpowers approached relative parity, Beijing adopted a dual-adversary posture with respect to both superpowers; in the 1970s, when American power appeared to slip, Beijing leaned to Washington's side against Moscow; and in the 1980s, as American power saw a resurgence, Beijing backed away at a strategic level from the United States and worked to improve relations with the USSR. In a new post–Cold War hegemonic system, there was no ready counterweight to American power. President George H.W. Bush's effort to use the 1990 Gulf crisis as a test case for a "new world order" was not reassuring in that regard. The Bush administration's remarkable facility at building an enormous military coalition to evict the Iraqis from Kuwait under American leadership and under authorizing UN resolutions seemed to Beijing to set a potentially dangerous precedent for the use of American military power in the post–Cold War international system. In addition, with the Soviet threat gone and with the late-1980s predictions of a looming Japanese threat to U.S. power collapsing with the bursting of the Japanese economic bubble, Washington began audibly to debate the implications of rising Chinese power for the United States.

In addition, the collapse of the USSR had immediate consequences for the PRC's bilateral relations with the United States. This was because the basis for Sino-American collaboration over the preceding twenty years—strategic cooperation against the USSR—had collapsed with the latter's dissolution. Over the decade since normalization with Washington, bilateral relations grew rapidly, bringing with them new issues and problems, but these were played down in the interest of strategic cooperation against Moscow. With the USSR gone, however, all of those issues now moved to the forefront of the relationship and increasingly cluttered the agenda—bilateral trade questions, human rights concerns, issues regarding the status of Tibet and Taiwan, and other problems. As the 1990s wore on, as bilateral problems increasingly dominated the agenda, and as Washington began to ponder what some Americans saw as an emerging "China threat," Beijing became increasingly uncertain about what exactly American China policy was.

Adding to these dilemmas was a growing sense of unease in Asia about China's rising strength. Foreboding about a rising Chinese threat to the region emerged in the early 1990s in Southeast Asia, exacerbated by persistent dire warnings from the Indian Defense Ministry. Slowly percolating Japanese misgivings were galvanized into more sharply realist evaluations in Tokyo about the implications for Japan of Chinese muscle flexing in the form of military exercises and missile tests conducted in a rather clumsy effort to influence political developments in Taiwan in 1995–96. These concerns reflected in part a realignment of perceptions with the eclipse of Soviet power in the region. For decades, the USSR had seemed the major security challenge in the region, but with the Soviets gone, the next biggest challenge seemed to be China. Where rising Chinese power in the 1980s had seemed useful as a counterweight to Soviet power, in the 1990s it was China that seemed the new big power on the block.

Further complicating Beijing's foreign policy prospects were changes in Taiwan. For decades after 1949, the ROC on Taiwan had been committed to the idea of one China. Over that period, the ROC under Chiang Kai-shek and, after 1975, under his son, Chiang Ching-kuo, had insisted that there was one China. On this Taipei agreed with Beijing; they simply disagreed about which regime—the ROC or the PRC—was the legitimate government of all of China. But the rapid democratization of Taiwan's politics after 1987 made possible the eruption into the island's politics of long-suppressed sentiments on behalf of Taiwan's independence. This sentiment emerged strongly in the 1990s, as even the KMT's leader, Lee Teng-hui, took steps to expand Taiwan's representation as a separate political entity in the international arena and to feed development of a Taiwanese national consciousness through policies of "Taiwanization." These trends transformed the dynamic of cross-strait politics and raised new doubts about whether Beijing's "peaceful unification" pitch to the island could succeed.

Finally, as the Cold War ended, Beijing faced a looming leadership transition. In 1991 Deng Xiaoping was eighty-seven, and many of the leaders in the coalition that had launched the reform era were comparably old. The CPC's chief, Jiang Zemin, appeared to be a weak leader, having been installed irregularly in the midst of the Tiananmen crisis in 1989, when Zhao Ziyang fell from power. In the two years following the Tiananmen events, China remained in the midst of the conservative economic retrenchment program put in place in the fall of 1988. Economic growth in 1990 slowed to just over 4 percent, and renewed impetus behind new liberalizing reform favored by Deng was uncertain.

In response to these various challenges, Beijing moved carefully and, generally speaking, adroitly. Although Deng retired from his last official post in March 1990, he remained active behind the scenes until 1994. In early 1992, in preparation for the convocation of the next party congress, Deng toured bastions of economic reform in China's south—Guangdong and Shanghai—and talked up the role of markets in reviving China's economic prosperity. With the Fourteenth CPC Congress convened later in the year, momentum had resumed behind economic reform, and in 1993 the party leadership adopted a landmark decision calling for sweeping reforms in China's state-owned enterprise sector, its banking system, its tax system, and its foreign trade regime. In this context, double-digit growth rates resumed in 1992 and 1993, provoking new dilemmas of controlling overheating and inflation. A concerted effort to recentralize some economic policy decisions and to reduce inflation in 1995–96 brought growth rates down to moderate 6 to 7 percent levels in 1997 that were revealed further into the next decade, when double-digit rates returned. The renewal of economic reform and growth in 1992 triggered a torrent of foreign investment in China, much of it from Taiwan and Hong Kong. The resulting boom revived interest in the PRC as a country undergoing revolutionary economic change even while its political order remained the object of scorn in the West.

Beijing's effort to deal with an international order under American hegemony was marked by caution. While seeking to avoid confrontation with Washington over many international questions, Beijing sought ways to blunt American dominance. One tactic was to seek "strategic partnerships" with other centers of power in the international system, beginning with Russia and France in 1997. Beijing sought to fashion these partnerships in the interest of a multipolar international order that would counterbalance American power. The efforts with respect to Moscow culminated in a new Sino-Russian treaty, signed by Russian President Vladimir Putin and Jiang Zemin in 2001. While committing both sides to promote a "global strategic balance," the treaty had limited value in constraining American power, given the degree to which both China and Russia depended on economic cooperation with the United States. The two also signed a joint communiqué calling for continued observance of the 1972 ABM treaty between Washington and Moscow, but this effort did nothing to stop the unilateralist Bush administration from renouncing the treaty and beginning deployment of a ground-based interceptor system in Alaska and California.

American dominance in the international system also convinced Beijing of the value of liberal multilateral institutions and regimes in constraining U.S. power. Its seat on the UN Security Council became an important tool in that regard, and Beijing was alarmed in 1999 when the Clinton administration intervened in the Kosovo crisis on humanitarian grounds by working through NATO rather than the UN. Beijing had been traditionally dismissive of multilateral institutions, despite its membership in the UN since 1971. It began attending UN disarmament forums in Geneva only in 1980 and began to sign onto arms control regimes thereafter.[9] In 1981 it conducted its last nuclear testing in the atmosphere and declared in 1986 that it would permanently ban such testing, and in 1984 it joined the UN's International Atomic Energy Agency. In the 1990s, Beijing's enlistment in such regimes accelerated. By the end of the decade it had acceded to most of the major international arms control regimes, including the Non-Proliferation Treaty in 1992 and its extension in 1998 and the Chemical and Biological Weapons Conventions in 1993. It signed the 1996 Comprehensive Test Ban Treaty but declined to ratify it until Washington did so, a prospect clouded by opposition to the treaty in a Republican-controlled Senate. In 1997 Beijing signed onto the Zangger convention on proliferation of fissile materials.

Beijing's new appreciation for multilateral organizations was evident at a regional level with its decision to participate in the ASEAN Regional Forum. Beijing's motivations were in part a consequence of the resolve of the Southeast Asian states to hang together on issues involving China rather than attempt to deal with Beijing bilaterally. China's clash with the Philippines for control of Mischief Reef in the Spratly Islands helped galvanize ASEAN solidarity against its rising power. The Chinese willingness to work through the ASEAN Regional Forum reflected an acceptance of new regional realities, but it also reflected Beijing's appreciation of the possibility of using it to blunt the reach of other external powers in the region, including the United States, Japan, India, and Europe.

More surprising was Beijing's initiative to help create a multilateral organization in Central Asia. The dissolution of the USSR presented Beijing with three new independent states on China's borders—Kazakhstan, Kyrgyzstan, and Tajikistan—and two more immediately beyond. Recognizing a power vacuum in a region of sensitive implications both for the PRC and for Russia, Beijing collaborated with Moscow in creating the Shanghai Five in 1996, which grew steadily in purpose and was reorganized in 2001 as the Shanghai Cooperation Organization, now including four of the five Central Asian states, along with China and Russia (see Chapter 13). NATO's Partnership for Peace exercises in Kazakhstan in 1998 demonstrated the potential for growing American influence in the region, which crystallized with the introduction of American bases in Uzbekistan in 2001 to support the war effort in Afghanistan. In these circumstances, the Shanghai Cooperation Organization fended off pressures for new membership by powers external to the region, instead accepting them as dialogue partners, following the ASEAN Regional Forum pattern. By that means, Beijing and Moscow sought to balance external influences—from the United States, India, Iran, and Turkey—in the region.

These diplomatic moves to deal with a U.S.-dominated international system were complemented by steps to accelerate PLA modernization. The effectiveness of American weapons in the 1991 Gulf War shocked and awed the PLA brass—much of the Iraqi hardware that American precision-guided weapons destroyed had been bought from China during the Iran-Iraq War in the 1980s. This shock prompted a new assessment of China's military modernization effort, which concluded that despite the efforts since 1985, Chinese military capabilities were falling even farther behind advanced levels. In response, Beijing redefined its defense doctrine as preparing to fight "local, limited wars under high-technology conditions." This imparted an even greater emphasis on upgrading the technological capabilities of the PLA, as well as initiating a new effort to acquire advanced weapons that China's defense industries could not produce, largely from Russia and Israel. As America loomed as China's most dangerous potential security threat—especially as trends in Taiwan raised the possibility of cross-strait conflict—Beijing bought weapons systems that might give the PLA the means to inhibit U.S. intervention on behalf of Taipei. It bought fourth-generation Sukhoi-27 and Sukhoi-30 fighter aircraft, quiet Kilo submarines, and Sovremenniy destroyers, which carry the supersonic antiship SS-N-22 missiles designed to interdict aircraft carriers, the American instrument of choice for intervention in the strait. Beijing also explored a concurrent interest in asymmetric capabilities—information warfare that might cripple American forces' reliance on computers and antisatellite weapons that might blind military satellites, on which American forces rely. All of these efforts did not reflect an effort to catch up with American military power across the board and match American capabilities force on force; little evidence supports the theory that Beijing was reaching for superpower capabilities to project military power far beyond China's immediate region.[10]

The persistent difficulty in the midst of these trends was presented by Taiwan, whose administration under Lee Teng-hui and, after 2000, under the Democratic Progressive Party leader Chen Shui-bian continued steps that seemed to prepare for an eventual move to formal independence. (The Democratic Progressive Party, which had been the opposition party, formally favored independence.) In addition to hard-line polemics against Lee and Chen, Beijing in the late 1990s began to deploy short-range ballistic missiles along its southeast coast facing Taiwan to underscore its readiness to use force to resolve the Taiwan question, despite its long-standing declarations that it preferred a peaceful resolution of the issue. But Beijing's principal tactic has been to rely on Washington to lean on Taipei to deter new steps that might provoke conflict in the Taiwan Strait. Both the Clinton administration in its second term and the Bush administration in the wake of the September 2001 terrorist attacks were amenable to such tactics and helped deflate support for steps toward independence, especially under Chen Shui-bian after 2005.

Domestically, the CPC leadership maintained a consistent facade of unity throughout the 1990s and into the new century. The aging party conservatives who had complicated Deng's reform politics during and after the 1989 Tiananmen crisis passed from the scene one by one in the early 1990s. The last and most senior of these, Chen Yun, died in 1995; once again demonstrating his acute political sense, Deng waited until 1997 to pass from the scene himself. Meanwhile, Deng had worked to establish institutionalized succession in the CPC's top leadership, elevating Hu Jintao to the Politburo Standing Committee in 1992. After a decade's preparation in roles immediately behind Jiang Zemin, Hu succeeded Jiang in the CPC's and PRC's top leadership positions in 2002–3—the first arranged transition from a retiring leader to a successor in the history of any major Communist regime. The broader Chinese leadership around both Jiang and Hu demonstrated a strong commitment to the reform policies launched by Deng and imparted new impetus consistent with Deng's overarching goal of building China's national strength.

## PROSPECTS FOR CHINA'S FUTURE

The history of China's interactions with the international system since World War II demonstrates the predominant influence of China's international context on the pursuit of its national agenda rather than the other way around. In particular, not only does the rise of China reflect the rise of a Chinese Communist leader—Deng Xiaoping—preoccupied with building China's power; it also reflects the even greater import of the emergence of an international context that made China's rise possible. As China's power continues to grow, it seems worthwhile to ask whether this dynamic might shift, allowing Beijing increasingly to impose its own national priorities on the international system.

Beijing's growing influence in the international order was reflected in its vigorous engagement with regions increasingly distant from China—in Africa, in the Middle East, and in Latin America. These efforts were motivated not by a strategic competition with other great powers, and especially the United States, in these regions; instead, they appear to have been motivated by China's increasing economic interdependence on the rest of the world. By 2006 China's total trade volume was sixty times what it was in 1978. In 1994 China became a net importer of oil, and by the first decade of the new century it was the second-largest oil importer in the world, behind only the United States. More broadly, the scale of China's interdependence in the world economy may be gauged by comparing the proportion of its trade volume to its overall GDP with that of other countries. In 2007 the U.S. interdependence figure was 26.8 percent, and Japan's was 27.3 percent. That of Italy, France, and Russia was roughly 55 percent, while the UK proportion was 62 percent. China's was a staggering 72 percent, surpassed among large economies only by that of Germany, at nearly 85 percent. This scale of interdependence reflected many realities—the slow growth of its domestic consumption sector and the rapid growth of its foreign trade, among other things. However, it also registered the potential vulnerability of China's economy to the ups and downs of the world economy.

Beijing's military power could also be expected to continue to develop as its economic strength and technological capabilities grew. Given the geopolitical complexities of the broader Asian region, however, it seems unlikely that it would tip the balance of power in the region anytime soon. China's "middle kingdom" position means that it is surrounded by significant centers of regional power—Russia, Japan, India, and the ASEAN bloc—and several secondary powers, including South Korea. Asia is home to seven of the world's ten-largest standing militaries—the remaining three being those of Iran, Turkey, and the United States—and five of eight of the world's declared nuclear states, not counting the United States. By all significant measures, Asia is by far the most heavily militarized region in the world—exceeding the Middle East or Europe and NATO—and most of the Asian powers pursued their own military modernization efforts. In these circumstances, it is easy to empathize with the strategic complexities that face defense planners in Beijing, as compared, say, to those in Washington, who must confront the geopolitical challenges of Mexico to the south, Canada to the north, and Cuba ninety miles off Florida's shores, discounting, of course, America's global responsibilities.

Judging by the record of Chinese interactions in the first decade of the twenty-first century, Beijing has proved to be an increasingly sophisticated player in international affairs. Driven by its increasing economic interdependence on the world economy and constrained by the limits of its hard military power, it sought to pursue its interests in a largely system-sustaining—not system-transforming—manner. Whether that pattern persists would seem to depend in a significant degree not only on the ambitions of Chinese leaders in Beijing, but also on the approach the international order adopts toward China.

# 13 ENTERING THE NEW CENTURY

The end of the Cold War produced widespread relief and in many circles exhilaration, but it also engendered considerable uncertainty about the future. Gone were the certainties that characterized the relatively stable world shaped by the powerful force of bipolarity following World War II. Missing now was the discipline imposed by the Cold War, which tended to limit freedom of maneuver within alliances (China's defection from the Soviet bloc may be viewed as an exceptional case proving the rule) and to subordinate other interests to the imperatives of the Cold War competition. It was not wholly in jest that policymakers and analysts lamented the passing of "the good old days of the Cold War." Now they had to come to terms with a new fluidity and attendant uncertainties in international affairs.

Questions abounded. In Asia, where the Cold War was imported from Europe and flared into three major conflicts, would the collapse of bipolarity remove the rationale for the American military presence and its structure of security arrangements? What would happen if a vacuum of power was thus created and long standing constraints removed from a region that was still heavily militarized and bristling with rivalries and collisions of interest? Would a Japan unanchored from the U.S. alliance feel compelled to assume a more assertive role and to flex its military potential in view of the rising power of its neighbor and historical rival China? How long would Americans be willing to underwrite the costs of a substantial military role in Asia and forgo the "peace dividend" from the ending of the Cold War? Would the Japanese be permitted to continue their "free ride" while competing commercially with their security guarantor? Similarly, would not the absence of the Soviet threat devalue the strategic importance of America's China connection, thereby making it more difficult to contain persisting political and economic tensions between the United States and the PRC?

An alternative scenario proceeded from a prospect not of American neo-isolationist withdrawal but of hegemony exercised by the sole remaining superpower. Would this put the United States on a collision course with a China aspiring to regional ascendance, in other words, a new Cold War? Might China and Russia thereupon join sides as a counterweight to American power in the way that the Sino-American relationship had been forged in the 1970s to resist a perceived Soviet drive to global dominance? Would the United States try to use its military preponderance to impose its will on matters of contention ranging from human rights to commercial disputes?

As it turned out, the United States did not seriously consider disengagement, from Asia or from Europe. As discussed in Chapter 14, potentially explosive issues and security structures designed to deal with them survived the end of the Cold War. America's role as a stabilizing force retained its logic in the new circumstances. The changes that ensued, perhaps surprisingly, tended to be incremental rather than transformative. The Japanese, far from ready to assume a more engaged military role, had to be prodded to take small steps in that direction. The Philippines, having the luxury of a receding Soviet threat to indulge in nationalist expression, ended the U.S. base rights but along with other American allies in Asia remained within the network of bilateral security treaties. In addition, Washington was able to negotiate military access rights in Southeast Asia, and it began developing closer military ties with India. In short, America retained a robust military presence in Asia even with the demise of its Cold War rival and the absence at long last of major conflict in Indochina. Stability and economic development were the watchwords in the period after the end of the Cold War, and America was widely perceived—if uneasily in some cases—as the balancing force and ultimate security guarantor for a region beset with rivalries and potential arms races.

## JAPAN'S ROLE IN INTERNATIONAL AFFAIRS

As the Cold War was winding down, the question arose whether Japan, which had become an economic powerhouse, was poised to take a more expansive role in international affairs. Its relentless acquisition of market share and high-profile buying sprees—from expensive impressionist paintings to such iconic properties as Rockefeller Center—reflected a strong and confident nation that might now be prepared to convert its economic might into a weightier geopolitical presence. The reality turned out to be somewhat otherwise.

Whatever geopolitical aspirations may have developed, Japan's asset bubble (inflated stock and property values) burst and the economy slipped into a period of deflation and stagnation persisting well into the new century. Rather than taking a more expansive role in international security affairs, Japan remained a "reactive state" whose geopolitical weight fell far short of its economic capabilities.[1] Even after Japan became a major investing state—as distinct from being predominantly a trading state before the 1980s—it did not follow the typical course of such states by adopting a more activist posture in foreign affairs.[2] Notwithstanding recurrent indications of interest in revising the constitution's Article 9 renouncing war, the steps taken toward playing a role in international conflicts were rather halting and reluctant. During the Gulf War of 1991 the Japanese were mocked for engaging in "checkbook diplomacy" rather than contributing military forces; in the postwar period Tokyo dispatched minesweepers, a contribution that could be defended at home as helping to ensure oil supplies. Next, military engineering troops were sent to aid the Cambodian peacekeeping operations. In both cases the troops were not permitted to engage in combat, but their deployment nonetheless established precedents by marking the first deployment of military forces abroad since World War II.

During the U.S. operations in Afghanistan after the September 2001 terrorist attacks, the Japanese sent naval units to the Indian Ocean to provide rear-area services. They came closer to combat operations during the U.S.-led campaign that ousted Saddam Hussein in Iraq. Armed engineering troops were sent to the southern region, where there was less likelihood that they would need to defend themselves. This mission was highly unpopular in Japan, and it was carefully limited to avoid entanglement in hostilities.

There was even less movement from the status quo in the case of Japan's relationship with Russia. The winding down of the Cold War had raised the prospect of a breakthrough in the long-frozen relations with Moscow. Japan's claim to the southernmost islands of the Kuril chain (the "Northern Territories" to the Japanese) was the obstacle blocking efforts to conclude a peace treaty formally ending World War II at long last. Gorbachev's visit in 1991 yielded little, but when Russian President Boris Yeltsin arrived two years later the two sides pledged to resolve the territorial dispute and conclude a peace treaty, and in a meeting in Khabarovsk in 1998 Yeltsin and Japanese Prime Minister Hashimoto Ryutaro agreed to resolve the issue by 2000. There was a precedent for negotiating the issue: In the 1950s, during a period of thaw in East-West relations, a compromise was almost reached according to which Moscow would return the two island clusters nearest Hokkaido while retaining the two larger islands. But even in the more relaxed atmosphere of the post–Cold War era, an accommodation remained out of reach as nationalist sentiment on both sides limited the room for give and take.

Japan's relations with China were marked by a high level of economic interdependence mixed with deep-rooted political tensions. The robust growth of Sino-Japanese trade and Japan's extensive direct investment in China gave both countries huge stakes in maintaining a healthy relationship. As discussed elsewhere (Chapter 12), it was the Dengist revolution beginning in the late 1970s, not the end of the Cold War, that opened the way for China to join in the remarkable economic development of the region and become integrated into the regional and global economy. Persisting political tensions had their roots extending still farther back in history, such as the Sino-Japanese War of 1895 (leading to the loss of Taiwan to Japan) and especially the Japanese invasion of the 1930s and World War II. An abiding mistrust of Japan has magnified Chinese reactions to Japanese acts perceived as reflecting an unexpurgated tendency toward militarism. Thus, repeated visits by Japanese leaders to the Yasukuni Shrine, which honors the nation's war dead, including convicted war criminals from World War II, and school textbooks sanitizing Japanese behavior during the war have evoked Chinese ire. Fear of a revival of Japanese militarism helps to account for the ambivalence the Chinese have shown toward the American military presence in the region. That presence may be seen as an effort to contain China's rise, on the one hand, but also as contributing to a balance of power in the region and constraining Japan's military ambitions, on the other. The alternative could be an arms race spreading in a chain reaction throughout the region.

Japan's deliberations over its role in security affairs were given sharper focus by menacing developments in its immediate neighborhood. North Korea, feeling vulnerable in the post–Cold War environment, pursued a nuclear program that, if left unchecked, could provide the spark for a chain reaction leading Japan and others in the region to follow the same course. A resolution of the nuclear issue was achieved in the mid-1990s, only to become unstuck a decade later. These nuclear crises bracketed another sobering event, North Korea's test in 1998 of a missile that overflew Japan.

Given the challenges it faced in the region, including the potentially explosive Taiwan issue, it is not surprising that Tokyo did not opt to move out of the embrace of the U.S. alliance system. In the wake of the 1995–96 Taiwan Strait crisis, Washington and Tokyo revised the guidelines for implementing their bilateral security treaty, redefining the scope of its application potentially to include a Taiwan contingency and expanding Japan's part in joint security affairs. Accordingly, insofar as Japan moved toward a more assertive geopolitical role, it proceeded toward heightened strategic collaboration with America, as reflected also in its decision to join the United States in designating the Taiwan issue as among their "common strategic objectives."

Prompted by the threat of a North Korea armed with nuclear missiles, Japan agreed to join the United States in developing a multibillion-dollar missile-defense shield, a joint project that could establish another new precedent by causing Tokyo to breach its ban on exporting arms.[3] The Korean issue further aggravated Japan's relations with the ROK and China, the latter two taking a more conciliatory approach to actions by Pyongyang that Tokyo regarded as increasingly threatening.

## THE KOREAN NUCLEAR ISSUE

Pyongyang pursued a nuclear arms program to provide a deterrent and bargaining power, requirements that became more urgent after the loss of support from its big Communist patrons. This pursuit ran up against concerns on the part of America and its allies over the dangers posed to their troops, and beyond that the threat posed to the nuclear nonproliferation regime (notably the 1968 nonproliferation treaty, the NPT). The prospect of nuclear weapons in the hands of a "rogue" state with a record of terrorist actions lent the North Korean program an especially menacing character. This prospect was all the more alarming given the danger of nuclear arms being disseminated to other pariah states or even to nonstate terrorist groups.

Prior to the first crisis over North Korea's nuclear program, there had been promising steps toward relaxing tensions on the peninsula.[4] In 1985 Moscow had agreed to supply the DPRK with light-water nuclear reactors—the kind of reactor less suitable for producing weapons-grade fuel—on condition that Pyongyang join the NPT, with its commitments to accept international inspections and not to disseminate nuclear arms. Six years later, in December 1991, high-level talks between North and South Korea produced an Agreement on Reconciliation, Nonaggression, and Cooperation and Exchange,[5] in which the two sides recognized each other's legitimacy during an interim period leading to unification. Later that month they agreed to renounce production of nuclear weapons, including a pledge not to possess nuclear-processing facilities. A North Korean party plenum late that month endorsed the agreements and appointed Kim Jong Il, the "Great Leader's" son, supreme commander of the armed forces, a major step in confirming his position as his father's successor.[6] In other measures designed to improve the atmosphere, Washington announced the withdrawal of U.S. nuclear arms from Korea, and the annual U.S.-ROK Team Spirit military exercises—a subject of strident protests from the North—were suspended for 1992. For its part, Pyongyang signed an agreement with the International Atomic Energy Agency (IAEA), the UN affiliate for monitoring compliance with the NPT, to permit inspections of its facilities. IAEA inspectors arrived in North Korea in mid-1992.

The situation deteriorated, however, with Pyongyang objecting to the resumption of Team Spirit and the IAEA demanding to conduct "special inspections" of suspect nuclear sites. Pyongyang resisted this demand by invoking an escape clause in the NPT permitting withdrawal from the treaty to avoid jeopardizing "supreme national interests." In early 1993 it announced its withdrawal from the NPT, the first country to do so.[7] The developing crisis was defused temporarily in mid-1993 when Washington offered security assurances and Pyongyang suspended its NPT withdrawal, but the thorny inspections issue remained unresolved. After the North Koreans missed an IAEA deadline set in early 1994, the agency referred the matter to the UN Security Council for enforcement action.[8] China, which was a crucial supplier of food and fuel to the DPRK, possessed leverage that Washington persistently urged it to use and reportedly warned the North Koreans that it would not veto Security Council sanctions. In fact, China abstained from a vote by the IAEA board to suspend assistance to the North Korean nuclear program; Pyongyang responded to the vote by expelling the remaining inspectors and refusing further cooperation.

Former president Jimmy Carter now entered the picture, traveling to the DPRK in June 1994 in a private capacity—though with a State Department official in his party—and meeting with Kim Il Sung, who acceded to Carter's request to allow the inspectors to remain and to freeze North Korea's nuclear program until the next round of U.S.-DPRK talks.[9] The talks were interrupted by Kim's sudden death in July, but resumed a few weeks later and yielded an "Agreed Framework" for resolving the crisis. According to the agreement, which was signed in Geneva in October, the United States undertook to organize an international consortium to supply light-water reactors to the DPRK for producing energy in exchange for Pyongyang's commitment to freeze the existing reactors' operations and to permit IAEA inspections. The consortium established the Korean Peninsula Energy Development Organization, with South Korea as the prime contractor. The North Koreans were also to be provided fuel oil for energy until the reactors were in operation. The United States and the DPRK also agreed to take steps toward normalizing their relations. Such steps were taken, including the first visit ever by a North Korean to the White House—by a senior leader who appeared in his military uniform when seeing President Clinton in October 2000—followed a few days later by a trip to Pyongyang by Secretary of State Madeleine Albright.

The concern underlying the first crisis centered on the nuclear complex in Yongbyon, where the North Koreans were suspected of unloading irradiated fuel rods from a reactor that could be reprocessed for plutonium used in producing nuclear weapons. There was speculation that the DPRK had enough plutonium for one or two bombs comparable to those used on Japan in 1945.[10] The second crisis arose in 2002, the second year of the administration of the younger George Bush, when the United States charged that Pyongyang had reneged on the Agreed Framework provisions by undertaking a clandestine uranium-enrichment program—the other way to produce nuclear weapons. In the months preceding the new crisis, the Bush administration, which had expressed scorn for the Agreed Framework, labeled the DPRK a member of the "axis of evil" (along with Iran and Iraq, which was invaded in 2003), included North Korea in its revised nuclear targeting strategy, and declared a doctrine of preemption against presumed threats to American security. The North Koreans initially acknowledged the uranium program, according to American officials, but thereafter they denied it. Washington now proceeded to insist on the "complete, verifiable, and irreversible dismantlement" of North Korea's nuclear programs.

The situation having deteriorated in late 2002 and early 2003 after Pyongyang's reported acknowledgment of a uranium-enrichment program, Washington along with its allies Japan and the ROK decided to halt the oil supplies provided according to the 1994 deal (the light-water reactors were never built, and the project was officially abandoned in 2006); Pyongyang responded by reactivating its nuclear facilities at Yongbyon and announcing its intention to withdraw from the NPT. It also pulled out of the 1992 agreement with Seoul to keep the peninsula free of nuclear arms. Initial contacts were established in April 2003 in Beijing between American and North Korean representatives to address the crisis, and that August the first of several rocky rounds of six-party talks on the nuclear issue opened in the Chinese capital.[11]

The six nations—the two Koreas, the United States, Japan, China, and Russia—approached the talks with a variety of aims. Pyongyang seemed to be using its nuclear program as leverage to extract security, economic, and diplomatic concessions, principally from the United States. The other five shared an interest in a denuclearized peninsula, but they also had disparate aims vis-à-vis the North. The hard-line Bush administration was determined to dismantle the DPRK's nuclear activities and was vocal in denouncing its human rights abuses. Japan remained closest to the U.S. approach, with a special interest in a final accounting for the Japanese citizens who had been kidnapped by North Korea; Prime Minister Koizumi Junichiro went to Pyongyang for a historic summit in 2002 and secured the release of some of them, but patently flimsy explanations for the fate of the others led to a breakdown of talks on the issue. Expectations of progress toward normalizing relations were also dashed.

Washington's other ally, the ROK, had been sobered by the heavy burdens shouldered by West Germany after the collapse of the Communist East German regime and shuddered at the prospect of far greater effects from a collapse of the DPRK. Moreover, a generational shift was occurring in the South: the emergence of younger cohorts with a more relaxed view of the North than held by the older generations steeled in the confrontations of the Cold War. (This shift was registered in a poll released in mid-2005 in which two-thirds of South Koreans of military age said they would side with the North in the event of a war between the United States and the DPRK.[12]) Kim Dae Jung, the longtime opposition leader who once faced execution by the old regime, was elected president in December 1997 and introduced a "sunshine policy" toward the North that sought accommodation in place of confrontation. He and Kim Jong Il held a historic summit in 2000. Seoul was now focused on improving relations with the North and averting a collapse of the DPRK.

China too feared a collapse of the regime in the North and an inundation of refugees, already a problem. The Chinese also had a strategic interest in maintaining North Korea as a buffer zone and having a large contingent of American troops tied down on the peninsula rather than available for a confrontation with China. As well, Beijing had an interest in keeping the North Korean issue as a bargaining chip in other areas, such as the Taiwan question. For these reasons Beijing was inclined to resist American pressure to use its leverage—as a supplier of food and fuel—to compel Pyongyang to take a more conciliatory approach. But if Beijing wanted a stable North Korea, it also had a fundamental interest in a denuclearized peninsula in order to avert a regional arms race that could lead to the nightmare of a nuclear-armed Japan. As for Russia, though it signed a new friendship treaty with the DPRK in 2000, its mainly economic interests were served by maintaining peace on the peninsula. A project such as a proposed pipeline to South Korea crossing the North would give Russia better access to a major market while giving North Korea, which would receive transit fees, a stake in an interdependent environment.

The six-party talks proved difficult and contentious. After the second and third rounds, held in the first half of 2004, Pyongyang accused the United States of hostile policies toward it and refused to attend the planned fourth round. Then in February of the next year Pyongyang declared that it had become "a full-fledged nuclear weapons state" and was suspending its participation in the talks. American intelligence believed that the North had increased its stockpile of weapons-grade plutonium fourfold during the two years of balky talks, enough to make about nine nuclear weapons.[13] Eventually, in July 2005, with Beijing again providing the venue for U.S.-DPRK consultations as well as playing a mediatory role, the North Koreans agreed to resume the talks and end their yearlong boycott.

A breakthrough in the negotiations finally yielded a statement of principles based on a draft prepared by the Chinese. A major obstacle had been Pyongyang's insistence on a right to peaceful nuclear energy and Washington's equally adamant insistence that the North Koreans had forfeited this right under the NPT and could not be trusted with any nuclear program. (A parallel standoff was taking place regarding Iran's nuclear ambitions.) Difficulties were also posed by the "sequencing" of the steps leading to a final resolution of the issue. Both the North Koreans and the Americans made compromises, though achievement of agreement also required a level of generality and ambiguity that portended further difficulties. The statement of principles, adopted on 19 September 2005, included the following key principles:

- The six parties reaffirmed the goal of the talks to be "the verifiable denuclearization of the Korean Peninsula." Though the United States had withdrawn its nuclear weapons from the peninsula and the ROK reaffirmed its pledge not to possess these arms, Pyongyang might object to the American nuclear umbrella over the South under the U.S.-ROK alliance and seek to probe growing fissures in the relationship.
- The United States said it "has no intention" of attacking North Korea. This fell short of Pyongyang's demand for security guarantees and left open the possibility

of Washington changing its intention if the nuclear issue was not defused to its liking.

- The DPRK pledged to abandon all nuclear weapons and existing nuclear programs and to return "at an early date" to the NPT and IAEA safeguards. This formulation—use of the plural "programs"—would seem to meet Washington's concern over the uranium-enrichment program, though Pyongyang was now refusing to admit to such an activity.
- The DPRK stated its "right to peaceful uses of nuclear energy." The other parties expressed their "respect" for this and agreed to "discuss, at an appropriate time," the provision of a light-water reactor to the DPRK. The United States acceded to pressure from the other parties by dropping its insistence that Pyongyang had forfeited a right to even civilian nuclear facilities. The offer to discuss a light-water reactor at an "appropriate" time left this crucial issue wide open for varying interpretations.
- The United States and other parties stated a willingness to provide energy assistance to North Korea, and the ROK reaffirmed its proposal to provide two million kilowatts of electric power. This reflected Seoul's eagerness to use economic aid to prop up the regime in the North.
- The six parties agreed to take "coordinated steps" to implement the consensus achieved "in a phased manner in line with the principle of 'commitment for commitment, action for action.'" This somewhat labored formulation addressed the knotty question of the sequence of the implementing steps; again, the devil would lie in the details of interpretation.
- The DPRK-Japan dispute over the abducted Japanese citizens found expression in an undertaking by the two sides to normalize relations by resolving "unfortunate past and outstanding issues of concern."[14]

An arduous road lay ahead in translating these guidelines into concrete actions. Indeed, within hours of the signing of the agreement, Pyongyang issued a statement spinning its interpretation of the terms covering the most problematic elements, the light-water reactor and sequencing of steps. The statement conditioned the beginning of the abandoning of the DPRK's nuclear programs and its return to the NPT on first receiving a civilian nuclear reactor. Prospects for implementing the agreement became further clouded when Pyongyang balked after Washington took measures against financial institutions accused of abetting North Korean counterfeiting and money laundering. Having left the nuclear issue dead in the water, Pyongyang took another defiant step by launching seven missile tests in July 2006 (on the Fourth of July Washington time), including a long-range missile that tumbled into the Sea of Japan after less than two minutes. Reacting to efforts led by Japan and the United States to obtain Security Council sanctions, Pyongyang threatened unspecified "stronger" action in retaliation. The North Koreans emphasized that they no longer felt bound by the moratorium on missile testing they had accepted in 1998 and renewed during Japanese Prime Minister's Koizumi's visit in 2002.[15] The missile tests were not, however, in violation of international law or treaties (unlike the expulsion of nuclear inspectors and exit from the NPT before the required six-month notice).

## NUCLEARIZATION OF THE SUBCONTINENT

The Simla agreement of July 1972 had led to a period of stability in the subcontinent after the 1971 war between India and Pakistan that led to the creation of the new state of Bangladesh. The Soviet intervention in Afghanistan at the end of the decade, however, set in motion a cascade of events with momentous consequences. The U.S. response, which included lifting the arms embargo imposed on Pakistan and providing substantial supplies in the fight against the Soviet presence in Afghanistan, strengthened the hand of General Mohammad Zia-ul-Haq, who had ousted and executed Bhutto. Zia pursued a policy of Islamization at home and nurtured close ties with the Islamist resistance in Afghanistan. Eventually, with the Soviet withdrawal followed by civil war and chaos, the Pakistani military, in particular its Inter-Services Intelligence, developed a close relationship with the fiercely fundamentalist Taliban as it swept to power. Then, in one of history's ironic twists, the United States enlisted the Pakistanis as a key ally in the invasion of Afghanistan to oust the Taliban and hunt down the terrorist Al-Qaeda organization that had been sheltered by the Taliban.

India, looking after its own interests, had remained discreetly quiet about the Soviet move into Afghanistan, while enhancing its ties with Moscow, a major arms supplier.[16] Meanwhile, there had been promising developments in Kashmir in the 1970s when India allowed the "Lion of Kashmir," Sheikh Mohammed Abdullah, to engage in political activity after a period of house arrest and exile, but his death in the early 1980s was followed by renewed unrest and secessionist sentiment.[17] Indian-Pakistani relations became strained by a series of confrontations. A dangerous situation of competing military exercises arose from Indian resentment over Pakistani support in the late 1980s for Sikh separatists seeking an independent Khalistan. Another focus of tension was the Siachen Glacier, in an inhospitable area of Kashmir where there were conflicting territorial claims: between India and Pakistan over Kashmir, between India and China over Aksai Chin, and involving all three over the part of Kashmir that Pakistan had ceded to China provisionally pending a final border settlement in the region.[18]

In these deteriorating circumstances, including Pakistani support for the renewed flaring of the insurgency in Kashmir through arms and training, the subcontinent became overtly nuclear when India conducted a series of nuclear tests in May 1998 followed later that month by Pakistan. India's defeat at the hands of the Chinese in 1962 had spurred it to undertake a nuclear program, which bore fruit with a test in 1974. Pakistan may have also been induced to begin its nuclear effort after a defeat, the humiliating dismemberment in 1971. Neither side adhered to the NPT, India charging that the nuclear powers had failed to meet their obligation to divest themselves of nuclear arms, and Pakistan demanding the right to match its rival in going nuclear. The dangers inherent in this situation were demonstrated a year after the nuclear tests when another confrontation in Kashmir, in the Kargil area, almost led to an all-out war. Pakistan, perhaps calculating that nuclearization of the subcontinent would inhibit India's use of its conventional arms superiority, infiltrated troops across the Line of Control and (in an echo of events during the Sino-Indian border conflict), an Indian patrol sent into the area disappeared. With the enemy occupying the heights, the Indians had to cope with severe logistical and topographical challenges, which they met by resorting to air strikes and artillery barrages that forced a Pakistani withdrawal.[19] President Clinton, in a step that helped prepare for notably improved American relations with India in the new century, threw his influence behind an appeal to defuse the situation.

Early in the new century two explosive incidents for which India blamed Pakistan—a lethal terrorist attack on the Parliament in New Delhi in December 2001 and five months later a massacre of women and children at an Indian garrison in Kashmir—raised a nuclear sword of Damocles over the subcontinent. Armies mobilized along the border, the Indian leadership contemplated a military offensive, American officials sought to defuse the situation, and finally New Delhi decided against actions that might elicit a Pakistani nuclear response.[20] These episodes may have had a cathartic effect akin to that of the Cuban missile crisis; in any case, nerves became settled and steps were taken to create a more propitious atmosphere for Indian-Pakistani dialogue, including a summit meeting in January 2004, a cease-fire agreement, and India's first declared force reduction in Kashmir. An impasse over Pakistan's demand that the Kashmir issue be given priority and India's insistence on elimination of terrorism was broken by the sides' agreement to hold talks on a "composite" agenda. A new Indian government formed by the Congress Party, which had returned to power in mid-2004 after the defeat of the Hindu nationalist Bharatiya Janata Party, sought to impart new momentum to the ameliorating trend. The new prime minister, Manmohan Singh, architect of economic liberalization policies introduced by an earlier Congress-led government in the 1990s, traveled to Kashmir in late 2004 to offer unconditional talks to those willing to renounce violence and to dangle an economic package of more than five billion dollars to "win the hearts and minds" of the people there.[21] Another step forward came the next year when the two sides agreed to open a bus service across the Line of Control in Kashmir (between Srinigar and Muzafarabad, the respective capitals of the parts controlled by India and Pakistan) to allow visits by families and friends. India acceded to Pakistan's objection to a requirement for passports, on the ground that they would treat the Line of Control as an international border, by permitting issuance of "entry permits" as documents. In an echo of the Ping-Pong diplomacy in 1971 heralding a new Sino-American relationship, the first bus from Srinigar left from a cricket stadium. This "cricket diplomacy" was pursued further in 2005 when President Pervez Musharraf attended a match in India between these two cricket-mad countries.

Meanwhile, the two rivals in the subcontinent were being wooed by the outside powers. The less rigid international structure after the Cold War freed Washington from an either/or choice between Pakistan and India or between combating terrorism and enlisting India as a counterweight to a rising China. Thus Pakistan escaped from the pariah status where it had fallen because of the nuclear tests and Musharraf's military coup as well as incursions across the Line of Control in Kashmir (Musharraf was head of the armed forces at the time of the Kargil incident); the United States now needed the Pakistanis in the war against the Taliban and in the hunt for Al-Qaeda leader Osama bin Laden (who had arrived in Afghanistan in 1996). Musharraf took risks in cooperating with the United States, risks that he was suspected of hedging by proceeding less than all out against jihadists for fear of alienating Islamist elements in his country. This caution was also reflected in his treatment of A.Q. Khan, a national hero known as the father of Pakistan's nuclear bomb; confronted by American intelligence showing Khan to be a serial proliferator supplying nuclear materials to several countries, Musharraf only put him under house arrest and refused to allow the Americans to interrogate him. Notwithstanding tensions arising from Musharraf's effort to balance domestic and international concerns, Washington rewarded his contribution to the antiterrorism campaign. Thus, in March 2005 it authorized the sale of F-16 fighter jets to Pakistan, ending a fifteen-year embargo. Washington had cut off aid to Pakistan in 1990 as required by law if the latter was believed to be pursuing a nuclear program.

The Bush administration, like its predecessor in putting a premium on enlisting India as a counterweight to a rising China, decided to relax controls on India's nuclear program as it did with Pakistan. In a significant—and controversial—step a few months after permitting the sale of jets to Pakistan, it sought to remove a long-standing irritant in U.S.-Indian relations by offering to lift a ban on sales of civilian nuclear equipment. An agreement was signed during Bush's visit in March 2006, the first visit to India by an American president since Clinton's in 2000 and only the second in twenty-eight years. According to this deal, unprecedented in offering nuclear assistance while allowing the recipient to expand its nuclear arms production, India would separate its civilian and military nuclear programs, only the former to be subject to international inspections. Moreover, India refused to commit itself to ending production of fissile material—the five official nuclear states under the NPT had voluntarily ceased producing fissile material—or to put its fast-breeder reactor program on the list of civilian facilities open to inspection.[22]

The deal drew criticism for its implications for the NPT regime; other countries might now be inclined to question the value of adherence to the NPT and to embark on a nuclear arms program. In particular, it might be seen as undercutting the case against North Korea and Iran for pursuing nuclear programs. Washington defended it by drawing a distinction between India as a democracy and the members of the "axis of evil."[23] In any case, the Bush administration's decision reflected its willingness to revamp the NPT and was consonant with its skepticism toward inherited multilateral agreements.

In the fluid post–Cold War environment, Washington's moves to cultivate India to counterbalance China did not cause a polarization of Sino-Indian relations, as typically developed during the Cold War. Instead, the two sides steadily enhanced their ties in parallel with the warming U.S.-Indian relationship. This trend was dramatized by a visit in April 2005 by the PRC premier, Wen Jiabao, which produced a joint statement declaring that Sino-Indian relations "have now acquired a global and strategic character."[24] The Chinese attached "great importance" to India's status in international affairs, a formulation stopping short of endorsing India's bid for a permanent seat on the Security Council but contrasting with Beijing's negative posture toward Japan's similar bid. Wen's visit covered a wide range of commercial ties (India's export of grapes and bitter gourds, among other items) and yielded a pledge by the two sides to increase their bilateral trade to 20 billion dollars or more by 2008 (in 2004 it had reached 13.6 billion dollars, compared with U.S.-Indian trade that year of 20 billion dollars).

The two sides signaled their intent to seek a breakthrough on the border issue, which had poisoned their relations in the 1960s but had been quiescent in recent years as the two sides took measures to demilitarize the border. Pledging to seek "a fair, reasonable and mutually acceptable solution" to the border issue, they produced an agreement on the "political parameters and guiding principles" for a settlement of the thorny boundary question.[25] The guidelines specified a range of considerations—such as historical evidence, national sentiments, the actual situation on the border, and geographical features—that could give negotiators room for give-and-take and mutual concessions. According to the agreement, this process should lead to "a package settlement" covering all sectors of the Sino-Indian boundary. The significance of the agreement was that a political decision had been made to seek a settlement, in which historical and legal issues in the territorial dispute would be subordinated to broader interests. (A precedent was the Sino-Russian border question; once the political decision had been reached, a breakthrough became possible, even though the final details of a settlement took years to be hammered out.)

Helping to smooth the way to productive boundary negotiations, the two sides confirmed removal of two sources of antagonism in the past, the borderlands of Tibet and Sikkim. India not only acknowledged PRC sovereignty over Tibet but also said that it would not allow "anti-China political activities" by Tibetans in India. As for Sikkim, the former principality whose incorporation into India had drawn a hostile response from Beijing, the Chinese made an unequivocal reference to "the Sikkim State of the Republic of India." The more relaxed situation was reflected in the reopening in July 2006 of direct border trade, the first since the border war in 1962.

### INDIA, PRC SET OUT GUIDING PRINCIPLES FOR A BORDER SETTLEMENT

Art. III. Both sides should, in the spirit of mutual respect and mutual understanding, make meaningful and mutually acceptable adjustments to their respective positions on the boundary question, so as to arrive at *a package settlement* to the boundary question. The boundary settlement must be final, *covering all sectors* of the India-China boundary.

Art. IV. The two sides will give due consideration to each other's strategic and reasonable interests, and the principle of mutual and equal security.

Art. V. The two sides will take into account, inter alia, historical evidence, national sentiments, practical difficulties and reasonable concerns and sensitivities of both sides, and the actual state of border areas.

Art. VI. The boundary should be along well-defined and easily identifiable natural geographical features to be mutually agreed upon between the two sides.

Art. VII. In reaching a boundary settlement, the two sides shall safeguard due interests of their settled populations in the border areas. (emphasis added)

"The Political Parameters and Guiding Principles for the Settlement of the India-China Boundary Question," accessed at http://meaindia.nic.in/treatiesagreement/2005/11ta110420051.htm.

Notwithstanding moves to prepare the ground for fruitful negotiations, there were enduring constraints from both sides: China's sensitivity to instability in Tibet, and Indian concerns over vulnerable borders. These complications were in evidence during the Dalai Lama's visit in early November 2009 to the Tawang tract, the disputed area at the junction of India's Arunachal Pradesh, Tibet, and Bhutan.

## EMERGING TRADE ISSUES IN SOUTHEAST ASIA

The Cambodian settlement and end of the Third Indochina War ushered in a tranquil period in this long-tormented area. The three Indochinese states were accepted into ASEAN, and Vietnam rapidly mended relations with its former antagonists, China and America. The 1990s saw high-level Sino-Vietnamese exchanges, including a summit between the party chiefs in 1992 signifying full normalization between Communist countries, and a border agreement was reached in 1999.

Meanwhile, the Clinton administration moved to put the decades of U.S.-Vietnamese conflict behind, a process abetted by Vietnamese cooperation in searching for missing American troops (of whom none were found to be living despite deep suspicions harbored by some Americans). The watchword during Bill Clinton's election campaign in 1992—"It's the economy, stupid"—was translated into economism in foreign affairs, the focus being on international economic relations. After Washington and Hanoi exchanged diplomatic recognition in 1995, negotiations for a trade agreement were successfully completed in 2000, the year that President Clinton visited Vietnam to mark the emotional end to the long conflict. Within four years trade between the two countries exceeded six billion dollars, the United States having become Vietnam's leading trade partner. It is a measure of the post–Cold War environment that in the new century the most contentious issues in relations between these old antagonists have been commercial, as in American demands for a curb on imports of Vietnamese shrimp.

If international trade and commerce lay at the center of foreign affairs after the end of the Cold War, there was a corresponding potential for disputes over trade issues and jolts from the onrushing tide of globalization. The flow of capital into the rapidly developing economies of Southeast Asia held dangers as well as opportunities. A rapid influx of short-term capital led to an overinvestment bubble, overvalued local currencies, and currency speculation.[26] If hot money could pour in, it could as easily rush for the exits. Starting with the collapse of the Thai baht in 1997, a contagious financial crisis swept the area (and the globe). In addition to the shock of seeing their economies in turmoil, the affected countries felt resentment toward the corrective prescriptions of the International Monetary Fund and Washington. The crisis deepened a growing sense of regional identity and spurred efforts to devise collective initiatives for coping with the challenges of capital mobility and globalization—as well as trade blocs elsewhere.[27]

As noted earlier, the Southeast Asian countries embarking on the export-led road to economic development had to compete for markets in the developed world; in the 1980s and 1990s, however, an evolving complementarity was reflected in growing intraregional trade and investment.[28] Still, the underlying pattern of export-driven economies persisted into the new century, as reflected in their high level of exports as a percentage of GDP. This was especially the case with Singapore, the area's richest country, where exports had reached 168 percent of GDP in 2004. (That is not a misprint; exports can exceed GDP when most of their components are imported and thus not counted as domestic production.)[29]

America's trade deficit with Asia and its interest in unimpeded access to the dynamic economies there generated tensions across the Pacific. The effort to give a stronger collective voice to the region's interests met with resistance from Washington, concerned over a loss of influence. One potential source of tension was the creation of a regional organization known as ASEAN Plus Three (Japan, South Korea, and China), which convened an East Asian summit in December 2005 to discuss formation of a new Asian community, the brainchild of the then prime minister of Malaysia, the prickly Dr. Mahathir bin Mohamad (who envisaged a "caucus without Caucasians"). Embraced by China, this group had the underlying purpose of offsetting America's postwar dominance in the region. Significantly, the United States was not invited, meaning that this became the first major regional meeting in which it was not a participant. (This development was foreshadowed in 1997 by the inaugural ASEAN Plus Three summit, also without U.S. participation.) The impact was greatly diluted, however, by the insistence of other members of ASEAN Plus Three to add to the summit Australia, New Zealand, and India, thereby reducing Chinese influence and strengthening the pro-American presence.[30]

In other developments in Southeast Asia, the financial crisis of 1997–98 was accompanied by a significant political result in the region's largest country. After massive demonstrations fueled by economic discontent and anger over corruption, longtime Indonesian dictator Suharto was toppled and a process of political liberalization arose that culminated in the new century in the country's first directly elected president, Susilo Bambang Yudhoyono. Unfortunately, the country was rewarded with a series of terrorist bombings that seemed part of the global outbreak of Islamist terrorism. The attacks in Indonesia—bombings in Bali in 2002 (causing more than two hundred deaths) and again in 2005, bracketing attacks in Jakarta in the two intervening years—were regarded as the work of Jemaah Islamiyah, a regional affiliate of Al-Qaeda, or of remnants of that organization after its losses from effective antiterrorist intelligence work in response to the first Bali bombings.[31] The much lower number of deaths in the second Bali bombings, around twenty, and the less sophisticated methods used also reflected the effectiveness of regional cooperation as well as American and Australian contributions.[32]

## STRATEGIC REALIGNMENT REVISITED?

One model for characterizing the post–Cold War international landscape is that of unipolarity, with America left as the sole superpower and exercising unchallenged hegemony. In these circumstances it is not surprising, particularly in the light of realist international relations theory, that lesser powers might join forces as a counterweight to predominant American power. A competing model holds that realist interpretations have been superseded by the growing economic interdependence wrought by globalization and transnational commercial entities. In this view the rest of the world needs American markets and investment, not to mention the stability conferred by the largely intact U.S. security structures in East Asia and elsewhere. What, then, are the signs that American hegemony in Asia has been challenged?

As discussed in Chapter 10, a strategic realignment occurred in the 1970s as the United States and China developed a relationship after two decades of hostility in order to offer a counterweight to what was perceived as a relentless Soviet drive for global hegemony. This realignment clearly was not based on ideological affinities but was responsive to classic realist calculations of balance of power. In the unipolar post–Cold War environment there have been indications that China and Russia have sought to form a strategic alignment to counterpose American dominance in Asia. Again, ideological considerations were not involved; the collapse of the Soviet Union and the chaos that ensued were object lessons for Beijing on how not to pursue reform. Notwithstanding ideological tensions, however, the former Communist country and the country desperately trying to preserve Communist rule were able to find common ground in the period after the end of the Cold War.

Joint statements issued during a series of Sino-Russian summit meetings were threaded with warnings against the dangers inherent in a unipolar world order. Take, for instance, the one issued by the summit in November 1998 between President Jiang Zemin and his Russian counterpart, Boris Yeltsin, the sixth summit since the demise of the Soviet Union.[33] Holding pride of place in a series of principles enunciated in the statement was one calling for a multipolar international environment in order to build "a balanced, stable, democratic and nonconfrontational new order"—in other words, an order not dominated by a hegemonic power. The two sides deplored attempts to bypass the Security Council, where they could exercise their veto power to check unilateral American actions or those by organizations dominated by the United States. The statement specifically cited the Kosovo issue, where NATO undertook military action to curb Serbia's repressive actions against the predominately Albanian population.

The new century saw the trend toward a deeper sense of mutual interests between China and Russia culminate in a Treaty of Good Neighborly Friendship and Cooperation signed in July 2001.[34] This fell well short of a mutual security alliance, requiring the sides only to consult in order to deal with a threat to either country, with no commitments to taking action. They did, however, pledge to develop "a strategic cooperation relationship" as promised at a summit in 1996. An underlying continuity in their relationship dating back to 1982—when Brezhnev took advantage of Sino-American tensions over the Taiwan arms issue to make an overture to Beijing—was registered in the treaty's assurances of support by each side for the other's "national unity" and territorial integrity. Taiwan was mentioned specifically, while for Russia there was resonance in its concern over maintaining control over restive ethnic groups within its new boundaries (the Chechnya case being the most troubling).

The strategic cooperation relationship had been given concrete form in military sales from Russia to China, enabling the former to profit from the latter's vast foreign currency holdings while supplying advanced weaponry such as submarines and fighter aircraft. The Russian supply link was all the more important for Beijing given the arms embargo

**PRC, RUSSIA SIGN TREATY FOR A "STRATEGIC COOPERATION PARTNERSHIP"**

The two parties to the treaty will enduringly and comprehensively develop a strategic cooperation partnership of good neighborliness, friendship, cooperation, and trust as equals. . . .

China supports Russia's policy of preserving the national unity of the Russian Federation and its territorial integrity.

Russia supports China's policies on preserving the national unity and territorial integrity of the People's Republic of China . . . .

Russia holds that there is only one China, that the Government of the People's Republic of China is the sole legitimate government representing the whole of China, and that Taiwan is an indivisible part of China. . . .

If a party to the treaty believes that there is a threat of aggression against one of the parties, undermining peace and involving its security interests, the two parties will immediately make contact and hold consultations in order to eliminate the threat that has arisen.

Treaty of Good Neighborly Friendship and Cooperation Between the People's Republic of China and the Russian Federation, 16 July 2001, Xinhua News Agency, 16 July 2001; *Beijing Review*, 2 August 2001, 8–9.

imposed by the United States and the European Union after the Tiananmen Square crackdown in 1989. Still another step was taken toward closer military relations when the two countries staged joint exercises in August 2005. These exercises, involving combined arms operations, began in the Russian Far East and then moved on to China's Shandong coastal province and the Yellow Sea. There were potential implications for a Taiwan conflict in these exercises, something the Chinese would not mind others inferring, but Russia would be loath to become implicated in this way and probably finds such exercises a way to promote the arms supply relationship.[35]

The exercises were billed as aimed at strengthening the two sides' capability for jointly countering "terrorism, separatism, and extremism"—the mantra they have recited for the purpose of putting themselves on the side of the international antiterrorism campaign while asserting their special interest in combating separatist challenges (e.g., in Xinjiang and Chechnya). That purpose was central to the creation of a regional organization, the Shanghai Cooperation Organization (SCO),[36] which evolved out of efforts to achieve boundary settlements and confidence-building measures along the borders after the collapse of the Soviet Union. The grouping was originally established in 1996 as the Shanghai Five, comprising China and the four successor states to the USSR having borders with China—Russia, Kazakhstan, Kyrgyzstan, and Tajikistan. Annual summit meetings produced treaties on fostering mutual trust and reducing military forces in the border regions. It became the SCO five years later with the addition of Uzbekistan in recognition of the need for regional cooperation in combating Islamist terrorism—the Islamic Movement of Uzbekistan being a major regional threat. A convention on combating "terrorism, separatism, and extremism" was signed and an antiterrorism center established in Bishkek, the Kyrgyz capital. Representatives of the four Central Asian members attended the Sino-Russian joint exercises in 2005 as observers.

The SCO has had an ambiguous relationship with the United States, on the one hand finding common interest in countering terrorism and on the other resisting American advances into Central Asia as a part of the campaign in Afghanistan (for example, with logistical airbases in Uzbekistan and Kyrgyzstan). In the latter respect the organization served the strategic interest of providing a counterweight to the American presence in the region. This was given expression in July 2005 when the SCO demanded that Washington set a deadline for withdrawing from the bases established in Uzbekistan and Kyrgyzstan to support the military effort in Afghanistan. The relationship had become further complicated by tensions between Washington's interest in enlisting support for counterterrorism and its desire to foster political liberalization in Central Asia, an area marked by repressive regimes under leaders held over from the Soviet era. Two opposite developments occurred in 2005: a revolt in Kyrgyzstan that ousted its longtime autocrat and led to election of a new leader in balloting regarded by outside observers as largely valid, and a crackdown in Uzbekistan by its strongman, Islam A. Karimov, who was supported by China and Russia. Resentful over American criticism and a UN operation removing endangered Uzbeks fleeing after the crackdown, Karimov set a six-month deadline for U.S. evacuation of the airbase in his country. In contrast, the new Kyrgyz leadership agreed to permit U.S. use of the airbase on its territory "until the situation in Afghanistan is completely stabilized."[37]

**SHANGHAI COOPERATION ORGANIZATION TARGETS TERRORISM**

The SCO attaches special importance to make every effort to ensure regional security. All members will closely cooperate with each other in implementing the Shanghai treaty on the crackdown on terrorism, separatism and extremism, including to establish the SCO antiterrorism center in Bishkek, Kyrgyzstan. In addition, the member states will work out corresponding documents of multinational cooperation in a bid to curb illegal arms smuggling, drug trafficking, illegal migration and other criminal activities. . . .

Declaration of the Shanghai Cooperation Organization, 15 June 2001, Xinhua News Agency, 15 June 2001.

Meanwhile, China and Russia were further consolidating their relationship in the wake of the friendship treaty. As in the case of the Sino-Indian border, the one between Russia and China remained quiet as the two sides sought to foster an atmosphere conducive to achieving a final boundary settlement. A major breakthrough in negotiations occurred within a few years of Gorbachev's visit to Beijing in 1989 that normalized relations, and by the end of the 1990s demarcation of the entire boundary had been almost completed. The Gordian knot tying the hands of negotiators pursuing a final settlement concerned two islands right next to Khabarovsk at the confluence of the Amur and Ussuri rivers and another, uninhabited island on the Argun, a tributary of the Amur to the west. Both sides pointed to the friendship treaty signed in 2001, which included an affirmation that there were no territorial disputes between the two, as imparting the political momentum that culminated in a final border agreement in October 2004.

The agreement was achieved through a compromise that simply finessed the issue of the application of international law to riverine borders. Though Gorbachev in his watershed Asian policy statement in Vladivostok in 1986 had conceded to the Chinese that the *thalweg* (central channel of navigable rivers) principle should apply in delimiting the river boundaries, Moscow resisted an application of the principle that would turn over to

China the big island alongside Khabarovsk that the city regarded as integral to its life. The compromise avoided using waterways in determining the boundary by drawing the line across the islands, leaving most of the big island to Russia and awarding to China the remainder as well as the nearby lesser island.

Given the logic of realpolitik aligning Russia with China in counterposition to a dominant America, did the deepening Sino-Russian relationship amount to a new strategic triangle?[38] To a certain extent it has, but the fluidity of international relations after the end of the Cold War attenuated the impact of the Sino-Russian alignment. Whereas in the 1970s the Soviet Union, perceived as intent on establishing global predominance, had deeply troubled relations with the other two sides of the triangle, the United States as the unipolar power after the Cold War has been in many essential respects a partner of China and Russia in an increasingly interdependent environment. American markets, investment, and technology were crucial to their economic development. Though Beijing remained acutely sensitive regarding American military support for Taiwan, and the U.S. presence in Central Asia caused unease in Russia as well as China, those concerns have been offset in significant measure both by the need for economic cooperation with the United States and the unwelcome prospect of instability in Asia were the unipolar power to withdraw from the region. Similarly, given their troubled relations, neither China nor Japan could contemplate with equanimity a power vacuum resulting from American withdrawal and the prospect of an arms race and heightened tensions.

# 14 CHANGE AND CONTINUITY

The end of the Cold War was one of the most dramatic and decisive turning points in the twentieth century, but in Asia, a principal arena and thrice the scene of large-scale combat, it shared a starring role in history with other developments that had transformative effects on the regional geopolitical landscape. This was so both because the Cold War ended in Asia in a much less sweeping manner than in Europe, and because of the impact of the other developments, namely, the rise of China (with origins antedating the end of the Cold War) and the repercussions of the terrorist attacks on America in September 2001. More broadly, the issue of terrorism was one of a large list of transnational phenomena acquiring heightened salience in the post–Cold War Asian landscape: health, environmental degradation, migration, crime, capital volatility, and so on.

One contrast with Europe throws into sharp relief the less decisive impact the end of the Cold War had in Asia. Starting with the extraordinary scene in Eastern Europe in late 1989, the Communist dominoes were swept off the board in all of Eurasia except in East Asia. The Mongolian People's Republic, for decades a Soviet satellite, followed closely behind the Eastern Europeans. At the end of 1991 came the implosion of the Soviet Union, the original homeland of socialism, and the emergence of fifteen nation-states in its place. Within a few years Yugoslavia met a similar fate.

Contrast those astonishing changes with the situation in East Asia, where the Communist regimes in China, North Korea, and Indochina (except for Cambodia) remained intact. As we have seen in previous chapters, the end of the Cold War certainly did have significant effects in this region. North Korea's economy was severely buffeted; Vietnam was forced out of Cambodia and then joined ASEAN; geopolitical tensions were greatly reduced with the removal of the U.S.-Soviet contest. Yet significant residual issues from the Cold War era resisted transformation and continued into the new century as sources of contention and in some cases of potential conflagration. Notably, the Korean peninsula remained divided, a flashpoint made the more incendiary by the perils of nuclear proliferation; and the Chinese civil war, in the form of Beijing's irredentist claim to Taiwan, persisted in posing the threat of a broader conflict with imponderable military and economic effects. There was also a bilateral issue left over from the end of World War II, Japan's claims on the southernmost Kuril Islands, and various islands off the East Asian coast were subject to competing claims to sovereignty.

One respect in which Cold War structures survived in Europe as well as in Asia was that of the American security networks. NATO not only survived but began a process of expansion, embracing former members of the Warsaw Pact and even taking in parts of what had been the Soviet Union. At the same time, the hub-and-spokes American security system in Asia, with some modification (such as the termination of the agreement on bases in the Philippines and New Zealand's de facto removal from ANZUS), stayed in place despite doubts in the early post–Cold War years about whether Washington would draw down its presence in the region. Indeed, this uncertainty afforded the United States even greater access to countries in Southeast Asia that had remained outside the alliance system but now wanted to retain the American presence as a stabilizing influence in a more unpredictable environment.

Alongside the enduring features of the Asian landscape was one development that marked a dramatic change: the democratization of several authoritarian regimes, mainly military, a shift also found in Latin America. In the 1990s, after the end of the Cold War, South Korea, Taiwan, and Indonesia underwent this evolution, holding elections and managing successions without violence or manipulation. They thus joined the mature democracies of Japan and India, Australia and New Zealand, and a broader, somewhat more problematic club of pluralist states such as the Philippines (which had seen off a dictatorship in 1986), Thailand, Malaysia, Bangladesh, Pakistan, and Sri Lanka. This development threw into sharper relief the absence of significant political change in the Communist-ruled states as well as Myanmar (Burma).

## COMMUNIST REGIMES IN EAST ASIA

One way to account for the survival of the Communist-ruled regimes in East Asia is to note the high degree of independence those Communist parties enjoyed. The Chinese and Vietnamese Communists gained power largely on their own (the huge aid provided the Vietnamese in the Second Indochina War serving to offset the American intervention and enabling the Vietminh to complete the revolution it had launched after World War II). Until the exigencies deriving from the strategic triangle had impelled Hanoi to move deeply into the Soviet embrace, it had tried to maintain its independence while balancing pressures from its big patrons. As for Pyongyang, even though the Red Army, as it had done in Eastern Europe, imposed the Communist system on North Korea, a fierce commitment to independence thereafter developed, with neither Moscow nor Beijing able to exercise dominant influence. In addition, as we have seen, Mao and his lieutenants nursed grievances against Moscow that in due course erupted into outright rivalry and even armed confrontation.

In Eastern Europe, by contrast, the Communist systems became inextricably linked in the minds of the people entrapped in the Soviet bloc with suppression of their national identities and aspirations. Regaining independence thus meant discarding the Communist system, and this became possible when Gorbachev made clear that the Brezhnev Doctrine of limited sovereignty was no longer to be applied (replaced by the "Sinatra Doctrine," meaning each country could go its own way). These dynamics also operated in the case of Yugoslavia, which, though not a member of the Soviet bloc after 1948, was viewed by the smaller nationalities (the Serbs being the largest) as an artificial alliance from which they demanded independence. Thus, given the differing contexts in Eastern Europe and East Asia, a common drive for independence produced quite opposite results with the end of the Cold War. (Albania and Romania stand out as exceptions, both having maintained a prickly independence during the Cold War but succumbed to the region's tsunami of anti-Communist revolt. Mongolia, however, while geographically distant, shared with the Eastern European satellites the experience of Soviet domination and reacted accordingly when Moscow's empire crumbled.)

## THE CHINA QUESTION

Thrown into sharp relief against the background of Japan's notable stability in domestic and foreign affairs since World War II, the Chinese experience has been marked by tumultuous upheavals in domestic affairs and sharp twists and turns in the foreign arena. Consider the domestic scene in the first decades after the war: the Communist triumph in the civil war, collectivization drives, the Great Leap Forward, the Cultural Revolution, all punctuated by Mao's propensity for permanent revolution. The PRC's foreign relations during that time were marked by sharp turns as Beijing wrestled with the implications of bipolarity for its basic interests: first an alliance with Moscow, then competition over leadership of the Communist movement after finding Moscow's leadership of the alliance to be adverse to Chinese interests, and finally the collapse of the alliance and China's retreat into the isolationism of the Cultural Revolution.

The Dengist revolution aimed at establishing conditions of stability that would enable China to embark on a spectacular trajectory of economic development—an annual economic growth rate of just under 10 percent in the three decades after the advent of Deng's reforms in 1978. This meant maintaining the Leninist one-party system while avoiding both the upheavals of the Maoist era and the "stability of cadres" of the Brezhnev era in the Soviet Union marked by an ossified bureaucracy and economic stagnation. Though his first two handpicked successors got ahead of the leadership consensus and were purged, Deng managed to ease out the veteran leaders of his generation and install a system of orderly replacement and rejuvenation to ensure both continuity and adaptability in the leadership. A telling measure of his success was that in the first decade of the new century, in an experience unique among major Communist states, leadership succession without a death or purge had become the norm.

Beijing's turn to what it called an independent foreign policy in the early 1980s ended the period in which it pivoted sharply from one posture to another in trying to come to terms with bipolarity. The Chinese pursued a flexible approach as they opened their economy to market forces—"Market-Leninism"—and integrated with the global economy. The extraordinary rise of China, marked by years of economic growth measured in double digits, had a significant impact on regions increasingly distant—in Africa, the Middle East, Latin America. Its efforts to engage with and exert influence on the international order have been motivated not by a strategic competition with other great powers but by its increasing economic interdependence with the rest of the world. By 2006, China's total trade volume was sixty times what it was in 1978, when Deng consolidated his power as paramount leader. In 1994 China had become a net importer of oil, on its way to becoming the second-largest oil importer in the world. As has been discussed (see Chapter 12), by the turn of the century China's interdependence in the global economy reached a level comparable to Germany's and far surpassing that of the United States and Japan. This high level of interdependence reflected many realities, such as the slow growth of China's domestic consumption sector and the rapid growth of its foreign trade, which became sources of tension with its trading partners.

China's military power, fueled by double-digit annual increases in the defense budget, also grew alongside the rising economic strength that made it possible. This raised the question of whether China's rise would pose a challenge to the international order akin to that of Germany at the turn of the twentieth century, known then as the German question. There are significant differences, of course, among them being that Germany had joined the scramble for colonial possessions but China has been intent on securing access to resources and markets but not territory (putting aside territorial disputes with neighbors). Would an increasingly muscular China, economically and militarily, be tempted to throw its weight around in pursuit of its goals? Would it compete with a fading superpower for regional if not global influence and status? Would it find itself on a collision course with that superpower or with competing centers of power such as Japan or India?

Given the geopolitical complexities of the Asia-Pacific region in the early years of the twenty-first century, the rise of China did not portend a tipping of the balance of power anytime soon. China's position in a highly militarized region, which includes five declared nuclear powers, imposes considerable constraints on any overweening ambitions (see Chapter 12).

Given its global economic interdependence, its imposing domestic challenges (e.g., lifting hundreds of millions out of poverty, providing a better safety net to mitigate the effects of wrenching change, managing the effects of adverse foreign economic developments, abating environmental degradation), and the limits on its military power, China perforce has sought to pursue its global interests in a largely system-sustaining, not system-transforming, manner. That may not be a prospect Mao would have contemplated with equanimity.

## THE PERENNIAL TAIWAN ISSUE

Aspects of deep-rooted continuity as well as significant evolution have characterized the Taiwan question, one of the seemingly intractable issues arising in Asia in the early years after World War II (the division of Korea and Kashmir being others in particular).[1] As we have seen, the Korean War caused a reversal of the Truman administration's decision to stay out of the Chinese civil war, the expectation having been that the Communists would complete their revolution by capturing the Nationalists' redoubt on Taiwan. Interpreting the North Korean invasion in 1950 as part of a global strategy by Moscow to expand its dominion, Washington in effect froze the Chinese civil war by interposing the Seventh Fleet in the Taiwan Strait to prevent attacks from either direction. Then, with the erection of the American alliance system in East Asia linked to a global Western security structure, the Taiwan question was drawn into the bipolar force of the Cold War, now deeply implanted in Asia.

But as we have also seen, a perception came to be shared by Washington and Beijing of an expansionist and aggressive Soviet Union on the march, producing a transforming impact on Sino-American relations. This required, as an enabling condition, an accommodation on the Taiwan issue, one that was linked to U.S. disengagement from the Vietnam War and the prospect of a reduced American role in Taiwan. It took nearly seven years from President Nixon's breakthrough visit to China in 1972 before the two sides could overcome the Taiwan obstacle to normalization of relations, which required that the United States withdraw its troops from Taiwan and end its security treaty with the ROC while switching diplomatic recognition from the latter to the PRC. This did not, of course, resolve the Taiwan issue—though the Chinese very likely expected an early resolution—because the United States retained a residual security link to Taiwan by offering to supply arms (after the one-year moratorium while the U.S.-ROC treaty elapsed according to its terms) and insisting on a peaceful resolution of the issue.

The stubbornly persisting gap between the two sides reflected fundamental differences: Sovereignty of the PRC over Taiwan was a bedrock demand that could be finessed but not removed, and successive American administrations, while "acknowledging" Beijing's claim to Taiwan, insisted on continuing the arms supply to the island in order to avert a forcible move by Beijing to bring Taiwan under its sovereignty. If anything, American leaders would find the issue even more constraining after Taiwan became a democratic, pluralist state while the mainland remained under the domination of a regime that squelched dissent and trampled on human rights. As mentioned in connection with Sino-Soviet normalization (Chapter 11), Ronald Reagan's 1980 campaign rhetoric on upgrading Taiwan's status and the resumption of arms transfers to the island led to a new crisis, one that produced the third of the canonical "three communiqués"[2] underpinning the relationship (the first two being the Shanghai and the normalization communiqués). Once again, however, the can was kicked down the road; endless disputes arose over whether the United States was in fact capping and "gradually" reducing the quantity and quality of arms. (How was inflation to be taken into account; how was replacement of obsolescent equipment to be counted against the cap; did an increase of the threat from the mainland justify a corresponding enhancement of the arms being supplied to Taiwan?)

Beijing, its expectations of a resolution of the Taiwan issue having been raised by the normalization agreement (expectations that may have rested on a misreading of Washington's intentions on arms supplies to Taiwan), issued a conciliatory appeal to Taiwan on New Year's Day 1979, the official date of the normalization communiqué. In a "Message to Compatriots in Taiwan," Beijing declared as a "fundamental policy"—that is, a long-term commitment, not a tactical maneuver—that it would seek a "peaceful reunification," thus jettisoning the decades-long call for "liberation" of Taiwan and taking a step toward meeting Washington's requirement for a peaceful resolution of the issue. It offered to "take present realities" into account and to respect the status quo on Taiwan while pursuing peaceful reunification. It also announced the end of the symbolic alternate-day shelling of the offshore islands and called for the "three links"—transportation, postal, and trade—to be established.

The August 1982 agreement on arms sales to Taiwan not only failed to resolve the issue but was destined to be shredded, particularly when George H.W. Bush, during the presidential election campaign of 1992, authorized the sale of 150 advanced F-16 fighter aircraft that would be produced in Texas (he won Texas but lost the election).[3] In contrast to the extensive analysis by the U.S. military and intelligence communities to which the proposed sale of an advanced fighter (the FX) was subjected at the beginning of the Reagan administration (the proposal was withdrawn after it was deemed not to be necessary for Taiwan's defense and after anguished debate within the administration), the F-16 sale was approved after only a pro forma review—not to mention that the full quantity requested by Taiwan was approved. (As a measure of the extent of U.S. arms transfers to Taiwan nearly two decades later, Washington announced in 2008 the sale of six billion dollars' worth of advanced weapons.)

The new administration of Bill Clinton, like Reagan's earlier and George W. Bush's in the early years of the new century, found itself constrained to adjust China policies to stubborn realities.[4] At first, though, the Clinton administration's problem was not Taiwan but an attempt, soon discarded, to link improvement of the PRC's human rights practices with normal trading relations. But the administration was destined to be confronted by a new dimension of the Taiwan issue: the rise of identity politics in Taiwan with the emergence of a sense of identity separate from the mainland. This undercut the useful fiction used by the United States in the Shanghai Communiqué—that "all Chinese" on either side of the Taiwan Strait regarded Taiwan to be a part of China (though perhaps it was more factual than fictional at the time inasmuch as dissenters from that position were silenced or in exile). Now, with even a Nationalist (Kuomintang) president, Lee Teng-hui, seeking more "international space" for Taiwan, new tensions arose as democratic politics in Taiwan collided with Beijing's interest in closer relations. These tensions were punctuated by the PRC's military exercises in the strait and lobbing of missiles into the waters near Taiwan at the time of the first direct presidential election, in 1996, prompting the United States to send two aircraft carrier forces to the area to convey its "abiding interest" in a peaceful resolution of the issue. Tensions accumulated further when the leader of the pro-independence Democratic Progressive Party (DPP), Chen Shui-bian, was elected Taiwan's president in 2000.

The younger Bush's administration, entering office in 2001, was strongly influenced by neoconservative thinking that called for a more robust challenge to America's foes and competitors (some of the former composing the "axis of evil"). In Asia this meant moving away from the Clinton administration's treatment of the PRC as a prospective "strategic partner" and instead viewing it as a competitor. Expressive of the new mentality was what

Bush said about Taiwan after an incident in April 2001 in which a U.S. reconnaissance plane collided with a PRC fighter plane and had to land on the Chinese island of Hainan. Asked what he would do in the event of a threat to Taiwan, the president said he would do "whatever it took" to defend the island. There was also talk during that time of removing the "strategic ambiguity" in Washington's commitment to Taiwan's defense—one offering sufficient commitment to deter Beijing from using coercion but not so much as to encourage Taiwan to take provocative moves toward independence. Neoconservatives wanted an unambiguous commitment to defense of the island.

Once again, however, a new American administration found itself adjusting its China policies in the face of resistance by Beijing on issues like Taiwan or trade. As in the case of the Korean nuclear issue, the Bush administration in its second term moved from confrontation to engagement with the PRC. There was a notable shift toward reversing the direction of pressure from Beijing to Taipei, with the administration warning the DPP-led government against disturbing the status quo by pressing ahead toward Beijing's redline of Taiwan independence. Washington's move toward engagement with the PRC was eased by the election by a landslide of a Nationalist leader, Ma Ying-jeou, as president in March 2008, and the defeat of a referendum calling for application of membership to the UN under the name of Taiwan.[5] The new government, with Beijing reciprocating, signaled an interest in expanding the links across the strait that the PRC had long urged. Agreements on expanded trade and travel ties were achieved that November during a visit by the head of the Association of Relations Across the Taiwan Strait, the most senior PRC official to visit since 1949.[6] This process was significantly furthered by a trade pact signed in June 2010 that lowered tariffs on several hundred goods and deepened cross-strait interdependence.[7] There were symbolic overtones in the choice of venue for the signing: Chongqing, Chiang Kai-shek's wartime capital and site of coalition negotiations between the Nationalists and Communists after the war (discussed in Chapter 3). The lesson to be drawn may be that where political negotiations failed, promotion of economic links offers a way to close the gap separating the decades-long adversaries.

The new Taiwan leader's interest in promoting practical ties with the mainland while trying to cool the Taiwan issue, after more than a decade of events approaching the boiling point, was registered in his call for "mutual nondenial" of each side's existence.[8] Though it was a negative formula, combined with the expanded ties across the strait it served to buy time while leaving the formal status of Taiwan in suspension. Beijing issued a white paper on Taiwan in February 2000 that specifically added an indefinite refusal by Taipei to negotiate on reunification as a condition that would trigger use of force, but the atmosphere at that time was much more charged than the one arising after Ma's election.[9]

Beijing's offer on this issue exhibits some resemblance to the status accorded Hong Kong after its reversion in 1997—the formula of "one country, two systems"—but with possibly significant differences. Drawing on a provision of the PRC constitution, Beijing established a "Special Administrative Region (*qu*)" for Hong Kong and pledged to allow a "high degree of autonomy"—except in foreign and defense affairs, which were reserved for the central government—for fifty years.[10] As "Hong Kong, China" it could develop relations with other states or international organizations so long as that did not imply independent statehood (e.g., UN membership). The new entity was granted "independent judicial review, including that of final adjudication," though in practice Beijing has insisted upon exercising final interpretation of provisions of the Basic Law (formally by the Standing Committee of the National People's Congress). As Beijing's gloss on the Basic Law explains, Hong Kong courts "as local courts cannot handle cases concerning the exercise of sovereignty by the highest state administrative organs."[11] How does this compare with the contours of an agreement proposed by Beijing for Taiwan?

In the Shanghai Communiqué the Chinese referred to Taiwan as a "province" (*sheng*), but the United States carefully avoided defining the island's formal status by "acknowledg[ing]" the PRC's position that it is "a part" of China. Paralleling its move after diplomatic normalization toward the U.S. position by dropping the call for "liberation" of Taiwan in favor of "peaceful reunification," Beijing began avoiding references to Taiwan as a province in the context of reunification proposals (though the term is used in other contexts, particularly historical, such as obituaries of persons who were "born in Taiwan Province"). In proposing terms of reunification, Beijing refers to Taiwan by using a generic term for *area* or *region* (*diqu*), thereby leaving the formal relationship of the island to the PRC open for negotiation or consultation. (Taiwan president Ma used that term in referring to the Taiwan "region" and the mainland "region.")

PRC President Hu Jintao used the thirtieth anniversary of the "Message to Compatriots in Taiwan" to strike a flexible note on the matter of Taiwan's desire for international "space." Provided that they did not have implications of an independent Taiwan, Hu declared, "fair and reasonable" arrangements for Taiwan's participation in international organizations could be devised through "pragmatic consultations."[12] This prospect took concrete form in May 2009 when a Taiwan representative—the minister of health—participated in the World Health Assembly of the World Health Organization, a UN body, the first such participation since the ROC lost its seat in the UN in 1971. Under the name "Chinese Taipei," the representative was included in the group of "Observers of Non-Member States."[13] In addition to the liberalized bilateral ties since Ma's election, another factor in this breakthrough was the threat posed at the time by swine flu. Beijing had blocked Taiwan's role in WHO efforts during the SARS outbreak six years earlier, but in the context of improved cross-strait relations, a functional issue provided an opportunity to pursue cooperative actions despite fundamental differences.

In applying the principle of "one country, two systems" to Taiwan, Beijing seems to have broadened its offer compared with Hong Kong by saying Taiwan could retain its economic and social system without reference to a time limit, by permitting it to retain its armed forces without reference to a mainland role, and by granting it final judicial review without reference to an overriding role for Beijing. The devil lurks in the details, of course, but foreign media distort the evolution of Beijing's position by using a shorthand stereotype: Beijing regards Taiwan as "a renegade province" that it seeks to recover by force if necessary. The direction of the evolution points rather to a model akin to Hong Kong's, though with a greater range and firmer guarantees of autonomy for Taiwan.

## THE U.S. "GLOBAL WAR ON TERROR"

Another major turning point, along with the end of the Cold War and the rise of China after the Dengist revolution, was the extraordinary terrorist attacks on the United States in September 2001, with hijackers crashing four American commercial planes (three into buildings, including the Pentagon) and causing thousands of casualties. Asserting that nothing would be the same again, Washington declared a "global war on terror," the first battle of which soon ensued with the invasion of Afghanistan and toppling of the Taliban regime that had harbored the organization, Al-Qaeda, that had plotted the attacks.

A year after the attacks of September 2001, the George W. Bush administration issued a major document, *The National Security Strategy of the United States*,[14] which served much the same purpose in the antiterrorist strategy as the secret NSC-68 had in the Cold War (see Chapter 7). As in the earlier document, with its alarmist appraisal of the global situation after the Soviet Union gained possession of the atomic bomb, the Bush strategy statement depicted a "dramatically" changed challenge to the United States in which the "gravest danger . . . lies at the crossroads of radicalism and technology."[15] The great struggle in the previous century against totalitarianism having been successfully completed, the United States now was "menaced less by fleets and armies than by catastrophic technologies in the hands of the embittered few."[16]

This strategy, designed to cope with a security environment that "has undergone profound transformation" since the collapse of the Soviet Union, may be called the Bush Doctrine of preemption. In the early years of the Cold War, preemption, meaning an attack reacting to an *imminent* threat from an adversary, was distinguished from preventive action, which was advocated by some hard-line Cold Warriors to forestall *potential* moves by the Soviet Union (or China) to acquire the capability of posing a threat of nuclear attack. In circumstances in which traditional concepts of deterrence "will not work against a terrorist enemy," however, this distinction has been blurred if not simply erased. Mobilization of troops and deployment of missiles might portend an imminent threat that would trigger preemptive action in a traditional geopolitical setting, but in an environment bristling with a potential conjunction of weapons of mass destruction (WMD) and shadowy groups of terrorists, "a reactive posture" is no longer regarded as an option.[17]

The Bush administration undertook two major offensives following the terrorist attacks of September 2001, both aimed at "regime change." The first, in the immediate wake of the attacks, toppled the Taliban regime in Afghanistan that had harbored Osama bin Laden and his Al-Qaeda network. Three years after the U.S. intervention, elections were held and the first popularly elected president in Afghanistan's history, Hamid Karzai (a Pashtun, the tribal base of the Taliban), assumed office. Reflecting the delicate project of accommodating tribal and religious differences after the devastating civil war that followed the Soviet departure and led to the Taliban's gaining of power in the 1990s, a Tajik (the ethnic group that was a major instrument in the American offensive) and a Hazera Shiite became vice presidents. The country continued to face the disruptive effects of surviving warlordism and the remnants of the ousted Taliban and its allies.

**THE BUSH DOCTRINE OF PREEMPTIVE—OR PREVENTIVE—WAR**

America is now threatened less by conquering states than we are by failing ones. We are menaced less by fleets and armies than by catastrophic technologies in the hands of the embittered few. . . .

The nature of the Cold War threat required the United States—with our allies and friends—to emphasize deterrence of the enemy's use of force, producing a grim strategy of mutual assured destruction. With the collapse of the Soviet Union and the end of the Cold War, our security environment has undergone profound transformation. . . .

Given the goals of rogue states and terrorists, the United States can no longer solely rely on a reactive posture as we have in the past. The inability to deter a potential attacker, the immediacy of today's threats, and the magnitude of potential harm that could be caused by our adversaries' choice of weapons, do not permit that option. We cannot let our enemies strike first. . . .

The United States has long maintained the option of preemptive actions to counter a sufficient threat to our national security. The greater the threat, the greater is the risk of inaction—and the more compelling the case for taking anticipatory action to defend ourselves, even if uncertainty remains as to the time and place of the enemy's attack. To forestall or prevent such hostile acts by our adversaries, the United States will, if necessary, act preemptively.

*The National Security Strategy of the United States*, 17 September 2002, accessed at http://georgewbush-whitehouse.archives.gov/nss/2002.

The second offensive, the invasion of Iraq in March 2003 that removed Saddam Hussein and his Baathist Party from power, illustrates the difficulties in applying the doctrine of preemption. The principal justification for the action was the claim that Hussein was reconstituting his program of WMD, and that the danger of these weapons falling into the hands of terrorists made it imperative for the United States and its "coalition of the willing" to take military action to forestall such a frightful eventuality. As senior American officials graphically put it, there was no time to wait before seeing "a smoking gun becoming a mushroom cloud." In any event, however, no WMD program was found, and ties between Hussein's regime and Al-Qaeda seemed very tenuous at most. Critics of Washington's decision making, pointing to the insurgency and terrorist acts that ensued in Iraq, have argued that the Bush administration's loose definition of preemption led to an ill-advised action with highly undesirable consequences, such as the conversion of Iraq into a breeding ground and test bed for the very terrorists it was intended to forestall.

The WMD issue, which had already arisen in the 1990s in such potentially explosive conflict situations as Korea and South Asia, had become all the more fraught after September 2001. We now turn to those areas to look at how these deep-rooted issues acquired even more acute implications in the context of the war against terror given the dangers of WMD being transferred to terrorist groups or rogue states.

## THE KOREAN PENINSULA

With the unification of Vietnam and the fall of the Berlin Wall, Korea stood out for being divided by a Cold War line that remained in place, with an uneasy armistice persisting over decades and no peace treaty in sight. The surrounding circumstances, however, underwent significant change; in particular, the end of the Cold War vastly reduced the odds of confrontation over Korean issues between outside powers. But this move toward a less volatile environment had an ominous counterpoint, the North Korean aspirations for a nuclear capability colliding with Washington's acute sensitivity to the prospects of nuclear proliferation, including dissemination of nuclear arms to "rogue" states and terrorist groups. The administration of George W. Bush was skeptical of the agreement signed by its predecessor, and its stigmatizing of the North Korean regime as a member of the "axis of evil" acquired a still sharper edge after another member, Iraq, became the target of invasion and occupation. That action and the preceding invasion of Afghanistan and overthrow of its Taliban regime offered menacing precedents for the Korean issue, though Washington repeatedly denied an intent to force a regime change and engaged in the multilateral talks addressing the North Korean nuclear question.

The generational change in South Korean politics altered the context of the confrontation over the DPRK's nuclear aspirations. Seoul's "sunshine policy" and growing economic investments in the North contained the potential for strains in its alliance with the United States, and correspondingly for opportunities for Pyongyang to probe fissures in that alliance. Washington began taking steps to adjust to an evolving situation while maintaining its commitment to the ROK's security. Thus, during Secretary of Defense Donald Rumsfeld's visit in October 2005 for the annual security consultative meeting, a joint statement reaffirmed the American commitment, including specifically "the continued provision of a nuclear umbrella."[18] But Washington accompanied this recommitment with plans for reducing and consolidating its force presence, a 33 percent reduction, which would bring troop levels down to twenty-five thousand and reduce the frictions between the American presence and the South Korean citizenry. Not only that, but by lowering troop concentrations near the front lines—where they traditionally served as a tripwire ensuring an American response should the North again invade—the United States would reduce the possibility that its troops would be hostages to Pyongyang's threats in a crisis and thus inhibit Washington's response.

The stalled nuclear talks became reenergized after a North Korean nuclear test in October 2006 (estimated by U.S. intelligence as subkiloton in size), which Pyongyang said was "entirely attributable to the U.S. nuclear threat, sanctions, and pressure."[19] Both China and Russia deplored the test, and American Secretary of State Condoleezza Rice, visiting Beijing shortly afterward, sought to cultivate common ground with the Chinese while the Bush administration backed off from a more confrontational stance. Rice said the United States would not pressure the Chinese, who—in a signal of their own readiness to apply pressure on Pyongyang—revealed in a statistical report that they had delivered no oil to the DPRK in September,[20] and the State Department now enjoyed more flexibility in dealing with the North Korean issue. Bilateral talks with the North Koreans, once taboo in this administration, led to removal of one of the obstacles to renewed negotiations within the six-party framework: sanctions against a Macao bank for money laundering of North Korean funds. Pyongyang began shutting down the Yongbyon reactor in July 2007; in a quid pro quo, a South Korean ship made the first delivery in what was to be a down payment of fifty thousand tons of fuel oil, part of the total of one million tons agreed to be supplied as the denuclearization process took place.[21]

Negotiations within the six-party framework as well as bilateral talks between U.S. and North Korean representatives yielded an agreement in October 2007 that moved the denuclearization process forward, at least on paper. Pyongyang agreed to begin disabling its nuclear facilities and to provide a "complete and correct declaration" of all its nuclear programs by the end of the year—a commitment that, typically, became subject to further wrangling and delays.[22] The Bush administration had now relaxed its demands for North Korean acknowledgment of its suspected uranium program, a cause of the administration's earlier scrapping of the Clinton-era Agreed Framework, and of its role in proliferation (such as to Syria, where the Israelis had conducted an air strike to demolish a suspected nuclear reactor).[23]

A pledge to begin cultural exchanges between Americans and North Koreans was realized when the New York Philharmonic performed in Pyongyang in February 2008, an event that inevitably evoked memories of the role of Ping-Pong diplomacy in the period of preparation for the breakthrough in Sino-American relations in the early 1970s. Reflecting the new atmosphere, President Bush sent a personal letter—termed "cordial" by the White House—to Kim Jong Il looking forward to reciprocal moves leading to normalization of U.S.-DPRK relations.

Meanwhile, Seoul's "sunshine policy" toward the North produced a summit meeting between Kim Jong Il and ROK President Roh Moo Hyun in October 2007, the second encounter at this level since World War II (the first being the one in 2000). The two leaders signed a declaration pledging "to reduce military tension and to resolve disputes through dialogue and negotiations," and they undertook to open road and rail links, to increase investment in free trade zones in the North, and to make a disputed area in the Yellow Sea a joint fishing zone.[24] These moves served Seoul's interests in enhancing security by promoting economic ties with the North, at the same time encouraging its economic development as a gradualist way toward eventual reunification while avoiding the trauma of the German precedent. For Pyongyang the attraction was the prospect of economic growth without political change. A complicating factor was soon introduced, however, when the succession of left-leaning presidents was broken by the election by a large margin in October 2007 of a businessman, Lee Myung Bak. North-South relations were not a major issue in the election, which turned on Lee's claims to more effective stewardship of the economy.[25] Lee did, however, express an interest in improving relations with the United States after a period of tension over policies toward the North, which may have prompted Pyongyang to revert to old habits by labeling him a "U.S. sycophant." Sensitive to being perceived as vulnerable to economic pressure, Pyongyang defiantly declared that the North would be "able to live as well as it wishes without any help" from the South—this at a time of flood damage to its crops and soaring global grain prices.[26]

The fitful, protracted, frustrating nuclear negotiations, which had produced the Agreed Framework in the 1990s, only to see that collapse in the early years of the new century, finally yielded a concrete "action for action" agreement as pledged in the 2005 accord (see

Chapter 13) that in effect reconstructed the earlier one (though in the meantime giving the North Koreans time to produce more plutonium and to conduct a nuclear detonation). In June 2008 the DPRK handed to the Chinese a sixty-page declaration accounting for its plutonium production dating to the early 1990s, and the United States reciprocated by lifting some economic sanctions and pledging to remove North Korea from the list of countries sponsoring terrorism.[27] On the day after delivery of the declaration, the North Koreans destroyed the cooling tower of the Yongbyon nuclear reactor, allowing international media to cover the event—while imposing a blackout on DPRK media.

By September, however, the familiar pattern reappeared of Pyongyang barring international inspectors from the Yongbyon site and resuming processing of plutonium in protest against Washington's refusal to remove North Korea from the terrorism blacklist until agreement had been reached on a plan for verifying compliance with denuclearization.[28] The situation was complicated by internal discord in Washington and perhaps in Pyongyang. The verification plan pushed by the United States would have permitted wide-ranging access to North Korean military and other sites, a demand attributed to pressure from hard-line elements in the administration suspicious of negotiations with Pyongyang.[29] North Korean resistance to this demand may have also reflected discord within Pyongyang or even be related to Kim Jong Il's weeks-long absence from public view, possibly because of a stroke. In a telltale nonappearance, he missed celebrating the eightieth anniversary of the founding of the DPRK in September 2008. He was eventually reported by North Korean media as making appearances, though dates were not disclosed; coinciding with his reported reappearance, Pyongyang agreed to resume disabling the plutonium plant and accepted a looser inspection program in response to Washington's removal of the DPRK from the list of sponsors of terrorism.[30]

In a potentially significant signal, Kim had his first reported meeting with a foreign official since the apparent illness when he received a senior Chinese party functionary on 23 January 2009, three days after the inauguration of American President Barack Obama.[31] Both North Korean and Chinese media reported Kim as saying that he remained committed to dismantling the DPRK's nuclear program. Pyongyang's message seemed to be that the "Dear Leader," now recovered, was able and willing to engage with the new president, who for his part had expressed willingness during the campaign to enter into dialogue with hostile states. The changed context, however, did not remove the familiar pattern of wild swings from agreement to crisis (or brinkmanship). In April 2009 North Korea launched what it termed a satellite into orbit but what Washington and others called a test of a long-range missile, one that failed according to tracking data showing the rocket and payload falling into the sea beyond Japan.[32] After the UN Security Council issued a statement—a notch below a resolution, reflecting Chinese and Russian concerns—that reproved the North Koreans for conducting the test, Pyongyang responded with characteristic indignation: suspending participation in the six-party talks, expelling UN inspectors, and several weeks later, on 25 May, defiantly conducting its second nuclear test followed by test-firing short-range missiles. On this occasion the Security Council responded more forcefully, including strong protests by China and Russia.[33] The ROK, for its part, announced that it would join the Proliferation Security Initiative, the group of more than ninety states that have agreed to interdict shipments suspected of trafficking in unconventional weapons. China, India, and Pakistan are not members of the initiative, and Seoul had refrained from joining previously to avoid provoking the DPRK. The latter was indeed provoked, declaring on the twenty-seventh that it was no longer bound by the 1953 armistice and that it would respond with "a powerful military strike" if its exports of arms were intercepted.[34]

After a couple of weeks of negotiations, the Security Council produced its toughest response thus far, a unanimous resolution (no. 1847) on 12 June applying an extensive package of sanctions that lent greater authority to what had been a posse-like Proliferation Security Initiative.[35] The Security Council did not, however, authorize the use of military action under Article 42; instead it invoked Articlε 41, which provides for "measures not involving the use of armed force." The resolution included the following provisions:

- Expressed "gravest concern" over "a clear threat" to international peace and security posed by the North Korean actions.
- Condemned in "the strongest terms" the 25 May nuclear test.
- Demanded that Pyongyang return to the NPT and IAEA safeguards.
- Banned financial services for the DPRK related to weapons of mass destruction.
- Called on member states to inspect shipments suspected of carrying banned arms or technology, excluding small arms; if the state under whose flag a suspect vessel is registered refuses to be inspected, it must direct the vessel to a convenient port for inspection. If the flag state refuses to cooperate, member states are directed to file a report to the Security Council.

Though these provisions fell short of authorizing the use of force, thereby avoiding calling Pyongyang's bluff in its warning that forcible inspection would be an act of war, the Security Council's strong language and broad range of sanctions represented a significant tightening of the screws on the North Koreans. Even in the absence of force, a ban on use of ports and refueling facilities by suspect North Korean vessels could have something of the effect of a blockade given their limited range.

Pyongyang's bellicose defiance of the international community may have been yet the latest effort to extract concessions in later negotiations and to put the new Obama administration on the defensive. It may also be related to a North Korean succession issue and Kim's health problems—he appeared noticeably gaunt in photos during this period; Kim may have been showing that he was still firmly in control, or there may be competitive moves by potential contenders in a succession struggle to demonstrate toughness. Indeed, the North Korean leaders at this juncture may have opted to forgo negotiations altogether in favor of developing a nuclear arsenal in the interests of regime survival—or success in the succession sweepstakes. The question of a successor for Kim became still more salient with speculation that his youngest son, Kim Jong Un, had been anointed as his political heir.[36]

Whether or not the succession question was a factor, Pyongyang pursued the familiar script of following up a period of provocative behavior with relatively conciliatory gestures as Kim's health improved and speculation surrounding his son faded in the second half of 2009. These gestures included the release to former president Clinton of two American journalists who had been sentenced to a harsh prison term, freeing a South Korean, and taking steps to enhance relations with the South.[37] The Chinese also weighed in, with Premier Wen Jiabao visiting Pyongyang in October 2009 to help nudge the North Koreans to return to the six-party talks while consolidating China's ties with the DPRK.[38] In December Pyongyang received President Obama's special representative and agreed on the need to resume negotiations, following this up with an authoritative 2010 New Year's Day joint editorial affirming the DPRK's commitment to a nuclear-free peninsula and calling for better relations with the United States.[39]

As in its departure from the adversarial posture taken toward China in its early years, the Bush administration, despite internal disputes, had repeatedly relaxed its demands on the DPRK, in effect returning to its predecessor's priority of eliminating the North's plutonium program, the basis of its inventory of nuclear weapons. Thus, the June 2008 declaration did not provide such an inventory, nor did it address the suspected uranium-enrichment program or proliferation activities—topics that were "acknowledged" in a separate message to the United States.[40] The administration's increasingly pragmatic policies toward China and the DPRK were closely related, given the potential Chinese influence on Pyongyang. Washington must have found some satisfaction in Beijing's willingness to use its economic and political leverage to push Pyongyang toward an accommodation on the nuclear issue. A measure of China's potential leverage can be found in its exports to North Korea, which by 2005 had exceeded one billion dollars after a 122 percent increase over ten years (the DPRK's exports to China were less than half that amount).[41] Beijing has in fact played a significant role in facilitating negotiations, but it has its own set of constraints limiting its responsiveness to American pressure. Like the South Koreans, the Chinese shudder at the prospect of a collapse of the DPRK, and not only for the economic and other effects of mass migration it would unleash. Beijing needed to balance an effort to avert a nuclear arms race in the region with avoidance of a loss of North Korea as a buffer zone, with the resulting expansion of the American presence to China's borders. From the Chinese perspective, a successful settlement of the North Korean nuclear issue undergirded by credible American security guarantees to Pyongyang would offer a prospect of achieving the stability Beijing cherishes.

The North Korean nuclear issue offered a sobering lesson, one that opponents of nuclear proliferation could not find reassuring, which is that the nuclear card could be used to exert pressure on adversaries and thereby improve one's hand in negotiations or in deterring regime change. Successive U.S. administrations were impelled to accept Pyongyang seriously as a negotiating partner, even if it implied concessions to a reviled regime. This afforded Pyongyang leverage in its pursuit of a peace treaty ending the Korean War, normalization of relations with the United States and other powers, and above all survival of the regime.

## REVISITING JAPAN AND ARTICLE 9

The U.S.-Japanese alliance, the keystone of the American security structure in the Asia-Pacific region, has been one of the most enduring elements of continuity in the postwar era. As has been discussed (Chapter 13), the end of the Cold War raised the question of which direction Japan would take, whether toward more independence from Washington or toward a continuing close and perhaps even intensified relationship. The latter tendency prevailed, particularly with Prime Minister Koizumi's efforts to define a more robust role within the alliance relationship in the first years of the new century, and this was further deepened by his successor, Abe Shinzo (elected in September 2006), grandson of the strongly pro-U.S. Kishi Nobusuke (prime minister at the time of the 1960 revision of the security treaty). A heightened security role may have been prefigured in Abe's decision upon becoming prime minister to create a new position of national security adviser.

The North Korean nuclear and missile programs placed Japan's security role in sharp relief. As the cabinet chief secretary, Abe had raised the idea of a preemptive strike after the North Korean missile launchings in July 2006. Like the question of the extent to which Japan is allowed under Article 9 of its constitution to participate in peacekeeping actions abroad or to come to the aid of an ally, Pyongyang's potential threat poses tricky constitutional issues. If an imminent threat is perceived, must Tokyo wait for an actual attack before responding? Japan has committed to spending billions of dollars on erecting a shield against incoming missiles as part of U.S. plans for missile defense in the region. Would it be able, politically and legally, to shoot at missiles aimed not at Japan itself but at its ally?[42] In this connection, however, it bears noting that the mutual defense clause of the 1960 treaty covers attacks only on territory under Japan's administration and thus does not obligate Tokyo to come to its ally's aid otherwise.

In May 2007 the Diet enacted legislation establishing procedures for a national referendum—after approval by two-thirds of both houses of the parliament—for constitutional revision. At the time the defense minister remarked that it was unreasonable under the constitution that Japan could not act militarily to support UN Security Council resolutions.[43] Constitutional reform, however, remained a quite uncertain prospect, given the political backlash evoked by even the modest steps Japan has taken since the early 1990s to play a role in military activities abroad. Abe's prime-ministerial career proved to be short-lived, lasting only a year and being buffeted by charges that Japan's closer cooperation with the United States was harming its relations with its neighbors. The leader of the opposition Democratic Party, Ozawa Ichiro, whose party had inflicted a crushing defeat on the Liberal Democratic Party in upper-house elections in July 2007, capitalized on discontent with the Japanese naval mission in the Indian Ocean supporting the war effort in Afghanistan. Abe explained that he was resigning in the hope that a more popular successor could manage an extension of the law authorizing that mission.[44] His successor, Fukuda Yasuo, the son of a former prime minister, did in fact manage that, but only by using a two-thirds majority in the lower house to override the opposition-controlled upper house—the first such use of this affront to consensus since 1951.[45] (Fukuda, like his predecessor, lasted only a year, being replaced in September 2008 by a former foreign minister, Aso Taro, the fourth prime minister in two years.[46])

That the subject of this drama was nothing more than a risk-free refueling mission in the Indian Ocean underscored the grindingly incremental pace by which the Japanese were willing to move toward a more robust role in international security affairs. The logistical support for U.S.-led operations in the Gulf and Afghanistan along with the potentially more consequential participation in the missile defense project—in 2008 the Diet rescinded a mandate for space to be used only for peaceful purposes and allowed space technology for national security uses, which could mean satellites for missile defense purposes[47]—reflected a gradual evolution toward becoming a more active partner within the long-standing alliance with the United States.

The possibility of a different direction, however, was raised by an upheaval in Japanese politics when Ozawa's party won elections to the lower house in 2009 and Hatoyama Yukio (yet another descendant of a former leader) became prime minister, breaking the LDP's almost continuous grip on power for more than half a century. The new government, as part of efforts to demonstrate its divergence from LDP policies, expressed an intent to be more Asia-oriented and less bound to Washington. This introduced complications into U.S.-Japanese relations as illustrated by Hatoyama's backpedaling from a deal on relocating a U.S. Marines base from a populous area in Okinawa to an alternative site on the island. Still, no Japanese leader could ignore the geopolitical realities of a highly dangerous region, and Hatoyama reversed course to accept most of the agreement (which included moving a substantial number of Marines to Guam). Declaring in May 2010 that it was unrealistic to remove the entire American military presence from Okinawa, Hatoyama cited North Korea and "the state of the wider region" in stressing the role of the alliance "as a deterrent force."[48] His remarks took place while North Korean leader Kim Jong Il was being embraced by China's leaders during his visit there, and following the sinking in March of a South Korean warship that Seoul and a multinational inquiry blamed on the North.

Hatoyama's vacillations and failure to deliver on campaign pledges led to plummeting public support, causing him to announce in June—a few weeks before upper house elections—that he was stepping down, thus becoming the fourth prime minister to resign in as many years.[49] He took specific note of the role of the U.S. alliance in this development, saying that it had "proved impossible in my time" to reduce the country's dependence on the American security umbrella.[50] The possibility of a more independent posture was thus pushed further into the future.

## THE SOUTH ASIAN CONFLICT

The nuclearization of the subcontinent added a volatile new dimension to the Indian-Pakistani conflict, but it is open to question whether this fundamentally changed the situation. The world shuddered at the prospect of two nations locked in conflict since their twin birth turning to nuclear weapons during a period of sustained tension. It could be argued, however, that a nuclear standoff produces a firewall against escalation; the potential of unacceptably high levels of mutual devastation from a nuclear exchange induces a strategic stability, constraining adversaries against escalating confrontations to a point where nuclear war might be triggered. This notion has been adduced by some Cold War theorists to argue that mutual assured destruction served a stabilizing role that allowed the world to avoid nuclear holocaust during the long era of superpower rivalry.

This does not present an altogether reassuring prospect in a situation like that of the South Asian conflict. In what is called the stability/instability paradox,[51] rival states secure in the belief that their opponents will not risk escalating a conflict to the nuclear stage are therefore less constrained at lower levels of conflict; thus, there is stability at the strategic level but instability below that. For there to be overall stability, the rivals must have a shared sense of where redlines lie beyond which a strategic response is required. This is further complicated by the great disparity in conventional forces between the South Asian opponents. Should Pakistan, directly as at Kargil or through Islamist terrorists (who were believed by India to have been responsible for the carnage from attacks on the parliament in New Delhi in 2001 and in Mumbai in 2006 and 2008), persist in provocations aimed at keeping the Kashmir issue alive and an insurgency in play, the Indians might decide that a threshold of toleration had been crossed and launch a major horizontal thrust into the enemy's heartland, which in turn could evoke a desperate recourse to nuclear retaliation by the Pakistanis. Given their propinquity and the fundamental stakes at issue in their confrontation, the two sides face the risk that unauthorized use of nuclear weapons—the A.Q. Khan experience hardly inspires confidence in the security of Pakistan's control over its nuclear technology—or hair-trigger reactions in conditions of heightened tensions could lead to an escalation that breached the barrier against nuclear use and produced the first nuclear exchange in history. The resignation in August 2008 of Pakistani President Pervez Musharraf, who had become extremely unpopular but had formerly been head of the army and had played an important role in stabilizing relations with India, raised concern over whether the squabbling political leaders could maintain firm control over the country's nuclear arsenal. Moreover, the dramatic resurgence of the Taliban in Pakistan and Afghanistan added to concerns over destabilizing trends in a region bristling with nuclear arms.

Notwithstanding the constants of Indian-Pakistani conflict and the enduring Kashmir dispute, India's international role evolved significantly after the end of the Cold War and the concurrent introduction of economic reforms that opened the country to foreign investment and the global economy. Freed of Cold War pressures that drove India into the Soviet embrace as its enemies Pakistan and China moved closer to America, New Delhi was able to fashion an omnidirectional foreign policy that afforded a broad scope for flexibility and balance.[52] This was reflected in the emergence in the new century of "strategic partnerships" with a wide array of major powers: America, China, Russia, and Japan. Meanwhile, economic reform brought India into the global economy, though following a growth model—producing annual percentage gains in the upper single digits—that significantly diverged from the East Asian version: Instead of exporting labor-intensive, low-priced manufacturing goods, India has emphasized services and high-tech production (and relied more on consumption than investment for growth, which in the long run may be more sustainable and less subject to global vicissitudes).[53] India's industrial production accounted for only a fifth of its total output, compared with two-fifths of China's, but this began to change as manufacturing increased at a faster rate despite the constraints of an underdeveloped infrastructure.[54]

Though Pakistan retained some leverage with the United States deriving from the latter's need for cooperation in the antiterrorist campaign, India's broad-based and flexible foreign policy in the post–Cold War environment served to marginalize international support for Pakistan's claim to Kashmir. This reduced pressure on India to offer territorial concessions and correspondingly placed the onus on Pakistan to desist from aiding the insurgents and thus to acquiesce in the status quo. A warming trend in the early years of the new century included summit meetings and secret talks exploring a modus vivendi that would defuse the Kashmir conflict.[55] New Delhi's strengthened diplomatic and strategic hand was also reflected in the offer from Washington to permit the transfer of nuclear technology to India while allowing it to maintain its military nuclear program (Chapter 13). In addition to loosening the NPT regime's restraints against transfer of nuclear equipment and fuel to a nonsignatory, the agreement did not extract from India a commitment to forswear conducting future nuclear tests, adding to its nuclear weapon inventory, or producing weapons-grade fuel; instead, India could reprocess nuclear fuel and build stockpiles as a hedge against cutoffs of supplies in response to further nuclear tests.[56] India did, however, offer a unilateral moratorium on testing, and the Bush administration notified the American Congress, in a letter that remained secret for nine months, until September 2008, that it would terminate nuclear trade if India conducted a test.[57] Ironically, one of the hurdles the deal had to surmount—as it did that September—was approval by the forty-five-nation Nuclear Suppliers Group, which was established at American initiative in the wake of India's first nuclear test, in 1974. The group, whose purpose is to control nuclear trade, may well have taken the Indian moratorium into account in granting its approval, but it did not require its members to end nuclear trade with India should New Delhi end the moratorium. (It was reported, however, that the group's members agreed not to sell sensitive technologies dealing with enrichment and reprocessing of nuclear fuel.[58])

The Bush administration's willingness to compromise the NPT regime—aided by India's clean track record on nonproliferation—reflected not only its readiness to break free from constraints imposed by international commitments (as, for example, the ABM treaty) but also strong commercial interests and the strategic goal of cultivating India as a potential counterweight to a rising China. Though for its part India would not want to invite the interpretation that it was becoming aligned with the United States at the expense of its other strategic relationships, significant areas of shared interest had arisen between two states whose relations had once been so prickly: combating terrorism, for one, and military cooperation in such areas as peacekeeping and maritime security in the Indian Ocean and adjoining regions.

## REGIONAL INTEGRATION

While Europe pressed ahead (if at times haltingly) in regional integration, including geographical expansion into the old Soviet bloc and monetary union among states in the continental core, Asia registered only piecemeal, incremental moves toward developing multilateral institutions. As previously noted, this divergent pattern is understandable given the different historical contexts. Where the Europeans had experienced calamitous results from the Westphalian system and its national rivalries, for the Asians the transformative emergence of nation-states after World War II signified the ending (though complicated by the Cold War) of centuries of penetration and domination by outside powers. This was not an achievement to be traded away lightly.

The most developed Asian organization, ASEAN, succeeded in fostering a sense of regional identity, and this enabled it to play an important diplomatic role in ending the Third Indochina War (in Cambodia), but its institutional minimalism and its members' dedication to the Westphalian system constricted its evolution into a genuine security body (the muscle applied in Cambodia came from outside powers). Illustrative of its feebleness was the failure of the foreign ministers' annual meeting in July 2008 to address the confrontation between Thailand and Cambodia over an ancient temple and surrounding land along their borders. Thailand rejected having the matter referred to ASEAN mediation, leading Cambodia to take the issue to the UN Security Council, a move that had the other members wringing their hands.[59] In 1994 ASEAN spawned a broader grouping designed to address security issues in the Asia-Pacific region, the ASEAN Regional Forum, comprising a wide range of representatives gathering at the time of the annual ASEAN meetings. These gatherings have included foreign ministers from the United States, the European Union, Japan, China, the ROK, and India, among others. Still, as the name indicates, this served as a talk shop (and stage for entertainment by costumed foreign ministers) rather than an organization likely to forge instruments of collective security.

Likewise, the broad organization dedicated to economic cooperation in the region, the Asia Pacific Economic Cooperation forum, offered not much more than an annual venue for dialogue among the leaders on both sides of the Pacific. President Clinton sought to give it more heft by turning it into a summit meeting, but real progress in economic integration has come from free-trade agreements, some of which are bilateral arrangements. After the end of the Cold War and into the new century, there was an extremely steep rise in regional free-trade deals; in Asia there was an explosion of such deals, reaching about seventy by 2006.[60] ASEAN has been active in promoting free-trade agreements, including one with China that began in 2010, and a South Asian free-trade agreement, sponsored by the South Asian Association for Regional Cooperation, began in 2006. These tend to be circumscribed, however, by exclusion of "sensitive" items that remain protected, as in an ASEAN-Indian agreement's exclusion of nearly five hundred (mainly agricultural) products.[61]

Transnational issues, which gained salience in the new century, offered a prospect for stimulating regional integration in an effort to confront pressing problems of disease (SARS and avian flu, for example), environmental degradation, drug and human trafficking, and especially the threat of terrorist activity across borders. The Shanghai Cooperation Organization, which had its origins in confidence-building measures taken by China and bordering states that had been part of the Soviet Union, has had a central focus on shared antiterrorist concerns. As reflected in the group's mantra expressing opposition to "terrorism, separatism, and extremism," Russia and China in particular view these shared interests in terms of territorial integrity and suppression of minorities seeking greater autonomy (such as Chechens and Uighurs, respectively). Washington, hoping to show solidarity on an issue to which it attached transcendent significance, identified an organization—the East Turkestan Islamic Movement (the very name pulsates with alarm signals for Beijing)—as being a terrorist body, but this did not remove underlying differences over human and minority rights. The bloody crackdown on the uprising in Uzbekistan in 2005 led to tensions between the SCO and the United States, which had condemned the Uzbek regime's behavior. Russia and China expressed support for the Uzbek leader, and a few weeks after the incident the SCO demanded that Washington set final deadlines for vacating bases in Central Asia used for the operations in Afghanistan.

Uzbekistan expelled the Americans from their base in that country, and another U.S. base serving as a logistical hub supporting the international mission in Afghanistan, this one in Kyrgyzstan, became a subject of geopolitical maneuvering in early 2009 when the Kyrgyz president announced that the Manas base lease was going to be terminated. The president, Kurmanbek Bakiyev, made the announcement at a press conference with the Russian president in Moscow after the Kyrgyz had been promised more than two billion dollars in grants and loans. Though the Russians and Kyrgyz denied any connection between the aid and the decision to expel the Americans, an inference of a link was widely drawn given the circumstances and timing. Washington grumbled that the Russians were trying to have it both ways given their expressions of support for the effort in Afghanistan, but Moscow's moves were consistent with its desire to gain leverage in the "near abroad" and require the United States to take Russian interests into account in the region.[62] As it turned out, it was Kyrgyzstan that had it both ways, presumably pocketing the Russian aid while four months later agreeing to extend U.S. use of the base after Washington offered a sharply higher rent and accepted face-saving changes.[63]

Given the potential for conflict with the West over ideological, geopolitical, and energy interests, the SCO has been regarded by some as having the potential for becoming a military rival of the U.S. security system in Asia. An SCO summit meeting in August 2007, coinciding with a military exercise in the Urals involving six thousand personnel, issued a statement implicitly denying a legitimate U.S. presence in the region: "Stability and security in Central Asia are best ensured primarily through efforts taken by the nations of the region on the basis of existing regional associations." President Putin used the occasion to signal Russia's rediscovered assertiveness by announcing that it had resumed long-range strategic air patrols.[64] A convergence of interests between Moscow and Beijing was in evidence in a joint communiqué issued in May 2008 by PRC President Hu Jintao and new Russian President Dmitry Medvedev (his predecessor having become prime minister in order to remain in power without contravening constitutional limits on presidential terms). The two sides took a swipe at American plans for missile defenses "in some regions of the world" and condemned use of the human rights issue "to interfere with other countries' affairs," a standard shared grievance. They also signed a one-billion-dollar deal for construction by Russia of a uranium-enrichment plant. Meanwhile, their bilateral trade had risen from below eleven billion dollars at the beginning of the new century to more than forty-eight billion dollars seven years later.[65]

Notwithstanding some signs of polarization and a return to Cold War practices, an organization like the SCO fell well short of an alliance like that of NATO or the Warsaw Pact, with its integrated military structure under Soviet control. Moreover, polarizing trends were constrained by interests of the main SCO powers, China and Russia, in cooperation with the United States on important issues ranging from trade and investment to nonproliferation and transnational challenges. There were also differences in the behavior of a resurgent Russia and the emergent China. Where the former began showing signs of throwing its geopolitical weight around, particularly in Russia's "near abroad," China's behavior has been dictated mainly by economic considerations, some of which put its interests at conflict with the United States on such subjects as Myanmar and Sudan. On other matters, such as Taiwan and Japan, Beijing's economic interests have provided an incentive to foster cooperative trends.

Crosscurrents affecting the SCO were evident at its summit meeting in August 2008, which followed closely on Russia's invasion of Georgia and subsequent recognition of the independence of two enclaves almost universally recognized as being within Georgian sovereignty. The joint communiqué issued at the summit remained silent on this matter, a topic of high attention in much of the world, while a joint declaration offered less than full support for Russia. The six SCO states expressed "deep concern" over the "recent tension over the South Ossetian issue" and called on the sides involved "to solve existing problems peacefully." It evaded the sovereignty issues while applauding the peace plan worked out by Russia (and France). What lay behind this reticence to rally around one of their members, one that had drawn bitter condemnation from the United States, was reflected in the declaration's stress on "efforts aimed at preserving the unity [and] territorial integrity" of states.[66] This is standard fare in SCO declarations, and it did not appear in the passage on South Ossetia, but it is a major principle for China, with its concern over Taiwan and separatist tendencies in Tibet and Xinjiang. Also, the four Central Asian members, having been parts of the Soviet Union, had reason not to be enthusiastic about what could be viewed as a dangerous precedent.

The SCO declaration did, however, invoke themes shared by Russia and China in protest against American unilateralism. Thus, it called for strict compliance with the UN Charter and opposition to unipolarity, and it took another slap at the United States for pursuing "a global antimissile system." Registering a concern central to the organization's purpose, its discussion of Afghanistan focused on the need to combat drug smuggling and transborder crime.

A functionalist approach to cooperation, as distinct from geopolitical integration, has become increasingly salient in efforts to cope with various transnational and proliferation challenges. Thus, the World Health Organization played a central role in handling the outbreaks of SARS and avian flu in the early years of the new century. Consider also informal, non-treaty-based associations of states such as the Proliferation Security Initiative, devoted to combating international trafficking in illicit weapons (a notable success being the interception at sea of a shipment to Libya), and the Global Initiative to Combat Terrorism, designed to secure nuclear sites and prevent trafficking within borders. A vexing transnational issue such as piracy illustrates the potential for a pressing problem to prompt movement toward regional cooperation. Indonesia, Singapore, and Malaysia in 2004 began full-time patrols of the Malacca Strait, a major shipping corridor and a lifeline for energy destined for East Asia. At a meeting of the region's defense officials two years later, India offered to join these efforts. China, wary of military cooperation, remained absent,[67] but in a significant departure, Beijing decided in late 2008 to dispatch a naval force to combat piracy off the Horn of Africa. This marked the first Chinese naval deployment outside the Pacific.[68]

A functionalist approach has also been taken to address complex disputes in which territorial, economic, and transnational issues are intertwined. In 1992, for example, ASEAN issued a "Declaration on the South China Sea," an area of overlapping territorial and jurisdictional claims and one possessing rich natural resources as well as being a strategic seaway.[69] In addition to seeking to promote a code of conduct to avoid military collisions in the area, ASEAN sought to promote functional cooperation among the disputants that would foster a more favorable atmosphere for conflict resolution while not prejudicing territorial claims. Similarly, Japan and China, whose conflicted past injects a toxic brew of nationalism into disputes, agreed in June 2008 to allow Japanese investment in Chinese projects in the East China Sea for developing oil and natural gas deposits in exchange for a share of profits. This enabled the two sides to promote economic development while deferring thorny territorial issues.[70]

A region severely buffeted by the financial crisis of the late 1990s groped for ways to insulate itself from the capricious effects of globalization, including hot money and financial instability. One way was for the Asian countries to amass huge piles of hard currency, much of it invested in U.S. securities; this afforded leverage against external pressures for changes in currency rates (such as pressure from Washington for the Chinese to revalue their currency), and provided a war chest for repelling financial attacks such as occurred during that previous crisis. The foreign reserves of Thailand, where the 1997 crisis originated, increased by more than threefold in the following ten years; China's rocketed during that period from 126 billion dollars to 1.8 *trillion* dollars (soaring to an astonishing 2.4 trillion dollars by 2010); this was a widespread pattern in Asia at that time.[71] By 2006 the East Asians were planning to venture into coordinated efforts on the currency front. The Chinese, Japanese, and South Koreans, meeting at the sidelines of an Asian Development Bank meeting (a characteristic way for initiatives to be pursued in Asia), announced steps toward coordinating foreign exchange policy, including the possibility of an Asian Currency Unit—akin to the European precursor to the euro. These three countries, their relationships burdened by historical animosities that continue to fester, in late 2008 held the first of what would be annual summit meetings—an "epoch-making" development according to the Japanese prime minister.[72] In addition to regional political issues like the North Korean nuclear program, the summit discussed regional responses to the global economic crisis, such as currency swaps to prop up a country's beleaguered currency—the South Korean won, in the case of the first summit. At their summit in October 2009 the three states agreed to press forward toward an "East Asian community," which would include a common fund of currency reserves available to individual states to repel runs on their currencies.[73] If there was sufficient will to create a robust fund of this sort, it would reduce the need for each state to maintain large reserves, which in turn would lower the overall demand for dollars.

ASEAN also sought to promote regional integration by promoting free-trade areas, including with China and with India. Soaring commodity prices had enabled the region to recover from the previous decade's financial crisis. But even with a substantial rise in intraregional trade, the economies remained competitors in that they were trading in commodities and semifinished goods headed for developed countries; if China stimulated its domestic consumption, it would become more of a final destination for exports from within the region and make intraregional trade more complementary.[74]

Asia's emerging economies, even if better insulated from the vagaries of capital flows than in the 1990s, remained vulnerable to downturns in their export markets. This became painfully evident as a result of the fallout from the bursting of the credit bubble in the United States in 2008,[75] making it even more imperative that export dependence be reduced by development of domestic and regional markets and by improving social safety nets to allow consumers to spend rather than rack up excessive savings. The Chinese addressed this prospect in March 2009 in a major policy statement by Premier Wen Jiabao, who announced a 17.6 percent increase in spending on safety-net programs, and stressed that bolstering the consumer sector was "a long-term strategic principle and a basic point of departure for stimulating economic growth."[76] If Americans had overspent and undersaved, Asians had done the reverse. This mirror image was reflected in the following figures: Chinese consumption accounted for 35 percent of GDP; American consumption, 70 percent.[77]

Just as Japan's ascent to economic superpowerdom engendered tensions with the United States, so also did the rise of China produce frictions in Sino-American trade relations. Persisting imbalances and grievances over a perceived undervaluation of the renminbi led to American demands for corrective measures by the Chinese. These demands were tempered, however, by the symbiotic relationship between the two sides'

TABLE 14.1
Selected Asian Regional Organizations

| |
|---|
| ASEAN (Philippines, Thailand, Malaysia, Singapore, Indonesia, Brunei, Vietnam, Laos, Cambodia, Myanmar), 1967 |
| South Asian Association for Regional Cooperation (Afghanistan, Bangladesh, Bhutan, India, Maldives, Nepal, Pakistan, Sri Lanka), 1985 |
| Asia Pacific Economic Cooperation (Asian and Pacific Rim states), 1989 |
| ASEAN Regional Forum (Asian states, Canada, United States, EU), 1994 |
| ASEAN Plus 3 (ASEAN, China, Japan, South Korea), 1997 |
| Shanghai Cooperation Organization (China, Russia, Kazakhstan, Kyrgyzstan, Tajikistan, Uzbekistan), 2001 |

economies, the Chinese enjoying a huge export market while the Americans relied on Beijing to underwrite the U.S. deficit with purchases of Treasuries. Beijing did loosen its currency's peg to the dollar beginning in 2005, though it tightened it again when Chinese exports faltered during the Great Recession. Meanwhile, that recession induced a rise in the U.S. savings rate, from about zero to more than 5 percent in 2009, thus reducing the American appetite for Chinese imports. Economists disagree over the proper valuation of the renminbi, but some have contended that an upward revaluation would stimulate the Chinese consumers' purchasing power, discourage excessive manufacturing investment, and reduce the trade imbalance, all of which would ameliorate Sino-American economic relations.[78]

## THE ASIAN CENTURY?

While limited movement toward multilateral cooperation emerged in response to specific, often transnational issues, the geopolitical landscape of the post–Cold War era remained dominated by the continuing American presence. Nonetheless, the end of the Cold War, economic interdependence, and liberalizing political and economic trends lent a substantial measure of fluidity to regional relations. India's evolving role as a major power in the Indian Ocean, a key trade route, and as a rising economic powerhouse illustrates the shift from the rigidities of the past. Both Washington and Beijing have significant incentives for keeping their strategic and economic tensions under control, and there have been efforts in the region to moderate polarizing tendencies by collective consultation even if regional institutions remained less than robust. Indicative in this regard was the American decision to sign ASEAN's Treaty of Amity and Cooperation during the regional organization's annual meeting in July 2009, a move Washington had previously avoided. Beijing signed the treaty in 2006.

Some leaders, notably Australian Prime Minister Kevin Rudd (a Mandarin speaker), sought to promote the East Asian summit (see Chapter 13) as a framework for regional political, strategic, and economic consultation and cooperation. America's accession to the Treaty of Amity and Cooperation was interpreted by some as a precursor for membership in the East Asian summit, thereby making that grouping more inclusive and counteracting polarizing tendencies. Still, deep-seated divergences among the region's states—such as between authoritarian and democratic systems, not likely to be bridged in the foreseeable future—made the evolution toward regional institutions that were more than talk shops or brainstorming forums a long-term prospect.

Even if Asia lagged far behind Europe in developing regional bodies, it had progressed far from being a mere geographical expression: It had become Asia, a region with a sense of identity, growing self-confidence, and a record of dynamic economic growth that prompted many to dub the new century the "Asian Century." Asians had shown remarkable resilience in rebounding from economic crises, such as the capital flight of the late 1990s, the bursting of the technology bubble early in the new century, and perhaps most significantly, the Great Recession sparked by the collapse of the U.S. housing market in 2007 and the ensuing financial panic (a bubble fueled by the amassing of foreign exchange reserves by Asians after the 1990s crisis). In the case of the Great Recession, the world looked to Asia, especially China, to act as the economic locomotive to pull the global economy back from the brink of a depression—a notable reversal from the usual pattern. In a specific sign of a broad trend, the British bank HSBC, Europe's largest, cited the shift in the center of economic gravity toward Asia when announcing in September 2009 that it was relocating its chief executive from London to Hong Kong (actually a homecoming for the formerly named Hong Kong and Shanghai Banking Corporation).[79]

Asia's economic resilience also translated into political stability a decade after the turbulence attending the financial crisis of the late 1990s. In 2009, for example, the ruling parties in India (overcoming the customary anti-incumbent sentiment) and Indonesia (where the Suharto regime collapsed a decade earlier) gained reelection.[80] What remained in question was the extent to which Asia's accrual of economic strength would translate into geopolitical power and thus potentially produce a fundamental shift in the regional and global balance of power. Even within the economic sphere, interdependence did not readily translate into regional integration; the rapid proliferation of free-trade agreements in the first decade of the new century was not accompanied by a significant growth in the proportion of intraregional trade, which remained at half of the region's total foreign trade. This could change, however, as a growing middle class and rising domestic demand create a market for end-use products.

In becoming an assertive Asia, after having been largely a Western construct, the region had escaped the shackles of colonialism and then many of the constraints imposed by the Cold War. The shift of economic power toward the region was driven by the export-led maritime trade pioneered by Japan and then spreading down the Asian coast. Another, later trend, one that has been powered by China's dynamic growth and its huge appetite for resources, offered an opportunity for the Asian hinterland to participate more fully in these transformative developments. This has involved the building of roads and railways, ports and pipelines, and other infrastructure linking China and its continental neighbors and promoting trade and development beyond the maritime model.

Yet, while new frontiers of economic growth and cooperation were opening up, there remained substantial obstacles to Asia's ascent to a dominant role: The Asian states' fervent allegiance to the Westphalian system, surviving Cold War structures, ideological differences, economic rivalry, persisting nationalist conflicts and territorial issues in the world's most militarized region, all conspired to constrict efforts to promote geopolitical and economic unity and left considerable scope for a continuing American presence. Even developments tending to erode post–Cold War unipolarity and adherence to the Westphalian dispensation—supranational and regional institutions such as the European Union and ASEAN, international organizations such as the IMF and the WHO, multinational corporations and nongovernmental organizations, nonstate groups such as Al-Qaeda[81]—did not remove the continuing significance of the American role as a stabilizing and balancing force. Witness the persisting U.S. security structure—though the cornerstone alliance, with Japan, could not be taken so much for granted after the defeat in 2009 of the Liberal Democrats by the Democratic Party of Japan—and the evolving U.S.-Indian relationship as a counterbalance to rising Chinese influence. In this landscape the security architecture erected by Washington after the outbreak of the Korean War, while at times a source of tension and even resentment among the peoples of the region, stayed in place as the ultimate guarantor of stability, the default option in the absence of credible and effective multilateral institutions even in an era of increasing economic interdependence and the growing role of transnational and other non-Westphalian bodies.

# NOTES

## CHAPTER 1

1. The following discussion of the 1922 Washington Conference treaty system and its decline draws on these sources: Akira Iriye, *After Imperialism: The Search for a New Order in the Far East, 1921–1931* (Cambridge, MA: Harvard University Press, 1965); Akira Iriye, *The Origins of the Second World War in Asia and the Pacific* (New York: Longman, 1987), 2–39; Marius Jansen, *Japan and China: From War to Peace, 1894–1972* (Chicago: Rand McNally, 1975), 354–408. Alternative accounts of the Washington treaties may be found in Warren I. Cohen, *America's Response to China: A History of Sino-American Relations*, 4th ed. (New York: Columbia University Press, 2000), 87–97; and Michael Schaller, *The United States and China: Into the Twenty-first Century*, 3rd ed. (New York: Oxford University Press, 2002), 38–43. For succinct, analytical accounts of the broader international setting of the Washington treaty system and its breakdown, see William R. Keylor, *The Twentieth Century World: An International History*, 4th ed. (New York: Oxford University Press, 2001), 220–42; and Zara Steiner, *The Lights That Failed: European International History, 1919–1933* (New York: Oxford University Press, 2005), 707–54.

2. A vivid account of realism and its classical varieties, as well as of liberalism and its various strands, is Michael W. Doyle, *Ways of War and Peace* (New York: W.W. Norton, 1997).

3. This sketch of realism and the sketch of liberalism that follows owe much to the classical analysis of Hans Morgenthau in his enduring text *Politics Among Nations: The Struggle for Power and Peace*, 6th ed. (New York: Knopf, 1985), which argues that the pursuit of power derives ultimately from human nature and pervades human society. Morgenthau's "classical realism" differs from later versions of realism, often referred to as "structural realism" or "neorealism," which proceeds from the premise that the pursuit of power derives from the systemic nature and needs of international politics. The starting point for these later realist perspectives is Kenneth Waltz's *Theory of International Politics* (Reading, MA: Addison-Wesley, 1979). For a detailed comparison of the two strains of realist thought, see, in addition to the relevant portions of Doyle,

*Ways of War and Peace*, James E. Dougherty and Robert Pfaltzgraff, *Contending Theories of International Relations: A Comprehensive Survey*, 4th ed. (New York: Longman, 1997), 58–89.

4. Iriye, *Origins of the Second World War*, 2–3.

5. William G. Beasley, *Japanese Imperialism, 1894–1945* (Oxford: Oxford University Press, 1987), 122–41, 253–54.

## CHAPTER 2

1. Herbert Feis, *Churchill-Roosevelt-Stalin* (Princeton, NJ: Princeton University Press, 1957), 206–11.

2. Ibid., 238.

3. Ibid., 209; emphasis added.

4. U.S. Department of State, *Foreign Relations of the United States* (*FRUS*), *1943*, vol. 2, *The First Cairo Conference* (Washington, DC: U.S. Government Printing Office, 1961), 448–49.

5. Ibid., 251–57.

6. Winston Churchill, *Triumph and Tragedy* (Boston: Houghton Mifflin, 1953), 227–28.

7. For a classic centrist analysis, see Feis, *Churchill-Roosevelt-Stalin*, 498–558; for frequently cited different interpretations flanking Feis on the left and right, respectively, see Diane Shaver Clemons, *Yalta* (New York: Oxford University Press, 1970) and Russell D. Buhite, *Decisions at Yalta: An Appraisal of Summit Diplomacy* (Wilmington, DE: Scholarly Resources, 1986). See also Tsuyoshi Hasegawa, *Racing the Enemy: Stalin, Truman, and the Surrender of Japan* (Cambridge, MA: Belknap Press of Harvard University Press, 2005), 30–44. More generally, interpretations of the Cold War from a rightist perspective tend to emphasize ideological sources of Communist conduct, whereas those on the left side of the spectrum see Communist behavior as reactive to American efforts to make the world safe for capitalism.

8. U.S. Department of State, *FRUS, 1945*, vol. 3, part 2, *The Yalta Conference* (Washington, DC: U.S. Government Printing Office, 1955), 984.

9. Feis, *Churchill-Roosevelt-Stalin*, 513.

10. Buhite, *Decisions at Yalta*, 93–94, 102.

11. See especially Hasegawa, *Racing the Enemy.*

12. For an eyewitness account of Soviet behavior by the last American consul in Dairen before the Chinese Communists' takeover, see Paul Paddock, *China Diary: Crisis Diplomacy in Dairen* (Ames: Iowa State University Press, 1974).

13. U.S. Department of State, *FRUS, 1945*, vol. 2, *Proclamation to Japan* (Washington, DC: U.S. Government Printing Office, 1960), 1474–76.

14. An influential proponent was Gar Alperovitz, *Atomic Diplomacy* (New York: Penguin Press, 1985).

15. Hasegawa, *Racing the Enemy*, 193–95.

16. Ibid., esp. Chapter 4. For a study of the decision to use atom bombs, see Amir Aczel, *Uranium Wars: The Scientific Rivalry That Created the Nuclear Age* (New York: Palgrave Macmillan, 2009).

17. But see Robert Jervis, "Was the Cold War a Security Dilemma?" *Journal of Cold War Studies* 3, no. 1 (2001): 36–60.

## CHAPTER 3

1. Hu Qiaomu, *Thirty Years of the Communist Party of China* (Peking: Foreign Languages Press, 1954), 97.

2. O.B. Borisov and B.T. Koloskov, *Sino-Soviet Relations: A Brief History* (Moscow: Progress Publishers, 1975), 39–41. "O.B. Borisov" was the pen name of Oleg Borisovich Rakhmanin, a longtime Soviet China hand in the International Department of the Communist Party of the Soviet Union.

3. Barbara W. Tuchman, *Stilwell and the American Experience in China, 1911–45* (New York: Macmillan, 1971), 531.

4. Hans Morgenthau, preface to Tang Tsou, *America's Failure in China, 1941–1950* (Chicago: University of Chicago Press, 1963), ix–x.

5. Tsou, *America's Failure in China*, 591.

6. William H. McNeill, *America, Britain, and Russia: Their Cooperation and Conflict, 1941–1946* (London: Royal Institute of International Affairs and Oxford University Press, 1953), 99, 330–31, and 356; Herbert Feis, *The China Tangle* (Princeton, NJ: Princeton University Press, 1953), 95–100. The Four-Power Declaration is also known as the Moscow Declaration.

7. John Gittings, *The Role of the Chinese Army* (London: Oxford University Press, 1967), 303.

8. Mao Zedong, "On Protracted War," *Selected Works of Mao Tse-tung*, vol. 2 (Peking: Foreign Languages Press, 1965), 136–45.

9. On this perspective, see Roy Hofheinz, "The Ecology of Chinese Communist Success," in *Chinese Communist Politics in Action*, ed. A. Doak Barnett (Seattle: University of Washington Press, 1969), 3–77.

10. Hans van de Ven, *War and Nationalism in China, 1925–1945* (London: Routledge Corzon, 2003), 151–63.

11. For a detailed analysis of this ROC-Soviet diplomacy, see John W. Garver, *Chinese-Soviet Relations, 1937–1945* (New York: Oxford University Press, 1988), 182–209.

12. On the 3 January 1944 Vladimirov cable, see ibid., 253–54.

13. On Soviet calculations regarding the subordinate place of the CPC in the achievement of broader Soviet objectives in China, see ibid., 251–52.

14. Truman's instructions to Marshall on 15 December 1945 called on the general to inform Chiang that "a China disunited and torn by civil strife could not be considered realistically as a proper place for American assistance." U.S. Department of State, *United States Relations with China, with Special Reference to the Period 1945–1949* (the China White Paper) (Washington, DC: U.S. Government Printing Office, 1949), 605–6.

15. "Memorandum by the Policy Planning Staff" (PPS 39), 7 September 1948, U.S. Department of State, *Foreign Relations of the United States, 1948*, vol. 8, *U.S. Military Assistance to China* (Washington, DC: U.S. Government Printing Office, 1973), 146–55.

16. U.S. Department of State, *United States Relations with China—With Special Reference to the Period 1944–1949*, U.S. Department of State Publication 3573, Far

Eastern Series (Washington, DC: Division of Publications, Office of Public Affairs, August 1949).

## CHAPTER 4

1. Tsuyoshi Hasegawa, *Racing the Enemy: Stalin, Truman and the Surrender of Japan* (Cambridge, MA: Belknap Press of Harvard University Press, 2005).

2. See Theodore Cohen, *Remaking Japan: The American Occupation as New Deal* (New York: Free Press, 1997).

3. Paul J. Bailey, *Postwar Japan: 1945 to the Present* (Oxford: Blackwell Publishers, 1996), 26–29; Michael Schaller, *The American Occupation of Japan: The Origins of the Cold War in Asia* (New York: Oxford University Press, 1985), 60–61.

4. Hasegawa, *Racing the Enemy*, chapter 4.

5. State-War-Navy Coordinating Committee, "U.S. Initial Post-Surrender Policy for Japan," Document 150/4, *U.S. Department of State Bulletin* (25 December 1945): 423ff.

6. A useful side-by-side rendition of the 1889 Meiji constitution and the 1946 constitution is in Hugh Borton, *Japan's Modern Century* (New York: Ronald Press, 1955), 490–507.

7. Bailey, *Postwar Japan*, 31–52; J.W. Dower, *Empire and Aftermath: Yoshida Shigeru and the Japanese Experience, 1878–1954* (Cambridge, MA: Harvard University Press, 1988), chapter 9.

8. Bailey, *Postwar Japan*, 31–35.

9. Bailey, *Postwar Japan*, 44; John Welfield, *An Empire in Eclipse: Japan in the Postwar American Alliance System* (London: Athlone, 1988), 64–65.

10. See the analysis in Dower, *Empire and Aftermath*, 329–68.

11. U.S. Department of State, *Foreign Relations of the United States (FRUS), 1948*, vol. 6, *Japan* (Washington, DC: U.S. Government Printing Office, 1974), 858–62.

12. Carol Gluck, "Entangling Illusions—Japanese and American Views of the Occupation," in *New Frontiers in American–East Asian Relations*, ed. Warren I. Cohen (New York: Columbia University Press, 1983), 200.

13. The peace treaty and U.S.-Japanese security treaty are in U.S. Department of State, *United States Treaties and Other International Agreements 1952*, vol. 3, part 3 (Washington, DC: U.S. Government Printing Office, 1955), 3161–91 and 3329–40.

14. Bailey, *Postwar Japan*, 70–71; Dower, *Empire and Aftermath*, 369–72.

15. Schaller, *American Occupation of Japan*, chapter 9.

16. See Dower, *Empire and Aftermath*, 400–414, for the text of the letter and analysis; also see Welfield, *Empire in Eclipse*, 52–54.

17. See the data and sources cited in Bailey, *Postwar Japan*, 67.

18. Schaller, *American Occupation of Japan*, 289.

19. Ibid., 279.

20. Kent Calder, "Securing Security Through Prosperity: The San Francisco System in Comparative Perspective," *Pacific Review* 17, no. 1 (March 2004): 135–57.

21. On the evolution of Japan's party politics in this period, see J.A.A. Stockwin, *Governing Japan*, 3rd ed. (Malden, MA: Blackwell Publishers, 1999), 48–53; Gerald Curtis, *The Japanese Way of Politics* (New York: Columbia University Press, 1988), 4–18; and Bailey, *Postwar Japan*, 70–72 and 78–89.

22. Michael Schaller, *Altered States: The United States and Japan Since the Occupation* (New York: Oxford University Press, 1997), 114–23; and Michael Barnhart, *Japan and the World Since 1868* (New York: Edward Arnold, 1995), 159–61.

23. The classic account of the 1960 crisis is George R. Packard, *Protest in Tokyo: The Security Treaty Crisis of 1960* (Princeton, NJ: Princeton University Press, 1966). See also Welfield, *Empire in Eclipse*, 114–61; and Schaller, *Altered States*, 127–62.

24. See Stockwin, *Governing Japan*, 54–56; Curtis, *Japanese Way of Politics*, 18–30; and Bailey, *Postwar Japan*, 95–99.

25. The following discussion draws from Bailey, *Postwar Japan*, 60–61, 74–76, and 89–94; Takatoshi Ito, *The Japanese Economy* (Cambridge, MA: MIT Press, 1992), 52–69 and 196–200.

26. The classic study of the role of MITI is Chalmers Johnson, *MITI and the Japanese Miracle: The Growth of Industrial Policy, 1925–1975* (Stanford, CA: Stanford University Press, 1982).

27. Schaller, *Altered States*, 108–12; and Glenn D. Hook, Julie Gilson, Christopher W. Hughes, and Hugo Dobson, *Japan's International Relations: Politics, Economics, and Security*, 2nd ed. (New York: Routledge, 2005), 364–65.

28. A contemporary brief on this question is John K. Emmerson, *Arms, Yen and Power: The Japanese Dilemma* (Tokyo: Charles E. Tuttle, 1972).

## CHAPTER 5

1. The titles of some works on the Korean War reflect its unusual character. See Clay Blair, *The Forgotten War: America in Korea* (New York: Anchor Books, 1981); Rosemary Foot, *The Wrong War: American Policy and the Dimensions of the Korean Conflict, 1950–1953* (Ithaca, NY: Cornell University Press, 1985); David Rees, *Korea: The Limited War* (New York: St. Martin's Press, 1964). See also Bruce Cumings, *The Origins of the Cold War*, vol. 1, *Liberation and the Emergence of Separate Regimes, 1945–1947* (Princeton, NJ: Princeton University Press, 1981), and vol. 2, *The Roaring of the Cataract, 1947–1950* (Princeton, NJ: Princeton University Press, 1990); Gregory Henderson, *Korea: The Politics of the Vortex* (Cambridge, MA: Harvard University Press, 1968); John Merrill, *Korea: The Peninsular Origins of the War* (Newark: University of Delaware Press, 1989); Robert Simmons, *The Strained Alliance: Peking, Pyongyang, Moscow and the Politics of the Korean Civil War* (New York: Free Press, 1975); Allen S. Whiting, *China Crosses the Yalu* (Stanford, CA: Stanford University Press, 1960).

2. Tsuyoshi Hasegawa, *Racing the Enemy: Stalin, Truman, and the Surrender of Japan* (Cambridge, MA: Belknap Press of Harvard University Press, 2005), 267; Robert M. Slusser, "Soviet Far Eastern Policy, 1945–50: Stalin's Goals in Korea," in *The Origins of the Cold War in Asia*, ed. Yonosuke Nagai and Akira Iriye (New York: Columbia University Press, 1977), 136.

3. Kathryn Weathersby, "Soviet Aims in Korea and the Origins of the Korean War, 1945–1950: New Evidence from Russian Archives," *Cold War International History Project (CWIHP) Working Paper 8*, Woodrow Wilson International Center for Scholars, Washington, DC, 1993, 21–22.

4. Okonogi Masao, "The Domestic Roots of the Korean War," in Nagai and Iriye, *Origins of the Cold War,* 301.

5. Weathersby, "Soviet Aims," 22–23.

6. National Security Council, NSC 8, 2 April 1948, in U.S. Department of State, *Foreign Relations of the United States (FRUS), 1948,* vol. 6, *The Far East and Australasia* (Washington, DC: U.S. Government Printing Office, 1974), 1164–65, and NSC 8/2, 22 March 1949, in U.S. Department of State, *FRUS, 1949,* vol. 7, *The Far East and Australasia,* part 2 (Washington, DC: U.S. Government Printing Office, 1976), 969–78.

7. Bruce Cumings, *Origins of the Korean War,* vol. 2, *Roaring of the Cataract,* 388–98; Merrill, *Korea,* 135–43.

8. Merrill, *Korea,* 173.

9. Kathryn Weathersby, "'Should We Fear This?' Stalin and the Danger of War with America," *CWIHP Working Paper 39,* Woodrow Wilson Center, Washington, DC, 2002, 9, citing an internal Soviet account of the Stalin-Kim talks.

10. Weathersby, "Soviet Aims," 28–31; Weathersby, "'Should We Fear This?'" 9–11.

11. See Kathryn Weathersby, "To Attack, or Not to Attack? Stalin, Kim Il Sung, and the Prelude to War," *CWIHP Bulletin,* no. 5 (Spring 1995): 3.

12. Remarks to the Soviet ambassador, 19 January 1950, in *CWIHP Bulletin,* no. 5 (Spring 1995): 8.

13. Thomas G. Paterson, *Major Problems in American Foreign Policy,* vol. 2, *Since 1914,* 3rd edition (Lexington, MA: D.C. Heath, 1989), 398–99.

14. Dean Acheson, *Present at the Creation: My Years in the State Department* (New York: W.W. Norton, 1969), 357.

15. Ibid., 358.

16. See Soviet documents quoted in Weathersby, "Soviet Aims," 14–15.

17. The revisionist view is systematically presented in the monumental two-volume study by Bruce Cumings, *Origins of the Korean War.*

18. See the documents and analysis in Weathersby, "Soviet Aims" and "'Should We Fear This?'"

19. Weathersby, "'Should We Fear This?'" 15.

20. U.S. Department of State, *FRUS, 1950,* vol. 7, *Korea* (Washington, DC: U.S. Government Printing Office, 1976), 157–61.

21. Ibid., 148–54.

22. U.S. Department of State, *FRUS, 1950,* vol. 7, 202–3.

23. Ibid., 161–65.

24. Ibid.

25. Michael Schaller, *The American Occupation of Japan: The Origins of the Cold War in Asia* (New York: Oxford University Press, 1985), 263.

26. *U.S. Department of State Bulletin* 22 (27 March 1950): 467–72. For an account of discord within the administration over Asian issues such as Taiwan and Japan, see Schaller, *American Occupation of Japan,* esp. chapter 14.

27. Resolutions in U.S. Department of State, *FRUS, 1950,* vol. 7, 155–56.

28. Sergei N. Goncharov, John W. Lewis, and Xue Litai, *Uncertain Partners: Stalin, Mao, and the Korean War* (Stanford, CA: Stanford University Press, 1993), 161–62.

29. For an analysis of deliberations over this option, see William Stueck, *The Korean War: An International History* (Princeton, NJ: Princeton University Press, 1995), 61–83.

30. U.S. Department of State, *FRUS, 1950*, vol. 7, 240–41.

31. Ibid., 826.

32. Goncharov, Lewis, and Xue, *Uncertain Partners*, document 62, 273–74, and document 64, 276–78.

33. Ibid., document 63, 275–76.

34. Ibid., 183–99.

35. See John Lewis Gaddis, *The Cold War: A New History* (New York: Penguin Press, 2005), 60, citing a Soviet account available at www.korean-war.com/ussr.html.

36. Stueck, *Korean War*, 244–45, 250–52, 322–23, and 326–27.

37. Ibid., 330–39.

38. See the section "Korea as a Substitute for World War III" in Stueck, *Korean War*, 348–53.

## CHAPTER 6

1. The text of the Vietnamese declaration of independence is in Robert J. McMahon, *Major Problems in the History of the Vietnam War* (Lexington, MA: D.C. Heath, 1990), 35–37.

2. Evelyn Colbert, *Southeast Asia in International Politics, 1941–1956* (Ithaca, NY: Cornell University Press, 1977), 15–16.

3. This discussion follows the outstanding analysis in David Joel Steinberg, ed., *In Search of Southeast Asia: A Modern History* (Honolulu: University of Hawaii Press, 1987), 175–218 and 247–345; and in Nicholas Tarling, ed., *The Cambridge History of Southeast Asia*, vol. 2, *The Nineteenth and Twentieth Centuries* (New York: Cambridge University Press, 1992), 79–130 and 249–318.

4. Steinberg, *In Search of Southeast Asia*, 307.

5. Ayesha Jalal, *The Sole Spokesman: Jinnah, the Muslim League and the Demand for Pakistan* (Cambridge: Cambridge University Press, 1985).

6. Sumit Ganguly, *Conflict Unending: India-Pakistan Tensions Since 1947* (New York: Columbia University Press, 2001), 2.

7. Ibid., 15–23.

8. For an account of his commission's work, see Joseph Korbel, *Danger in Kashmir* (Princeton, NJ: Princeton University Press, 1954). For an account from an Indian perspective, see J.N. Dixit, *India-Pakistan in War and Peace* (London: Routledge, 2002), 111–21.

9. For a searching study of Washington's Cold War policy in South Asia up to 1956, see Robert J. McMahon, *Cold War on the Periphery: The United States, India, and Pakistan* (New York: Columbia University Press, 1994).

10. See George M. Kahin, *The Asian-African Conference* (Ithaca, NY: Cornell University Press, 1956).

11. Dorothy Woodman, *Himalayan Frontiers* (New York: Praeger Publishers, 1969), 262.

12. For a lucid, detailed account of the development of the Sino-Indian border dispute, see Neville Maxwell, *India's China War* (New York: Anchor Books, 1972). For an updated account placed in a broader context, see John W. Garver, *Protracted Contest: Sino-Indian Rivalry in the Twentieth Century* (Seattle: University of Washington Press, 2001).

13. John K. Knaus, *Orphans of the Cold War: America and the Tibetan Struggle for Survival* (New York: Public Press, 1999).

14. For a discussion of the security dilemma as one of the "taproots" of Sino-Indian conflict, see Garver, *Protracted Contest*, 16–22.

15. This contrast is developed in detail in Colbert, *Southeast Asia in International Politics*, 54–92, and in Gary R. Hess, *The United States' Emergence as a Southeast Asian Power, 1940–1950* (New York: Columbia University Press, 1987), 158–215. In addition, see the exhaustive study of the evolution of American policy in Robert J. McMahon, *Colonialism and Cold War: The United States and the Struggle for Indonesian Independence, 1945–49* (Ithaca, NY: Cornell University Press, 1981).

16. William J. Duiker, *The Communist Road to Power in Vietnam* (Boulder, CO: Westview Press, 1981), 32, 38–39.

17. Colbert, *Southeast Asia in International Politics*, 197.

18. Ibid., 226–28.

19. Ibid., 268–71.

20. See *Beijing Review* 22, no. 47 (23 November 1979): 18–20, and no. 48 (30 November 1979): 11–15.

21. The text of the Geneva Declaration is in U.S. Department of State, *Foreign Relations of the United States, 1952–54*, vol. 16, *The Geneva Conference* (Washington, DC: U.S. Government Printing Office, 1981), 1540–42.

22. *The Pentagon Papers: As Published by The New York Times* (New York: Bantam Books, 1971), 52–53.

23. George C. Herring, *America's Longest War: The United States and Vietnam, 1950–1975* (New York: McGraw-Hill, 1996), 47.

24. Ibid., 48–49; emphasis added.

25. Harold Hinton, *Communist China in World Politics* (Boston: Houghton Mifflin, 1966), 30–31.

## CHAPTER 7

1. *New York Times*, 28 October 2005.

2. Text of NSC-68 in U.S. Department of State, *Foreign Relations of the United States (FRUS), 1950*, vol. 1 (Washington, DC: U.S. Government Printing Office, 1977), 235–92. For a policymaker's account, see Dean Acheson, *Present at the Creation: My Years in the State Department* (New York: W.W. Norton, 1969), 346–47, 373–77. For a scholarly retrospective, see Ernest May, ed., *American Cold War Strategy: Interpreting NSC-68* (Boston: St. Martin's Press, 1993).

3. U.S. Department of State, *FRUS, 1950*, vol. 1, 240; emphasis added.

4. Ibid., 237.

5. Ibid., 280.

6. Acheson, *Present at the Creation*, 420.

7. For a detailed account of the evolution of policy in its domestic political and bureaucratic setting, see Robert M. Blum, *Drawing the Line: The Origin of the American Containment Policy in East Asia* (New York: W.W. Norton, 1982).

8. John Lewis Gaddis, *We Now Know: Rethinking Cold War History* (Oxford: Clarendon Press, 1997), 75–76.

9. See the U.S.-Philippines treaty in *United States Treaties and Other International Agreements 1952*, vol. 3, part 3 (Washington, DC: U.S. Government Printing Office, 1955), 3947–51.

10. U.S. Department of State, *FRUS, 1951*, vol. 6, part 1 (Washington, DC: U.S. Government Printing Office, 1977), 132–34.

11. John Foster Dulles, "Security in the Pacific," *Foreign Affairs* 30 (January 1952): 183.

12. Kent E. Calder, "Securing Security Through Prosperity: The San Francisco System in Comparative Perspective," *Pacific Review* 17, no. 1 (March 2004): 135–57.

13. See Karl D. Jackson and Wiwat Mungkandi, eds., *United States–Thailand Relations* (Berkeley: University of California Press, 1986), 86.

14. Arthur J. Dommen, *Conflict in Laos: The Politics of Neutralization* (New York: Praeger Publishers, 1971), 218.

15. See Nancy Bernkopf Tucker, *Patterns in the Dust: Chinese-American Relations and the Recognition Controversy, 1949–1950* (New York: Columbia University Press, 1983).

16. For the U.S. position, see Ely Maurer, "Legal Problems Regarding Formosa and the Offshore Islands," *U.S. Department of State Bulletin* 39, nos. 1–17 (22 December 1958), 1005–11.

17. Text of the memorandum in U.S. Department of State, *FRUS, 1950*, vol. 7 (Washington, DC: U.S. Government Printing Office, 1976), 161–65.

18. The Formosa Resolution may be found in Russell Buhite, ed., *The Far East*, vol. 4, *Dynamics of World Power: A Documentary History of U.S. Foreign Policy, 1945–73*, ed. Arthur M. Schlesinger (New York: Chelsea House, 1973), 213–14.

19. Zhou's statement is in *Keesing's Contemporary Archives*, vol. 10 (London: Keesing's Publications, 1955–56), 141–85.

20. For an examination of the wedge strategy, see Gordon H. Chang, *Friends and Enemies: The United States, China, and the Soviet Union, 1948–1972* (Stanford, CA: Stanford University Press, 1990).

21. See the ruminations of a veteran analyst of the Cold War: John Lewis Gaddis, *The Cold War: A New History* (New York: Penguin Press, 2005), 82–84.

## CHAPTER 8

1. Mao Tse-tung [Mao Zedong], "On the People's Democratic Dictatorship," 30 June 1949, *Selected Works of Mao Tse-tung*, vol. 4 (Peking: Foreign Languages Press, 1961), 411–23.

2. *Cold War International History Project* (CWIHP) *Bulletin*, nos. 12–13 (Fall–Winter 2001): 260.

3. John Gittings, *The World and China, 1922–1972* (New York: Harper and Row, 1974), 156.

4. *CWIHP Bulletin*, nos. 6–7 (Winter 1995–96): 5.

5. Ibid., 5–7.

6. Document in Sergei N. Goncharov, John W. Lewis, and Xue Litai, *Uncertain Partners: Stalin, Mao, and the Korean War* (Stanford, CA: Stanford University Press, 1993), 241–42, and discussed on 92–93.

7. Document in ibid., 242–43.

8. *CWIHP Bulletin*, nos. 6–7 (Winter 1995–96): 7–9.

9. For a searching if strained interpretation of the Stalin-Mao talks, see Goncharov, Lewis, and Xue, *Uncertain Partners*, 76–109; also see Gittings, *World and China*, 150–55.

10. See Mao's cable to Beijing, 7 January 1950, in Goncharov, Lewis, and Xue, *Uncertain Partners*, 246, and discussion on 100–101.

11. Text of documents in Goncharov, Lewis, and Xue, *Uncertain Partners*, 260–64.

12. *CWIHP Bulletin*, no. 16 (Fall 2007–Winter 2008): 154.

13. A. Doak Barnett, *Communist China and Asia* (New York: Vintage Books, 1960), 220, 348.

14. For Sino-Soviet economic relations, see Shu Guang Zhang, *Economic Cold War* (Stanford, CA: Stanford University Press, 2001).

15. "The Origin and Development of the Differences Between the Leadership of the C.P.S.U. and Ourselves," *Peking Review* 6, no. 37 (1963): 14.

16. *CWIHP Bulletin*, nos. 8–9 (Winter 1996–97): 250, n.2.

17. For a systematic statement of the dangers of Soviet revisionism for other Communists, see "On Khrushchev's Phony Communism and Its Historical Lessons for the World," *Peking Review* 7, no. 29 (1964): 7–24.

18. Text in *Communist China, 1955–9: Policy Documents with Analysis*, Harvard Center for International Affairs and the East Asian Research Center (Cambridge, MA: Harvard University Press, 1962), 144–51. See the discussion by Roderick MacFarquhar, *The Origins of the Cultural Revolution*, vol. 1, *Contradictions Among the People, 1956–1957* (London: Oxford University Press, 1974), 43–46.

19. MacFarquhar, *Origins of the Cultural Revolution*, vol. 1, 100–102.

20. See Donald S. Zagoria, *The Sino-Soviet Conflict, 1956–1961* (Princeton, NJ: Princeton University Press, 1962), 43–49.

21. Ibid., 61–64.

22. MacFarquhar, *Origins of the Cultural Revolution*, vol. 1, *Contradictions Among the People*, 48–56.

23. Zagoria, *Sino-Soviet Conflict*, 145–51; Zbigniew K. Brzezinski, *The Soviet Bloc: Unity and Conflict* (Cambridge, MA: Harvard University Press, 1969), 298–308.

24. Roderick MacFarquhar, *The Origins of the Cultural Revolution*, vol. 2, *The Great Leap Forward, 1958–1960* (New York: Columbia University Press, 1983), chapters 4 and 5.

25. The draft document is found in appendix 1 in Shu Guang Zhang, *Economic Cold War*. See also sources cited in Lorenz M. Lüthi, *The Sino-Soviet Split* (Princeton, NJ: Princeton University Press, 2008), 74–78.

26. Zagoria, *Sino-Soviet Conflict*, 195–99; MacFarquhar, *Origins of the Cultural Revolution*, vol. 2, *Great Leap Forward*, 92–94; Aleksandr Fursenko and Timothy Naftali, *Khrushchev's Cold War* (New York: W.W. Norton, 2006), 158–82.

27. *CWIHP Bulletin*, nos. 6–7 (Winter 1995–96): 155–59.

28. MacFarquhar, *Origins of the Cultural Revolution*, vol. 2, *Great Leap Forward*, 68–71.

29. Fursenko and Naftali, *Khrushchev's Cold War*, 178–79.

30. Khrushchev-Mao talk, 31 July 1958, in *CWIHP Bulletin*, nos. 12–13 (Fall–Winter 2001): 250–60.

31. Deng was notably blunt with the Soviets. See his remarks in September 1960, *CWIHP Bulletin*, no. 10 (March 1998): 173.

32. See text in William E. Griffith, *The Sino-Soviet Rift* (Cambridge, MA: MIT Press, 1964), 399.

33. *CWIHP Bulletin*, nos. 6–7 (Winter 1995–96): 208–11.

34. See Thomas J. Christensen, *Useful Adversaries: Grand Strategy, Domestic Mobilization, and Sino-American Conflict, 1947–1958* (Princeton, NJ: Princeton University Press, 1996), 194–241; Chen Jian, *Mao's China and the Cold War* (Chapel Hill: University of North Carolina Press, 2001), chapter 7.

35. *CWIHP Bulletin*, no. 10 (March 1998): 181.

36. *CWIHP Bulletin*, nos. 6–7 (Winter 1995–96): 174.

37. Zagoria, *Sino-Soviet Conflict*, 209.

38. *CWIHP Bulletin*, nos. 6–7 (Winter 1995–96): 211.

39. Ibid., 226–27.

40. See Soviet statement in Griffith, *Sino-Soviet Rift*, 439.

41. Andrei Gromyko, *Memoirs* (New York: Doubleday, 1989), 251–52; Vladislav Zubok and Constantine Pleshakov, *Inside the Kremlin's Cold War* (Cambridge, MA: Harvard University Press, 1996), 224–25; Chen Jian, *Mao's China*, 188–89; Lüthi, *Sino-Soviet Split*, 95–104.

42. CPSU letter to CPC, 27 September 1958, in *CWIHP Bulletin*, nos. 6–7 (Winter 1995–96): 226–27.

43. Chinese statement of 1 September 1963 in Griffith, *Sino-Soviet Rift*, 382.

44. Zagoria, *Sino-Soviet Conflict*, 211–14; MacFarquhar, *Origins of the Cultural Revolution*, vol. 2, *Great Leap Forward*, 96–99; John R. Thomas, "The Limits of Alliance: The Quemoy Crisis of 1958," in *Sino-Soviet Military Relations*, ed. Raymond L. Garthoff (New York: Praeger, 1966), 114–49. For an analysis arguing that the Soviets and Chinese were in agreement during the Taiwan Strait crisis, see Morton H. Halperin and Tang Tsou, "The 1958 Quemoy Crisis," in *Sino-Soviet Relations and Arms Control*, ed. Morton H. Halperin (New Delhi: English Book Store, 1967), 265–303.

45. Soviet statement of 21 September 1963 in Griffith, *Sino-Soviet Rift*, 439.

46. *CWIHP Bulletin*, no. 10 (March 1998): 173, 177; documents in Griffith, *Sino-Soviet Rift*, 351, 373; Chen Jian and Yang Kuisong, "Chinese Politics and the Collapse of the Sino-Soviet Alliance," in *Brothers in Arms: The Rise and Fall of the Sino-Soviet Alliance, 1945–1963*, ed. Odd Arne Westad (Stanford, CA: Stanford University Press, 1998), 272.

47. See Soviet Government Statement, 21 September 1963, in Griffith, *Sino-Soviet Rift*, 434–35. Also see Lüthi, *Sino-Soviet Split*, 137–38.

48. Soviet statement of 21 September 1963 in Griffith, *Sino-Soviet Rift*, 440.

49. John Gittings, *Survey of the Sino-Soviet Dispute, 1963–1967* (London: Oxford University Press, 1968), 327; MacFarquhar, *Origins of the Cultural Revolution*, vol. 2, *Great Leap Forward*, 257–60.

50. "Origin and Development," 399–400.

51. William R. Keylor, *The Twentieth Century: An International History* (New York: Oxford University Press, 1966), 306.

52. Gittings, *Survey of the Sino-Soviet Dispute*, 58.

53. *CWIHP Bulletin*, nos. 12–13 (Fall–Winter 2001): 267, 269.

54. Ibid., 262–70.

55. *CWIHP Bulletin*, nos. 8–9 (Winter 1996–97): 261.

56. Soviet statement of 1 September 1963 in Griffith, *Sino-Soviet Rift*, 382.

57. Griffith, *Sino-Soviet Rift*, 400.

58. Zagoria, *Sino-Soviet Conflict*, 3–6.

59. *Long Live Leninism* (Peking: Foreign Languages Press, 1960).

60. Beijing's position on peaceful transition was advanced in a statement presented to the 1957 Moscow conference. See note 22.

61. See Zagoria, *Sino-Soviet Conflict*, 343–69.

62. CPC Central Committee to CPSU Central Committee, 14 June 1963, "A Proposal Concerning the General Line of the International Communist Movement," in Griffith, *Sino-Soviet Rift*, 259–88.

63. "Open Letter from the CPSU Central Committee to Party Organizations and All Communists of the Soviet Union," 14 July 1963, in Griffith, *Sino-Soviet Rift*, 289–325.

64. Griffith, *Sino-Soviet Rift*, 163.

65. See Carl A. Linden, *Khrushchev and the Soviet Leadership, 1957–1964* (Baltimore, MD: John Hopkins Press, 1966), esp. chapter 10.

## CHAPTER 9

1. William J. Duiker, *The Communist Road to Power in Vietnam* (Boulder, CO: Westview Press, 1981), 179.

2. Ibid., 213–14.

3. Ibid., 186–99; George C. Herring, *America's Longest War: The United States and Vietnam, 1950–1975* (New York: McGraw-Hill, 1996), 74–75.

4. William R. Keylor, *The Twentieth Century: An International History* (New York: Oxford University Press, 1966), 371; Arthur M. Schlesinger, Jr., *A Thousand Days: John F. Kennedy in the White House* (Boston: Houghton Mifflin, 1965), 163.

5. Arthur J. Dommen, *Conflict in Laos: The Politics of Neutralization* (New York: Praeger Publishers, 1971), 86–87.

6. Text of the agreement in ibid., 415–23.

7. Emphasis added; see the analysis in Donald S. Zagoria, *The Sino-Soviet Conflict, 1956-1961* (Princeton, NJ: Princeton University Press, 1962), 350–55.

8. Schlesinger, *A Thousand Days*, 302–3.

9. Zagoria, *Sino-Soviet Conflict*, 352–53.

10. *The Pentagon Papers: As Published by The New York Times* (New York: Bantam Books, 1971), 87–88.

11. Herring, *America's Longest War*, 85–89.

12. Ibid., 95.

13. Ibid.; Duiker, *Communist Road to Power*, 203.

14. Herring, *America's Longest War*, 105–8.

15. Ibid., 108–10.

16. *Pentagon Papers*, 216.

17. Emphasis in the plenum document; quoted in Duiker, *Communist Road to Power,* 222.

18. Donald S. Zagoria, *Vietnam Triangle: Moscow/Peking/Hanoi* (New York: Pegasus, 1967), 109; Duiker, *Communist Road to Power,* 224.

19. Zagoria, *Vietnam Triangle,* 110–11.

20. Duiker, *Communist Road to Power,* 225.

21. *Pentagon Papers,* 232–33.

22. Ibid., 234–42; Herring, *America's Longest War,* 130–31.

23. Robert S. McNamara, James Blight, and Robert Brigham, *Argument Without End: In Search of Answers to the Vietnam Tragedy* (New York: Public Affairs, 1999), 167. For the NSA report, see *The New York Times,* 2 December 2005, and the NSA Web site, www .nsa.gov/vietnam/indes.cfm.

24. Herring, *America's Longest War,* 133–37. The text of the Gulf of Tonkin Resolution is in Russell Buhite, ed., *The Far East,* vol. 4 of *Dynamics of World Power: A Documentary History of U.S. Foreign Policy, 1945–73,* ed. Arthur M. Schlesinger (New York: Chelsea House, 1973), 490–91.

25. *Pentagon Papers,* 373–78; Herring, *America's Longest War,* 140–41.

26. U.S. Department of State, *Foreign Relations of the United States (FRUS), 1964–1968,* vol. 2, *Vietnam* (Washington, DC: U.S. Government Printing Office, 1996), 174–85; quotation on 175.

27. *Pentagon Papers,* 372.

28. *FRUS, 1964–1968,* vol. 2, *Vietnam,* 180.

29. Ibid., 183.

30. Ibid., 185.

31. *Pravda,* 11 February 1965.

32. Duiker, *Communist Road to Power,* 240–42.

33. See Richard Wich, "Chinese Allies and Adversaries," in *The Military and Political Power in China in the 1970s,* ed. William W. Whitson (New York: Praeger, 1972), 298–99.

34. See "Comment on the Moscow Meeting," *People's Daily* and *Red Flag,* 22 March 1965, in *Peking Review* 8, no. 13 (26 March 1965): 7–13.

35. *Pentagon Papers,* 411–12.

36. Herring, *America's Longest War,* 171.

37. Duiker, *Communist Road to Power,* 250.

38. Herring, *America's Longest War,* 163–64; Chen Jian, *Mao's China and the Cold War* (Chapel Hill: University of North Carolina Press, 2001), 221–29.

39. Henry Kissinger, *White House Years* (Boston: Little, Brown, 1979), 1226; see also Chen Jian, *Mao's China,* 215–21.

40. See Wheeler's report to the president, 27 February 1965, in *Pentagon Papers,* 615–20.

41. Robert McNamara, *In Retrospect* (New York: Times Books, 1995).

42. Henry Kissinger, "The Vietnam Negotiations," *Foreign Affairs* 47 (January 1969).

43. Kissinger, *White House Years,* 226.

44. *Public Papers of the Presidents of the United States,* 3 November 1969 (Washington, DC: U.S. Government Printing Office, 1969).

45. See Kissinger's account, *White House Years*, 277–82.

46. Ibid., 282.

47. *Public Papers of the Presidents*, 30 October 1970; Herring, *America's Longest War*, 257–62.

48. Duiker, *Communist Road to Power*, 283–88.

49. Kissinger, *White House Years*, 486.

50. Stanley Karnow, *Vietnam: A History* (New York: Viking Press, 1983), 629–31; Herring, *America's Longest War*, 265–66.

51. Kissinger, *White House Years*, 1009; for his account of the operation, see 1002–10.

52. Richard Wich, *Sino-Soviet Crisis Politics: A Study of Political Change and Communication* (Cambridge, MA: Harvard University Press, 1980), 234–35.

53. Ibid., 245–47.

54. Kissinger, *White House Years*, 980–81.

55. Ibid., 1017–18; Herring, *America's Longest War*, 269.

56. *Public Papers of the Presidents*, 25 January 1972; Kissinger, *White House Years*, 1043–44.

57. Wich, *Sino-Soviet Crisis Politics*, 219–20.

58. Karnow, *Vietnam*, 638.

59. Kissinger, *White House Years*, 1098; Duiker, *Communist Road to Power*, 291–95.

60. Kissinger, *White House Years*, 1098.

61. Ibid., 1178–86; Herring, *America's Longest War*, 273–75.

62. Kissinger, *White House Years*, 1189–90.

63. A transcript of the Kissinger-Zhou talks is available at www.gwu.edu/~nsarchiv/.

64. Cited in Arnold R. Isaacs, *Without Honor: Defeat in Vietnam and Cambodia* (Baltimore, MD: John Hopkins Press, 1983), 20–21.

65. Wich, *Sino-Soviet Crisis Politics*, 266.

66. Isaacs, *Without Honor*, 34.

67. Ibid., 36.

68. See, for example, Zhou Enlai's remark to the DRV aid negotiator in "77 Conversations Between Chinese and Foreign Leaders on the Wars in Indochina, 1964–77," *CWIHP Working Paper 22*, Cold War International History Project, Washington, DC, May 1998, 192.

69. Kissinger, *White House Years*, 1412.

70. Ibid., 1469–70.

71. Available at www.aiipowmia.com/sea/ppa1973.html.

72. Kissinger, *White House Years*, 235.

73. Quoted in Michael R. Beschloss, *Taking Charge: The Johnson White House Tapes, 1963–1964* (New York: Simon and Schuster, 1997), 213–14.

## CHAPTER 10

1. The analysis in this section updates that in Richard Wich, "Chinese Allies and Adversaries," in *The Military and Political Power in China in the 1970s*, ed. William W. Whitson (New York: Praeger, 1972), 297–303.

2. "Carry the Struggle Against Khrushchev Revisionism Through to the End," *Peking Review* 18 (June 1965): 5–10.

3. See in particular Luo's statement on the V-E Day anniversary that May, "Commemorate the Victory over German Fascism! Carry the Struggle Against U.S. Imperialism Through to the End," *Peking Review* (14 May 1965): 7–15; the quotes are from this source; emphasis added. For textual exegeses, see Harry Harding and Melvin Gurtov, *The Purge of Lo Jui-ch'ing: The Politics of Chinese Strategic Planning*, R-548-PR (Santa Monica, CA: Rand Corporation, 1971); and articles by Uri Ra'anan and Donald Zagoria in *China in Crisis II*, ed. Tang Tsou and Ping-ti Ho (Chicago: University of Chicago Press, 1968).

4. "The Historical Experience of the War Against Fascism," *Peking Review* (14 May 1965): 14–22.

5. "Long Live the Victory of People's War," *Peking Review* (3 September 1965).

6. Roderick MacFarquhar and Michael Schoenhals, *Mao's Last Revolution* (Cambridge, MA: Harvard University Press, 2006), 20–27.

7. "Refutation of the New Leaders of the CPSU on 'United Action,'" *Peking Review* (12 November 1965): 10–21.

8. New China News Agency (NCNA) (Beijing), 24 May 1965. Also called Xinhua, this is the PRC's official press agency.

9. See Ho Lung (He Long), "Democratic Tradition of the Chinese People's Liberation Army," *Peking Review* (6 August 1965): 9–30.

10. "Make Our Army a Great School of Mao Tse-tung's Thought," *Peking Review* (5 August 1966): 8–10.

11. See Richard Wich, *Sino-Soviet Crisis Politics: A Study of Political Change and Communication* (Cambridge, MA: Harvard University Press, 1980), 59–61.

12. Ibid., 97–112 and passim. For further discussion drawing on extensive archival sources, see Genrikh Kireyev, "Strategic Partnership and a Stable Border," *Far Eastern Affairs*, no. 4 (1997); Yang Kuisong, "The Sino-Soviet Border Clash of 1969: From Zhenbao Island to Sino-American Rapprochement," *Cold War History* 1, no. 1 (August 2000): 21–52; Lyle J. Goldstein, "Return to Zhenbao Island: Who Started Shooting and Why It Matters," *China Quarterly* (December 2001): 985–97; MacFarquhar and Shoenhals, *Mao's Last Revolution*, 309–13; M. Taylor Fravel, *Strong Borders, Secure Nation* (Princeton, NJ: Princeton University Press, 2008).

13. Wich, *Sino-Soviet Crisis Politics*, 189–91.

14. Ibid., 199–200; MacFarquhar and Schoenhals, *Mao's Last Revolution*, 313–14. For a secret Soviet report on the Kosygin-Zhou meeting, see *Cold War International History Project (CWIHP) Bulletin*, nos. 6–7 (Winter 1995–96): 191–93.

15. Wich, *Sino-Soviet Crisis Politics*, 78–79 and 114.

16. Richard Wich, "The Tenth Party Congress," *China Quarterly* (April–May 1974): 243–45.

17. *Peking Review* 11, no. 48 (29 November 1968): 30–31.

18. *Public Papers of the President of the United States: Richard Nixon, 1969* (Washington, DC: U.S. Government Printing Office, 1971), 1–4.

19. Wich, *Sino-Soviet Crisis Politics*, 88–89.

20. Henry Kissinger, *White House Years* (Boston: Little, Brown, 1979), 699.

21. Wich, *Sino-Soviet Crisis Politics*, 81, 88.

22. The Nixon administration's efforts to develop a new relationship with China are discussed in *RN: The Memoirs of Richard Nixon* (New York: Grosset and Dunlap, 1978); Kissinger, *White House Years*, 162–94 and 684–787; John H. Holdridge, *Crossing the Divide: An Insider's Account of the Normalization of U.S.-China Relations* (Lanham, MD: Rowman and Littlefield, 1997). The official documentary record is in U.S. Department of State, *Foreign Relations of the United States (FRUS), 1969–1972*, vol. 27, *China 1969–1972* (Washington, DC: U.S. Government Printing Office, 2006).

23. Richard M. Nixon, "Asia After Viet Nam," *Foreign Affairs* 46 (October 1967): 111–25.

24. *CWIHP Bulletin*, no. 11 (Winter 1998): 166–68, 170–71.

25. Wich, *Sino-Soviet Crisis Politics*, 257–60.

26. The basic documents in the developing Sino-American relationship are in Robert S. Ross, *Negotiating Cooperation: The United States and China, 1969–1989* (Stanford, CA: Stanford University Press, 1995), appendix A. This work also provides a detailed, closely analyzed account of two decades of negotiations, drawing on extensive sources and interviews.

27. For an account of the impact of the Nixon shocks, see John Welfield, *An Empire in Eclipse: Japan in the Postwar American Alliance System* (London: Athlone Press, 1988), 295–300.

28. *Peking Review* (18 August 1978): 7–8.

29. Bruce Cumings, *Korea's Place in the Sun: A Modern History* (New York: W.W. Norton, 1997), 358–59; Don Oberdorfer, *The Two Koreas: A Contemporary History* (New York: Basic Books, 1997), 23–26.

30. Neville Maxwell's account, *India's China War* (New York: Anchor Books, 1972), though drawing mainly on Indian sources (he was a foreign correspondent based in New Delhi during this period), takes India to task for its actions leading to the border war of 1962. For an analysis by a China scholar writing shortly after the events, see Harold C. Hinton, *Communist China in World Politics* (Boston: Houghton Mifflin, 1965), 273–307.

31. *Peking Review* (8 November 1962): 21.

32. Maxwell, *India's China War*, 439–40.

33. For an analysis in terms of a window of opportunity for Pakistan, see Sumit Ganguly, *Conflict Unending: India-Pakistan Tensions Since 1947* (New York: Columbia University Press, 2001), chapter 2; Sumit Ganguly, *The Crisis in Kashmir: Portents of War, Hopes of Peace* (Cambridge: Cambridge University Press, 1999); J.N. Dixit, *India-Pakistan in War and Peace* (London: Routledge, 2002), 139–52.

34. Dixit, *India-Pakistan*, 155–57; Ganguly, *Conflict Unending*, 46.

35. Ganguly, *Conflict Unending*, 71.

36. Text in Ganguly, *Conflict Unending*, 164–67.

37. Kissinger, *White House Years*, 868.

38. Dixit, *India-Pakistan*, 184.

39. See Kissinger's extended account in *White House Years*, chapter 21, "The Tilt: The India-Pakistan Crisis of 1971."

40. Ibid., 913.

41. For an insider's account of Indian calculations and planning, see Dixit, *India-Pakistan*, chapter 6.

42. Kissinger, *White House Years*, 901. See also Raymond L. Garthoff, *Détente and Confrontation: American-Soviet Relations from Nixon to Reagan* (Washington, DC: Brookings Institution, 1985), 267–78; Robert Jackson, *South Asian Crisis: India, Pakistan, and Bangla Desh* (New York: Praeger, 1975).

43. Garthoff, *Détente and Confrontation*, 451.

44. For accounts of developments discussed in this section, see ibid.; Henry Bradsher, *Afghanistan and the Soviet Union* (Durham, NC: Duke University Press, 1983); Thomas T. Hammond, *Red Flag over Afghanistan: The Communist Coup, the Soviet Invasion, and the Consequences* (Boulder, CO: Westview Press, 1984); Alvin Z. Rubinstein, *Soviet Policy Toward Turkey, Iran, and Afghanistan* (New York: Praeger, 1982).

45. *CWIHP Bulletin*, nos. 8–9 (Winter 1996–97): 133.

46. Ibid., 133–61.

47. Ibid., 141.

48. Ibid., 141–43.

49. Vladislav M. Zubok, *A Failed Empire: The Soviet Union in the Cold War from Stalin to Gorbachev* (Chapel Hill: University of North Carolina Press, 2007), 260–61.

50. *CWIHP Bulletin*, nos. 8–9, 164.

51. Robert M. Gates, *From the Shadows: The Ultimate Insider's Story of Five Presidents and How They Won the Cold War* (New York: Simon and Schuster, 1996), 132.

52. Ibid., 146.

53. See Brezhnev's statement on the intervention, *Pravda*, 13 January 1980; *Current Digest of the Soviet Press* 32, no. 2 (13 February 1980): 1–4.

54. For this view see Richard F. Staar's foreword to Anthony Arnold, *Afghanistan: The Soviet Invasion in Perspective* (Stanford, CA: Hoover Institution Press, 1985).

55. *New York Times*, 1 January 1980.

56. Ross, *Negotiating Cooperation*, 50–53.

57. Richard Wich, "Tenth Party Congress."

58. MacFarquhar and Schoenhals, *Mao's Last Revolution*, chapter 21, "Zhou Under Pressure."

59. For insider accounts of American policy making, see Jimmy Carter, *Keeping Faith: Memoirs of a President* (New York: Bantam Books, 1982); Cyrus Vance, *Hard Choices: Critical Years in America's Foreign Policy* (New York: Simon and Schuster, 1983); Zbigniew Brzezinski, *Power and Principle: Memoirs of the National Security Adviser, 1977–1981* (New York: Farrar, Strauss, Giroux, 1983); Michel Oksenberg, "A Decade of Sino-American Relations," *Foreign Affairs* 61, no. 1 (Fall 1982): 1175–95. U.S. and Chinese documents as well as interviews are marshaled in Ross, *Negotiating Cooperation*, 92–162. We have benefited also from discussions with American and Chinese officials.

60. Personal communication.

61. *Peking Review* (22 December 1978): 10–11.

62. Alan D. Romberg, *Rein In at the Brink of the Precipice: American Policy Toward Taiwan and U.S.-PRC Relations* (Washington, DC: Stimson Center, 2003), 144.

63. Text in Ross, *Negotiating Cooperation,* 269–70.

64. *Peking Review* (22 December 1978): 11.

65. See the PRC government statement, 16 December 1978, ibid., 8–9.

66. See Ross, *Negotiating Cooperation*; the Taiwan Relations Act is in appendix B, 273–83.

67. Gates, *From the Shadows,* 120–22.

68. Ibid., 122.

69. Ibid., 122–23. Gates accompanied the director of the CIA, Stansfield Turner, on a secret trip to China in late 1980 to work out arrangements for the facilities. He became defense secretary during George W. Bush's second term.

**CHAPTER 11**

1. Brisk, insightful accounts of these developments can be found in Geoffrey Hosking, *The First Socialist Society* (Cambridge, MA: Harvard University Press, 1990), chapter 15; Stephen Kotkin, *Armageddon Averted: The Soviet Collapse* (Oxford: Oxford University Press, 2001). For the ultimate insider's version, see Mikhail Gorbachev, *Memoirs* (New York: Doubleday, 1996).

2. Gorbachev, *Memoirs,* 215.

3. Kotkin, *Armageddon Averted,* 15–16; see also Gorbachev, *Memoirs,* 216.

4. See especially Reagan's address to the conservative Heritage Foundation, 3 October 1983, in *Presidential Documents,* vol. 19 (10 October 1983). For a critical dissection of the Reagan Doctrine, see Raymond L. Garthoff, *The Great Transition: American-Soviet Relations and the End of the Cold War* (Washington: Brookings Institution, 1994), 692–716.

5. Ezra Vogel, *Japan as Number One* (Cambridge, MA: Harvard University Press, 1979); Clyde V. Prestowitz, Jr., *Trading Places: How We Allowed Japan to Take the Lead* (New York: Basic Books, 1988.)

6. John Welfield, *An Empire in Eclipse: Japan in the Postwar American Alliance System* (London: Athlone Press, 1988), 446–47; Paul J. Bailey, *Postwar Japan: 1945 to the Present* (Oxford: Blackwell Publishers, 1996), 140–43.

7. Eduard Shevardnadze, *The Future Belongs to Freedom* (London: Sinclair-Stevenson, 1991), 58.

8. *Pravda,* 26 February 1986. See also versions in Foreign Broadcast Information Service (FBIS), *Daily Report: Soviet Union,* 26 and 27 February 1986.

9. *Pravda,* 29 July 1986. See "condensed text" in *Current Digest of the Soviet Press* 38, no. 30 (27 August 1986): 1, 3–8, 32.

10. *Beijing Review* (15 September 1986): 5.

11. *Pravda,* 23 July 1987.

12. *Pravda,* 8 December 1988.

13. See for example *Pravda,* 23 December 1985.

14. Garthoff, *The Great Transition,* 726–29.

15. Ibid., 726–27; Kotkin, *Armageddon Averted,* 61.

16. Text in *New York Times,* 15 April 1988.

17. *Washington Post,* 15 April 2002.

18. See Richard Wich, "China and the Superpowers," in *Détente in Asia?* ed. Leslie Palmier (London: Macmillan, 1992), 114–15.

19. Ibid., 122, n.6.

20. Ibid., 116–17.

21. Bruce Cumings, *Korea's Place in the Sun: A History* (New York: W.W. Norton, 1997), 464–65.

22. For an account of Moscow's shift in Korea policy, see Don Oberdorfer, *The Two Koreas* (New York: Basic Books, 1997), chapter 9.

23. *Pravda*, 18 September 1988, in *Current Digest of the Soviet Press* 40, no. 38 (1988).

24. Text in FBIS, *Daily Report: East Asia-90-194*, 5 October 1990.

25. Oberdorfer, *Two Koreas*, 202.

26. For an account of the development of Sino–South Korean relations, see ibid., chapter 10.

27. For Cambodian developments from the Vietnamese invasion to the Paris settlement, see Michael Leifer, "Powersharing and Peacemaking in Cambodia," *SAIS Review* 12, no. 1 (Winter–Spring 1992): 139–54.

28. The founding document is in Michael Haas, ed., *Basic Documents of Asian Regional Organizations*, vol. 4 (Dobbs Ferry, NY: Oceana Publications, 1974), 1269–71.

29. For a searching analysis of the early evolution of ASEAN as a security and diplomatic community, see Michael Leifer, *ASEAN and the Security of South-East Asia* (London: Routledge, 1989).

30. See David Capie and Paul Evans, *The Asia-Pacific Lexicon* (Singapore: Institute of Southeast Asian Studies, 2002).

31. Donald E. Weatherbee, *International Relations in Southeast Asia: The Struggle for Autonomy* (Lanham, MD: Rowman and Littlefield, 2005), 68.

32. The text of the treaty is at www.aseansec.org/1217.htm.

**CHAPTER 12**

1. On Soviet assistance in modernizing the PLA, see John Gittings, *The Role of the Chinese Army* (New York: Oxford University Press, 1967), 119–57.

2. Chen Yi, speech to the Eighth CCP Congress, "The Present International Situation and Our Foreign Policy," in *Eighth National Congress of the Chinese Communist Party*, vol. 2, *Speeches* (Peking: Foreign Languages Press, 1956), 341.

3. The pioneering research on the "third front" program is Barry Naughton, "The Third Front: Defense Industrialization in the Chinese Interior," *China Quarterly*, no. 115 (Autumn 1988): 351–86.

4. Barry Naughton, *The Chinese Economy: Transitions and Growth* (Cambridge, MA: MIT Press, 2007), 71–72.

5. For a comprehensive account of the Great Proletarian Cultural Revolution, see Roderick MacFarquhar and Michael Schoenhals, *Mao's Last Revolution* (Cambridge, MA: Harvard University Press, 2006).

6. Deng Xiaoping, "Speech at the Opening Ceremony of the National Conference on Science," 18 March 1978, in *Selected Works of Deng Xiaoping (1975–1982)* (Beijing: Foreign Languages Press, 1984), 101–16.

7. For a comprehensive analysis of the economic reforms, see Naughton, *Chinese Economy*, 85ff.

8. Deng Xiaoping, speech to the 4 June 1985 meeting of the Central Military Commission, in *Selected Works of Deng Xiaoping*, vol. 3, *1982–1992* (Beijing: Foreign Languages Press, 1994), 131–33. For a detailed analysis of the 1985 shift in PRC defense doctrines and its implications for PLA modernization, see Paul H.B. Godwin, "From Continent to Periphery: PLA Doctrine, Strategy, and Capabilities Towards 2000," *China Quarterly*, no. 146 (June 1996): 464–87.

9. On China's approach to multilateral arms control regimes, see Michael D. Swaine and Alastair Iain Johnston, "China and Arms Control Institutions," in *China Joins the World*, ed. Elizabeth Economy and Michel Oksenberg (New York: Council on Foreign Relations Press, 1999), 90–126.

10. A solid comprehensive analysis of PLA modernization is David Shambaugh, *Modernizing China's Military* (Berkeley: University of California Press, 2003). On recent developments, see also David Shambaugh, "China's Military Modernization: Making Steady and Surprising Progress," in *Strategic Asia 2005–2006: Military Modernization in an Era of Uncertainty*, ed. Ashley J. Tellis and Michael Wills (Seattle, WA: National Bureau of Asian Research, 2006), 387–422.

## CHAPTER 13

1. Kent E. Calder, "Japan as a Post-Reactive State?" *Orbis* (Fall 2003): 608.

2. Ibid., 605.

3. *New York Times*, 3 April 2004; *Washington Post*, 11 July 2004.

4. For accounts of the origins and development of the crisis, see Don Oberdorfer, *The Two Koreas* (New York: Basic Books, 1997), chapters 11–15; Michael J. Lazar, *North Korea and the Bomb* (New York: St. Martin's Press, 1995).

5. Foreign Broadcast Information Service, EAS-91-240, 11–13.

6. Oberdorfer, *Two Koreas*, 260–65.

7. Ibid., 276 and 279–80; *New York Times*, 1 February, 9 February, and 13 March 1993.

8. Oberdorfer, *Two Koreas*, 306–7.

9. Ibid., 326–36.

10. Ibid., 306–7.

11. See the chronology in *Washington Post*, 11 February 2005.

12. *New York Times*, 17 August 2005.

13. *Washington Post*, 10 July 2005.

14. *New York Times*, 20 September 2005; *Washington Post*, 20 September, 21 September, and 25 September 2005 (see the last for a deconstruction of the terms of the agreement).

15. *New York Times*, 5 and 7 July 2006.

16. Sumit Ganguly, *Conflict Unending: India-Pakistan Tensions Since 1947* (New York: Columbia University Press, 2001), 79–83.

17. Ibid., 88–91.

18. Ibid., 83–85.

19. Ibid., 114–29.

20. See the account by Steve Coll in the *New Yorker*, 13 and 20 February 2006, 126–39.

21. *New York Times*, 18 November 2004.

22. *Economist*, 4 March 2006.

23. *Washington Post*, 3 March 2006.

24. "Joint Statement," Xinhua News Agency, 12 April 1998.

25. The guidelines are available at http://meaindia.nic.in/treatiesagreement/2005/11ta1104200501.htm.

26. Linda Y.C. Lim, "Whose 'Model' Failed? Implications of the Asian Economic Crises," *Washington Quarterly* 21, no. 3 (Summer 1988): 25–36.

27. Richard Stubbs, "ASEAN Plus Three," *Asian Survey* 42, no. 3 (May–June 2002): 440–55.

28. Ibid., 448–49.

29. *Economist*, 15 October 2005.

30. *New York Times*, 13 December 2005; *Washington Post*, 14 and 15 December 2005.

31. For an account of terrorist networks in Southeast Asia, see Sally Neighbors, *In the Shadow of Swords* (New York: HarperCollins, 2004).

32. *Washington Post*, 2 October 2005; *New York Times*, 3 October 2005; *Economist*, 8 October 2005.

33. "Joint Statement," Xinhua News Agency, 23 November 1998.

34. *Beijing Review* (2 August 2001): 8–9.

35. *Washington Post*, 15 August 2005.

36. See the SCO declaration, 15 June 2001, Xinhua News Agency (Beijing), Lexis-Nexis.

37. *New York Times*, 12 October 2005.

38. For a view of Sino-Russian relations as a tactical partnership falling short of a strategic alliance, see Bobo Lo, *Axis of Convenience: Moscow, Beijing, and the New Geopolitics* (Washington, DC: Brookings Institution Press, 2008).

## CHAPTER 14

1. For an analysis of the Taiwan issue by a former State Department official and longtime observer of Sino-American relations, see Alan D. Romberg, *Rein In at the Brink of the Precipice: American Policy Toward Taiwan and U.S.-PRC Relations* (Washington, DC: Stimson Center, 2003). For an extensive reconstruction of the negotiating process, see Robert S. Ross, *Negotiating Cooperation: The United States and China, 1969–1989* (Stanford, CA: Stanford University Press, 1995). For a close study of the U.S.-Taiwan-PRC triangle, see Nancy Bernkopf Tucker, *Strait Talk: United States–Taiwan Relations and the Crisis with China* (Cambridge, MA: Harvard University Press, 2009).

2. See the PRC-U.S. joint communiqué, 17 August 1982, in Robert S. Ross, *Negotiating Cooperation* (Stanford, CA: Stanford University Press, 1995), 270–72.

3. Romberg, *Rein In at the Precipice*, 150–53.

4. For an insider's account, see Robert Suettinger, *Beyond Tiananmen: The Politics of U.S.-China Relations, 1989–2000* (Washington, DC: Brookings Institution, 2003).

5. *New York Times*, 23 March 2008.

6. *New York Times*, 5 November 2008.

7. *New York Times*, 30 June 2010.

8. *New York Times*, 15 April 2008.

9. The white paper is available at www.china-embassy.org/eng/7128/.html.

10. Text of the PRC-UK Joint Declaration on Hong Kong's reversion is in *Beijing Review* 27, no. 40 (1 October 1984). Text of the Basic Law accessed at www.constitution.org/cons/hongkong.txt.

11. See *Beijing Review* 33, no. 15 (9–15 April 1990): 7–9.

12. Alan Romberg, "Cross-Strait Relations: 'Ascend the Heights and Take a Long-term Perspective,'" *China Leadership Monitor*, no. 27 (Winter 2009): 18, accessed at www.hoover.org/publications/clm.

13. *New York Times*, 30 April 2009.

14. Accessed at www.georgewbush-whitehouse.archives.gov/nsc/nss/2002.html.

15. Ibid., cover letter.

16. Ibid., 3.

17. Ibid., 9–11.

18. *New York Times*, 22 October 2005.

19. *New York Times*, 12 October 2006.

20. *New York Times*, 3 October and 1 November 2006.

21. *Washington Post*, 15 July 2007.

22. *Washington Post*, 4 October 2007.

23. *New York Times*, 9 May 2008.

24. *Washington Post*, 5 October 2007; *New York Times*, 5 October 2007.

25. *New York Times*, 20 October 2007.

26. *New York Times*, 4 April 2008.

27. *Washington Post*, 27 May 2008, which lists the remaining sanctions.

28. *New York Times*, 25 September 2008

29. *Washington Post*, 26 September 2008.

30. *Washington Post*, 12 October 2008.

31. *New York Times*, 24 January 2009; *Washington Post*, 24 January 2009.

32. *New York Times*, 6 April 2009.

33. *New York Times*, 15 April and 26 and 27 May 2009; *Washington Post*, 15 April and 26 May 2009.

34. *Washington Post*, 27 May 2009.

35. *Washington Post*, 13 June 2009.

36. *Washington Post*, 3 June 2009.

37. *Washington Post*, 18 and 24 August and 9 November 2009; *New York Times*, 23 August 2009.

38. *New York Times*, 7 October 2009.

39. *New York Times*, 1 January 2010; *Washington Post*, 1 January 2010.

40. *Washington Post*, 2 July 2008.

41. *Economist*, 22 July 2006.

42. *Economist*, 25 November 2006.

43. *Washington Post*, 15 July 2007.

44. *New York Times*, 14 September 2007.

45. *Washington Post*, 12 January 2008.

46. *New York Times*, 25 September 2008.

47. *Economist*, 27 September 2008.

48. *New York Times*, 5 and 21 May 2010.

49. *New York Times*, 2 June 2010.

50. *New York Times*, 3 June 2010.

51. Sumit Ganguly, *Conflict Unending: India-Pakistan Tensions Since 1947* (New York: Columbia University Press, 2001), 122–23.

52. See C. Raja Mohan, "India and the Balance of Power," *Foreign Affairs* (July–August 2006): 2–16. This issue of the journal carried four articles grouped under the rubric "The Rise of India."

53. Gurcharan Das, "The India Model," *Foreign Affairs* (July–August 2006): 17–32. For analyses of India's economic development, see Arvind Panagariya, *India: The Emerging Giant* (New York: Oxford University Press, 2008); and Arvind Subramanian, *India's Turn: Understanding the Economic Transformation* (New York: Oxford University Press, 2008).

54. *New York Times*, 1 September 2006.

55. See Steve Coll, "The Back Channel," *New Yorker*, 2 March 2009, 38–51.

56. *Washington Post*, 28 July 2007.

57. *Washington Post*, 3 September 2008.

58. *Washington Post*, 12 September 2008.

59. *Economist*, 26 July 2008.

60. *Economist*, 29 July 2006.

61. *Economist*, 6 September 2008.

62. *New York Times*, 20 and 22 February 2009.

63. *New York Times*, 24 June 2009.

64. *Economist*, 25 August 2007; *Washington* Post, 18 August 2007.

65. *Washington Post*, 24 May 2008; *New York Times*, 24 May 2008.

66. *New York Times*, 29 August 2008; the text of the declaration was accessed at www.dbroca.uz/?act=news& code=1&nid=9622.

67. *Economist*, 10 June 2006.

68. *New York Times*, 27 December 2008.

69. See Donald E. Weatherbee, *International Relations in Southeast Asia: The Struggle for Autonomy* (Lanham, MD: Rowman and Littlefield, 2005), 133–39 and 153, n.19.

70. *Economist*, 21 June 2008.

71. *New York Times*, 25 September 2008.

72. *New York Times*, 14 December 2008.

73. *International Herald Tribune*, 12 October 2009.

74. *Economist*, 31 October 2009.

75. For the decline in Asian exports, see *New York Times*, 22 January 2009.

76. *New York Times*, 5 March 2009.

77. Barry Naughton, "The Scramble to Maintain Growth," *China Leadership Monitor* no. 27 (Winter 2009), accessed at www.hoover.org/publications/clm.

78. *Economist*, 1 August 2009; *New York Times*, 3 August 2009.

79. *New York Times*, 26 September and 27 November 2009.

80. For a discussion of Asia's economic and political response to the financial crisis of 2008, see "Briefing: Emerging Markets and Recession," *Economist*, 2 January 2010, 25–28.

81. See Richard N. Haass, "The Age of Nonpolarity," *Foreign Affairs* (May–June 2008): 44–56.

# SELECTED BIBLIOGRAPHY FOR FURTHER READING


**BACKGROUND**

Aczel, Amir. *Uranium Wars: The Scientific Rivalry That Created the Nuclear Age*. New York: Palgrave Macmillan, 2009.

Alperovitz, Gar. *Atomic Diplomacy*. New York: Penguin Press, 1985.

Feis, Herbert. *Churchill-Roosevelt-Stalin*. Princeton, NJ: Princeton University Press, 1957.

Gaddis, John Lewis. *The United States and the Origins of the Cold War, 1941–1947*. New York: Columbia University Press, 1972.

Hasegawa, Tsuyoshi. *Racing the Enemy: Stalin, Truman, and the Surrender of Japan*. Cambridge, MA: Belknap Press of Harvard University, 2005.

Iriye, Akira. *The Origins of the Second World War in Asia and the Pacific*. New York: Longman, 1987.

Schaller, Michael. *The American Occupation of Japan: The Origins of the Cold War in Asia*. New York: Oxford University Press, 1985.

**DECOLONIZATION, NATIONALISM, AND REVOLUTION**

Colbert, Evelyn. *Southeast Asia in International Politics, 1941–1956*. Ithaca, NY: Cornell University Press, 1977.

Cumings, Bruce. *The Origins of the Korean War*. Vol. 2, *The Roaring of the Cataract, 1947–1950*. Princeton, NJ: Princeton University Press, 1990.

Ganguly, Sumit. *Conflict Unending: India-Pakistan Tensions Since 1947*. New York: Columbia University Press, 2001.

McMahon, Robert J. *Colonialism and Cold War: The United States and the Struggle for Indonesian Independence, 1945–49*. Ithaca, NY: Cornell University Press, 1981.

Tsou Tang. *America's Failure in China, 1941–1950*. Chicago: University of Chicago Press, 1963.

U.S. Department of State. *United States Relations with China, with Special Reference to the Period 1945–1949*. Washington, DC: U.S. Government Printing Office, 1949.

## THE COLD WAR PERIOD

Chang, Gordon. *Friends and Enemies: The United States, China, and the Soviet Union, 1948–1972*. Stanford, CA: Stanford University Press, 1990.

Dommen, Arthur J. *Conflict in Laos: The Politics of Neutralization*. New York: Praeger Publishers, 1971.

Garver, John W. *Protracted Contest: Sino-Indian Rivalry in the Twentieth Century*. Seattle: University of Washington Press, 2001.

Goncharov, Sergei N., John W. Lewis, and Xue Litai. *Uncertain Partners: Stalin, Mao, and the Korean War*. Stanford, CA: Stanford University Press, 1993.

Herring, George C. *America's Longest War: The United States and Vietnam, 1950–1975*. New York: McGraw-Hill, 1996.

Leifer, Michael. *ASEAN and the Security of South-East Asia*. London: Routledge, 1989.

MacFarquhar, Roderick, and Michael Schoenhals. *Mao's Last Revolution*. Cambridge, MA: Harvard University Press, 2006.

McMahon, Robert J. *The Cold War on the Periphery: The United States, India, and Pakistan*. New York: Columbia University Press, 1994.

Ross, Robert S. *Negotiating Cooperation: The United States and China, 1969–1989*. Stanford, CA: Stanford University Press, 1995.

Stueck, William. *The Korean War: An International History*. Princeton, NJ: Princeton University Press, 1995.

Welfield, John. *An Empire in Eclipse: Japan in the Postwar American Alliance System*. London: Athlone Press, 1988.

Wich, Richard. *Sino-Soviet Crisis Politics: A Study of Political Change and Communication*. Cambridge, MA: Harvard University Press, 1980.

Zagoria, Donald S. *The Sino-Soviet Conflict, 1956–1961*. Princeton, NJ: Princeton University Press, 1962.

## POST–COLD WAR AND THE NEW CENTURY

Haas, Richard N. "The Age of Nonpolarity." *Foreign Affairs* (May–June 2008).

Kotkin, Stephen. *Armageddon Averted: The Soviet Collapse*. Oxford: Oxford University Press, 2001.

Lo, Bobo. *Axis of Convenience: Moscow, Beijing, and the New Geopolitics*. Washington, DC: Brookings Institution Press, 2008.

Mohan, C. Raja. "India and the Balance of Power." *Foreign Affairs* (July–August 2006) (and three other articles under the rubric "The Rise of India").

Naughton, Barry. *The Chinese Economy: Transitions and Growth*. Cambridge, MA: MIT Press, 2007.

Oberdorfer, Don. *The Two Koreas*. New York: Basic Books, 1997.

Romberg, Alan. *Rein In at the Brink of the Precipice: American Policy Toward Taiwan and U.S.-PRC Relations*. Washington, DC: Stimson Center, 2003.

Shambaugh, David. *Modernizing China's Military*. Berkeley: University of California Press, 2003.

Weatherbee, Donald E. *International Relations in Southeast Asia: The Struggle for Autonomy*. Lanham, MD: Rowman and Littlefield, 2005.

# INDEX